The Creative Power

"A feast of creative thought from Bill Smith's Odyssey working with famous corporations, integrated into a broad conceptual framework of management. Scholars, students, and policy-makers will find this book a satisfying source of insight and inspiration."

William E. Halal, Professor of Management, George Washington University, author of *Technology's Promise: Expert Knowledge on the Transformation of Business & Society*

"Reading *The Creative Power* is a Formula-One spiral through the dynamic links between being 'purpose-full' and 'power-full' at any level of one's focus: leading ourselves, our organizations, or our world. Bill Smith's own story guides the reader agilely through both his far-reaching, multi-dimensional intellectual quest and his astoundingly practical discoveries. You are challenged to recognize the invisible, ubiquitous potential that lies untapped in one's purpose. You may be transformed in your appreciation of its quantum nature. And you will have at hand new approaches for activating and channeling that power in yourself and others."

Janet L. Greco, Ph.D., Co-President, Transition One Associates

"Smith tells his own story and adventures in understanding perform-ance and living in organizations, and then connects this to the evolving and developing theory of power. Smith presents the dimensions of power—control, influence and appreciation—and then examines these intertwined strands of power in organizations from the rational-legal of Weber and Taylor to the systemic, holistic, and purposeful of Follett, Trist, Thompson, Ackoff, and Bohm."

Alan M. Barstow, Ph.D., Director, Academics and Outreach, Organizational Dynamics, University of Pennsylvania

Theorist and consultant William E. Smith presents a new philosophical lens for helping leaders see the advantages of a more holistic approach to improving organizations. This breakthrough book:

*   Introduces the AIC (appreciation, influence, control) philosophy, model, and process of purpose-power relationships as a next step in the evolution of organization and systems theory
*   Traces the roots of the AIC model from philosophy, theology, and science; its evolution in organizational theory; and indicates its actual and potential contribution to organizational practice
*   Translates the model into a transformative, strategic organizing process that can be used to organize at any level, in a way that will ensure the achievement of higher levels of purpose.

William E. Smith, Ph.D. is a Director of Organizing for Development, an International Institute (ODII.)

The Creative Power

Transforming Ourselves, Our
Organizations, and Our World

William E. Smith

Routledge
Taylor & Francis Group

NEW YORK AND LONDON

First published 2009
by Routledge
270 Madison Ave, New York, NY 10016

Simultaneously published in the UK
by Routledge
2 Park Square, Milton Park, Abingdon, Oxon OX14 4RN

*Routledge is an imprint of the Taylor & Francis Group,
an informa business*

© 2009 William E. Smith

Typeset in Times New Roman by
Florence Production Ltd, Stoodleigh, Devon
Printed and bound in the United States of America
on acid-free paper by Sheridan Books, Inc.

Library of Congress Cataloging in Publication Data
Smith, William E.
    The creative power: transforming ourselves, our organizations, and
    our world/William E. Smith.
        p. cm.
    Includes bibliographical references and index.
    1. Organizational change.   2. Organizational behavior.
    3. Organizational sociology.   I. Title.
    HD58.8.S6424 2008
    658.4′063—dc22   2008018651

ISBN10: 0–415–39361–2 (hbk)
ISBN10: 0–415–39360–4 (pbk)
ISBN10: 0–203–88878–2 (ebk)

ISBN13: 978–0–415–39361–4 (hbk)
ISBN13: 978–0–415–39360–7 (pbk)
ISBN13: 978–0–203–88878–0 (ebk)

I dedicate this book to the memory of Turid Sato. She was one of the first to see the full transformational potential of the philosophy and model of organization developed in this book. She herself was a model of the kind of influence power we would later find to be at the center of the most effective organizations. She was herself transformed by her experience with the model and left the World Bank to help set up the organization ODII, Organizing for Development, an International Institute, to promote it. It was her courage and foresight that gave birth to three of its most important applications. The first set the stage for the transformation of the electricity sector in Colombia. The second was its most intensive and extensive in Thailand. The third was its highest global-level application in which ten countries created "A New Paradigm for Development." She became my life partner and soul mate till her tragic death on October 15, 1997.

Contents

List of Illustrations   xii
Acknowledgments   xv

Introduction   1

PART 1
The Starting Experience: Theory and Intuition   5

1 Learning to March: Experience of Control   7

Turbulent Contexts   *7*
    Trinidad: a Trial by Fire   10
    An Insight from Rome   13
    Rewards for Innovation?   15
    Stumped Again   20
The Classical Literature and Control-Centeredness   *23*
    First Concepts of Organization   23
Purpose and the Classical Period   *27*

2 Learning to Dance: Experience of Influence   32

Reading the Music   *32*
    Power   34
    Taking the First Steps: Consultants, Tools, and
       Answers   36
The Dance Begins   *41*
    The Dance Takes Form   45
    The AIC Form in Embryo   46

Open Systems and Influence   48

Organization Environment Relations   49
The Move to Process   50
Stakeholders   55
Purpose in the Open-Systems Phase   57

3 Learning to Fly: Experience of Appreciation   60

The Academic Opening   60
The Breakthrough Intuition   63

Stakeholders as Dancing Partners: Anchoring the
Concept of Influence   73
New Levels and New Depths   74

**4 International Development: Examples and Evolving
Concepts of Wholeness**   75

The World Bank Experience   75

Santa Marta, Colombia   75
Santa Marta Effects   83

New Levels Outside of the World Bank   86

Thailand Does It All   86

*The Literature on the Emerging Phase: Embracing
Wholeness   91*

Beyond Open Systems   91

Summary   102

**PART II
The Philosophy, Theory, Model, and Process**   103

5 The Emerging Philosophy: The Nature of Purpose   106

Insights from Religion, Philosophy, and Science   106

The Common Message from Religions   108
Science Demurs   113
Philosophy, Purpose, and Manifest Power   113

*The Emergent Philosophy of Organization: Purpose →
Time → Power   121*

Unconscious Purpose   124

*Practical Synthesis of Conscious and Unconscious
Purpose   131*
Summary   133

6 Building the Theory   134

Purpose and Power Fields   134

   Power Fields Are Organized Dimensionally   136
   A Natural Example   136

The Brain and Five-Dimensional Organization   141

   The Reptilian Brain   142
   The Mammalian Brain   143
   The Neocortex   144

Our Visual System   145
Color as a Five-Dimensional Language of Power   146

   Color Perception   146

Summary: The Contribution of the Dimensional
   Perspective   154

7 Building the AIC Model   156

The Dimensional Perspective   156

   Purpose, Zero Dimensions, and the Complementarity
      Link to Wholeness   156
   One-Dimensional Organization   157
   Two-Dimensional Organization   158
   Three-Dimensional Organization   158
   Four-Dimensional Organization   161
   Five-Dimensional Organization   162
   Fractal Dimensions   165

The Nine Basic Manifest Powers   170

   The Power Relationships as Holons   172
   Appreciative-Centered Organization: Five-Dimensional
      Mind Space   173
   Influence-Centered Organization: Four-Dimensional Timing   175
   Control-Centered Organization: Three-Dimensional
      Physical Space   179

Summary   180

8 The Process in Practice   183

Principles in Process   184

   Purpose   186

Making the Impossible Possible: The Appreciative Field   190

   (A-a) Discovery   192
   (A-i) Diplomacy   192
   (A-c) Visioning   192

Orchestrating the Dance of Influence   196

(I-a) Evaluation   197
(I-i) Negotiation   197
(I-c) Strategy   198
Leadership Role   199

The Control Phase: Action as Feedback   202

(C-a) Appraisal, Reflection   203
(C-i) Working Agreements   203
(C-c) Operations, Action   203

Summary: Back to the Center   204

PART III
**Implications for Ourselves, Our Organizations,
and the World**   207

9   Implications for Ourselves   209

Phase 1: Discovering Our World   210
Phase 2: Telling the Story   210
Phase 3: Committing to Action   212
The Power Map   218

Implementing Appreciation   219
Implementing Influence   220
Implementing Control   221

Creating the Power Map   222
How to Interpret the Power Map   224

Interpretation of the Fifth or Mind/Spirit
   Dimension   226
Interpretation of the Fourth or Relational
   Dimension   227
Interpretation of the Third Dimension   227
Preferred Ends and Means—Second and First
   Dimension   228
Interpreting Zero-Dimensions   229

The Power Map and Leadership   230

Leading Appreciative-Centered
   Organizations   230
Leading Influence-Centered Organizations   231
Leading Control-Centered Organizations   232

Summary   234

**10 Implications for Cultures, Institutions, and
Organizations** 235

Cultures as Context 236
Institutions and Long-Term Values 239
Organizations as Individuals 240
Power Patterns for Organizational Effectiveness 242

 Effective Appreciative-Centered Organization 242
 Effective Influence-Centered Organization 244
 Effective Control-Centered Organization 246

*Illustration of Practical Use of Value Priorities
 and Sequence 247*

 The Action/Learning/Organizing Process 249
 Priorities as Identified by the Community Meeting 251

Summary 256

11 The Humpty Dumpty Rule 260

Exploring the Potential 260
Facing the Reality 269

 Fifth Dimension: Spiritual System 271
 Fourth Dimension: Political System 272
 Third Dimension: Executive System 272
 Historical Test 272
 An African Test 276
 The Feminine–Masculine Test 276
 Practical Impact of the Appreciative Level 278

Summary 283

12 Reflections 284

The Three Transformations 284

 Transforming Ourselves 284
 Transforming Our Organizations 287
 Transforming Our World 291

Appendix 293
Notes 305
References 311
Index 319

Illustrations

Figures

1.1	BOAC award and three levels of organization	18
1.2	AIC pattern in classical literature	27
1.3	Etzioni's nine powers	27
2.1	Parsons' three levels	33
2.2	Smith Charmoz model	42
2.3	Summary of Ozbekhan's planning process	52
3.1	Trist and Emery's organizational environments	66
4.1	Stakeholder's Colombia power project	77
4.2	Jantsch's model	96
5.1	The AIC pattern in major religions	112
5.2a,b	From two to three dimensions	117
5.3	Rummel's five spaces	119
5.4	The essence and manifestation of purpose	123
5.5	Freud's model of consciousness	125
5.6	The Jungian powers	129
5.7	The model of Purpose	131
6.1	Cube three dimensions	138
6.2	Concave and convex surfaces	138
6.3	The triune brain	143
6.4	The triune production of light as photons within an atom	147
6.5	The physics of color	148
6.6	Color opponency	150
6.7	Larvae of the fruit-fly	153
7.1	Color and three-dimensional organization	158
7.2a,b	Lightness to darkness	160
7.3	Creating the virtual torus	161
7.4	The virtual torus	162
7.5	Cross section of torus	163
7.6	Infolding and outfolding in 5 dimensions	163
7.7	Interfolding tori	164

7.8	Colors and dimensions	166
7.9	Fractal trees	167
7.10	Fractal image of AIC field relationships	168
7.11	The religio: power relationships in five dimensions	172
7.12	Ideals: fifth dimension	174
7.13	Manifestation of purpose in five dimensions	175
7.14	Values	176
7.15	Rhythm Based Time	177
7.16	Manifestation of purpose in four dimensions	178
7.17	Goals	179
7.18	Manifestation of purpose in three dimensions	180
8.1	Appreciating the whole	192
8.2	Thai village decimation	193
8.3	International network	195
8.4	Functions of influence	196
8.5	Priority maps	200
8.6	Stakeholder analysis	201
8.7	Control phase	202
9.1	The three circles of power	213
9.2	Color choices in five-dimensional space	223
9.3	Summary of ideals, values, goals	225
9.4	Sample scores	226
9.5	Power and leadership functions	231
10.1	The philosophical aspects of cultural difference	237
10.2	The AIC model of culture	238
10.3	The nine powers	241
10.4	Effective appreciative organization	243
10.5	Effective influence organization	245
10.6	Effective control organization	247
10.7	Integration of action learning	248
10.8	AIC systems generic values map	251
10.9	Priorities as identified by the community meeting	252
10.10	Internal strategic planning priority issues	253
10.11	Distribution of valuations in AIC fields	254
11.1	The Humpty Dumpty rule	261
11.2	Appreciative-centered ideals	263
11.3	Power map for humanity	271
11.4	AIC pattern in political system	273
12.1	Influence: engaging the issues	289

Tables

10.1	Balanced towards Appreciation I-a	309
10.2	Balanced towards Influence I-I	309

10.3	Balanced towards Influence I-I	310
10.4	Balanced towards Control I-c	310
A.1	Power map worksheet	293
A.2	Scoring sheet for ends and means (first and second dimensions)	295
A.3	Your power (ends and means in 1 and 2 dimensions)	298
A.4	Your power map (interpretation of all five dimensions)	299
A.5	Appreciative-centered environments (fifth dimension)	300
A.6	Influence-centered environments (fourth dimension)	301
A.7	Control-centered environments (third dimension)	302
A.8	Power resolution and transformation (zero dimensions)	303

Color Plates

Color plates are positioned between pages 160 and 161

C-1	Origin of our color perception
C-2	Purpose as the source of power: the five-dimensional language of color
C-3	Colors and three-dimensional organization
C-4	Color complementarity—opponency and wholeness
C-5	The three-dimensional perspective: dark to light
C-6	The four-dimensional perspective: dynamic cycles
C-7	The five-dimensional perspective: infolding and outfolding
C-8	The dimensional organization of AIC
C-9	Purpose and power
C-10	Reciprocal power
C-11	Organizing: the appreciative phase
C-12	Organizing: the influence phase
C-13	Organizing: the control phase
C-14	Life organizing and color
C-15	Colors for power map

Acknowledgments

Those who made significant contributions directly to the intellectual and practical creation of this work are fairly well recognized in the text. Consistent with the theme of this book I would like to acknowledge those unsung in the text but who formed the essential causal texture of the environments that supported my work. This includes Marilyn and my three children, Graham, Michele, and Michael who had to bear the brunt of my initial obsession with the work and had to teach me that a walk in the park to feed the ducks is just as important as creating new theories of organization.

It includes the faculty and students of the wonderful incubator the Social Systems Science (S^3), program at the Wharton Graduate School of the University of Pennsylvania. The constructive opponency between the two ends of Vance Hall provided by the steel and diamond clarity of Russell Ackoff and the wistful poetical approach of Eric Trist provided a perfect soil for the creation of the AIC concepts developed here. However, without Tom Burns and Tom Gilmore as faculty to give critical support to my complex evolving thesis at its most critical stage of development I wouldn't have made the rapidly approaching time limits for completing the work. It fell to John Eldred, another student colleague to keep on picking me up and putting me back together again like Humpty Dumpty after the many personal life crises I faced during the decades of long struggle to produce this work.

Cover Design

The cover design is by Graham Smith, Illustrations. Graham is the author's son and has, along with his siblings, grown up with the ideas and practice as they developed. He and Michael, his younger brother who is also a graphic artist, have been sources of inspiration and practical suggestions for the graphics in the book. Michael contributed the Humpty Dumpty image in Chapter 11.

Graham's choice for the cover is a simple seedling with three sprouts representing the oneness of the whole and its division into three parts.

This living organizational entity is centered in a context of light and air of the appreciated world and grounded in the earth of the controlled world. The overall tone of green represents the transcendent spirit of appreciation the author attempts to evoke in his understanding of nature's process of organizing.

Introduction

As a Management Trainee for British Overseas Airways Corporation (BOAC), some 40 years ago, my life was transformed by an assignment given at the end of that program. We had to write a paper on the effects of organization and management theory on practice. I am finally finishing that assignment with this book. The book, far from showing a one-way relationship between theory and practice, shows how human intuition and experience can combine, transform, and even transcend both theory and practice. It traces the emergence of a new philosophy, model, and process of organization from the stimulus provided by that first paper.

The journey takes us from applications in the private sector; from individual management experience in improving the performance of airlines; to consulting at the organizational level with applications in the pharmaceutical and chemical industries to the design of multinational corporations. It shifts to the public sector with the creation of a new paradigm for the design of World Bank projects, which then moves to the design of whole sectors of economies, whole countries, and to the design of the global development system itself. The book traces the evolution of a new philosophy, theory, and model of organization called AIC for appreciation, influence and control. The terms describe the three fundamental power relationships that form the base of the new model. The journey then returns to its origin people working in organizations trying to improve their own lives while contributing to improved organization that will leave the world a better place because of their joint efforts.

Part I: The Starting Experience: Theory and Intuition

Each chapter of Part I describes a phase of the three cycles of time that frame the AIC theory developed in the book. Each chapter interweaves the struggle of practitioners, typified by the author, acting against the backdrop of available theories and philosophies from the field of organization and beyond trying to extract or create middle-ground principles and models that better address the uniqueness of their situation, experience, and style.

Chapters 1–3 acquaint us with descriptions of both the personal experience and the historical evolutions that lead to the discoveries explored in this book. We explore control-centered, influence-centered, and appreciative-centered spaces in the context of classical organization theory, open-systems, and whole-systems thinking. We become acquainted with the concepts and practices associated with each space through stories of practice and its limitations. We review the literature and its evolution from control-centered thinking, through influence and then to the emerging appreciative-centered thinking.

The story in the three chapters is one of addition, not replacement; the gifts of the classical period remain. The gifts of the open-system space are added to those of the classical period. The new space of whole systems is added to that of both the classical and open-systems spaces. At the end we will see that all three spaces were always there and some writers, especially Mary Parker Follet, a writer in the classical period, saw and dealt with all three right from the beginning.

Chapter 4 unites the perspectives of the first three chapters through the stories of application to the design of projects and programs in the field of International Development.

Part II: The Philosophy, Theory, Process, and Model

Part II is the influence part of the book; it is the middle ground that joins together reflections from science, philosophy, and religion with learning from practice to produce an organization process that builds in the wisdom derived from all sources.

Chapters 5–7 paint a broad picture of the theoretical, philosophical, and spiritual evolution that lies behind the development of the AIC concepts and their current practice. It expresses the driver as a philosophy drawn from the intuitive insight that purpose is the source of power. This insight could generate many different models, but in this book we develop a model of power relationships. Similarly there are dozens if not hundreds of different approaches that can be used to implement the philosophy and model. Chapter 8 describes the generic process that is drawn from this combination of reflection and practice. It describes the process in a way that allows it to be adapted to any organizational issue the reader might face.

Though every instance or use of the model has to be reduced to some form of technology and technique in order to implement, we advocate strongly against reducing AIC to a specific technology or set of techniques to be used in every instance. To do so negates the foundational philosophy that every person is unique, and every situation is unique. Every person has their unique expression of the three powers and every situation has its own latency for manifestation of the three powers. The joy and sorrows of living, the joy and sorrows of work are to be found in this engagement of the actor and the situation. It is here, the center of the organizing process that the full expression of the power of purpose to create and re-create is found. It cannot and should not be reduced to formulae. The joy of creation comes when the whole is engaged in fully appreciating a situation, when all the stakeholders engage fully with both the positive and negative forces to discover the best pathways, and then fully informed actors take responsibility for the decisions that they make knowing that they are fully "informed" with all the many levels of meaning of that word.

Part III: Implications for Ourselves, our Organizations, and the World

Part III is the future, or appreciative-centered part of the book. It takes our understanding of the philosophy, the model, and experience with the process to draw out implications that might stimulate the reader to research, extend, deepen, and apply both the ideas and the practice:

1   What would happen if we obeyed the Humpty Dumpty law—the appreciative principle that you never separate the parts, ourselves and others, from the whole?
2   What is the potential if at every level of purpose we added the appreciative level?
3   What would happen if we treated the appreciative influence and control fields equally?
4   What are the realities we would have to face in order to achieve that potential?

To explore these questions we use the logic of the philosophy, model, and process developed in Part II.

This multi-dimensioned story is really three books in one. It is my story as a practitioner, an amateur in the truest sense of that term, one who loves his work and has been transformed by it. It is also a story of my profession searching to understand why organizations do not seem to achieve the potential that reading of the early pioneers and my first actual experience of organization led me to expect. In this sense it is also a story of an emerging field of "Organizational Sciences" that is broadening the historically narrow perspective of "Organization and Management." Organization and Management is based on a view of organizations as formal hierarchically controlled entities as studied in Business Schools, while Organizational Sciences seeks to include what we know about the organization of life into our theories and practices. Finally, it is a story of the human spirit that has the power to transcend current difficulties, frameworks, models, and theories to see ourselves as an *essential*, meaningful part of the whole, the universe of life.

Each part and each chapter within each part weaves together these three perspectives. I have tried to make each chapter stand alone as much as possible and use cross reference to other chapters where further explanation of ideas or practical applications might be found.

How to Read the Book

The book itself attempts to model the concepts in action. It treats each chapter and each part as a whole each reflecting in a different way its part of the whole message of the book. As a reader, consistent with the three-in-one theme of the book, you will have your own preference for each of the three perspectives—the practical, the theoretical, and the spiritual. If you are more practical and are willing to suspend your disbelief about new concepts and their rationalization you might take a leap of faith and begin the book at Part III and even complete the Power Map in Appendix II that shows how the pattern of AIC (appreciation, influence, and control) powers reveal themselves within you. Chapter 9 will explain this and Chapters 10–12 will extend your concept of application to your organizations and your world.

If you are more theoretical in perspective and want to know what new ideas are being explored and tested you should begin with Part II and then move on to Part III. In that part you can decide whether you want to go from application to yourself, in Chapter 9, to application to organization in Chapter 10, or to the world in Chapter 11.

Finally, if you have a more holistic or spiritual priority and have difficulty separating the practical from the theoretical and the spiritual then jump in wherever you like or read the book as is.

Part I

The Starting Experience

Theory and Intuition

The chapters of Part I acquaint us with personal experience of control and the evolution of organizations theory and its basis in concepts of control.

Chapter 1 begins with the story of the experience that followed the initial stimulus from J.A.C. Brown and the early classical writers on management. It recounts a progression of learning at three airports, in Lima, Trinidad, and Rome. It is also apparent as I tell this story that I had a control-centered view of organizations and how improvement is achieved. The progression leads to what appeared to be an almost accidental but enormous increase in performance at Rome that I could not account for. It did not fit into a control-centered vision, nor could any explanations be found in the available management literature, which again was primarily control-centered. The chapter takes the opportunity to review the available literature and show how the control focus came about and how the literature dealt and did not deal with influence and appreciation. The gap between my experience and available knowledge was powerful enough to motivate me to learn more and leave England to pursue an MBA at Indiana University.

Chapter 2 begins with the literature, symbolized by the contribution of my mentor at the time, James D. Thompson. In my master's thesis I tried and failed to account for the performance increase I experienced in Rome. It is Thompson, though, who gives me my first clue to the mystery, that power is the key. The literature with his and his colleagues' contribution takes a huge leap as it begins to see organizations as open systems. The exponential increase in the number of variables introduced into the consideration of what makes organizations effective as open-systems thinking introduced environmental factors into our thinking was enormous. It caused a whole new way of thinking about organization that we are still grappling with today in such forms as Chaos and Complexity Theory. With hindsight I could see that we had entered into a new level, a new dimension.

The chapter reviews how my colleagues and I translated such concepts into consulting practices and the design of multinational organizations. It ends with a description of the development of the first precursor to the Appreciation, Influence, Control (AIC) process for integrating individual, team, and organization development. The results from this series of applications, although they replicate the same kind of performance achieved in Rome raised similar questions. We now had a set of practices that we could make work, but others carrying out the same practices in different conditions could not necessarily replicate the results. So what were the underlying principles that could be applied anywhere by anyone?

Chapter 3. The search for those principles provided the motivation for me to make another huge shift and, in mid-career, pursue those answers through a PhD program in Social Systems Sciences at the Wharton Graduate School of Business, University of Pennsylvania. My thesis, which I applied to the design of projects for Rural Development in the World Bank setting did, finally, uncover the principles and produce the first round of the AIC framework. The chapter tells how the idea was created, and describes the contributions of Eric Trist, Russell Ackoff, and Hasan Ozbekhan to the new framework.

Chapter 4 describes how the framework was applied to the design of World Bank projects, then whole sectors of the economy. It proceeds to tell how its application spread through a whole country—Thailand—and caused a change in its Constitution to allow the large group meetings the process required. It was used to help the organization of the continent of Africa's response to the "50Years is Enough" campaign against the World Bank. Finally, it was used by a conference of ten countries to create a New Development Paradigm; a new way to look at the organization of international development.

The chapter reviews the body of organization literature that attempts to deal with the "whole," our appreciative-centered, multi-dimensional level of organization that directly contributed to the development of the AIC philosophy and process. It also notes some of the related literature that has appeared since then or that has only come to my attention while writing the book.

The chapter begins with the first person to openly muse, in relationship to organizations, on the "totality" of what we know; Kenneth Boulding. He realized that that totality is not knowledge but an image. The chapter covers Sir Geoffrey Vickers—the first person to use the word "appreciation" in this organizational sense. He saw it as the field beyond the realm of rational decision-making that policy makers must draw on. We review the considerable contributions of Erich Jantsch who linked appreciation to ideas of evolving consciousness

In reviewing work that was introduced after the development of the AIC concepts the chapter briefly covers the contributions of D. Cooperider's "Appreciative Inquiry," Gareth Morgan's "Imaginization," Joseph Nye's "Soft Power," Lyotard's "Generative Conversations," Peter Senge's "Presence," and Michael Jackson's "Creative Holism" and Clegg's extensive review of the literature on power.

1 Learning to March
Experience of Control

Turbulent Contexts

To be part of an overseas airline after World War II was to be at the center of major global, cultural, and technical change. Global power was shifting from the British Empire and Europe to the United States. The social structure of England was becoming more turbulent as forces for democracy and the demands of the new technology gave more power to the lower classes. The masses needed to be educated to handle the new technologies, and women, who had saved the British war effort by working in the factories, could never be satisfied again with the kitchen. I was a beneficiary of this huge shift and was the first of my working-class neighborhood to go to a university, all paid for by the Liverpool City Council.

In joining one of the two major global airlines of the time—BOAC and Pan-American Airlines—I was to be a part of the new highway. Just as the railroads had paved the way to extend the industrial revolution, so the airlines were paving the way for a new vision in which the world would shrink as all countries could be reached in hours instead of days or weeks. The aviation industry accelerated the process of development and innovation brought on by the advances made during the war. The management of time became as important as the management of space. Telecommunications, the neural network linking this highway, would accelerate the introduction of a new and infinitely available resource that would characterize the times as the age of information.

The airlines and the aviation infrastructure of airports, hotels, and telecommunication themselves would bring the demands of a new culture of technology wherever they went. There was a correct way to build, fly, maintain, and manage aircraft that would be the same in any culture no matter who or which class carried out the service or flight operations. All overseas employees found themselves at the center of this confluence and had to find ways to cope and in so doing became co-creators of an emerging new order.

The United States having focused on building large transport aircraft and bombers to support the war effort was able to develop a huge lead in international aviation. Being less bound by social structures it was also able to take a lead in codifying a new idea demanded by the new technologies; that organization and management of the new complexities mattered and therefore we had to learn and teach new ways to organize, lead, and manage.

When I joined British Overseas Airways Corporation as a management trainee in 1961 the Corporation very much reflected this confluence of transitions. Its culture was an amalgam of three different cultures. The culture of top management was more like that of the Foreign Office, a diplomatic service. Its flight operations drew more on the military culture and all operational staff wore uniforms. The emerging technical, managerial culture resulting from the introduction of such new disciplines as meteorology, aeronautical engineering, aircraft maintenance, complex demands for communication, and logistics to manage ground handling of cargo, mail, and passengers, was not really recognized or valued as something different, requiring a different kind of attention or a different kind of management.

The job I trained for was placed at the nexus of that change. Before the war the piston-driven aircraft that used to link the strands of the Empire had very short ranges. In 1936 a flight of 1,200 miles from Alexandria to Khartoum would involve five stops and take 15 hours. The numerous stops were called stations and each required a Station Officer. Station Officers were responsible for the organization of everything on the ground that affected the aircraft. They were responsible for calculating the weight and balance of the aircraft and for the preparation of flight plan and weather information. They had to look after passenger accommodation and catering as well as the handling of mail and cargo. They had to be prepared for any eventuality, natural catastrophe, political turmoil, and accidents that could affect service.

In prewar times the job had a romantic connotation, as the stations were located in far-off places such as Karachi, Burma, Bangkok, Hong Kong, and the Seychelles. There would be very few flights, allowing plenty of free time to enjoy the local social life with the status and perquisites approaching those of a diplomat.

By the 1960s, when I joined the airline, the technical and managerial component was reaching a critical stage as new and larger jets carried four times as many passengers and made fewer stops. The stations were becoming the complex highly technical multi-agency places they are today. They were becoming centers or corridors of technical innovation, and housed numerous agencies, customs, immigration, health, agriculture, and tourism all of which influenced flight operations and passenger, mail, and cargo handling. Peter Jones, one of my fellow trainees has collected many of the stories that reflect the adventure, the humor, and some of the nostalgia for those times and placed them on a website (Jones 2008).

It was for these reasons that BOAC had added a three-month management studies program to the end of its 2-year technical training for Station Officers in the program I attended. The lack of such training and lack of value given to engineering and management was already a factor in the tremendous brain drain from England to the United States that had begun in the 1950s. The BOAC training by today's standards was very rudimentary. As I recall, it consisted of a rather academic introduction to economics, law, and then management. In spite of this, the requirement to write a paper on the effect of organization and management theory changed my life by introducing me to the literature that was emanating principally from the United States.

At the end of the Station Officer training we were sent to a station for a six-month probationary period as proxy managers. We would act as airport managers but the actual manager was there to support us. I was posted to Lima; it was a BOAC station, meaning that it was controlled by staff directly hired by BOAC. Most stations, as we will see later, were controlled by local airlines—not BOAC itself.

At the airport, Callao, there was only one flight per day. This meant that there was no time pressure. At most airports, aircraft had to be turned around from arrival to departure in 45 minutes. We had 24 hours transit time. It was not surprising, then, that BOAC had never had a single delay since the inauguration of the flight several years earlier. This was tough to face as a neophyte; there was no way I could do better, I just had to avoid making a mistake that could cause a delay or give bad service to passengers.

Fortunately, we had an excellent airport manager, an Anglo-Peruvian who had had British military training. He gave me my first practical lessons in control. After every flight he would call a meeting of everyone involved and we would review not only everything that went wrong—which was generally very little—but he would also get us to look at what could have gone wrong. He made us see a causal connection between every element of the flight support systems, from passenger reservations, all the way through to passengers eating on the flight and disembarking at the next port of call.

He tied this together with links to the military and British culture with ceremony. As each flight departed he would have all staff line up in order of height and salute-off the aircraft. This became quite an attraction for the local Peruvians and people would come to the airport just to watch the wonderful anachronism of the send-off of the BOAC flight. Local airlines would try to imitate the send-off, but without the background culture of discipline and meaning, their staff were not very committed and it showed in their unpressed uniforms, floppy caps, and diffident line up.

This view of management as foreseeing and controlling all the variables that affect performance received another boost when I was introduced to "Methods." England was beginning to get the message about modern management. An executive from Imperial Chemical Industries, Dr J. Faraday had received some notoriety for his role in introducing "Methods" into the Corporation. BOAC hired him to introduce similar management efficiency into the company. All managers and professionals were to receive Methods training. The training was really an introduction into Scientific Management. It was a sophisticated form of what the airport manager from Lima had taught me. You had to understand how all the variables in a system were connected and you had to design methods to link them in the most efficient way possible.

Trinidad: a Trial by Fire

The three islands in the Eastern Caribbean—Antigua, Barbados, and Trinidad—had been identified as the worst performers on the whole of BOAC's network in terms of punctuality and customer service. Three Station Officers were sent to the islands to help improve performance. I was sent to Trinidad and Tobago, West Indies.

Our airport operations at most stations were handled by the local airlines, in this case British West Indian Airlines (BWIA). My image of Trinidad had been formed by the romantic images of Station Officers of the past, and by tourist advertisements for Tobago. I imagined myself on the beach seeing our flight arriving over the horizon then jumping into my Land Rover to go to the airport. Instead I found myself at Piarco, in a very urban setting, at least an hour from the nearest beach. I did, though, as previous Station Officers, find myself at the nexus of the cultural, social, political, and technical changes that characterized that phase of BOAC's development.

Trinidad had just one year earlier, 1962, become independent from Great Britain. Expatriate positions, so associated with the colonial past were looked on with great suspicion. BWIA had been a BOAC subsidiary since 1949 but as part of independence had been bought out by the government of Trinidad and Tobago. Given the end of our story, the evolution of a more holistic approach to organization and management, which causes us to include the external environment we influence and the context that we have to appreciate, I could have no better introduction. However, I was oblivious to the fact that any of this had anything at all to do with effective management. I was all of 24 years old and had never managed anything before.

I will never forget the day of my initiation. It was late afternoon. The temperature was competing with the humidity at about 95 degrees when I went out to see my very first flight at Piarco. As a newly minted, fully-fledged Station Officer, I was resplendent in my new uniform; my crisp white shirt, neatly pleated navy blue trousers, and stiff blue cap. The sun sparkled on the gold of the three brand new stripes on my epaulettes.

The new Boeing 707 was majestic, as the hot air from her whining engines made the rich green hills surrounding Piarco shimmer. With an almost satisfied sigh the engines wound down and her gleaming frame came to rest. I strode out to meet her at an appropriately brisk military pace, fully mindful of my Peruvian experience, I reached the end of her wing before I noticed—I was alone.

The cavalcade of steps, baggage trolleys, air-conditioners, catering vans, and fuel trucks that were supposed to greet the arriving plane had not moved. I turned and signaled to the steps to approach—they did not move. By the time I located the local duty officer and had him order the steps and air-conditioners in place we had a very hot, sweaty, and angry load of passengers and crew to deal with.

BWIA had never before had a BOAC representative at the airport. The local duty officer had assumed I would take over control of BOAC flights, the porters and drivers had no idea who I was. They probably thought I was an engineer or flight-crew member—it was my first day at the airport—and so they did not heed my signals. In addition, they never took responsibility themselves for moving to the aircraft—they always waited for a signal from the duty officer.

Such was my introduction to a host of similar problems of misunderstandings, differences in expectations, problems of personality, politics, and cultural differences—all the problems of getting things done through others, amplified by working in a different culture. Nothing in my two years of management training had prepared me for this. The multi-racial management and staff of BWIA, newly independent from Great Britain, were not about to pay too much attention to this fresh-faced graduate.

The situation was made painfully clear in the first couple of months. I used BOAC's traditional approach to the problem. I made lists of all the problems and put them into a report copied to my Area Manager, the BWIA Traffic Superintendent, and the local Manager. I would then arrange a meeting with local management to obtain BWIA's agreement to correct the problems. Nothing ever happened as a result of these meetings, they just became harder and harder to arrange. I soon learnt a lesson I still teach today; not to introduce anything new or negative in writing first, if at all.

I then turned to my newly acquired Methods skills. I discovered that at least 75 percent of our delays came from the passenger handling system—checking in passengers, assigning seats, boarding passengers, and completing customs and immigration documents. There was a huge bottleneck in the system.

The basic document for recording passenger information was called the passenger manifest. The manifest was typed up at the check-in desk as each passenger reported in. Until the last passenger arrived, the seat plan, flight documentation, fuel calculation, load and balance calculations, customs, and immigration clearances could not be processed. Once the last passenger checked in, there was always a chaotic hustle to complete the procedures. The haste, as much as anything, caused problems that led to delays—miscalculations and errors in documentation, missed signatures, and erroneous passenger counts.

I was able to analyze the flow of the system and come up with several designs for eliminating 95 percent of our delays. The revised system we adopted worked by pre-manifesting passengers and circulating the pre-manifest with an estimated number of passengers to all departments. When the last passenger checked in, it was only the adjustments that had to be communicated. Similarly, once passengers started to board, control of the flight and its documentation was moved from the check-in counter inside the terminal to the boarding gate at a ramp close to the aircraft. The shift of control-point saved an average of ten minutes scurrying time on each flight. The system was hugely successful and virtually eliminated passenger handling delays.

However, one day, after the system had been in use for several weeks, a woman who was one of the senior Traffic Assistants came on duty. She had been on holiday during the introduction of the new system. Under the old system, the most senior women were given the task of manifesting passengers, because of their typing skills and because of the critical nature of the manifest to the passenger handling system.

When she arrived at her position and saw the unfamiliar pre-manifest with passengers' names already on it she exclaimed, "What is this? This is no good—the old way is much more accurate." She proceeded to tear it up and returned to the old way. Naturally, I was furious and let her know in no uncertain terms how the whole new system depended on the pre-manifest. She seemed unduly calm, and other local staff that had been very positive about the results of the new system seemed reluctant to intervene. A week or so later, I was asked to the office of my own Area Manager and he presented me with a complaint about my handling of the incident from the local Station Manager.

Although I was able to explain the incident I had a sense that something more than this single event was operating. It took several months before I fully understood what had happened. I had spent so much time focusing on the task of improving passenger service that I had been totally unaware about my effect on people. In particular, I had been unaware of my effect on the local Station Manager. I had been training his staff and the staff had come to regard me as a source of knowledge; they would come to me when they had technical problems. I had been changing his systems. Every time he would come to the duty office and see something different he would ask, "What is happening here?" The staff would reply, "Oh, Mr. Smith says we should do this now." Wherever he turned his head "Mr. Smith says . . . Mr. Smith won't allow us to . . . Mr. Smith believes that . . ." He had begun to feel a stranger in his own station. It wasn't long before he found a way to remind this youngster that Piarco Airport was his world and I had better start realizing that. He had no need to tell the senior Check-in Agent what to do. She knew how he felt and she delivered the lesson I have never forgotten.

We did re-establish the system. I continued to train staff, that is, everyone who had a direct role in affecting performance. I also took personal responsibility for improving the systems and procedures. I would move from section to section, from passenger handling to cargo to flight operations improving systems and procedures and training staff. Performance in each section would improve for a while and then fall backward as I paid attention to other sections.

Performance did improve erratically but at great personal expense and effort. So I learned very early on that success has to be everyone's success, and for everyone to feel that success they have to be involved. You cannot be a hero or a martyr by doing everything yourself. I still needed some new insight and that was to come from my next posting—Rome.

An Insight from Rome

> Congratulations, Fiumicino [Rome Airport] has just jumped ahead of Kai-Tak [Hong Kong Airport] and is now first in punctuality and passenger service.

The telex arrived in September 1967 after only 6 months of my new posting to Fiumicino, Rome's International Airport. As Station Officer I still had no power to direct local staff. I had to coordinate with the local manager to review and suggest improvements in performance. Any implementation of those suggestions was up to the local manager.

The telex both surprised and perplexed me. BOAC had about eighty overseas agency airports (those not controlled directly by BOAC but by local airlines) and it measured performance every month by recording punctuality and keeping track of the number of positive and negative reports from passengers to provide an indicator of passenger service.

Fiumicino was a very large airport, a transit point for routes going south to Africa, to the Middle- and Far-East. Its performance had been consistently modest; it fluctuated around the mid-way mark, fortieth out of eighty stations. I was surprised at the telex because we had managed to improve performance so quickly; I was perplexed because it had taken so little effort in comparison to Trinidad. I fully expected the performance to decline again as it had at Piarco. It did not; it stayed in the first three during the rest of my 2-year stay in Rome.

How did this happen? What did I do? What did Rome staff do?

Operating in the background, no doubt, I had an overall impression or sense of direction from the organization literature I had been exposed to as part of BOAC's management training. However, it was the direct experience in Peru and Trinidad that had most conscious impact on how I went about the job.

In Peru there was nowhere to go but down. It was a BOAC-controlled station so we could tell our staff what to do. Callao had so few flights that I could be present at each one and intervene directly to avoid error and help improve performance. In Trinidad, as one of the worst performers, there was nowhere to go but up. My strategy of training, systems change, and then personal presence had results but they depended on my being there. Once I left a section performance would drop.

At Rome there were so many flights that I could not possibly use the same approach. I could never see more than one-tenth of the flights in any week. I knew not to make the mistake of producing negative reports as a vehicle for change. I knew that I had to develop a relationship with the local manager and have him be a part of anything I wanted to change. I knew that everyone had to be involved. The size of the operations was so much bigger than Trinidad and the 24-hour operation made it impossible to be in touch with everyone on a personal basis.

The first step of my "Methods" plan was to create some vehicle to communicate with everyone; all staff handling BOAC and our partners' flights. I would then go on to carry out a systems analysis, which would obviously take a much longer time than in Trinidad. I started a modest newsletter consisting of only one or two sheets. The newsletter reported the statistics of each section's (traffic, cargo, catering, flight operations, engineering, and so on) performance over the last month. If performance improved I would try to find details of specific actions that had contributed to the performance increase. In order to uncover these stories I went around each of my shifts and asked who had put in a special effort to create the improvements. I put these stories in the newsletter. Soon staff began to respond—when they saw me coming they knew I was looking for something good. I wanted to find what was working well. Traditionally, supervisors and other officers came looking for problems—things that were not working well. If we had a special performance problem I would ask one of the local staff with some artistic talents to produce a cartoon for me illustrating, humorously, the effects produced by the problem. For example, one month, when the rate of mishandled baggage was high, the artist produced a cartoon of a very attractive half-naked lady sauntering down the Via Veneto with a sign—"**Better On A Camel**."

After only one month I was surprised when our performance jumped from fortieth to about eighteenth. In the ensuing months, contrary to my experience in Trinidad, the performance level did not drop. Rome stayed in the top two or three positions of the league for the remainder of my 2 years posting. Once it became evident that performance was not dropping, that something extraordinary had happened, I began to seek the cause. As part of my systems analysis I began to look at what had changed. I assumed that the staff had found small ways to improve things that together added up to a huge performance increase. Something must have changed in the design or management of the systems of aircraft and passenger handling.

I visited every department, analyzed the systems, and talked with staff from the Senior Duty Officers to the humblest porters, yet in more than a year I could not find any evidence of a change in the system that could be recorded, nothing specifically or concretely had changed. Even when we looked at the more amorphous categories, such as climate and team spirit we could sense small shifts but nothing dramatic enough to account for the leap in performance and the maintenance of the new level over time.

As I looked for causes the only concrete source of difference I could find was the newsletter. We could not ascribe the difference to personality—I had not changed that much since Trinidad. I also knew that if I told my colleagues to start a newsletter, following the same kind of guidelines, they would not necessarily get similar results. I knew of several airports that used such newsletters but they did not achieve high levels of performance. The performance leap had something to do with the situation in Rome, it must have some relationship to the way I went about the work, my attitude, or approach. It also must have something to do with the impact of the newsletter itself. I tried to find what linked all three by talking to other managers. When back in London, I contacted people in Management Training but they could not help. One of my fellow trainees, Peter Farey, had joined the Methods group, he was very interested and gave me more help and resources for Methods, but nothing spoke of something bigger, which I sensed was operating throughout the airport.

Rewards for Innovation?

The events in Rome might have been one more step in a fairly conventional and privileged airline career had it not been for another critical incident that complemented and completed the major lesson from Trinidad. The BOAC Area Manager for Italy was based in the city while I was based at the airport. He was used to the airport representative keeping regular office hours. It was very easy for him as Area Manager to call and have someone at the airport to answer his questions. I did not keep regular hours—I was a budding scientific management analyst—I had worked out a point system indicating the number of problems and degree of difficulty of each flight and made up a schedule to cover the most points, i.e. the most difficult flights. My hours were different every day, some days I did not work office hours at all.

Although copies of this schedule were sent routinely to the Area Office, the manager did not pay much attention to it and there was no regular meeting forum where such matters were discussed. The Area Manager was a colonial type with public (private) school education and a reputation for being difficult. I was one of the new graduate intake of trainees from a redbrick university with a working-class background. We clashed over requests for small amounts of money for my unusual and, therefore, non-budgeted activities—money to fund the newsletter, small prizes, and parties to reward the Italian staff for their improvements in performance. I was worried enough about the clashes to ask advice from the older and much wiser senior engineer who seemed to get on well with the Area Manager. His advice was very simple. He said:

> "Bill, the Area Manager is a bully. He sent the last guy in your job out with an ulcer. You just have to tell him to f . . . off."

There was no way I could follow his advice literally but I did interpret it as having to stand up to the Area Manager. This I resolved to do and was just waiting for an opportunity. It came soon enough in the form of a telephone call in which he complained strongly about my not being at the airport for something that was important to him. Without using any of the four letter Anglo-Saxon words recommended by the engineer I did get really angry with him and reminded him of the number of times I submitted my schedule to him, how it was based on a point system allowing me to cover the most difficult flights. I reminded him that this was not convenient for me because I worked different hours every day but it was the most effective use of my time. Then I added the zinger—my job was to make the airport more effective not to be a lackey for him. He was almost apoplectic on the other end of the phone. He immediately scheduled a meeting to discuss the incident. I could tell by his tone and the arrangement he made that this was a critical meeting and would probably be the basis for a negative report to London.

I had read somewhere that when you are really worried about something you should imagine the worst that could possible happen: you should then accept that that is going to happen and then make a list of everything that you can do to make it better. I accepted that a negative report was going to go in. However, the list I made ended up being a list of every single contact I had had with the Manager since my arrival. Every single one was negative; from minor affronts, to failure to listen, and numerous examples of his unwillingness to support what I was doing in spite of the evidence of results. The final item, for our culture, was quite serious—I was in our local agent's office when the Area Manager had called and was openly critical of my not doing my job (i.e. to be there for him).

When I went to his office for the meeting, under the stress of emotion, I had mistaken the time of meeting and was an hour late. Rather than making him angry the lateness seemed to unnerve him a little, he probably thought I had done this on purpose and was going to be a harder nut to crack than he thought. His dark mahogany desk was immaculately clear. He began:

"Now, Smith, I want to go over our recent incident."

He pulled out a single piece of paper from a drawer and began to read. It was a fairly accurate rendering of my angry conversation with him. This was clearly the text that would go into a report to London.

I looked straight back at him and acknowledged:

"Yes, that conversation sounded awful, and very angry. But your telephone call was the straw that broke the camel's back."

I then pulled out my three sheets of paper from my BOAC-issued briefcase and began to read very deliberately the list of each contact I had had with him since arriving at Rome. I noticed him becoming more uncomfortable as the list went on until in the end I didn't have the heart to read the last one in which he was undermining his own staff to our local agents. He just stood up and said:

"Smith, I certainly see that we have had an awful lot of misunderstanding so let's go have a coffee and we'll talk this through."

I thought that was the last of the incident but what happened next only confirmed how totally innocent I was of any political awareness or skills. Without sending any official letter to London, the Area Manager was voicing informal concerns about the radical changes at the airport and the strange goings on there. As a result, a team of Traffic Inspectors was sent to examine the airport. Not having any idea of the real reason for the inspection I welcomed the inspectors with open arms. Here at last was a chance to show what I was trying to do and hopefully get some support, if not from the Area Manager at least from London. As they represented the technical system and were equally innocent of the political motivation for the inspection they were quite impressed and I was nominated for a Q for Quality award. The award was part of BOAC's latest general methods campaign that had moved on to Deming's work on Total Quality.

The Area Manager had to give me the award and I have always kept the picture not only for its personal meaning but also for its symbolism. The photograph in Figure 1.1, as well as showing the award for the results I could not explain, also symbolizes the three levels of culture that were in transition, and in play in the Rome situation:

1   I represented the technical control system, which was just beginning to be understood as having different kinds of management needs than the more traditional role or class-oriented management system of the British.
2   The Area Manager represented that role-oriented class system that was being pressured by the rapid evolution and complexity of technology. He also represented my complete failure to be aware of the role of influence and politics in management.
3   The picture of the Queen represented the appreciative field, the British culture that itself was under great global pressure to change with the loss of the colonies and the resistance of newly independent countries such as I experienced in Trinidad. The Q for Quality poster in the background also presaged the important lesson of control; that in the end results depend on "Me" not "You." The three relationships of A, I, and C were there right from the beginning.

The Area Manager was eventually removed from Rome and overseas assignments but not before I had one more culture clash that would result in my decision to leave BOAC and England.

Figure 1.1 BOAC award and three levels of organization

We had a visit from the General Manager for Europe, another of the colonial types. It was shortly after Fiumicino had topped the list of airports for punctuality and service. I was working at the airport and had just come from accompanying a VIP to one of our aircraft when I saw ahead the Area Manager for Rome, talking to the General Manager for Europe. The GM called me over and began to exchange the usual niceties:

"Ah, Smith, how are you enjoying Rome? How's the wife?"

he asked in his impeccable southern accent. Then after a few more exchanges with the Area Manager and myself, he asked:

"Oh, Smith, would you step aside a moment, there is something I'd like to say."

Knowing that the performance results had just been published and Rome had again performed excellently I prepared to answer his questions with all the modesty my bursting pride could muster:

"By the way, Smith, I noticed you didn't call your Area Manager, Sir!"

I was so taken aback I just blurted out in obvious anger and disappointment:

"Of course I didn't call him Sir, I know his name. I only call passengers whose name I don't know, Sir!"

The bitterness and strength of my reply surprised even me. I tried to back peddle:

"You have to understand that I am the first age group not to complete military service; I missed it by only thirty days. I have not developed the habit of calling people Sir."

Too late, the damage had been done, the reply came:

"I, too, Smith, did not complete military service for medical reasons, but I call my superiors Sir."

Nothing was said, then or later about Rome's performance.

At that time I took a narrow view of the incident and saw it as another part of the class struggle. I couldn't possibly perform any better—and this is the reward. The future does not look good.

Today, as I look at the incident I realize that I was being taught the hard way the second half of my lesson from Trinidad. Designing and doing good work is not enough unless you involve those affected by the work, those below you, those alongside you, and those above you. I often wonder if I had had more natural political gifts or if I knew what I know now about power what would have happened in Trinidad and Rome.

However, I did resolve that it was now time to learn more. I would go to the source of most of the new information, a place that valued professional organization and management—America. I researched American Universities and decided to complete an MBA at Indiana University because of the work of one man: James D. Thomson, a sociologist who seemed to be speaking that broader language, that scope beyond technology that my reading and experience embraced. He was even beginning to speak of power. The MBA was a very new idea then and at that time I would be one of only 200 MBAs in England.

Stumped Again

In order to complete the story of Rome we have to jump out of our time sequence and take us two years later to my master's thesis. I was so taken with the sense that something more was operating than I could see, that I made the study of the Station Officer role and its effect on performance the subject of my thesis.

I wanted to find out from every Station Officer who held the job (there were more than 100) how in practice they carried out their jobs and whether the differences affected performance. I knew that I had not followed a traditional approach to the job. I hoped to find other Station Officers who had achieved similar success but by different means. BOAC would be able to use the results to improve the design of their training programs and possibly the selection of staff to be Station Officers. I was still operating from the role-level assumptions that you could solve all organizational problems by the proper design of jobs and organizations, systems and procedures.

I used the information from experience that you had to look at the Station Officer's role, the people above him who controlled him, and then the people alongside him and the people below him; a full circle of influence, although I did not understand it as such at the time. I constructed questionnaires for the Station Officer and each of the constellation of roles around him—his Area Manager, who knew both the Station Officer and his counterpart the local Airline Manager, and his Functional Manager, based in London, who knew his technical capabilities—and last, I constructed a questionnaire for the local Airline Manager who had to work closely with the Station Manager on a daily basis.

The questionnaires attempted to establish two things:

1   What were the factors that most contributed to successful performance?
2   How did the Station Officer actually go about his job?

Measures of performance for each station were already available from published information.

I expected the profile of a successful Station Officer to come out quite differently from traditional expectations. As the management of the airlines had been drawn from the military after World War II their model unconsciously followed military norms. I expected that the highest level of performance on agency stations on which Station Officers had no command or control would differ considerably from the military model. Using new insights gained from my mentor Thompson I also suspected that each of the key roles of the Area Manager, the Functional Manager, and the Station Officer himself would have different interest in and expectations of the Station Officer so would create different profiles for success. Each of them would have a very different view of what constituted Station Officer performance.

It took a major feat of organization on BOAC's behalf to contact 100 Station Officers scattered around the globe and distribute and return their questionnaires. As the questionnaires were returned I could hardly wait for the results. I would stay up late at night in the Business School's brand new computing room, punching the data from each questionnaire onto IBM cards. In 1969 computer processing was still quite primitive. My excitement was high as the reams of green-lined computer paper folding into neat piles gave the expectation of profoundly sophisticated scientific results. My first real research! I had all the variables covered from every point of view possible; I had the human insight and experience of having carried out the job myself; I had this new-found power of the computer to apply any mathematical or statistical process to my data. How could I fail?

I processed the BOAC Area Managers' questionnaires, which were to produce a profile of what characteristics and key behaviors they thought most contributed to high performance. I correlated these profiles with information on station performance during that particular Station Officer's tour of duty. The results would provide two kinds of data—both how well the Area Manager understood what factors affected performance and what those factors were.

I ran the correlation for the Area Manager's questionnaires. There was no significant correlation!:

> OK, so what do they know anyway? They are the furthest from understanding what the job is.

I turned to the London questionnaires of the Functional Traffic Managers. Again there was no significant correlation!:

> What is happening—they at least should have some idea!

With rising anxiety I turned to the local managers' profile:

> They should know. They see the Station Officer in action on a daily basis. Oh no—there is no significant correlation here either!

Now close to panic, I turned to the last group, the Station Officers themselves:

> They must correlate; they know what it takes to do well. There must be some correlation here. Let me cross my fingers!

Alas! There was no correlation! My heart sank:

> What am I to do? This can't be true! There is no significant correlation at all between any of the profiles and station performance! Did this mean that nobody, not even the Station Officers themselves, really know what accounts for performance?
> This can't be.

I checked and re-checked, but there it was—no correlation!

After a sleepless night thinking of all the costs, the trips around the world, the long burdensome task that headquarters had undertaken to coordinate and distribute the questionnaires and their return—all for no result. What could I do? What would I tell them?

The next day, in desperation, I joined all the computer cards together and challenged the computer. OK, you go through this mess and tell me if anything at all correlates with station performance. The results emerged— a number of seemingly unconnected items from the questionnaires began to give promising correlations. In terms of content, they did not seem to add up to any recognizable theme. Suddenly I noticed that almost all of the responses came from one group of questionnaires—the local Airline managers. There was no pattern relating Station Officer characteristics to performance, but there was a relationship between local Airport Managers and performance even though the questionnaires were not designed to pull that out. The questions were an accident of the design.

The answer then hit hard and clearly. Of course, it was true that the Station Officers' profiles did not correlate with performance. It was not they but the local Airline Manager who most affected performance. The local Airport Manager had control of the staff and resources that most affected performance. In practice Station Officers had very little influence on performance.

The implications for agency policy were enormous. If your goal in sending Station Officers to agency stations was to improve performance, as was the case of the three of us sent to the Eastern Caribbean, you were wasting your time. If a station were performing consistently badly the most effective route would be to change the agent. This policy was later pursued in the Caribbean. BOAC replaced BWIA as handling agents and hired independent contractors over whom they had more control.

With great luck the research results proved very illuminating and useful to BOAC. However, they only increased the enigma of the results from Rome for me. They seemed to confirm the more traditional hypothesis that more direct control correlated more with increased performance. I did not have that kind of control at Rome and I had made a significant difference in performance. The point was further proved by the results after I left Rome; performance returned to the mid-range levels. Was there something different between low levels of performance increase and exceptional levels?

At least the more traditional managers breathed a sigh of relief. The much more expensive direct control of local managers, overall, was more effective than the more indirect but much less expensive influence of expatriate liaison officers. Nothing I could do with the questionnaires revealed any correlation between their characteristics or modes of operation and high performance. I was back at square one. I was little further along. The university had not proved as productive a locale for discovery as I hoped.

In terms of my own quest the research seemed to be telling me that we don't really know what are the causes of high performance such as Rome. In the case of Rome the factors appeared to lie in the properties of the system as a whole and not in the behaviors or characteristics of the individual actors—the Station Officer, local manager, or the higher levels.

The Classical Literature and Control-Centeredness

First Concepts of Organization

Although in hindsight it is painfully obvious that a position such as that of a Station Officer at a critical juncture in time, and at the nexus of so many cultural, social, and political waves, was very dependent on factors in the context and on a network of relationships he could not control. The very lack of formal control at agency stations meant that to be successful the Station Officer had to learn other forms of power. Yet the topic of power in relationship to effectiveness was not even mentioned in our training or in informal briefings. Our focus was on the technology and anything that interfered with that was a problem to be solved on an incident-by-incident basis.

Surprisingly, though, power has always been an issue in organization theory right from its origins. Max Weber (1864–1920), for example, although trained in law, was a sociologist who spent his whole career as an academic at the University of Berlin. His sociological training, which included studies of religion and the development of civilizations, gave him a broad approach to his study of economic development and organizations. He was concerned with why people obeyed commands. He divided the problem into two parts: situations in which people were coerced into obeying orders—which he called *power*—and ones in which people obeyed orders voluntarily—this he called *authority*. Organizations, he believed, were concerned with the latter—authority. This can be seen in AIC terms as a division between control and appreciation. He further divided authoritative organizations into three types:

1   **Charismatic**: that draws its power from the almost supernatural or spiritual power of its leaders.
2   **Traditional authority**: that draws its power from the traditional relationship between groups. Such authority is based on custom and changes slowly with changes in custom.
3   **Rational Legal**: that draws its power from the logic of the mechanism or laws required to achieve very specific goals.

Already we can see the beginnings of the triune pattern of relationships we have labeled appreciation, influence, and control (AIC):

a   Charismatic has a transcendent or spiritual quality that evokes appreciation;
b   Traditional has a focus on group relationships that evokes influence;
c   Rational, with its concern for logic and efficiency evokes control.

However, of the three types of organizations it was the control type under the label of bureaucracy that received the dominant emphasis in the modern industrial world. With his interest in religion Weber was able to link the rational organization of the economic system to the particular moral outlook of the Protestant religion. With their greater emphasis on this world Protestants needed to stress that salvation was achieved through hard work, often labeled the "Protestant Ethic." This was not easy because economic activity in the pre-industrial world was not regarded as a worthy activity.

From those early days, often referred to as the Classical period, improvement of organizations was viewed almost entirely from a control-centered view. The appreciative-centered view, labeled by Weber as *Charismatic* was recognized, but regarded as not relevant to the development of the prevalent industrial form of organization. Similarly, the natural forms of folk organization based on social relationships, or influence-centered organizations, which Weber labeled as *Traditional Authority* became equated with control. Influence and appreciative power, of course, still existed, and were used naturally by organizational actors but they were not addressed in a formal way. Many of the stories recounted in Peter Jones' collection are actually stories of serendipitous appreciation and influence. It is precisely because they didn't fit into the control framework that they became interesting stories.

The scientific revolution was sweeping the country in many fields—medicine, physiology, chemistry to name a few. The rational approach toward scientific inquiry was replacing old methods of knowing. The field of management was no exception—scientific management was, in fact, an attempt to convert traditional, influence-centered, organization into rational, control-centered organization, and appreciative-centered organization was ignored:

> The rational and bureaucratic organization was socially and morally legitimized as an indispensable form of organized power, based on objective technical functions and necessary for the efficient and effective functioning of a social order founded on rational-legal authority.
>
> (Reed 2006)

From then on most organization theory became management theory, dealing with the management of the kind of industrial organization produced by the scientific revolution. Even the reactions to the problems inherent in such an approach were still framed within this narrow view of organization.

> Taylor's "scientific management" [was] directed towards a permanent monopolization of organizational knowledge through the rationalization of work performance and job design.
>
> (Ibid.: 29)

The scholars who reacted, for example, to such rational technical approaches espoused by Frederick W. Taylor (1916) still emphasized human factors but considered within a control-centered view of organizations. When Gouldner surveyed the literature in 1959 he saw two distinct approaches to organization: the "rational" and the "natural." The rational took an engineering approach to organization—it could be designed and shaped to meet specific goals. The "natural" systems approach viewed organizations as systems that adapted to the laws of nature in spontaneous and indeterminate ways. Following Darwin, system survival was the goal and adaptation the major process. The emphasis was still on single organizations and organization theory was the theory of managing those single organizations.

So within this field of the single control-centered organization operating under the norms of Weber's bureaucracy, Gouldner (1959) saw three distinct patterns:

1   **Mock bureaucracy**—in which groups or organizations pretended to follow rules but only actually did so when "enforcers" were present.
2   **Representative bureaucracy**—in which different groups agree to follow rules based on common values. In mines, for example, this might be safety. The miners follow the rules because it will avoid accidents to them, and the managers because it will cut costs and increase efficiency.
3   **Punishment-centered**—in this pattern rules arise because groups try to coerce or control each other. It was the need for this kind of control that led to the formation of Unions. They could impose rules on management in relationship to overtime, health, safety, job boundaries, and so on.

So the control-centered, bureaucratic view of organization became the whole: it provided the principal perspective, the lens through which organization/management theory was developed. Gouldner split this whole into three parts. Again, it is not too difficult to perceive the underlying AIC relationships that still persist inside this sphere of control-centered organization:

•   **Mock bureaucracy** leaves freedom in the hands of the workers—appreciation;
•   **Representative bureaucracy** depends on group values and relationship—influence;
•   **Punishment-centered** depends on control.

Amitai Etzioni, who similarly operates in the control or bureaucratic sphere, also illustrates the recursive nature of the three relationships. He identifies three kinds of power that are very close to those of Gouldner (Figure 1.2). He creates a two-dimensional pattern of nine power relationships in which each dimension contains the three AIC relationships (Figure 1.3).

The second dimension correlates the three kinds of power with three levels of different ways or means of manifesting them, which he describes as "Degrees of Involvement." Together they form a matrix of nine types of power relationship.

Etzioni believed that the most common types of power, which he conceived as compliance to authority, were 1, 5, and 9 (Pugh *et al.*: 33). Coercive power produces alienative behavior and alienative behavior produces coercion. Similarly, remunerative power and calculative involvement, and normative power and moral involvement both are mutually causative. A church is an example of 1, a factory of 5, and a prison of 9.

Aic Pattern in Classical Literature		
Etzioni	**Gouldner**	**AIC**
Coercive	Punishment	Control
Remunerative	Representative	Influence
Normative	Mock	Appreciation.

Figure 1.2 AIC pattern in classical literature

Etzioni's Nine Powers			
	Degrees of Involvement		
Type of Power	Moral (a)	Calculative (i)	Alienative (c)
Normative (A)	1	2	3
Remunerative (I)	4	5	6
Coercive (C)	7	8	9

Figure 1.3 Etzioni's nine powers

Purpose and the Classical Period

Actual implementation of the concept of bureaucracy, although it had enormous success in making organizations more efficient, further reduced the treatment of people as "wholes' by separating action taken in the "bureau" from the whole human being. Human imaginations, ideals, emotions, values not related to the definition of the task, but which might have been captured if knowledge from "Charismatic' and "Traditional Authority" organizations had been included in our theories and organizational practices, were kept outside of consideration. The conduct of the *bureau* or *office* was separated from the conduct of the human. Human goals were organizations goals. Personal and social values were subordinate to economic values of the firm if not illegitimate. The personal was separated from the official. Human ideals were to be dealt with in church but not in the modern organization. The wholeness of the officeholder as a human being was broken. Only the goals of the bureau were legitimate.

Under these conditions it is no surprise that human purpose was not a central concern of the classicists. Purpose was treated primarily from the organization's perspective and then only at the level of goals. Implicitly people belonged to organizations to serve the organizations purpose. The organization's goals shaped the definition and description of organization theory. When Weber discarded charismatic and traditional power he did so on the basis that the kinds of purpose they pursued could not easily be specified so were less susceptible to rational-legal power.

So the first step in reduction from holism in organization can be described as putting aside the study of appreciative-centered (charismatic) and influence-centered (traditional) organization in the belief that only the principles of the control-centered (rational-legal) were appropriate to the design of modern organizations.

A remarkable exception to the flow of classical management and organization theory occurred in the work of Mary Parker Follett. Writing in the 1920s through to her death in 1933, she produced insights into the nature of purpose and power that are still as fresh and relevant today as they were then. Like Weber, as a student of philosophy, political science, and history she was able to take a very broad approach to her understanding of organizations. Unlike Weber, an academic, she also had a great deal of experience. For example, she helped create educational and recreational centers for young people in Boston. She also served on many boards. She did not accept Weber's reduction of organization to the rational-legal. As a member of various public-sector statutory boards she was able to study organization, management, and leadership in its very broad social domains, so she naturally included her intuition and experience of "charismatic" or appreciative-centered organization and "traditional authority" or influence-centered organization that are more easily found in the public sector. When she was invited by industry to review problems of organization she found the problems were the same as those she found in the public sector—those of control, power, conflict, and participation.

She instinctively never separated workers from their natural social relationships. She understood the starting point was purpose. You had to learn how to guide men's conduct in both work and social relationships. In this she was one of the first writers to understand the value of psychology as a tool for improving organizations.

In *Dynamic Administration* she introduces the concept of both power and purpose:

> No word is used more carelessly by us than the word "power." I know of no conception which needs more careful analysis.
>
> (1945: 96)

She looked to psychology for insights questioning whether men had an instinct or drive for power or whether men sought power for specific ends. She quoted jurists who believed that people sought a reciprocal balance of power—people do not like to receive favors without reciprocating to restore a balance of power.

Relying more on her own intuition and experience she suggested that we think more of *power with* than *power over*. She believed that "genuine power is capacity," so power was not a zero-sum game in which one gains power and another loses. "[T]he problem is how much power they can grow"; in this she was retaining the root meaning of the word power from Latin, i.e. *potere* reflected in the French *pourvoir* and the Spanish *poder*, to be able:

> In a store or factory I do not think the management should have power over the workmen or the workmen over the management. . . . It is possible to develop the conception of power with, a jointly developed power, a co-active, not a coercive power.
>
> (Ibid.: 101)

She also introduced the image of circularity of power, a concept that would not be fully developed till the 1980s through theories of process and systems learning. She saw circularity as the basic means for bringing about integration, i.e. how to get the whole system working together:

> Circular organization is the basis of integration. If your business is so organized that you can influence a co-manager while he is influencing you, so organized that a workman has an opportunity of influencing you as you have of influencing him: if there is an interactive influence going on between you, power with may be built up.
>
> (Ibid.: 112)

It is this holistic integrative perspective, centered in influence, which gives her work written 70 years ago, before systems thinking was introduced such a modern ring:

> We must observe every case of behavior as a whole; this must never be forgotten in the study of social situations.
>
> This appreciation of "total behavior" brings us back again to our formula: the will or purpose of a man or group is to be found in that activity which is a constant function, or a combination of such functions, of some aspect of his environment . . . this formula, with its implied definition of behavior as a function of the interweaving between the activity of organism and activity of environment, gives us a new approach to the social sciences.
>
> (Ibid.: 54)

It is, especially, her concept of the interpenetration of purpose, action, and power that foreshadows concepts not broached till the advent of quantum sciences. These concepts almost jump out from history. They are not pursued at all in the mainstream of organization and management literatures for decades because of a focus on control-centered organization:

> It now seems clear that we must look for purpose within the process itself. We see experience as an interplay of forces, as the activity of relating leading through fresh relating, to a new activity, not from purpose to deed and deed to purpose with a fatal gap between,
>
> You cannot coordinate purpose without developing purpose; it is part of the same process.
>
> It could be put this way. Purpose is always the appearing of the power of unifying, the ranging of multiplicity into that which is both means and ends, the One holding Many.
>
> (Ibid.: 56)

She also foreshadowed the idea that the brain and our patterns of neural activity might account for the fundamental patterns we keep on repeating at the individual, organizational, and cultural levels:

> Both psychologist and sociologist note that as the number of integral reflexes involved in behavior increases the immediate stimulus recedes further and further from view as the significant factor. The stimulus becomes the total situation of which the total behavior is a function. As the psychologist finds that what the bee is really doing is laying up honey in its home, that it is only incidental that it sips from this flower or that, so in studying social relations we find that a situation of which behavior is a constant function is usually very complex.
>
> The purpose in front will always mislead us. Psychology gives us an end as moment in process.
>
> Through our observation of human relations, through the teachings of psychology, we learn then that from our concrete activities spring both the power and the guide for those activities. Experience is the dynamo station; here are generated will and purpose. Further and of the utmost importance, here too arise the standards with which to judge that same will and purpose.
>
> (Ibid.: 54)

Unfortunately, at that early stage in the early 1960s I had only read her work and that of the other classical writers in reviews, Fayol on administration, Taylor on scientific management. The Hawthorne experiments carried out between 1927 and 1932 by Elton Mayo came the closest of anything I read in giving an explanation for what happened at Rome. In the Hawthorne experiments Mayo had experimented with the effects on productivity of changing working conditions only to find that the conditions didn't cause the increases in productivity; he found it was the attention paid to employees and their freedom to pursue their own means of production that most affected performance (Trahair 1984). I still felt there was some bigger principle operating but Mayo's results certainly gave me hope to keep on searching.

At this early stage of my career I had been operating as an individual and discovering that aspects of the organization where I was working contained elements and processes that affected my performance. I had begun to learn AIC at its most elementary level. I had learned that I had to manage not just downwards to my own work (control), but I had to work with colleagues I could not control (influence), and also had to manage upwards to understand my boss and the large system he represented (appreciation).

Management of difference, power, and politics were emerging as salient issues and so also was the role of culture. However, at that time I had no way of understanding or incorporating them into what I was doing and the available literature proved of little direct help.

So it was with great anticipation I set out to seek answers from the place where most of the literature and ideas about organization were originating—America.

2 Learning to Dance

Experience of Influence

Reading the Music

After 2 years of study as an MBA student I still did not have the answers. I was especially disappointed that the study on the role of the Station Officer did not reveal any insights on exceptional performance. The MBA did, however, bring with it some unanticipated benefits. The discovery of computers and the power to bring together knowledge, especially mathematics and statistics from the whole world and apply them to your unique problem opened up a whole new set of possibilities. Here was one new avenue to high performance. I began to appreciate what would later come to pass, through the Internet, that all knowledge, not just mathematics, could be funneled through that computer terminal. Everybody could become a Wizard of Oz by tapping the keys of the computer. My association with Jim Thompson did not give me direct answers on how to create conditions for exceptional performance but he at least provided the doorway to a new level of understanding of power.

The more traditional parts of the MBA did little to enhance my understanding of high performance of organizations. My first degree in England had taught me several modern languages; it seemed that the MBA added to my repertoire. I was now able to speak "accounting, production, marketing, finance, and economics." Jim Thompson was writing a book, *Organizations in Action* and, as students, we reviewed the draft chapters in his class. It proved to be a seminal work that has probably had as much influence on the field of organization as any other single book. Single paragraphs have inspired whole books if not whole schools of thought. For example, Harvard's Lawrence and Lorsch's (1967) basic work on organization and environment is rooted in this work. Jay Galbraith,[1] a DBA student of Thompson's while I was at Indiana, based his *Organizational Design* (1977) on Thompson's work. Eric Trist, who was later to become one of my own PhD mentors, also acknowledged his debt to James D. Thompson.[2]

Organizations in Action (Thompson 1967) provided a turning point in management thinking and began to lay down the underpinnings of the synthesis that was to become AIC. The first half of the book presents the idealization of an organization operating under "norms of rationality." Thompson develops a series of propositions about the factors that affect the structural design of organizations that could be tested. In the second half of the book, he recognizes the limits of the structural approach as the limits of rationality. He sees structural design as subject to the administrative process. The administrative process, in turn, is influenced by the interests of powerful groups and the personalities of powerful individuals. Design, then, is not solely the resulting rational structural relationship between the divisions of labor. It is subject to the irrationality of competing goals and the personalities and interests of its members. An understanding of goal agreement and power processes becomes essential to the design of organizations.

In one fell swoop he was taking us away from the ideal of improving organizations through the design of their structures and was pointing us towards a new area of process and power. As Trinidad and Rome showed, I had no concept of how to deal with "the irrationality of competing goals, interests and personalities," I had no concept of "power processes"; they were just problems to be solved on a piecemeal basis.

Just as I had discovered, the hard, piecemeal way at the individual level, the underlying principal that you needed a three-level approach to your job—you had to manage upward, sideways, and down—Thompson showed the same principal operating at the organizational level (see Figure 2.1).

Using Parsons' (1967) concept, he suggested that organizations have three very different levels of responsibility and control. Each demand very different perspectives and action. Our airport operations provide an example of the technical level—they were protected from daily exigencies

Parsons' Three Levels (The A, I, C interpretations have been added by the author)			
	EXIGENCIES	LOGIC	DEGREE OF CERTAINTY
INSTITUTIONAL (Appreciative) A	Obtaining legitimization from surrounding community. Providing meaning.	Open system logic.	Low
MANAGERIAL (Influence) I	Mediating between technical units and procuring resources for them.	Mediating between open and closed systems.	Medium
TECHNICAL (Control) C	Processing materials efficiently.	Closed system rationality.	High

Figure 2.1 Parsons' three levels

affecting other departments by the Area Manager. He also mediated with entities outside of the airline that affected airline operations; the government, area businesses, and social groups. The underlying principal was that the technical core could operate as a closed or control-centered system protected from contingencies by a surrounding managerial level. It could then afford to operate more efficiently undistracted by interference from other departments. The managerial level had to mediate the relationship between multiple internal and external stakeholders so success depended more on influence than control skills. The institutional (A) level dealt with the whole that affected the operation of the whole of BOAC in Italy. Although the Area Manager was the point man for this success, at this level it involved the whole institutional pattern embedded in BOAC's culture as modified by its whole history with Italy. When the Area Manager was fulfilling ceremonial functions, meeting VIPs, attending flight inaugurations, he was fulfilling this diplomatic, institutional role.

The last column of Figure 2.1 shows that the role of each level is to reduce uncertainty for the next level. The institutional level reduces external uncertainties of the whole through the creation of policies that limit the amount of variables that the managerial level has to consider. It gives a bounded space in which the managers can be free to apply their coordinative influence skills. Similarly, the managers reduce the uncertainties associated with coordination between departments in order to leave the technical operation free to control their operations efficiently.

We now had the beginning of the AIC framework, its vertical first dimension. The key shift from the classical period lay in the recognition of the different function or purpose carried out by each level. The classical view held that each level in the hierarchy was a control point that divided its responsibility into smaller components and handed control of those to lower levels. The functions of management were the same at each level except for the size of the unit. Now with Parsons' distinction we could see that management at each level completed very different types of task requiring very different processes. Thompson then made it clear that these processes were power process.

Power

As we saw in the last chapter, the idea of power has been central to the study of organization and management since the beginning. By 1957, Dahl noted that there were so many ways in which different cultures, different disciplines, and different people looked at power that many thought that its study was a bottomless swamp. He felt that we would probably never get to one "Theory of Power," but we would end up with many theories, each with a specialized application:

Thus we might never get through the swamp. But it looks as if we might get around it. We are not likely to develop a single "theory of power."

(Dahl 1957: 56)

A common thread in almost all of the writing on power up to that time was an emphasis on "power over." Power was something that you had that could make other people do what you wanted. Weber, for example stated:

"Power" (Macht) is the probability that one actor within a social relationship will be in a position to carry out his own will despite resistance, regardless of the basis on which this probability rests.

(Weber 1947: 52)

The principal dissenting voice, as we saw in the last chapter, was Mary Parker Follett who insisted on "power with." Dahl, likewise, took a more intuitive approach to power. In trying to grasp its essence he realized that power was a relationship between people. He developed a notation that enabled one to assess the relative degrees of power held by two or more people.

Emerson (1962) building on this notation and the concept of power as a relationship added the idea that power was the obverse of dependence:

Power: (Pab) The power of Actor A over actor B is equal to the amount of resistance on the part of B which can potentially be overcome by A.
Dependence: (Dab) The dependence of A on B is (1) directly proportional to A's motivational investment in goals mediated by and (2) inversely proportional to those the availability of those goals outside of the A–B relationship.

(p. 32)

In building on this insight, Thompson made two important contributions to the dialogue on power. First, he supports the conceptualization of power as a relationship, not a quantity, or a possession. Second, and more importantly from our point of view, he establishes the *multiplicative nature* of power in the task (influence) environment:

By considering power in the context of interdependence, we admit the possibility of A and B becoming increasingly powerful with regard to each other—the possibility that increasing interdependence may result in increased net power. It is the possibility on which coalitions rest.

(Thompson 1967: 32)

Thompson establishes the base for understanding that when we extend our reach from a focus on what we control to include consideration of and engagement with the influenced environment we can multiply our power. The recognition of the open-system relationships of the organization with its environment makes salient the interdependencies between them both. As dependency is the obverse of power then interdependencies are power relationships: they are the "power with" of Mary Parker Follett, or as I now prefer, they are influence relationships.

Thompson also gives voice to the second quality of this new domain of influence that is essential to the dance—time:

> The paradox of administration, the dual searches for certainty and flexibility, to a large extent revolves around the dimension of time. In the short run, administration seeks the reduction or elimination of uncertainty in order to score well on assessments of technical rationality. In the long run, however, we would expect administration to strive for flexibility through freedom from commitment—i.e. slack —for the larger the fund of uncommitted capacities, the greater the organization's assurance of self-control in an uncertain future.
>
> (1967: 150)

We are now building the core of our understanding of this influence-centered domain. Its core is mediating relationships over time, mediating upwards, downwards, and sideward between three levels, to harmonize the interests of all the parties.

Taking the First Steps: Consultants, Tools, and Answers

After the MBA I had a better sense of direction. I had a first rough framework around which I could build an approach to exceptional performance. I decided to find out how to flush out this framework by working at the interface between academia and practice—consulting. I stayed on in America and went to work with a nationally known consulting firm, A.T. Kearney, in Chicago. They had just split from McKinsey, which concentrated on the strategic aspect of organization whereas Kearney focused on the more operational side.

Unfortunately, during the 2 years or so I worked for them, I never had a chance to put the higher level perspective on the whole organization and its relationship to the task or influenced environment into practice. However, there were two studies out of the dozens I carried out that again made an unexpected contribution to the search: one, ironically, was the very first.

A colleague, Bruce Springborn, came to tell me that my first assignment was a labor turnover study for McDonald's. I was still not familiar enough

with the American culture to understand that this was a major assignment. I still confused hamburgers with hot dogs and thought that as the low
man on the totem pole I had been given a nominal assignment to study hot-
dog stands. He disabused my ignorance very quickly by explaining that
McDonalds had huge operations and were headquartered close to us near
Chicago.

I soon discovered that I was part of a nationwide study for a company
that had applied the most sophisticated of modern scientific methods to the
production and marketing of the lowly hamburger. McDonald's was
the epitome of modern management science. It even had a Hamburger
University. It had become one of the most successful organizations ever.
McDonald's belief in scientific methods made them a natural client for our
company, which prided itself on the introduction of Methods Time and
Motion (MTM) studies to industry. Our task was to apply our industrial
science to the study of labor turnover in both the companies franchised
and non-franchised stores. I was given appropriate training in MTM and
sent out to cover a score or so of appropriately selected stores in the
Midwest.

Due in part to the innocence of the neophyte and also, I imagine, because
of the shock of my experience with research in BOAC I kept a very open
mind. How people saw and explained things was not necessarily how they
were. My peripheral vision was wide open; I was certainly not going to
repeat the mistake of relying solely on the technical part of the problem.
In the late 1960s and early 1970s the franchise business and fast foods
were burgeoning. The market for fresh-scrubbed teenage male labor was
becoming saturated. It was getting harder to find teenage boys with the right
image and attitude. Turnover was increasing and of great concern to our
client. I noticed, after a few visits to stores, that there were no females in
McDonald's own non-franchised stores and relatively few females in their
franchised stores. Questioning did not reveal any overt policy not to hire
young girls or older women. So I began to find out why the stores did not
hire women. The best I could divine was that it was an implicit part of the
culture, part of the value system. The founder, Ray Kroc, who continued
to have a very strong influence on operations, was known for his Victorian
values. Unconsciously, he conveyed the message that mixing young girls
with young boys would produce more "hanky panky" than hamburger.
Managers were very reluctant to test that assumption.

I visited, without asking permission, a number of franchises of other
companies who did hire females. Far from lowering standards or increasing
problems of discipline I received the opposite impression—mixing young
boys and girls raised standards and considerably lowered turnover rates.
My conclusions were something of an embarrassment to my colleagues and
the partner in charge of the study. This was, after all, common sense. Who
needed a $500,000 study to come up with such a simplistic solution?

However, the suggestion, wrapped up in all the industrial engineering data about costs and turnover, was finally submitted to the company. McDonald's did shortly after start hiring both young and older women.

Here was the lesson again—the factors that most affect performance lie outside the management control system. In this case they lay in the cultural values of the founder. If this was true then maybe this is also a source for exceptional performance? But how can organizations become aware of this and take advantage of it by building this knowledge into the way they organize and conduct their affairs? My mistakes at Trinidad had made me aware, but I had no idea how to build that awareness into understanding or action by others. There was the additional problem that was now becoming a theme. Even when I acted on such insights the effects were problematic. The results in BOAC and in the study of McDonald's were very effective, but in both cases I had to step outside sanctioned procedure. In the case of BOAC not adhering to a nine-to-five schedule: at McDonald's making common sense rather than technical recommendations. The first caused anger and the second embarrassment.

It was also this study, linked to Mary Parker Follett's unique contributions, that triggered my awareness that possibly women and the natural way they go about things may also have something to contribute to exceptional performance. The process was given a very personal jolt by my daughter, Michele. We had a small sailboat and were preparing to go sailing. I asked our two sons Graham and Michael to hitch up the boat and load the sails and other equipment. I then turned to Michele and asked her if she would make the sandwiches. At all of 9 years old she turned to me with that special look that I have come to know as a special combination of "love and power" and asked:

"Dad, did you ask me to make the sandwiches because I'm a girl?"

She was absolutely right, I was a male chauvinist, and still may not have completed all twelve steps of recovery. Her question did put the issue of male and female difference forever at the forefront of my mind. It was the seed that would eventually bear fruit in association of the feminine with the appreciative. If we had more women in organizations at that time would we have more Mary Parker Folletts and more Micheles producing more appreciative approaches and less control approaches?

Our focus, however, in spite of all the other daughters who must have had been raising questions of chauvinism with their fathers, was still on the procedures and methodologies that assumed one could know or learn and then control everything necessary for success. Organizations were machines that required the right tools and techniques for their design, improvement, and maintenance. Action outside this sphere was seen as illegitimate.

If the McDonald's incident pointed to the need to enlarge our concept of the organization field beyond a center of control, beyond the masculine perspective, the next incident shows the issue of the centrality of power raising its head again, but this time in a way that did not involve interpersonal relationships.

A big part of the consulting firm's revenue came from executive compensation studies and job evaluation. After several months of working on the monotonous and tedious systems for evaluating jobs and determining executive compensation I started to look for ways to eliminate some of the drudgery. Computers were very new to business in those days and were totally alien to departments working on organization and human resources but an understanding of their power was one of my gifts from Indiana. In my spare time I started to work on ways to use the computer to reduce the amount of repetitious calculations. In order to do this I had to understand the rationale behind the point systems being used. I was very surprised to discover that they were heuristics, rules of thumb—there was no real basis.

In practice, both consultants and clients often worked backward from the results they wanted to allocation of points in the system. The heuristic nature of the process was revealed in the linear relationship between the points allocated. For example, one of the usual factors in evaluating the worth of a job is the level of education required. The evaluation plan would allocate points to each of the levels: high school diploma, bachelors degree, master, and doctoral. Similar points would be attached to such factors as degrees of experience, size of budgets controlled, and so on. In each case the progression of points from low to high would be linear, i.e. 20, 40, 60, 80, 100, and so on.

Common sense tells us that not all of these relationships could possibly be linear. For example, for many jobs education beyond a master's degree may be a detriment. A PhD may not add anything to the ability to do the job and may make the PhD less motivated. In such cases the curve of value for education should peak at the master's level and drop at the PhD level.

Using the power of the computer I was able to create a program that truly reflected the values of a large group of people into an internally consistent compensation plan. In order to produce non-linear relationships I had to engage the help of the transportation division, which was using massive programs to solve routing problems. They showed me how to use linear programming to produce non-linear relationships.

To get a value I would have a group of people declare what they believed a job was worth. They could give a very precise single value or a very wide range if they had little idea. We would then ask them what factors they thought accounted for performance in the job and whether there were any relevant levels they could identify. Again, they could be very precise or very vague. We would run a factor analysis and choose the three or four factors that most accounted for performance. The program was able to show which values truly predicted worth, and eliminated those that did not.

The program could also be used the other way round; you could reveal the relevance of the existing values in any job-evaluation system. The program revealed the lack of correlation between declared values and those paid for. It also revealed that in most plans there was no significant correlation between performance and compensation. Much of executive compensation was and probably still is determined by the implicit values determined by competitive forces in the larger social system. They have little to do with the difficulty of the work, the level of education, and so on, the typical things that are measured in job evaluation. For example, jobs in the public sector that require the same or greater levels of education, experience, and skill are often paid significantly lower than the private sector. Industries that are in very favorable economic situations pay more for the same jobs than less fortunate industries.

Again, Thompson's insight on power processes proved critical. Compensation had less to do with performance or merit than it had to do with power. Its rationality was in the internal distribution of salaries within a given organization. The inter-organizational or inter-sector distribution was based more on power. The source of that power was in the larger social system and was correlated with the ability to control and influence the allocation of resources. Those who had little power over resources were rewarded less well.

There are larger consequences for society of such distribution. We tend to value those people and organizations that are wealthy and believe that they are doing something right or better. The approach to management and organization in the public sector, for example, is derided for not being as efficient as the private sector. Yet efficiency comes with control and the public sector has much less control of the factors that affect its performance than does the private sector. The organizing process required when you don't have control is much more difficult and less subject to norms of efficiency. On a job-evaluation scheme the skill involved should be rated higher. Public-sector envy of the supposed efficiency of the private sector encourages the application of control-centered organizing strategies to the public sector, which proves very costly where influence- or appreciative-centered strategies would be more effective and much less costly.

The bulk of the consulting assignments I was involved in had little to do with the large issues that I sensed needed to be addressed and the larger principles that had to be discovered. I was not able to follow on a consistent basis the new perspective I had received from Jim Thompson. Now, I was at a loss: the universities didn't have the answers I was looking for, nor did the consulting firms, so I gave up looking for people who already knew. I would just have to take a job and work on the issues however I could.

The Dance Begins

It was 1971 when I decided to join the International Division of a U.S.-based pharmaceutical company, G.D. Searle. For most of the time I worked in a group called the Staff Coordination Group (SCG), headed by John Berquam. It operated as a think-tank for the President of the International Division, Woody Ensor. We would take on any problems that did not fall to the regular functions such as Marketing, Production, Finance, Human Resources, and R & D. I had found a place where I was at the nexus of many streams of action and it was characterized by Thompson's key influence word "coordination."

The company was growing even more rapidly overseas than it was domestically. It expected to double its volume of international sales every 5 years. This rapid growth caused two major problems that it fell to me to examine. The first was the structuring of international operations, their relationship to headquarters and its subsidiary companies. The second was the development of the division's own management talent. How should managers be developed in order to cope with such rapid growth? For the first time I would be able to go beyond the behaviors of individuals and look at some of those factors at play in the larger social and cultural systems. I had an opportunity to look at a whole organization through the "power" lens that Thompson had provided for me.

The rapid growth of the company, especially in its international operations was causing severe growing pains. Corporate product managers were licking their lips at the size of overseas markets and wanted greater control over international activities. There were strong moves to disband the International Division and to form a Global Organization. It fell to me to carry out the necessary organizational research.

I saw the necessary three levels—the institutional, managerial, and technical—as the Corporate Headquarters, the International Division, and International Subsidiaries, operating in the context of the pharmaceutical industry. I compared that pattern with the same three relationships in multinational companies in other industries. From this information, and following Larry Greiner's (1972) concept of organizational evolution I constructed a model with my colleague Remy Charmoz, also from the Staff Coordination Group (see Figure 2.2).

What is salient in the Figure 2.2 is the evolution of three levels of organization and the power relationships between each of them over time. The translation of mutual adjustment, planning, and policy and procedure as appreciative, influence, and control power, of course were not in the original. What changed in each phase of evolution of multinational companies were the locus of control and the nature of power relationships.

Phase 1: In the earliest phase of internationalization, when overseas units are very small and scattered, controls of key resources such as finance

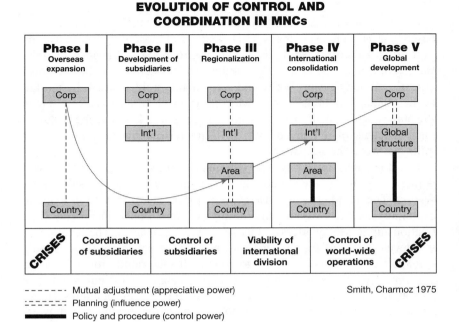

Figure 2.2 Smith, Charmoz model
(Smith and Charmoz 1978)

are kept very much in the hands of Corporate Headquarters. Corporate Headquarters minimizes risk by using local distributors and participating in joint ventures. This allows the corporation to "learn the ropes." Often, returns on the original investments are held as reserves against future losses. During this phase, there are no systems to process international information, no international staffs, and no plans or strategies. Decisions are made through direct personal contact as problems arise, "mutual adjustment." Control is located at the corporate office, because new operations need cash. However, in practice there is not a great deal of control or influence over the daily operations. An overload at the top provokes a move to Phase II. Either too many decisions must be made, or not enough decisions are made. Whatever the case may be, the result is that the subsidiaries go their own way.

Phase II is marked by subsidiary development and the appointment of an international executive and staff. The executive acts to support the subsidiaries and allocates capital accordingly. Large subsidiaries therefore get the most attention, because they require most of the investment. The locus of control now moves into the hands of the subsidiaries, which initiate, propose, and act. The Corporate Headquarters is essentially left out of the process because of its lack of knowledge. Up to this point, there has been little movement of people to the International Division, and U.S.-centered thinking still predominates. The very small numbers of international staff ensure that they too cannot exert a great deal of influence or control over the international subsidiaries. Power is exercised on a basis of personal contact between the international executive and both corporate offices and the subsidiaries. By the end of Phase II, however, the international executive becomes overwhelmed. He is continuously traveling and has little, if any, time left to plan. Subsidiary managers begin to run their subsidiaries according to their own needs, not the Corporate Headquarters'. Competition between subsidiaries develops over new areas and territories.

Phase III introduces a phase of consolidation between the subsidiaries into areas or regions, e.g. Northern and Southern Europe. Area international executives are added, as well as staffs. This is the stage of development that BOAC was at in which Area Managers had a great deal of influence but not control over operations. The increased demands for coordination required a regional plan, which in turn replaced personal contact as control moved from subsidiary to region. By now the corporation recognizes the international group as a source of investment and is no longer satisfied with informal personal decision-making. Use of return on investment criteria is instituted either across the board or is modified for the differential risk levels of countries. The international president is now a politician, a buffer. Since little data is available for making decisions, the domestic executives are ignorant of the international affairs. The international president must simultaneously get support from domestic product divisions and ward off ignorant staff groups who want information and may flood the fledgling subsidiaries with procedures.

The International President may be seen as a block by both international and domestic subsidiaries. At this point, the domestic subsidiaries and corporate offices realize how little they know about the international group and notice that the international group is a competitor for capital, research and development, people, and so forth. The problem at this point, however, is to prevent a move to a global structure that would be premature, because corporate staffs are still ignorant about international affairs, and there are no planning and information systems to provide a link with the corporate office.

Phase IV is marked by international consolidation. In this stage, control moves to the international CEO to bring order and rationality to the dispersion characterizing the previous three periods of development. This period is one in which the corporate officers take a real and direct interest in the International Divisions. The size of investments and interdependency of areas dictate a greater degree of centralization. International consolidation is marked by executive international committees, planning and evaluation systems, more sophisticated financial measures, and task forces.

By now the International Division rivals the Domestic Divisions even more. There is an increasingly greater need for worldwide data and for a global mechanism to overcome parochial local interests. The corporate staff want more control and information at this point; the area managers resent the planning and control. The international executive may again moderate a still-ignorant staff, since the corporate officers might press prematurely for the kind of "planning control" that is better suited for the next phase of development.

Phase V, which can be termed "global development," is marked by corporate control. Through the increased contacts of the previous phase, corporate and domestic product groups have a more realistic awareness of foreign operations. The "planning" coordination provided by the International Division is now superfluous. Phase V is also marked by significant improvements in global information and planning systems. Most companies maintain some form of international specialist coordination. This role is more integrative than controlling.

The transition to a global product structure constitutes a metamorphosis. There are changes in the financial control system designed to handle such factors as national variations, profits by product and region, and transfer pricing. Different and multiple standards of evaluation appear; careers and compensation practices are changed; new committees and staffs evolve. Most important, an international mentality gets created to various degrees. All together, we feel these changes were more significant and dependent on cultural change than any of the other crises the company had experienced. They constituted a "way of life" for which the organization was not sufficiently prepared.

G.D. Seale, we felt, was at the crisis point between Phases III and IV, the viability of the international division. Corporate Headquarters wanted to jump to Phase V—Global Development. However, it needed the development process of Phase IV to prepare itself for the enormous cultural shift that a global perspective brings. It had not developed the human, informational, or financial systems to be able to successfully carry out the planned transition.

I was privy to the political maneuvering as strong-willed, ambitious men at all four levels battled for more influence and control. The research pointing out the problems was very well received and I thought that at last we could bring rationality to the power process and avoid the mistake and huge cost of moving too rapidly to Phase V. However, each party tended to take out of the research only the points that supported his or her own point of view and then continued the battle with sharper tools.

For me it confirmed that organizations are not run on norms of rationality but on norms of power. It reinforced the necessity of working at least three organizational levels to obtain all three of the institutional, managerial, and operational perspectives. It also identified the horizontal or coordinative level of power, which could also be expressed as power relationship. What is important is that it stressed the importance of lateral power, the second dimension:

a   mutual adjustment as appreciation;
b   planning and coordination as influence;
c   standard procedures as control.

The original research paper that Remy and I wrote on this topic was actually titled "Coordinate Line Management," it was an attempt to give a label to what we felt was a different and missing level and type of management that was even more necessary in the International Division than in the Domestic Divisions. We were looking for a term that distinguished the type of power required for lateral communications that was different and more complex than vertical control. We borrowed the concept of "coordinative" from Thompson. We were experiencing the different field of relationships that we eventually called "influence-centered."

The whole exercise provided the realization that any change process had to actually deal with power relationships. Explanation from research, however valid, was not up to the task. The question still remained, of course, how is all of this built into an organizing process that any organization could use?

The Dance Takes Form

The answer to this question began to take form at Searle when I began to tackle the second problem, the development of international managers and organizations to handle the doubling in size of the International Division every five years. Here my colleagues at SCG and I began, at first intuitively, to provide a development processes that incorporated some of these features.

I began by reading the literature on management development and interviewed staff from multinational companies with the best reputation for management development. At that time most management programs consisted of classroom training in which managers talked about management. Some of the better programs instructed managers in the handling of the primary business systems—finance, human resources, marketing, and production—a mini MBA. The unstated purpose of most programs seemed to me to be indoctrination by Corporate Staff groups to make sure that line managers did their homework right—i.e. they filled in the right accounting forms, followed personnel procedures correctly, and so on. They had little to do with generating the kind of performance I had seen possible in BOAC and later in Searle. Some programs had begun to shift towards a human-relations and participative approach, but they too seemed more concerned with boosting the stature of human resource specialists than contributing directly to performance. Very few of the human resources staff designing and running these programs had any line management experience.

The AIC Form in Embryo

I found little that I could use directly to help the managers of our relatively small international units. Even if we could adapt some of the programs to make them more performance-oriented, it was impractical to take overseas managers away from their operations for several weeks at a time.

We eventually decided on a different approach. We would treat the development of the manager of a subsidiary and the development of his staff as part of a business planning process. The planning process, however, would be a group process in which the top management team worked together with the help of an outside consultant. In this sense I was building on Thompson's idea that planning is the primary coordinating process. Because of this we called the program the Management Planning Process (MPP).

Building on the lessons from Rome and Trinidad and Parsons' insights through Thompson, we created a three-level integrated development process. The three vertical levels, the first dimensions of the emerging model, were top, middle, and lower level managers for each subsidiary. In this sense we were using power in the senses of capacity, 'potere' in Latin or 'pourvoir' in French. We were ensuring that all three organizational powers, institutional, managerial, and technical were involved. The lateral second dimension consisted of three different means or tracks that we integrated into this whole: individual leadership development, team development and organization, and systems development. We ensured that each job was seen in context, and each manager would see his part in the whole and learn how to coordinate upwards, sideward, and downward.

We met three or four times a year off-site. Each session carried out activities at all three levels. In the first session we would begin by having the groups develop images of what the company and the industry might look like in the future. At the individual level we integrated a career development process into the program. Each manager, then, not only received information about himself, his values, leadership style, political skills, and so on, he learned this in the context of planning work, and changes in organization, so that each would support the other. This approach was applied in the same way to the design of business systems such as the financial and information systems. When outside experts were needed they operated through the MPP. For example, all staff would be involved in the design of a new financial system, or a new information system.

We began by working with one of our best-performing subsidiaries, our Canadian operation, headed by Guy Labrosse. Together we made significant improvements, not as dramatic as Rome but much better than average. For our second trial we moved to one of our worst International operations, an English Medical Instruments Division. The results were similar; the company had not made a profit since we acquired it five years earlier. Within eighteen months it had made its first profit. After two years it was performing so well that it received the classical corporate reward—it was sold.

The program was very successful and for the first time I began to see results getting closer to those of Rome. However, they were now brought about by a process that involved the whole organization. We were beginning to understand and realize the leverage supplied by the influence-centered approach. It achieved so much more in less time. We were proving the multiplicative power of influence first indicated by Thompson. It involved less work for me and, apparently, had much less of the negative results that occurred in Trinidad, Rome, and the consulting firm. I say "apparently" because there were no ill-effects from all the people involved but in the distance there were without my knowledge others who were upset by the success of the program.

The political upheavals I referred to in describing the Corporate–International–Global structural problems began to affect the International Division. In spite of the findings of the research the company did decide to jump to Phase V—Global Management. The International Division was to be gradually dismantled. The Corporate Human Resource group would then become the Human Resource group for the International Division. It was only then that I heard that I was regarded as a threat to this group even though I had no contact with them. Again, I had no idea why. Later I learned that MPP was regarded as a human resource-type program and they wanted involvement. More than that I was getting more practical results, faster and at much less cost than the organization development programs they were running. Consistent with many organization development programs at that time, the Corporate group focused on team building but made little attempt at integrating into the whole of management and organization.

Now under the globalization strategy they wanted to take over the program. I explained that one of the reasons that MPP was successful was that it was line- and not staff-controlled. It was a business program with a business priority not a staff development program. Senior line managers took part in the program and made integrated decisions based on the results.

The Corporate Human Resource group thought that this constraint was a refinement and they had enough influence with senior management to have the program accepted. I thought that this would be a good opportunity to take time out and reflect on our learning by pursuing a PhD. The Corporate Human Resource department offered help if I promised to stay on a year and find someone to run the MPP program corporation-wide. I agreed and found Ken Murrell who was just graduating with his PhD from George Washington University. As I predicted, Ken found that he was unable to get the support he needed from a base in Human Resources. He eventually went back to academia.

I felt that some key strands were beginning to link together that gave hope of being able to extract the underlying principles of exceptional performance in a way that they could be used by anyone in any type of organization. I knew that you had to think in terms of wholes and that every part of the whole also had to operate at three levels: upwards, sideward, and downwards. Obviously, at Searle I had not defined the whole large enough and didn't see that Corporate Human Resources would see MPP as a threat.

We had a beginning two-dimensional matrix of three levels and three different means of coordination in each. I knew that we had a lot more to learn about the power processes that held the whole matrix together. Now would be a good time to push forward with a concerted effort to identify the principles and find means to communicate them. This would be a good time to take time out to really think this through.

In the account above we referred directly to the writers, scholars, and colleagues in the organization and management field who had a direct impact on our work. In order to provide the context for the next chapter, we now have to go back to fill out the picture of where our practical effort fits within the whole field of organization theory at that critical stage of evolution.

Open Systems and Influence

Consistent with what we have already learned about the individual level and the organization level, the organization field as a whole is also influenced by fields outside of its control. The major evolutionary advance referred to as open systems was triggered by developments outside the field of organization in biology and information systems. Bertalanffy, a biologist, saw the potential for aiding all sciences by studying the similarity of systemic relationships that existed in all disciplines (1950). He coined the term "general systems theory" for this new science.

Kenneth Boulding (1956) first saw the potential of this kind of thinking for organizations and March and Simon (1958) first identified the organization as a "sociological unit" comparable in significance to the individual organism in biology, Katz and Khan (1996) wrote the first book applying open-systems thinking to organizations. However, as we saw above, it was James D. Thompson and his *Organizations in Action* (1967) who first developed an open-systems model of organization that transcended the division between Gouldner's rational and natural systems to create a "contingency" model, as it later became known, that incorporated them both.

Thompson noted that classical organizations theory relies on a rational perspective employing "closed system," or as we would say "control-centered" logic. He argues that a view of an organization as a natural system requires an "open system" logic:

> Having focused on control of the organization as a target each (Scientific, Administrative Management and Bureaucracy) employs a closed system of logic and conceptually closes the organization to coincide with that type of logic. If instead of assuming closure, we assume that a system contains more variables than we can comprehend at one time or that some of the variables are subject to influences we cannot control or predict, we must resort to a different logic.
>
> (1967: 12)

To this end he linked the open-, natural-, and closed-system perspective to Parsons' three levels of organizational responsibility and control— technical, managerial, and institutional. It was these three levels, as indicated earlier that were to provided the basic pattern forming the vertical dimension of the AIC model.

Organization Environment Relations

Once organization theory opened up to consider environmental relation-ships, a huge space at a new level, and in a new dimension was created. There were now three spatial distinctions:

1 the organization
2 the task environment, and
3 the rest of the environment.

This addition of two levels of environment to the organizational equation multiplied exponentially the number of factors that needed to be taken into account to understand organizational functioning.

Jay Galbraith (1973), a DBA student of Thompson's at the same time as I was completing my MBA, also used Thompson's insights to begin to understand the demand of such an information-processing viewpoint for the design of complex organizations. He began to uncover the more subtle patterns of control and coordination that were required in modern organization. Our understanding of control and coordination patterns in multinational organizations was part of this work and was published by Galbraith (1978). The single chief at the top of the hierarchy could not ensure high performance through control alone. Success was contingent on environmental actors who could not be controlled. Competing areas of organizations might even demand dual control, so the idea of the "matrix" organizations with two centers of control was born. In any case, from this point on the management of lateral relationship in organization became just as important as the management of hierarchical relationships.

The Move to Process

Clearly, the three different functions of organization at the institutional, managerial, and technical levels required different kinds of management, different climates, and styles of operation. Such complexity could not be achieved by line control, which assumed that each level was simply a more detailed rendering of higher level goals. As all the contingencies and constraints affecting each element of the influenced environment could never be known a new level of thinking was required. The idea of process as the key to understanding organizations began to replace the concept of structure. The organization was required to institutionalize processes for learning from its environment; middle level managers needed new processes for mediating the very different open-systems perspective of the institutional level with the closed-system perspective of the technical system:

> To deal with the situation of such great complexity, the organization must develop processes for searching and learning, as well as for deciding.
>
> (Thompson 1967: 9)

The idea of process supplanted the idea of structure as the answer to appropriate organizational design. We would from then on make the major conceptual and dimensional leap from three- to four -imensional thinking by centering our thinking in organizing *as process* rather than *organization as structure*.

The dynamic of seeing process as structure over time became an essential building block for insight and innovation, Lawrence and Lorsch in researching patterns of Integration and Differentiation caused by organization environmental relationships (1967) noted the importance of time. They observed, for example, how it took varying amounts of time to obtain feedback from different organizational impacts on the environment. These differentials dictated varying spans of attention from managers. Some products required short time horizons and other long:

> The paradox of administration, the dual searches for certainty and flexibility, to a large extent revolves around the dimension of time.

In the short run, administration seeks the reduction or elimination of uncertainty in order to score well on assessments of technical rationality. In the long run, however, we would expect administration to strive for flexibility through freedom from commitment—i.e. slack—for the larger the fund of uncommitted capacities, the greater the organization's assurance of self-control in an uncertain future.

(Thompson 1967: 150)

Elliott Jacques (1967) went even further; he suggested that time spans of discretion determined the actual value of a manager's contribution to an organization. For example, factory workers on piecework would receive feedback on their performance within the hour so they had times span of discretion one hour long. Foremen may not know till the end of the day how well they were doing while their supervisors would not know till the end of a whole week. The highest paid executives, those with the longest spans of discretion or feedback from results, were those who were responsible for long-term investment of ten or more years, e.g. executives in high technology or with huge capital investments.

The excitement about entry into this new world created by extending the boundaries of organization thinking to include the environment was palpable at the time. Paul Weis (1971) for example, in pulling together a group of authors who he thought represented the new wave declared:

Conceptually, the life sciences are entering a phase of maturation . . . one comes to the realization that the trend from naïve micro deterministic causality toward macro deterministic "system" theory is inexorable. The urge to fit our concepts to our expanding knowledge is breaking through the old constraints that tend to hold knowledge and understanding captive.

(p. vii)

In the same book Hasan Ozbekhan, also a faculty member at Social Systems Sciences, introduced his seminal work *Planning and Human Action*, it was this work that shifted our focus to view organizing as a process on planning.

The influence of Hasan's work on AIC, was to present the matrix of three vertical and three horizontal power relationships as a planning process. He was broadening Thomson's view of planning as coordination, a primarily influence task, to include the whole organizing process. He translated Thompson's institutional level into a "Normative" planning process, his planning level into "Strategy" and technical into "Operations." The structural spatial view derived from Parsons had now moved up one dimension to include time; it was now a *process* view.

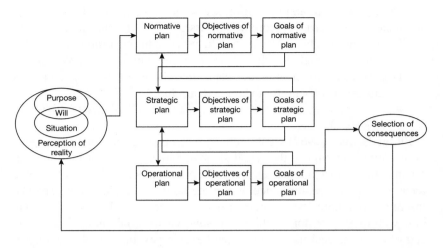

Figure 2.3 Summary of Ozbekhan's planning process

1   Hasan argued that the difference between objective reality and our perception of the situation by a planner makes planning an essentially human process in which difference of personality, values and knowledge matters and affects our choice of ends and means.

2   The centrality of purpose is very evident to him:

> Purpose and the will to pursue purpose is the engine that drives planning. This again emphasizes the human aspects of motivation over the more technical aspects of planning.
>
> (Ozbekhan 1971: 215)

3   He also acknowledged the importance of the unperceived and unconscious aspects of purpose, will-power and motivation that result in the unintended consequences of planned action.

4   He also addressed the multi-leveled, interactive, dynamic processes of planning:

> Three distinct qualities of planning are the normative dealing with the values of the whole system, the strategic dealing with the relationship between the parts of the system, and the operational dealing with the specific allocation of responsibilities and resources. Each level is also divided into similar phases which deal with acquisition of knowledge, selection of means, and establishment of ends.
>
> (Ibid.: 216)

In particular, it was the continuous loop of process that captured our imagination:

- Implementation of operations is not an end point; an accomplishment that is complete.
- Implementation is another aspect of feedback.
- The environment is now changed and managers have to appreciate how it has been changed.
- There is no beginning and end only continuous process.

Peter Senge, too, in his *Fifth Discipline* (1994), building on Forrester's work on system dynamics (which uses computers to simulate the complex creation and interaction of systems feedback loops) popularized the use of feedback loops for understanding dynamic complexity. Much of this complexity comes from impaired awareness or lack of understanding of differential rates and types of feedback "Cause and effect are not closely related in time and space" (1994). He and his colleagues created a set of archetypal causal loops that described many common problematic situations in organization, e.g. limits to growth, shifting the burden, eroding goals.

He or one of his co-authors also developed a version of the three AIC relationships. In Appendix 1 of the *Fifth Discipline* he notes that each of the five disciplines can be perceived of at three different levels:

- **Practice**—what you do (C)
- **Principles**—guiding ideas and thoughts (I)
- **Essences**—the state of being of those with high levels of mastery in the disciplines (A).

For example, for the fifth discipline—Systems Thinking—he identifies:

- **Essences (A)**
  - Holism
  - Interconnection
- **Principles (I)**
  - Structure, Influence Behavior
  - Policy Resistance
  - Leverage
- **Practice (C)**
  - Systems Archetypes
  - Simulation.

This open-systems phase of evolution began with insights from other fields. This process of expanding perspective has continued. Meg Wheatley, for example, provided one of the most popular summaries of this search in *Leadership and the New Sciences* (1992). Building on a series of new science books that sought to explain the new thinking to laymen, e.g. Fritjof Capra 1978, Herbert Nick 1987 and Michael Talbot 1986, she set out to introduce three branches of science—quantum physics, self-organizing systems, and chaos theory and to draw out their implications for organizational designs and practices.

She noted the "seemingly spontaneous developments that happen in widely separated places and disciplines." But the three themes that are interwoven in her work are relatedness, self-organization, and self-reference. She quotes Robert Haas, then CEO of Levi Strauss:

Relatedness

We are at the center of a seamless web of mutual responsibility and collaboration . . . a seamless partnership with interrelationships and mutual collaboration.

(Wheatley 1992: 140)

This point hits at the core function of the influence phase to relate upwards to the normative or appreciative, to relate sideward to internal and external stakeholders and to relate downwards to subordinate control systems.

Self-Organization

One thing I feel especially intriguing about self-renewing systems is their relationship with the environment . . . Here are structures that seem capable of maintaining identity while changing forms. Form and function engage in a fluid process where the system may maintain itself in its present form or evolve to a new order.

(p. 90)

Again this hits at the core of influence—relationships over time.

Self-Reference

More than any other science principle I've encountered, self-reference strikes me as the most important. If management practice is ever to be simplified into one unifying principle it will be found in self-reference.

(p. 146)

This points to purpose being our center and source of power; everything is referenced back to the purpose of the self, individual, organization or community.

Stakeholders

As we noted in the Introduction, one of the major practical developments arising from the focus on the task or influenced environment was the development of the stakeholder concept. Although the use of the word stakeholder originated in Stanford Research Institute in the context of survey research, our contemporaries at Wharton's Social Systems Sciences Program were major developers of its application to organizational design and process (Freeman 2004). Our attitude to stakeholder theory at the time is summed up by our colleague Ed Freeman:

> As a pragmatist these questions do not seem very interesting to me. I have come to believe that whatever the academic verdict is on what is now called stakeholder theory, at least from a "managerial point of view" it is simply "a good idea that is useful to executives and stakeholders."
>
> (p. 8)

The word stakeholder had been coined at Stanford Research Institute (SRI) by the group of Robert Stewart, Marion Doscher, Igor Ansoff, Eric Rhenman, and others as a way of organizing their environmental scanning process (an organization's stakeholders are anyone who affects or is affected by the organization). However, in the context of an approach to organization and management it was used heavily at Wharton by Ackoff, Emsoff, Howard Perlmutter, and Eric Trist, then synthesized by Ed Freeman in his 1984 book, *Strategic Management: A Stakeholder Approach*. Ian Mitroff, who was visiting Social Systems Sciences at the time as part of the initial process, wrote *Stakeholders of the Organisational Mind* (1983).

In practice the concept of stakeholders gives a very practical approach to extending management thinking into the influenced field of International Development. In Rural Development, for example, no hierarchical control could be effective in managing the thousand of complex relationships involved. The need for practical tools for engaging with the influenced environment was paramount. For example, when I introduced the concepts to the World Bank in 1976 they spread very quickly through the whole development field. Freeman (1984) summarizes this very practical perspective as follows:

> I would summarize *Strategic Management: A Stakeholder Approach* in the following logical schemata:
>
> 1   No matter what you stand for, no matter what your ultimate purpose may be, you must take into account the effects of your actions on others, as well as their potential effects on you.
> 2   Doing so means you have to understand stakeholder behaviors, values, and backgrounds/contexts including the societal context.

To be successful over time it will be better to have a clear answer to the question "what do we stand for".

3   There are some focal points that can serve as answers to the question "what do we stand for" or Enterprise Strategy. (The book laid out a typology which no one ever took seriously.)

4   We need to understand how stakeholder relationships work at three levels of analysis: the Rational or "organization as a whole"; the Process, or standard operating procedures; and the transactional, or day to day bargaining. (These levels are just the three levels in Graham Allison's *Missiles of October*.)

5   We can apply these ideas to think through new structures, processes, and business functions, and we can especially rethink how the strategic planning process works to take stakeholders into account.

6   Stakeholder interests need to be balanced over time.

(Ibid.: 10)

All these contributions helped to move us from a closed- to a more open-system view of organizations. External environmental relationships became equally as important as internal ones in determining the effectiveness of an organization. They helped us to move beyond the concept of hierarchical control as the sole engine of organizational power, to the concept of co-alignment.

The co-alignment we assert to be the basic administrative function is not a simple combination of static components. Each of the elements involved in the co-alignment has its own dynamics. Each behaves at its own rate, governed by forces external to the organization.

(Thompson 1967: 147)

And with that co-alignment comes a fundamentally new idea: the administrative process as a centering between many processes.

Thus in our view the central function of administration is to keep the organization at the nexus of several streams of action and because the several streams are variable and moving the nexus is not only moving but sometimes quite difficult to fathom.

(Ibid.: 148)

Pfeffer (1981), for example, counted eight different models of power; none of which covered the whole territory. The literature left users to draw whatever they could from any of them to apply to their own situation.

In the open-systems age the central goal of organization was still to increase control but now the whole new area of influence could be brought into that effort—it was *power with* in order to obtain *power over*. Scott and Raven's well known categorization of the five sources of power—reward, coercive, legitimate, referent, and expert—carries this connotation that power comes from "control over" these five major resources.

This belief in the goal of control led to many attempts to reduce influence to measurements that would all allow more control. Influence was still to be used in order to produce control. Many theorists used dependency theory and power relationships to calculate the probabilities of outcomes from influence relationships. If you couldn't count it you couldn't control it. However, so many factors and so many intervening variables had to be taken into account that the products were not very useful in practice. This led to a common view at the time that you could just not get much leverage out of the study of power.

Purpose in the Open-Systems Phase

The concept of purpose during this phase of open-system evolution was no more salient than in the classical period. As the field of consideration became broader to include the environment then the more general word "purpose" rather than the more specific expression of "goal" was used. Hasan Ozbekhan's treatment above is typical of this development.

Just as the classical phase had its unique exception, Mary Parker Follett, so did this phase; the work of Ackoff and Emery in *On Purposeful Systems* (1972), which, the authors themselves admit, is one that requires much study. That study formed a "right of passage" that Russ's PhD students dreaded.

Ackoff and Emery set out to "provide a way of looking at human behavior as a system of purposeful (teleological) events." They further wanted to do this in a very rigorous scientific way that would contribute to building one cohesive body of knowledge that would synthesize the findings of the various scientific traditions. They set out to build an understanding of purpose, purposeful states, and interaction of purposeful systems, including social systems and beyond. Using their operational research experience they were able to express the structural basis of their formulations mathematically as well as with logic. Although the authors are able to produce the mathematics to represent the possibilities, probabilities, and efficiencies built into these models, they readily admit that they are ideal measurements. Actually obtaining such measures to enter into the formulas is practically impossible.

They derive the concept of purpose from the structural concept deterministic causality. In a simplified translation they indicate that a function is a capacity to produce a specific type of outcome:

> Purposeful individual or system: one that can produce (1) the same functional type of outcome in different structural ways in the same environment and (2) can produce different outcomes in the same and different structural environments.
>
> (p. 31)

Ultimately, Ackoff and Emery were concerned with defining what a purposeful individual or system is and not so much with defining what exactly purpose is. They look at what a purposeful system does that a non-purposeful system does not. From their work, though, we can derive the view that purpose is a capacity to produce or co-produce outcomes. It is related to function but has greater degrees of freedom in terms of its capacity to choose outcomes and operate in different environments. It is this idea of greater degrees of freedom that I eventually realize as the dimensional organization of purpose and its relationship to power (the capacity to produce), which will be dealt with in greater depth in Chapter 7.

A major impact of the clarity of Russ's thinking on purpose is the recognition of human systems as ideal-seeking systems. We have all come to learn that the process of accomplishment is generally as rewarding, if not more so, than achieving the outcome:

> Man seeks objectives that enable him to convert the attainment of every goal into a means for attainment of a new more desirable goal. The ultimate objective in such a sequence cannot be obtainable; otherwise its attainment would end the process. An end that satisfies these conditions is an Ideal. . . .
>
> Thus the formulation and pursuit of ideals is a means by which to put meaning and significance into his life and into the history of which he is part.
>
> (Ackoff and Emery 1972: 237)

The hierarchy of purposes that Ackoff and Emery produce is then:

- ideals that are never reached;
- objectives, ends that can be achieved in the long terms; and
- goals that can be achieved in a very specific timeframe.

The hierarchy of ideals, objectives, and goals is fine to describe levels of purpose within a single organization; however, several writers understood that we needed a different purpose word to better reflect the relational nature of purpose in the influenced environment. Sommerhoff (1950) came up with a very useful concept of "directive correlations" to refer to the joint "goal directedness of coupled systems," i.e. organizations that have linked interests —suppliers, competitors. Emery and Trist (1965) built on this idea to explain the process of co-designing organizations as social and technical systems that were directively correlated. The job of socio-technical systems design was to jointly optimize the two systems. Directive correlation is another way of conceiving of the different kind of power process we encountered called "coordinative line management" where control was not possible.

By 1976 when I left G.D. Searle to pursue a PhD Program in Social Systems Sciences the organization field was in the turmoil of the open-systems revolution. The inclusion of the environment as part of the organizational field enlarged both the spatial field of the organization to include the issue of time, and the harmonization of multiple directively correlated actions of external stakeholders. Many practitioners, writers, and scholars were feeling the same phenomena and were coming up with different labels to describe them. The key issues marking progress and needing further synthesis were:

1   The idea of purpose needed to be refined and extended to go beyond the concept of a goal controlled by a single entity. Managers and organizations had to deal with "directively correlated" purposes that were determined jointly by several actors.
2   Internal and external lateral relationships had become as important as vertical-control relationships.
3   The concept of effectiveness through design of structures proved too rigid for the dynamic conditions of the new phase of evolution. Uncontrollable environmental relationships required the flexibility of adapting structures over time, i.e. process.
4   The idea of power was similarly being enlarged from the control of "power over" to include the influence of "power with" but this was still enough to make a complete model of power.
5   There was a realization that the "directively correlated" actions of many stakeholders could actually multiply the effect of individual action. Power was no longer a zero-sum game. Power could be created and multiplied.
6   The multiplication began in this newly defined influence space. Taking some poetic license we could say that this was the field where the feminine appreciation met with the masculine control to dance, testing out the possibilities for a longer term engagement that would multiply their energies.

All of these themes dealt with the extension of the control-centered view of the single actor and organization with a single purpose into the influence field of multiple actors with dynamically interrelated purposes. They did not yet deal with purpose, power, or organization of the whole. Systems theory declared that the whole was greater than the sum of the parts but did not deal directly with the qualities and operations that gave systems that property. They were still not dealing with the nature of wholeness; the very property that made systems greater than the sum of the parts. My experience with the effects of culture and the effects of the feminine were beginning to suggest that the undiscovered secrets of exceptional performance lay in understating the properties of wholeness.

It was an exciting time to begin a PhD program, to take up again the ideals triggered by the Rome experience. Could all of this new experience, information, knowledge, and wisdom be pulled together in such a way that everybody could have access to it? Could we really put such power to create exceptional performance in everyone's hands? This was the challenge I wanted to address in the program.

3 Learning to Fly

Experience of Appreciation

The Academic Opening

Serendipity, the unexpected insight, coincidence, or chance opportunity seems to have played a significant role in the journey so far. Perhaps the most important instance occurred in the choice of PhD program itself. I had been accepted into the Social Sciences PhD program at Michigan University with a full scholarship when I heard of a new program at the Wharton Graduate School of Business. From the previous chapter the reader will be aware that I had become familiar with the work of Russell Ackoff, Eric Trist, and Hasan Ozbekhan. I knew of their work independently but then learned to my astonishment that not only were they in the same area of the country, they were in the same university, and in the same department, Social Systems Sciences. I had no choice; I joined the program. My application there was accepted and I chose to go even though I received no financial aid. With three children in high school and college coming up, this was no small decision. I knew I would have a tough job supporting them while working on the PhD, but even here serendipity was to play a role again. It was one of the consulting assignments I took to support my family that ended up producing the insights that would finally answer my questions from Rome. Clearly, experience was giving me a message, any system looking for exceptional performance has to be open to receive such serendipitous inputs.

As I entered the doctoral program in 1976, I felt that all the major pieces of the puzzle were available. What I needed was the time, space, and support to devise a framework of concepts and fit them into an organizing process. The Graduate Program in Social Systems Sciences was initiated in 1974. Its nickname S^3 (S cubed) reflected its early origins in operations research. Its goal was to provide a new kind of education and experience that unified the scientific, methodological, and humanistic domains. It replaced conventional course work with Learning and Research Cells consisting of five to ten students and one or more faculty members. Students were expected to work on real-world problems as part of their research. Two research centers helped provide this bridge; Russell Ackoff's Busch Center and Eric Trist's Management and Behavioral Science Center.

Russell Ackoff was one of the founders of the Operations Research movement that grew out of Britain's desperate situation during World War II. In his *Redesigning the Future* (1974) and *On Purposeful Systems* written with F. Emery (1972), Russ articulated, as well as any one at that time, an eloquent argument for taking a whole systems approach to planning.[1] He was on the forefront of the *open-systems* movement and also argued forcefully that *aesthetic* and *ethical* values should be incorporated into our theories and practice of decision-making. His words resonated convincingly with my experience at Rome, and my subsequent work with managers of the subsidiaries of the multinational company.

Eric Trist, a gentle Celt with sparkling eyes, provided a wonderful counterpoint to Russ. Whereas Russ possessed an intellect of steel and diamond brilliance, Eric had the uncanny ability to help others find the diamond in themselves. A poet of the field, he breathed warmth and hope into every one he touched. As a student at Cambridge he had started reading English Literature when an encounter with Kurt Lewin, generally regarded as the founder of social systems science and initiator of the action research approach, caused him to take a deep interest in psychology. Lewin had introduced the concept of fields created from the subjective perspective of an individual's life space. His practical work, which incorporated this whole perspective was implemented through his creation of action research, which had a profound impact on some of the major policy issues of the time. For example, he worked on increasing the morale of combat troops, improving the effectiveness of psychological warfare, and changing the food habits of the population given shortages of some traditional foods. Although his principles were sound and had a great deal of success in practice his attempts to reduce his ideas to theoretical form ran into problems. He chose a form of topological mapping that essentially reduced force fields to two spatial dimensions. He devoted enormous effort to the process but it never took hold. His is a key case in the social sciences that would have benefited, as Einstein did, by moving to higher dimensional explanations. His two- and three-dimensional rendering of his topological concept just did not do justice to the greater breadth of his ideas or the potential already built into the action research process itself.

Lewin's impact on Trist was great and revealed more in his ecological approach and interest in action research rather than in field theory. It was Trist and Emery's translation of organization as three environments—internal, transactional, and contextual—as a field concept that had a major impact on the ideas developed in this book.

Trist's clinical experience as a result of his meeting with Lewin enabled him to make a leading contribution to the development of collaborative and interactive approaches that culminated in the success of the interdisciplinary teams in World War II. He received an OBE in 1946 specifically for his work with self-help participative processes that greatly facilitated the resettlement of British prisoners of war. Anyone who has attended a residential workshop owes something to this work. Workshops are mini-versions of the "social islands" that Eric and his colleagues created for the prisoners, a protected space in which, by operating under different norms, accelerated transformation or development can take place.

His post-war work moved from the level of individuals to the level of organizations. As a founding member of the Tavistock Institute of Human Relations in London, Eric influenced the creation of a movement that has spread under many labels from England to Scandinavia, and the U.S.A. to the rest of the world. His work in the coalmines of England produced the key concept that work must be designed "to jointly optimize the social and technical systems." In Scandinavia, the concept led to the creation of the movement labeled *Industrial Democracy* and in the U.S.A. to the *Quality of Work Life*. The influence of this pattern of thought reached its zenith when mainstream industry, epitomized by the U.S. automobile industries, finally adapted the approach and the hugely successful Ford Taurus, the first U.S. car designed from scratch using socio-technical design principles, rolled off the lines in the mid 1980s. (Volvo of Sweden had experimented since the late 1960s building cars with autonomous work groups, similar to those identified by Trist in the coalmines, rather than through the assembly line.)

By the time I joined the Social Systems Sciences department, Eric was already working on the third level, the application of the pattern to a socio-ecological perspective—the domain between organizations—the scale of "whole organizational systems" and "macro contexts." It was this contextual, inter-organizational approach that would be so helpful in unlocking the door to Rome's secrets.

Hasan Ozbekhan, of Turkish origin, had worked in strategic planning with General Electric and had attended the famous Club of Rome meetings in 1968. These meetings marked the beginning of the end for concepts of centralized planning. A new planning paradigm began to crystallize; one that would undermine the Soviet-style centralized planning process that had taken over most governments and even the corporate sector.

The social blueprint had reached its limits. At the conceptual or appreciative level control-centeredness as a means of dealing with whole populations was dead. The idea of *forecasting* futures was being replaced with the idea of *creating* futures. This collective learning would not be externalized into the design of political systems for some twenty years with the collapse of the Soviet System. From then on it was clear that in spite of a few remaining Stalinesque leaders, populations of large countries could never again be organized through command and control strategies. They were just too rigid, expensive, and self-defeating. It was clear that the influence centeredness of democracy was a human evolution and not just a Western political strategy. In fact, the West's political strategy still has a lot to learn in order to reach the full potential of human democratic values. Hasan, as we saw in the last chapter, had combined his insights and experience into a powerful image of the relationship between purpose, planning, and action.

There was a palpable tension between the two ends of the fourth floor of Vance Hall, the home of S³. One housed Russ's Busch Center and the other Eric's Managerial Behavioral Science Center. Russ's personal style of hard-edged intellect clashed with Eric' softer, poetic style. Russ tended to serve powerful authoritarian heads of corporations, while Eric served a motlier crew of middle level, intermediary organizations that had significant roles in the multi-organizational domain. Students tended to fall into one or the other camps. There were great rewards for any student who could withstand the tension of the two styles and incorporate them both into his work, but few could. The department became an unintended example of effective organization through what I discovered later as "opponent processing."

Attempts at resolving the tension between their two perspectives were a painful but rewarding input into my own work. The direct influence of Russ on my work was to provide the basic rigorous understanding of the nature of systems thinking. The effect of Eric's work has been more pervasive and personal. Eric influenced me to take the multi-organizational rather than the single-organizational approach. He also ensured I kept the human being at the centre of my systems thinking. For example, he prevented me from bringing in the natural scientific perspective that was producing new insights from quantum physics. He felt that the behavioral science already suffered too much from applying the physical to the social science inappropriately. Meg Wheatley (1992) did take up this perspective and some ten years later showed how it could provide very useful insights. In Part II and Part III I will show how I finally caught up with this special interest and its role in developing AIC.

The Breakthrough Intuition

When I was in the process of recruiting Ken Murrell to replace me at G.D. Searle he established a key connection that would lead to the break-through. He had a girlfriend who worked as an Administrative Assistant to Francis Lethem of Policy Advisory Services in the World Bank. At the end of the working day Ken went to Francis's office to pick up his girlfriend. Unfortunately, Francis had to keep her a little late. So feeling a little guilty, he took the time to engage Ken in a discussion of his plans on completing his doctorate. Ken explained how he was going to head up a very innovative corporate-wide program that integrated leadership, team, and organization development at G.D. Searle. Francis mused that that was exactly the kind of thinking that the World Bank needed. Ken gave my name to him and Francis did contact me.

It took almost three years before my contact with Francis produced any results. It was 1979 and the World Bank was in the last few years of Robert McNamara's leadership. McNamara had increased lending during his tenure from less than $1 billion in 1968 to about $12 billion in 1981 and had given the World Bank for the first time a very specific purpose—to reduce world poverty.

Before 1968 the World Bank had concentrated almost entirely on physical infrastructure projects. The governing principles of intervention were the same as those of the classical period of organization. The projects were designed very much on economics and engineering principles. The strategy failed to produce the rapid economic improvement or the decrease in poverty that the World Bank's shareholders expected. The sum of many economic and engineering projects did not add up to improvement in the whole performance of countries.

McNamara introduced a host of new initiatives each of which required the creation of a new department—Rural Development in 1973, Urban Development in 1975, and Population in 1979. Added to the pressure for increased levels of investment, and the demands of an analytically more rigorous project appraisal process, the largely economic and technical culture of the World Bank had to cope with integration of new social disciplines that came with the new departments.

I was working as a consultant with one of those new departments: Rural Development. I was carrying out an action research project covering six very different rural development projects. The major breakthrough came as a result of a critical challenge made by Gus Schumacher, a Project Officer for the World Bank. We were attending a very pivotal meeting headed by Francis Lethem who had become quite adept at managing the very much undervalued and arcane art of introducing new ideas into the World Bank setting.

He had worked out an elaborate system for introducing new ideas to the protected conservative core of World Bank thinking. This, of necessity was the complete opposite of McNamara's control-centered approach. Francis instinctively understood that all innovation begins at the periphery. As part of this process of introducing the social sciences to the World Bank he sponsored relatively young or unknown scholars or practitioners to work on project issues. He would begin, for example, with a brown bag lunch then follow up with those who showed interest and take the connection to the next step—a suggestion for a study or a small project. His office would provide seed money for such efforts. In this fashion Francis had a major, but largely hidden, influence on introducing the World Bank to the dimensions of the social sciences necessary for the success of the new departments. World Bank staff had a role in selecting issues or project components and providing steering committees to guide the studies. Through his own modesty and political skills Francis was able to walk that

delicate line between innovation and conservatism that was so profession-
ally dangerous in the World Bank if not in any major institution. At that
time I knew very little about international development. I benefited from
his umbrella to introduce new ideas from my previous experience and from
social systems science to the design of World Bank projects.

A report from the Operations Evaluation Department (OED), the
independent evaluation arm of the World Bank, had recently flagged
organization and management as a key factor in the failure of World Bank
projects. Francis had heard from Ken Murrell some of the innovations I had
introduced into the design of multinational companies. Francis felt that such
input from the private sector might prove beneficial to the design of World
Bank projects. He asked me to scan a wide range of both high performing
and low performing projects to get a feel for the key issues.

The rapid review surprised us both. It revealed that, if anything, the World
Bank was already relying too much on management control systems
championed by McNamara from his Ford and NASA experiences. The
implicit model of project management assumed a degree of control over
projects very similar to the kind of control exercised by private sector companies over their own projects. However, success of development projects
relied much more on complex social, political, and technical elements
emanating from what Thompson called the task environment, which were
not subject to management control.

The World Bank's design process, implemented through the very strict
project planning cycle introduced as part of McNamara's project philosophy,
was based very much on systems engineering principles that assumed
implicitly a high degree of control. The project planning process was the
core competency of the World Bank's operations and was widely regarded
as the best of all the development agencies. It relied very heavily on analysis
and created tight boundaries around projects to ensure managerial control
and to protect the project from uncontrollable environmental factors.

Our action research team found that the design process produced
structures and plans that were too rigid for their dynamically evolving
contexts. They relied on numbers that were arrived at with many assumptions that could not in practice be justified. Project plans were unable to
withstand the changes in policies, staffing, and political relationships that
were so typical of the development landscape. The semblance of control
was kept, at least on paper, and at great cost, during the period of intense
World Bank identification, preparation, appraisal, and supervision of the
projects. Once this presence was removed project performance often
deteriorated as under-weighted, unforeseen factors, and unintended
consequences flooded into the breach. At that time as many as 65 percent
of the World Bank projects we reviewed did not meet their goals.

It was then, for the first time, I was able to use the whole systems
perspective that I had been developing since my connection with Thompson

and that was now being honed by exposure to Russ, Eric, and Hasan. I suggested alternative whole systems rather than a management systems approach; one in which the relationship between the project and its environment was conceived of as a single whole. From the very first moment when the World Bank begins to identify a project, through all the phases of preparation, implementation, and review, the project should be perceived and managed as a set of project/environmental relationships. This would require greater ownership and participation of implementers in the design and a greater degree of coordination of projects with other organizations in their environment.

Ben Thoolen of the new Rural Development Group was particularly enthused about such an approach. Successful rural development required not only improved agriculture but also health, water, transportation, markets —it required a whole integrated approach. It was this integrated approach that went so much against the grain of the engineering, economic mentality and was almost impossible to implement under the rifle shot project approach. Ben had an ongoing cultural struggle on his hands to create the conditions for the integrated or "synthetic" regional approach rather than "analytical" project approach to rural development.

One of the "synthetic" or integrative conceptual tools I introduced was Emery and Trist's model of environmental relations.

Using this model they described events within project boundaries as taking place within *the internal environment*. When discussing actors outside the project boundaries such as credit banks, beneficiaries, and other third parties who exchanged goods and services with the project they referred to *the transactional environment*. When discussing events of a more general social, political, or economic nature they referred to the *contextual environment*.

The goal was to approach project and program design from this integrative perspective. As this had never been done before the team adopted an

	Organization	Environment
Organization	$L_{1,1}$ Internal	$L_{1,2}$ Transactional
Environment	$L_{2,1}$ Transactional	$L_{2,2}$ Contextual

Figure 3.1 Trist and Emery's organizational environments

action research approach and encouraged project officers to take this larger view of design and apply it to their own projects.

The critical meeting, which would lead to the essential insight at the heart of this book, was part of the review process of these experiments. Gus Schumacher was working on a major rural development project in the northeast of Brazil. After a period of listening to the review he grew more and more uncomfortable, until he finally issued the challenge:

> Look these ideas are certainly helping us to broaden our view of the factors affecting project success but this academic jargon is impossible. I can't use words like "internal", "transactional", and "contextual" in the field, and if you have to use words like that to explain your concepts then they are no good for what we need: practical ways to teach people in the field how to do a better job.

The team had no way of knowing that this piece of "Yankee orneriness" was to provide the stimulus for the breakthrough we were seeking. Our team's initial reaction was to be defensive:

> Of course it takes new language, or language used in new ways to express new concepts, which then become new models and practices.

However, with my antennae tuned by the unanticipated consequences encountered in previous experiences in Rome, Trinidad, and in Searle I did listen and began to search for alternative more "practical" means of expressing the same ideas. From my language training I recalled:

> When you want to make something simple and understandable you make it active.

We returned to Francis's office and asked ourselves:

> What does the actor actually do in his relations to these three environments?

Within 20 minutes we had answers to the first two:

> The actor "controls" elements and people in the internal environment. However, you can't control people in the transactional environment but you can only "influence" them.
> But what do you in the contextual environment?
> What is it that we do to those environmental elements that affect project performance but which we can't control or influence?

At that meeting we couldn't identify a term that satisfied us. It took another 3 months to find, but the process of search produced the key insight.

The appropriate term to describe what we do in the contextual environment came from *The Art of Judgment* (1965) by Sir Geoffrey Vickers. Vickers was one of those rare individuals whose reflections on their experience cause them to see gaps in both traditional practices and formal or academic explanations and theories. He was a decorated World War I veteran and had experience as a solicitor, Director of Economic Intelligence, member of the Joint Intelligence Committee of the Chief of Staff, as an advisor to the National Coal Board in charge of manpower, training, and education, and had published six books and more than fifty scientific and professional articles.

While reflecting on the process of policy making he struggled with the inadequacy of the then current concepts of decision making, especially the individual, specialized, static emphasis implicit even in Simon's work, which he admired (Vickers 1965: Intro., p. 22, fn. 4). He felt much of the decision-making literature was concerned with the execution of policy and very little with its creation:

> I have had to question sciences in which I am not professionally qualified and sometimes (had to) supply my own answers, when theirs seemed ambiguous, inconsistent or absent . . . Even the dogs may eat the crumbs which fall from the rich man's table: and in these days, when the rich in knowledge eat of such specialized food at such separate tables, only the dogs have a chance at a balanced diet.
>
> (Vickers 1965: 11)

How do policymakers draw from their whole experience and the whole situation to decide on what policies are needed? Just as we struggled with a term to describe what we do in reference to the "whole" contextual environment that affects project performance, so Vickers struggled with how to describe the process of understanding the whole environment and the whole mental state that the decision makers brought to it.

WHOLE

> I need first a word to describe it and as I cannot find one in the literature, I must invent one. I will call it appreciation, following the ordinary usage in which we speak of "appreciating a situation". Reviews of policy are usually preceded by such an appreciation.
>
> (1965: 39)

The term appreciation was in fact used in this way by the British Military who carried out "appreciations" of the situation prior to military operations. Lawrence of Arabia, for example had the mission to appreciate the Arabian situation from the point of view of the whole of British interests; social, political, economic, military, religious. Every English student also knows the term from classes in literature—students are asked to appreciate a poem or novel, to understand how all the parts, words, metaphors, rhyme, meter, and imagery all combine to convey the artist's meaning or intent or at least explain the reader's reaction to it.

However, it was the joining of the concept of appreciation with that of influence and control that had such an unanticipated effect. At home I began to map the three environments using the three new terms. It was a beautiful summer afternoon while I was working in my study overlooking the garden. Free from travel, interviews, and consulting sessions I could now begin to pull together the results of the action research program using the new simple "action" language.

Seemingly out of nowhere I experienced a burst of ideas, connections, and implications that exploded with such energy that I could not contain it. I had to get up and pace from room to room, downstairs, through to the house, into the garden and back again, my body was racing to catch up with my mind:

> Appreciation, influence, and control are all power words . . .
> Internal, transaction, and contextual environments are power fields . . .
> Therefore all system environment relationships are power relationships . . .
> Appreciation, influence, and control are power fields . . .
> All these power relationships together form power fields . . .
> Every system then—abstract, human, physical—is a set of power fields that can be described in terms of appreciative, influence, and control relationships . . .
> Each of these A, I, C relationships have their own properties, their own substance, their own rules of engagement . . .
> Every individual, every team, every organization, every institute operates through these rules of relationship . . .

The implications of being able to describe every system, material, human, and intellectual in terms of AIC relationships had just began to sink in when the question came. It popped up out of nowhere in all its innocence. If individual/system/organization environment relationships are really power fields then . . .

Where does the Power come from?

Just as gently and just as innocently without any delay or effort the answer popped up . . .

Power comes from Purpose.

The gentle response belied the burst of implications and questions that both preceded and followed:

> If purpose is the source of power, then every purpose no matter how big or small creates a power field . . .
> Then the bigger the purpose the more the power . . .
> The real source of power is not knowledge, authority, wealth, or military might . . .
> The path to empowerment is through purpose . . .
> In rural development it does not matter that people are poor, have little formal education, have no military might, or political clout . . . Their ultimate power comes from purpose and how they translate that purpose through their fields of appreciation influence and control . . .
> Isn't this what the religions have always said?
> Doesn't this have something to do with the messages from people such as Gandhi and Martin Luther King?
> Doesn't this say something about the relationship between Religion, Philosophy, and Science?
> If Purpose creates power fields isn't it like mass and gravity? At the origin isn't mass really purpose and purpose mass? Isn't the ultimate AIC purpose, gravity, and mass?

As I paced through the garden I saw my wife, Marilyn, picking tomatoes. The words just bubbled and bubbled out as I tried to explain. She listened patiently, and then more patiently then finally asked me whether I would take some of the tomatoes into the kitchen. I was forewarned: from then on, all of this would take some explaining.

A thousand other questions, implications, thoughts, and feelings kept flowing. They imbued everything with a new meaning, a new context, a new color, and flavor. The resonance would not and has not stopped since then. However, I never did share, till many years later, the full nature of the insight into the connection between all social and natural sciences and even less did I share the profound experience of feeling connected through purpose to all things; that I had been transformed.

After returning to Washington, I shared the discovery of the new term "appreciation" and my insight that together "appreciation, influence, and control" were power fields created by purpose. The action research team accepted the basic idea and the terms appreciation, influence, and control to describe the three environments, however, they were afraid, with good reason, that using the concept of power at all would raise hackles with the World Bank orthodoxy. However, over time, the logic of three levels as causal factors affecting performance also made good "analytical' sense so proved enough to carry the day. The idea of purpose as the source of power stayed somewhat in the background.

In practice, it was the concept of appreciation even more than the concept of purpose or power that caused most controversy. The concept of appreciation required the designers and practitioners, in the first phase of organizing, to be open to the whole situation, to enter into it without pre-judgments and to listen to all possibilities. In practice, there was never a single case of application in the World Bank setting in which the idea of trusting the participants to create their own agenda of priorities was not resisted even when the AIC process had specifically been requested. In several dramatic cases the discussion would carry on till the very morning of a workshop's beginning.

Eric Trist, my PhD advisor had retired from Wharton, and Russ had taken on the role of my advisor. He could not accept appreciation as a form of power. He felt that control and influence were forms of power but appreciation was something else, something "clinical"; which implied that it might be OK in Eric's shop but not in his. I was willing to look for other labels, but that field that affected the whole, that was not subject to influence or control, was a reality for me. We eventually ended the advising relationship because changing the name did not change the reality. Hasan took on the role and played it very appreciatively; he was just there for me.

The difficulty in the academic world was mirrored in the international development field as instanced by the reaction of one of my most respected colleagues, George Honadle. After a presentation at an annual development conference George came up to me trembling with anxiety to warn me:

> "Bill, you really must drop the concept of appreciation, it is too far out, it will be your undoing."

However, the more I tried to find another word or another way to express the concept the more the label appreciation and the concept it represented grew in appropriateness, importance, explanatory power, and practical impact.

It was, of course, in this disputed field of appreciation that I found the answer to Rome. In contrast to Trinidad, Rome had all the control resources it needed; plenty of good modern equipment, well trained sophisticated staff. It had good collegial relationships and "espresso" diplomacy for raising and dealing with difficult issues. What it missed was a sense of meaning; that what each individual did mattered. The combination of the newsletter, and my being an appreciative rather than an influencing or controlling personality created a sense of a search for a larger purpose and gave each person a channel for expressing their part of the whole. I was lucky. If control conditions had been poor and influence relationships less effective the exceptional performance at Rome would never have happened. The reason I could not find answers to exceptional performance is that I was looking for it at the control level, I was not consciously aware of an influence or appreciative level. As Einstein had already taught us, the answer to our problems is never found at the level at which they are experienced.

The results of the action research program, the first articulation of the AIC philosophy, were published as *The Design of Organizations for Rural Development* (Smith 1980) co-authored with Francis and Ben Thoolen. It was the first paper to deal systematically with the concept of power in the design of Bank Projects and introduced the World Bank and the development world to the concept of stakeholders. It was very well received by the academic community and the three major International Centers for Rural Development.

Prof. John D. Montgomery of Harvard University's John F. Kennedy School of Government noted:

> Your staff working paper on the design of organizations for RD projects is a giant step forward for mankind. . . . I was astonished at the overlap in our findings though we approached the problem from quite different points of view.
>
> (Letter to F. Lethem, July 29, 1980)

Prof. William J. Siffin, Director, International Development Institute, Indiana University summarized the paper and made it the topic of the Institute's newsletter:

> Some months ago you sent me a copy of a truly exciting paper, "The Design of Organizations for Rural Development Projects" . . . The perspective which is built into the paper is powerful and sensible . . . The explicit acknowledgement of the relevance and reality of power is one of the refreshing—and distinctive features of this paper. The straightforward way in which the idea of power is handled strikes me as quite wise.
>
> (Letter to F. Lethem)

Guy Hunter, Overseas Development Institute, London wrote:

> I was glad to receive your paper . . . It is an extremely interesting and useful contribution . . . I would like to add that we are very interested in this attack on general theory. Indeed we are trying to evolve between us some better theoretical statements about agricultural administration.
>
> (Letter, May 28, 1980)

Stakeholders as Dancing Partners: Anchoring the Concept of Influence

The new concept of power was key to the success of the research. For practitioners, it was the concept of stakeholders that multiplied exponentially around the international development community. This probably indicated the greater latency for influence rather than appreciative concepts at the time.

As we noted above, the word stakeholder had been coined at Stanford Research Institute (SRI) however it was our Wharton group that developed it for application to the design of organizations.

In 1978, however, when I introduced the concept of stakeholders to the international development world there was no theory of stakeholders, it was just a very good idea. I saw it as a very practical anchor for understanding the influenced environment—it was the stakeholders' power field, the sum of the two-way relationships between the organization and its stakeholders. The reception of the paper confirmed the enormous latent need for concepts and practices that broke boundaries and limitations of control-centered design. The paper was translated into Spanish and French and sold more copies than any other paper in the previous 374 of the series.

In late 1980, Francis Lethem helped arrange the very first Search Conference to be held in the World Bank. It was addressed to improving the design of World Bank projects. Its appreciative-centered format was new in that all participants contributed equally to the outcome—there were no presenters. Eric Trist, Michel Chevalier, and Roger Schwass, all of the Environmental Studies program at York University Ontario and I, still at Wharton, facilitated the session. The realities of the World Bank experience were examined through the lenses of a number of case studies that mirrored a typical range of successes, failures, issues, and opportunities. Although the topic was improving World Bank projects the search took into account factors in the World Bank and forces outside of the World Bank. The result was an illuminating and powerful self-discovery for the participants. They were able to break out of the control perspective and see the need for stakeholder involvement.

Using our three-level approach they also examined the World Bank itself and its organization to support projects and programs. They discovered what they termed the "missing middle level" both within project design and the organization of the World Bank. Within the World Bank the missing middle level was a strategic role for middle managers. The participants saw middle management as translating orders from the top to the bottom; they were not mediating the country perspective with that of top management. The whole concept of "strategy," "stakeholder," and creating "enabling environments" emerged from that workshop to become part of the intellectual infrastructure of the World Bank. As a result of this effort, for example, one of our S^3 colleagues, Francisco Sagasti, was hired to lead a Strategic Planning group in the World Bank.

New Levels and New Depths

Between 1980 and 1984 the process spread principally through training workshops in which project officers learnt to apply the concepts to their own projects. Over the next 10 years its application moved upward from individual project application, through sector-wide, and outside of the World Bank to country-wide application until in 1992 it was ultimately applied to the design of the global development system itself. Along the way actual implementation of the concepts again produced several key insights that raised questions about what the process was actually tapping into and what it actually produced. The next chapter gives examples chosen to illustrate both the raising of the level of application and the new insights.

4 International Development

Examples and Evolving Concepts of Wholeness

The World Bank Experience

In 1981 the World Bank paper, *Design of Organizations for Rural Development* (Smith *et al*. 1980) came to the attention of Turid Sato, as she was taking a sabbatical at Harvard and MIT to study the new area, for the World Bank, of Institutional Development. Turid was one of those unusually colorful, energetic, and effective people that the World Bank produces. Several excellent portraits of such people are provided in Sebastian Mallaby's Book *The World's Banker* (2004). Turid Sato was the first woman to be hired into the World Bank's prestigious "Young Professional Program" and she delighted in telling the story of how she got there. She was Norwegian and was aware that the Bank had not hired any females into the program when she applied. Her name did not reveal her sex and she took great pains to make sure that nothing else in her application did. However, when she showed up for the interview she was told that the World Bank did not hire women for that program.

At that time the Japanese had just joined the World Bank as a major shareholder and insisted that the World Bank hire more Japanese. So the Human Resource Division went down the list of past candidates with Japanese names and invited them to re-interview. Turid Sato's name sounded Japanese so she ended up being interviewed and hired. This was one case in which the left hand of bureaucracy not knowing what the right hand was doing turned out well.

When Turid returned from sabbatical she arranged a series of seminars by all the five or six major contributors whose work she felt could advance the cause of institutional development and eventually settled on the AIC process as the most promising.

Santa Marta, Colombia

The first chance to move from research, training, and development came when Turid returned to Operations in 1984 as the Senior Loan Officer for Colombia, Latin America. She recounts her story of Colombia:

In late 1984, I had a new assignment as the senior loan officer for Colombia in the Country Programs Division. Over the holidays, while the Division Chief was on vacation, I acted for him. To my astonishment, a telegram arrived from the Colombian Finance Minister saying, in essence, "The electricity sector is bankrupt. Since the Bank has been supporting the sector for 30 years, can you help us solve this problem?" At first, I thought the message was exaggerated, but after some investigation and a workshop I organized at the Bank in January to assess the situation, it was clear that the crisis was real.

(Navia 1997)

In the mid 1980s Colombia's electricity sector had been buffeted by a series of adversities: worldwide recession, devaluation of the peso, and a lower rate of demand than the original forecast. The sector already had underway a number of large capital-intensive hydro projects that could not easily be postponed. Its tariff policies were not sufficient to provide internal generation of cash to pay for the investments. Institutional jealousies within the sector made the development of common strategies very difficult, many government agencies did not pay their electricity bills, and losses due to illegal tapping were estimated at 25 percent. As a result the sector faced an external debt of some $3 billion, approximately 40 percent of the country's entire foreign debt. It had an over-capacity in generation of 45 percent. Turid Sato, (using an informal version of AIC, i.e. she did not tell her colleagues that she was using any special process) organized a one-day workshop with several hours of appreciation of the problem from everyone's perspective, several hours of influence—people developing their own views of what the priority issues were and which stakeholders had to be involved in any solution—and their own best guess at what a solution might be—control.

At around 5 p.m., thanks to an engineer who hadn't said much, the group's thinking jelled. He said, "The Colombians need an institutional mechanism to provide oversight for the entire energy sector." Everyone agreed. A nationwide energy board would be the answer. In addition, it was time to stop new construction in the electricity sector, such as a planned $3 billion hydroelectric project called URRA, to make better use of installed capacity and increase tariffs.

(Navia 1997)

Going through the process, they realized that these recommendations would never be accepted coming from the World Bank, so Turid Sato planned a mission to Colombia:

So on a mission in February, 1985, my task was to find out if we could find a way of working together—the Colombians and us. From my studies at MIT and work I had done on institutional development at the Bank, I knew about a participatory process called Appreciation-Influence-Control (A-I-C). I thought this process might be useful.

When I proposed the A-I-C approach, which required all the stakeholders of the electricity sector to participate in a search for solutions, the Colombians were delighted—including the Minister of Mines and Energy, who was new and was seeking priorities and a platform.

(Ibid.)

Turid and the local World Bank representative, Mel Goldman, with the help of their Colombian counterparts, identified the most influential stakeholders in all three of the environments of the electricity sector—the ministers, permanent secretaries, heads of the utilities and their contractors, several mayors (as some of the utilities were municipal), congressmen, and several expert consultants and members of the opposition party. The special-interest groups who wanted to keep building more hydro-electric plants also wanted to attend and were invited.

The event was the first full-scale application of the principles of AIC. As the approach was quite different from the traditional ways of problem solving there was a good deal of apprehension and controversy. The fact that there was just a purpose and a process and no subject matter agenda made both the World Bank and senior Colombians very nervous.

- We planned to spend 1 day on listening to everyone's appreciation of the problem, the potential for solution and the realities that needed to be dealt with. This was to be carried out without comment or judgment,

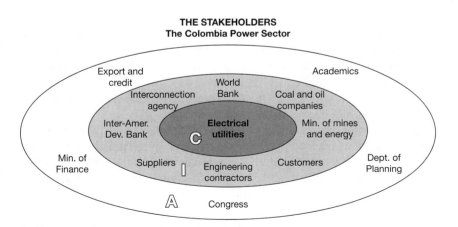

Figure 4.1 Stakeholder's Colombia power project

i.e. no attempt at influence or control (Part II will identify in more detail how and why the process works).

- On the second, or influence day, the participants were to self-select into groups based on what areas they felt had most leverage in bridging the gap between potential and reality.
- The final day was to be spent on working out how best to implement those priority areas.

When the World Bank team arrived, several days before the workshop, to finalize the logistics and materials a local team representing each of the ministries and agencies was assigned for support. In Turid Sato's words:

> When we arrived at Santa Marta, the small northern town where the conference was to be held, we encountered a major problem in the form of a new member of the local conference team chosen by the Minister of Planning. The new team member flatly vetoed the participatory approach already agreed to. She wanted a conventional "talking heads" conference and insisted that "the ministers want to make speeches, not participate in games." After many hours of exhausting arguments about the agenda, the two other facilitators (Bill Smith and Arnoldo Martinez came) said:

> "We can't run this conference the way they want it. Our only choice is to pull out. If you can't resolve the design issue we will leave in the morning."

They then left the meeting.

> After a final attempt to convince the local team, I felt I had run out of options.

> "If you insist on a traditional conference, I'll announce tomorrow at the opening that we cannot guarantee any results with a traditional format and therefore we will have to leave the management of the conference to you."

> (Personal papers in possession of the author)

Our local counterpart, aware that the last conference in Colombia of this kind ended up with a fist fight between two senators, changed her mind, but she still insisted that the ministers would never go along with the idea of having them work actively, and equally, with others in a search for solutions.

That night I was very restless and disturbed. It seemed as though everything that had happened since Rome—the successes, failures, excitements and disappointment, the support and opposition, the miracle of intuition—all boiled down to the opening of the next day's workshop. The next morning I woke up with an amazing clarity. I knew exactly what had to be done. I had breakfast with Turid and Arnoldo and told them:

> "We have to take out all the compromises we have made. And Turid, I even have to take out the compromises I made for you (Turid, for example, didn't want me to use pictures as the product of the appreciative phase but just let people write). As we don't have the support of the local group we have to give the process the best possible chance to do its work."

Apparently, I was speaking with such a quiet compelling authority that they raised no questions or objections, but Turid asked:

> "Bill, what's that on your forehead?"

Right between my eyes was a red spot where the tiny blood vessels must have burst during the night. We then wondered, but have never found out whether in fact that physiological result from deep thought might be the origin of "the third eye."

In the circumstances I knew something dramatic was called for. This intuition was verified when minutes before the start of the workshop the Minister of Planning, who himself had a huge investment in the electricity sector, came up to me and suggested that I change the design:

> "These things may work well elsewhere but Colombia is different. You have to change the design."

After initial opening statements by the four Ministers, I took the floor and acknowledged the difficulty of our joint undertaking. I explained that such difficult times called for dramatically new ways of looking at and dealing with issues. I asked the participants to "suspend their disbelief" as Aristotle might suggest, and for 24 hours try a dramatically different "theatre" in which to view the story of the sector's past and its possible futures. If at the end of the drama they could not see a way out of their dilemma we would hand control of the workshop back to them.

Borrowing from an incident described in Russ Ackoff's (1974) book *Redesigning the Future*, I went to the flip chart and uncovered a diagram showing the organization of the electricity sector in Colombia. I tore it off, rolled it up, and threw it away.

The sector no longer exists.

Underneath that diagram was a chart with the names of all the power plants in Colombia. I called out the names of each of the six major electricity plants one by one and for each I asked:

"Who is served by this plant?"

As participants raised their hands I made an explosive sound into the microphone blowing up each plant in turn:

Your plants are destroyed.
  You no longer have your jobs.
  You are no longer constrained by any ideas, relationships, structures, or physical plants that currently exist.
  You no longer have your positions, you are no longer Ministers, engineers, politicians, Bank members, consultants, and you have no special position or areas of responsibility
  You are all equally concerned Colombian citizens.
  Your only job is to create the best possible electricity sector to serve your children, your grandchildren, and your country.
  You have 24 hours to do it.
  So, let's go to it!

The participants were initially in shock—the room went totally silent— then Ministers, bureaucrats, engineers, economists, administrators, academics began to look at each other as though checking out their sense of reality:

"Is this really happening, is he crazy or are we crazy?"

They had expected speeches, lectures, and bureaucratic games. There was an anxious rumble then an occasional laugh that became infectious and soon rolled into booming energetic exchanges. A new energy and a new perspective were born that continued through the whole 3 days of the workshop. There was not even the whisper of a suggestion to return to a traditional format.

After they completed their image of the ideal sector the facilitating team asked participants to examine the realities that they would have to face if they were to make progress toward that ideal. The second day they used a system of causal mapping to allow participants to identify their beliefs about the most important priorities and to identify who had most influence in terms of enhancing and restraining achievement of their ideal. Participants were encouraged not only to indicate logically what they thought but also to give their personal feelings and values about proposals made.

The third phase was organized around groups with most responsibility for action. They organized themselves to decide three things:

- what they themselves could act on (control);
- what they needed to do in co-peration with others, and (influence);
- general recommendation for policy change (appreciation).

Their major recommendations included:

1 Institutional Reform: A "rector," or some kind of governing entity, for managing the electricity sector in the context of the whole—investment policy, financial reform, technology, and so on.
2 New Policy Direction: Freeze on new construction for five years; diversification from hydro-electric to other power sources via conversion of existing power plants (hydro-electric had gotten 90 percent of the investments in the sector over the previous 30 years); and geographic diversification (the majority of power generation was in one watershed).
3 Financial Issues: Change in the structure and levels of tariffs; and external borrowing to buy time.

It was in the last phase of the workshop that something very unusual for these kinds of meeting happened that was eventually to lead us to a deeper understanding of the nature of the appreciative field. The Minister of Mines and Energy had really risen to the occasion defying all predictions by the local team; he did turn up for group meetings on time, and contributed as an equal. He even called occasionally disruptive participants to honor the process and when one continued to be disruptive the Minister had him removed. He set an example for others to follow.

He was summing up and handing the microphone to anyone who wanted to make final comments about "los pasos a seguir," the next steps. The surprise was in the emotional nature of the response.

• For the first time we see the whole picture . . .
• For the first time we see the problem and it is us . . .
• We have this sense of change and we can see what we need to do . . .
• But for God's sake let's not drop the ball.

These were largely engineers; bureaucrats used to the dry formulations of policies and plans, yet their voices were cracking as they tried hard to control their emotions. The press had been kept out of the workshop but had been waiting outside for a final report. As they came in they wanted a statement and came up to me, thinking I was the World Bank representative. I pointed in Turid's direction and saw that she was putting on her sunshades to hide her tears.

Normally, the senior participants of such conferences would leave right away but they seemed to want to mill around with little need to speak. There was an unusual calm—a feeling that something extraordinary had happened. It was this depth of emotion, the sense of calmness and deep peace that was the surprise, which we would meet again and would come to understand in a much deeper way.[1]

The participants created a steering group to provide the guidance to pursue the last two items after the workshop. The steering group functioned as middle ground to mediate between the operational entities of the electricity sector and the National Planning and Financing Agencies. Known as a "Technical Energy Board," the body was eventually written into the permanent legal structure of the sector.

The workshop and its aftermath had a ripple effect that moved through the whole of the energy sector and the way it made decisions. Almost 10 years later there was a review of the sector by the World Bank's energy program ESMAP, in a report entitled "Power Sector Restructuring Program," Report No. 169/94 dated November 1994. It devotes a chapter to the design and implementation of the process and says:

> The restructuring of the sector was made in Colombia, by Colombians, for Colombians. . . . The role of ESMAP and the Bank and foreign consultants was limited strictly to ancillary support.

Trevor Byer, the manager of the ESMAP program in Colombia, believes that it was the process adopted by the World Bank, rather than the World Bank's technical advice, that facilitated the change in *attitude* that led to all the changes in policies. The World Bank facilitated a process for problem solving, leaving country officials to do their own diagnostic work and thereby learn more fully about their own problems and set their own future directions.

Jorge Eduardo Cock Londono, an energy economist who was one of the small group of facilitators at Santa Marta and who then became the Minister of Mines and Energy, had this to say:

> The participatory process in the power sector started in Santa Marta in 1985. It has continued, with many, many seminars, before arriving at a scheme that we are all pleased with. I believe the participatory approach was the only route to restructure this complicated sector. The challenge now is to implement it. This is my top priority.
>
> (ESMAP 1994)

By now I had become almost inured to finding that many of our most significant learning came from seemingly insignificant details or offhand comments that suddenly resonate and lead to critical insights. This process continued with our discovery about the deeper nature of appreciation during the Colombia project. The impact of the workshops was such that they began to spread to other sectors. When one of the Colombians explained this to us, he said:

> "People would say let's tackle this problem, but let us do it in the spirit of Santa Marta."

The word "spirit" captured our attention and we realized instantly that this was the deeper part the participants were experiencing. Spirit produced the deep emotion, the calmness, the need to be, without saying or doing anything. The appreciative phase either created or enhanced spirit. This is why bureaucrats and engineers were so moved to find that they cared so much that they were in touch with the spirit of the whole. Turid also found that whenever she was in appreciative space, tears would well up no matter what the subject was. I found that since that time in which I came to understand the deeper spiritual property of the appreciative field I never had another problem with explaining or conducting the appreciative phase. Since then I have never received the kind of objections that Russ's or my colleague George Honadle's raised. Apparently without knowing it something I was saying or the way I was presenting appreciation before this awareness created a dissonance. Once I understood and respected the spiritual quality of the appreciative field the problem just dissolved. The experience had a transformational impact on both Turid and me.

Santa Marta Effects

Although the process was very successful in the field it was very threatening to the traditional core of World Bank thinking. It really did empower the local project stakeholders and raised the question of ownership—why were the projects called World Bank projects; shouldn't they be "Country Projects." Equally, professionals whose reputations were built on their analytical abilities found it difficult to accept process approaches in which the primary analysis was carried out by the country. As the Head of the Colombia Division at the time wrote:

> Analysis is still the best way to define country needs and to define programs. While participative methods have their uses, they are no substitute for the primacy of analysis by Bank experts.
>
> (Letter to the author)

In addition, news of the success of training of World Bank staff in this thinking was beginning to reach the executive-level defenders of the World Bank faith. When Francis and Ben Thoolen first asked me to develop a series of training courses based on AIC I refused. I recognized that when facing World Bank professionals with my lack of experience in development and with World Bank staff's reputation for arrogance and disdain of the "new" social sciences, the result would not be very productive and possibly disastrous.

Francis and Ben, however, insisted. I agreed on condition that one of them or another World Bank member would always co-teach with me to provide the missing experience and vouch for the relevance of the new thinking to World Bank practices. I also asked to sit in on several training experiences the World Bank regarded as very successful. Jim Adams from the John F. Kennedy School of Government was running a series of seminars using Harvard's classical case method that was very new to the World Bank. I asked to attend as an observer. After the session Jim asked:

> "What do you think of the pedagogy? Will you be using it in the training?"

I had by now become inured to the fact that new ideas were dangerous and so my antennae were always up to sense where the reaction might come from. By the end of the seminar when Jim came to me my antennae were really vibrating at high alert. I replied:

> "What I am struck by, is not the pedagogy but the reaction of the Bank staff. I have never seen people under so much stress. They are very dedicated and extremely bright and they are very serious about doing the best they can for development. However, the conditions they are operating in are producing such stress that they are using these sessions to let off steam. It is clear that there can't be many opportunities for staff to vent in this way with their colleagues. So, this is very healthy at the clinical level but in the current Bank environment it can be very dangerous
>
> "It's clear then that any training I do will have to allow for this venting but we must find some way to reduce the danger."

After giving the matter some thought I decided to find a simulation that involved all the typical stakeholders of a development project actively involved in trying to solve problems and improve development. I called on a consulting colleague David Burnham, a former Harvard Business School graduate. He was, at that time President of David McClelland's consulting firm specializing in concepts of motivation. David suggested a case "Aire Libre," which involved a whole province in a Latin American country struggling over development and performance issues around the role of a sugar mill. We converted the case into a simulation in which the World Bank staff would take on the roles of Government Officials, the Church, the Military, left- and right-wing Church priests, and peasants, as well as a visiting World Bank team. To encourage realism the team even brought in uniforms and peasant dress, guns and other artifacts.

Playing stakeholders' roles had a very powerful and in many cases a transformative impact on World Bank staff—even 10 years later people would come up to me and our other facilitators and explain how the simulated incidents had impacted their ability to cope with real life situations.

However, the shift in power relationships that were replicated in the new philosophy was not lost on the traditional core of senior management.

The simulations weren't enough to disguise the voices of people who called for a greater role for country stakeholders in the design of World Bank projects. My prediction of danger proved only too accurate. Turid Sato learned that a Senior Vice President had staff planted in the workshops who reported to him what individual staff members were saying. She understood that there was a hit list and her name and almost all of the innovators were on it. When names on the list began to be refused expected promotions or be reassigned to less influential areas or not have contracts renewed Turid decided it was time to leave. She took advantage of one of the many World Bank reorganizations and accepted an early retirement package to start up a new organization based on the AIC philosophy, Organizing for Development, an International Institute, ODII.

The revolution continued, but outside of the World Bank. It soon returned, however, under the label of "participation." NGOs, emboldened by their own success with participation and their "50 Years is Enough" campaign were able to force the World Bank to make participation a part of the Program Planning Process. But, at its heart, their application was flawed.

In AIC terms, though the focus on participation was good, it was not enough, the influence phase of AIC is very participative, the appreciative phase is beyond participation—it helps to see the whole beyond the participants. The control phase is about individual people or individual organizations making final decisions in their own area of responsibility, which is not participative at all. In other words participation doesn't provide a whole organizing process.

However, even when participation was used in the right phase of the organizing process it was equally flawed. The whole point of the stakeholder concept was to bring the area of influence into the organizing process— this meant that the stakeholders involved had to be the one's who had actual influence and they had to be "engaged" in the organizing process. As the World Bank and most other development agencies did much of the planning for their development clients they did not engage their stakeholders they "analyzed them." Thus, stakeholder analysis—a control process—took place of "stakeholder engagement"—an influence process.

Even when stakeholders were "engaged" they were often nominally recruited from stakeholder groups but did not exercise any influence within those groups. It is common in developing countries to find professionals who make a living by attending donor workshops as "stakeholders" so that the donors could then check off the box that said that project stakeholders had been consulted.

When Mr Wolfensohn took over the World Bank in 1995, a whirlwind of country visits in his first year confirmed his suspicion that the countries' and NGO criticism of the World Bank were correct. The World Bank was too arrogant in dispensing its own analytical solutions to their problems. He began a process of confronting his own senior managers. Among these was the Vice President who had kept the hit list of innovators. By then he had become Vice President for Latin America. The Vice President led the charge for his region against Wolfensohn's initiative. In doing so he unwittingly signed a warrant for his own early retirement (Mallaby 2004: 113). The concepts, then, had managed to survive and received renewed energy from Wolfensohn.

New Levels Outside of the World Bank

In terms of my search I had now found two extra levels of organization, influence, and appreciation that could literally make the pursuit of purpose exponentially more "power-full." I now understood where the extra power for exceptional performance came from. We had also developed an organizing process built on these insights and it did produce exceptional results. The main question to be answered now became: *Is it replicable by others, and will it become self-organizing?* Some of this had already happened in Colombia but as our intervention was part of a World Bank process due to their institutional ambivalence I could not follow it up.

Turid Sato; John Karefa Smart, the former First Foreign Minister of Sierra Leone; Michael Marshall (the son of George C. Marshall), who had spent his career on international development and wanted to join ODII "to undo all the wrong that he had done using traditional principles"; Jim Kearns, a former VP from the World Bank; Greg Boyer; and I led the new organization. The organization shifted its approach from the World Bank to work with countries directly or through the United Nations, particularly its Management Development Programme.

Thailand Does It All

Experience with and reflection on the AIC process had led ODII to understand that people, organizations, and cultures had preferences for appreciative, influence, and control approaches. We understood, for example, that appreciative approaches were more "feminine" and Eastern in nature, that control approaches were more "masculine" and Western. Influence approaches were the dance between the masculine and feminine with their emphasis on relationships; they were more African and Latin. As ODII's thinking was primarily influenced by the West, we knew that we had to learn more about the most controversial part of our process— appreciation. Following the intuition from Mary Parker Follett and the challenge from my daughter, Michele, we would focus on women; and following our sensing about culture we would focus our efforts on Eastern cultures (see Nichol's model in Chapter 10, p. 237).

Turid Sato's network of influence led to a program in Thailand. She approached her colleagues in the Foreign Ministry of Norway to support a study of "Women's Organizing Abilities." She also linked with the head of the largest NGO in Thailand, the Population and Community Development Association (PDA). He was affectionately known as "Mechai." He was an international icon who almost single-handed changed Thailand's attitude and approach to the problem of AIDS and paved the way for similar approaches internationally. Who else could persuade three-piece-suited World Bank staff to distribute condoms in the red-light district of Bangkok?

Mechai had became so popular with international donors that he decided to branch out to tackle what he thought was the most important problem in Thailand—rural development. He requested ODII to train his staff. As a large part of our funding came from Norway to study women's organizing we joined with Thailand Development Research Institute (TDRI). We planned to use our normal AIC approach but within that pay special attention to the role of women.

ODII ran a four-day workshop for thirty-five trainees—ironically they were mostly male because few Thai women would be allowed or willing to travel between villages:

> Some 35 Thai participants got exposed to the AIC process by using it to design the village level workshops that they soon would be conducting. Within two weeks of the exposure to the philosophy, the methodology and logistic requirements, teams of five facilitators/researchers fanned out the country side to conduct the village planning sessions.
>
> The village development planning workshops brought together a variety of representatives in the villages, from village headmen to women community leaders to youth, aiming at having an equal number of men and women present.
>
> The villagers were taken through the three phases of the AIC process, looking at the present realities of their village and how they got there, brainstorming as many ideas as possible about their ideal village, discussing strategies of how to get from the present reality to their ideal visions, prioritizing the different options, and then setting action plans which they could commit to implementing.
>
> These workshops were followed by district level synthesis workshops where representatives from the village, one man and one woman, presented their priorities to government officials (such as officers from the Ministries of Health, Agriculture, and Education), development officers and to the other village representatives, in order to share information and ideas, discuss strategies and to look into possibilities of support for implementing their plans.
>
> (Naguchi 1996)

As ODII provided the funding for these workshops it was able to insist on one criterion that participants from villages be 50 percent men and 50 percent women. Our view was that you could not study women's organizing abilities out of context:

> The results of the program at the local level were presented at a policy conference in October 1991 on women in rural development. At this workshop, the Ministry of Interior announced a proposal for a new policy—namely that rural women would be represented in local decision-making bodies thus removing one obvious constraint which prevented women from using their full capacities to contribute to development. Conference participants also embraced the idea of NGOs playing a facilitative role in helping villagers design their own development programs and promote self-help. The policy workshop demonstrated to the stakeholders the kind of results possible from the process.
>
> (Ibid.)

Again, the ODII team ran into the same problem as in the World Bank. This time it was the government who feared the empowerment of villages. From 1932 Thailand had a military government that appointed a civilian administration. However, by the 1980s Thais were becoming disenchanted with the lack of progress. Local-level attempts at village development were viewed with suspicion and leaders in the field were actually being shot at.

It was at this time that Turid and I met Paiboon Wattanasiritham, Director of the Thailand Foundation for Rural Reconstruction Movement (TRRM) the very first NGO authorized in Thailand, and Dr Prawese Wasi a Magsaysay award winner for government service (Asia's equivalent of the Nobel prize).

Paiboon or Khun Paiboon as he is known—the prefix is a mark of respect—was originally a banker and had received a degree in economics from Hull University in England. However, he never forgot his country origins, Ayuthaya—"I'm a true rural boy at heart," he would say. He became the President of the Stock Exchange of Thailand and then the Senior Vice President of a commercial bank. He was in his next job as head of the Thailand Rural Reconstruction Movement when the ODII team met him. Prawase Wasi was a medical doctor, and like Khun Paiboon he emphasized the strong human values that emanated from their Buddhist background. For example, he advocated a philosophy of development very different from the West's "obsession with money."

> We must stay one step ahead of the world by remaining faithful to the right concept, or "sammaditthi", of development. It is one which focuses on goodness while interlocking the economy with mind,

family, community, culture, and the environment. All this provides basic happiness which can be measured by various indicators.

(Ibid.)

Turid and I had just finished the series of workshops with the PDA. It was not clear what, if any role ODII would have after that. We had given Paiboon and Prawase some of the materials we had been developing to help communicate our understanding up to that date about what AIC was and why we thought it worked. After reading the material overnight Prawase asked me at breakfast:

"Bill, do you have any Buddhist training?"

I laughed:

"No, but I do know why you are asking. What we have learnt about Appreciation sounds very like Buddhism, and that is, in fact, is why we chose Thailand to carry out this project. We believe appreciative principles and practices are very deeply embedded in Buddhist philosophy and culture."

The ODII team believes it was that resonance between the spiritual quality of appreciation and Buddhism that accounted for what happened next. Paiboon and Prawase with their deep Buddhist values trusted a process that was based on appreciative norms. They lent their hands and their hearts to the organization of an AIC workshop to bring together the government and the NGO community. Thereafter, as the extracts from Lynne Naguchi's (1996) and Brenda Furugganan and Prof. Mario Antonio G. Lopez (2002) papers show, there was a veritable explosion of AIC workshops that spread throughout Thailand producing a country-wide, self-organizing, self-replicating process that ended up changing the Thai Constitution.

The NGO/government workshop was held in January 1992, and was designed as the second half of a pincer strategy to counterbalance the grass-root work at the village level. In particular it was designed to overcome fears of subversion by popular grass-roots movements. Officially it was announced as enhancing the goals of collaboration between the government, NGO and private sector collaboration in rural development. The workshop consisted of sixty-five participants; approximately half of the Thai participation came from government and half from NGOs. Additionally it included Thailand's Chamber of Commerce and local representatives of the development assistance agencies or foundations, the United Nations Development Programme, the Canadian International Development Agency, the Ford Foundation, and the Friedrich Niemen Foundation. The goal was primarily appreciative, designed to change attitudes and perceptions of the reciprocal relationship between the government and NGOs.

The workshop succeeded in improving relations, and set in motion a process of institutional development. It helped to form an active partnership between the government, the NGO community, and the private sector. It spread from rural development into urban development, the private sector and into the universities. Finally, it reached to the level of the national government in late 1994 with the drafting of the Eighth Year National Economic and Social Development Plan (1997–2001). The Secretary General of the National Economic and Social Development Board (NESDB) the main governmental body that advises the cabinet on development planning and policy was open to the idea of participatory planning.

The setting for the workshop was located symbolically, in the Palace of Love and Hope. Its transformational importance was indicated by the number of reporters who covered the event—100 journalists to 65 participants.

The new perspective was followed up with an even more ambitious workshop attended by 1,500 people with even wider participation— business executives, farmers, slum organizers, monks and nuns, teachers, engineers, doctors and government officials, including the prime minister. It was at this workshop that the NGO Coordinating Committee on Development first proposed the use of the AIC process for the creation of the Eighth National Development Plan.

For the first time ever this National Plan emphasized human-centered development rather than purely classical economic development and involved all provinces in its development. Most significantly the workshop led to a 1997 Constitutional change in which citizens were given the right to unite and form associations. Under Sections 45 to 47, people had the right to organize:

> to conserve or restore their customs, local knowledge, arts or the good culture of their community and of the nation and participate in the management, maintenance, preservation, and exploitation of natural resources and the environment.

The Constitution also provided for NGO representation in all committees responsible for enacting laws related to education, health, and welfare.

ODII continued its work in many other countries and eventually moved up the systems hierarchy by tackling the design of the international development system itself. By then I felt I had achieved the dream of Rome: I knew what accounted for the highest levels of performance in organizations, the answer lay outside of the area of controllable variables and levels in which the field traditionally searched for improvements. What was required was a philosophy, model, and process that could deal with the whole beyond control. This included the wholeness of people, the wholeness of situations, both the explicate and the implicate order, the conscious and its unseen unconscious aggregate. At the end of the Thai experience, reviewing more than a decade of experience with the process we were able to point to six conditions that produced the transformations we were involved with:

- there was a latency in the whole (culture, industry, appreciated field) for the purpose;
- the purpose was one that transcended the particular interests of every stakeholder;
- that the whole system was represented in the process;
- that everybody in the process had equal opportunity to participate and to contribute;.
- the autonomy of every participant was respected (i.e. the group would not make decisions for any participant—no groupthink);
- the process was designed to create the best possible conditions for the equal use of all three powers—appreciation, influence, and control— that translated the purpose into action.

Invocation of all three fields has a transformative impact on people who care about the purpose. When people gain a new appreciation of their whole situation their world literally enlarges. They enter into a new *appreciative* space beyond the need to influence or control. Within that new appreciated world they see new options; they develop different priorities and more inclusive attitudes.

The whole organization field at that time was also struggling with the same issues, as the limits of theory and practice based on open-systems thinking began to emerge. The second half of this chapter presents the parallel progress reflected in the literature of the time.

The Literature on the Emerging Phase: Embracing Wholeness

Beyond Open Systems

The lessons from the open-systems or influence-centered phase, understanding dynamic organization environmental relationships, are still being absorbed both in theory and practice. The organizational field's attempts at understanding and practice with the next level of "whole" systems' perspectives really started in the mid 1980s. It s origins though were always there from the beginning, even if ignored. They were in Weber's recognition of a charismatic level. They were partially in Parsons' concept of the "institutional" level and Etzioni and Ozbekhan's "normative" level.

One of the first people to muse on the importance of understanding this level in a more comprehensive way relative to organization was the same person who introduced the concept of open systems to organizations, Kenneth Boulding. In his book *The Image* (1956), Boulding carries out a thought experiment in which he attempts to explore the limits of how he knows who he is, and what his world is in all of its extensions; philosophical, emotional, and practical.

He concludes that the word that represented the totality of all this information is not "knowledge" but "image." He then began to wonder about how this image is both created and changed. He explored, for example, the role of facts, values, and culture in forming and reforming that image. He discovered that if he were able to follow through on his intuition and understanding he would end up creating a new science with different substance and laws than our current science. He called that science "Eiconics." He noted, for example, that the world he knew best, that of economics, is pretty anti-eiconical. He noted that the fields of sociology and psychology are much more eiconical. He dubbed the social psychologist George Margaret, who combined both fields, the first eiconist. He also pointed to the field theories of Kurt Lewin as image-based. However, he confesses that of the people who influenced his development of the concept of image most did not come from any particular discipline. They were Chester Barnard and his *The Functions of the Executive* (1938), with the image of an executive as the receiver of information and giver of orders; Norbert Wiener with his image from *Cybernetics* (1948) of the executive at the center of a control system watching through feedback for deviation from ideal values; and third, from Weaver and Shannon's *The Mathematical Theory of Communication* (1949), with the image of organizations as sets of equations that parallel the concepts of mass and energy in physics.

Sir Geoffrey Vickers (1965), similarly, was struggling with the way people make decisions when they have to deal with this aggregate space. He wanted to "describe, analyze and understand the process of judgments and decision as they are encountered in business and public administration." He had no word to describe the whole arena and process that he felt were involved:

> I need first a word to describe it and, as I cannot find one in the literature I must invent one. I will call it appreciation, following the ordinary usage in which we speak of "appreciating the situation."
>
> (Vickers 1965: 39)

He was very aware of Simon's work and drew a great deal from it. His thinking, however, differs markedly. He illustrates the difference that consideration of the level of the whole takes us. Policymaking takes place in institutional space—beyond the individual's or organization's control.

1　I adopt a more explicitly dynamic conceptual model of an organization and of the relations, internal and external, of which it consists, a model which applies equally to all its constituent sub-systems and to the larger systems of which it is itself a part.

2　This model enables me to represent its 'policy makers' as regulators, setting and resetting courses or standards, rather than objectives, and thus in my view to simplify some of the difficulties inherent in descriptions in terms of "means" and "ends".

3　I lay more emphasis on the necessary mutual inconsistency of the norms seeking realization in every deliberation and at every level of organization andhence on the ubiquitous interaction of priority, values, and cost.

4　In my psychological analysis linking judgments of fact and value by the concept of appreciation, I stress the importance of the underlying appreciative system in determining how situations will be seen and valued. I therefore reject "weighing" (an energy concept) as an adequate description of the way criteria are compared and insist on the reality of a prior and equally important process of "matching" (an information concept).

5　I am particularly concerned with the reciprocal process by which the setting of the appreciative system is itself changed by every exercise of appreciative judgment.

(Ibid.: 22)

He reacts very strongly to the classical control-centered emphasis on "goal-seeking": some of the blame must be taken by psychologists who have made goal-seeking the paradigm of rational behavior . . . It shows a failure to appreciate relations in time; and enhanced capacity to appreciate relationships in time is clearly one of the distinguishing marks of our species

(Ibid.: 311)

He clearly points to the relationship essence of the influenced environment:

The goals we seek are changes in our relations or in opportunities for relating; but the bulk of our activity consist in 'relating' itself.

(Ibid.: 312)

In policy making he seeks the setting of governing relationships or norms rather than setting goals. In this space

the channels of dialogue differ strikingly from those within an organization. Instead of the trunk lines with their junctures and branches, which carry information up and down such an organization, a net of communication links each with all in a way both piecemeal and comprehensive and mediates mutual influence. This network—it is tempting to call it a reticular system—is indeed undergoing change.

(Ibid.: 32)

He notes, for example, that the shift from communication by speech to communicating by writing and reading brought about by the printing revolution caused major changes in this reticular system. He also notes that our new generation brought up on images, video, and TV will experience a similar shift.

If it was Mary Parker Follett, from the classical period, who most provided a base for building the AIC concepts, and if it was James D. Thompson who provided the framework for the dynamic relations between organizations and environment, then it was Erich Jantsch who most informed the appreciative level. In *Design for Evolution* (1975) he explores the acquisition of knowledge for human purposes. He maps a sweeping view of the new physical and social sciences into a turbulently ordered view of organization at all levels of existence. He provides a guiding image of ordered, dynamic complexity linking the physical, biological, social, and cultural worlds, balancing rational intellectual thinking with subjective feeling and values. He believed that there was an urgent need to explore the dynamics of those areas beyond the clouds "where human cultures are rooted and from which cultural change emanates as the powerful guiding factor of social and individual change" (Jantsch 1975: xv).

- The lowest level of the hierarchy of human knowledge is "know how," i.e. the control-centered level of *"ordering and implementing well perceived goal oriented action"*.
- The second level, our influenced level, is "know- what"—the setting of goals in a dynamic systemic context.
- The third, our appreciative level, is: "know where to" in which we strive for an overall sense of movements and direction . . . It is also the level of policy design.

(Jantsch 1975).

The three levels he notes coincide with Lazlo's (Jantsch 1975: xiii) (i) "mastering of change"; (ii) understanding the order of change or process; and then (iii) to the third level—the order of process or evolution. It is this third level of evolution, order of process, answering the question "where to" that captures the essence of this appreciative level, the relationship to the whole. It is through this perspective that we finally begin to develop a more complete concept of purpose.

For Jantsch, purpose provides order. It is the order we learn when taking an evolutionary approach. Purpose is meaning in this dynamic perspective and forms the core of any evolutionary myth. But this sense of purpose derived from this evolutionary appreciated world is developed in opposition or more exactly complementary tensions:

> arising from our interaction with reality this sense of purpose relies on a direct insight that is not developed in the laboratory or in the appreciated world. It is the direct experience of an objective purpose which may be sensed by "tuning in" to the evolutionary movement.
>
> (Jantsch 1975: 141)

His holistic approach, which, at that time, put him on the speculative fringe of the systems group includes all modes of insight, paradigms of physical and social science, artistic expression, mystical insight, and psychic revelatory process.

His design approach is avowedly dynamic focusing "on processes and their interaction, processes of a self-realizing and self-balancing type which unfold in continuous feedback linkage to their own origin." Within this design approach it is his evolutionary worldview that takes him to the third level of the whole:

> it is the event unfolding in space and time which is set in absolute; creation is continuously creating itself.
>
> (Ibid: xvi)

He points to new insight from physical and biological evolution, particularly to Prigogine's (1985) concept of "order through fluctuation."

One of the basic concepts applied to the design of individual, social, and cultural systems is the notion of a triplicate structure of levels of perception or inquiry:

> The rational approach [c] assumes separation between the observer and the observed, and focuses on an impersonal "it" which is supposed to be assessed objectively and without involvement by an outside observer; the basic organizing principle here is logic, the results are expressed in quantitative or structural terms, and the dynamic aspects are perceived as change.
>
> The mythological approach [i] establishes a feedback link between the observer and the observed, and focuses on the relationship between a personal "I" and a personal "Thou." Its basic organizing principle is feeling, the results are obtained in qualitative terms, and the dynamic aspects are perceived as process, or order of change.
>
> The evolutionary approach [a] establishes union between the observer and the observed and focuses on the "we," on the identity of the forces acting in the observer and the observed world; the organizing

principle is "tuning-in" by virtue of this identity, and the results are expressed in terms of sharing in a universal order

(Prigogine 1985: 84)

(I have added the (a), (i), and (c) to recall the secondary or means dimensions that recall the work of Etzioni and Gouldner and which becomes the means dimension of the AIC framework.)

In his design process these complementary views of reality enable him to rise above the classical reductionist view that stresses quantity to a more holistic view that stresses quality. Finally, he adopts a four-dimensional view that emphasizes the space/time view of process. In this he is one of the first writers to stress that the new view of dynamic relationship, of process represents a shift from three- to four-dimensional modeling.

Most of the book is then spent understanding the three evolving worlds of *consciousness*, *appreciation*, and *reality* in terms of the model. For example, in examining the feedback relationships between consciousness and reality he creates the following ordering of ideas. Notice that "purpose" is placed in spiritual space accessed through an evolutionary or open approach. The polar opposite of "purpose" is a "measure" existing in physical space and created though a rational approach.

In Part II we will draw more on this work but for now our emphasis is on Jantsch's contribution to our understanding of the "Appreciated World," the world we associate with the whole, the part of the world beyond our ability to control or influence.

Erich Jantsch's Model			
	Evolution approach (a)	**Mythological approach (i)**	**Rational approach (c)**
Spiritual space (A)	Purpose (telos)	Values	Laws (regularities)
Social space (I)	Ethics of whole systems	Individual ethics	Behavioral patterns
Physical space (C)	Oneness	Gestalt (quality)	Measure
The evolving norms in the feedback relations between consciousness and reality (re-ordered to make the underlying AIC pattern consistent with other charts in the text)			

Figure 4.2 Jantsch's model

The appreciated world is the product of our subjective self. It consists primarily of models projected onto it by consciousness—models of the world as it is and as it ought to be, and which return and govern consciousness in the disguise of powerful myths. To keep the model/myth cycle always open and flexible, to perceive and deal with reality through a fluid spectrum of models, is the most difficult task at the core of creative design.

(Ibid.: 189)

Building on Jantsch, then, the ultimate appreciative level (A) is our *appreciated world*, the ultimate level of influence (I) is our *consciousness* and the ultimate level of control (C) is reality. The means of accessing these levels, the secondary level is *evolutionary* (a), *mythological* (i), and *rational* (c). Purpose for him is an *ordering* that gives meaning at the spiritual level, which is manifest at the influence level *as human ethics* and at the control level as *measure*.

Jeffrey Stamps work as illustrated in *Holonomy: A Human Systems Theory* (1980) makes an enormous contribution to our understanding of the whole-part relationships by extending Koestler's original concept of the holon—a word he coined to express the whole–part relationship; "holos" coming from the Greek for whole and "-on" connoting the part as in electron and proton. He also adapts Paul MacLean's word "holonarchy" to describe the hierarchical structure of holons, the set of holons nested within holons in an infinite set of part–whole relationships. He uses this insight to construct a human systems theory that is both inclusive and evolutionary. This construct and Jeffrey's courage in pursuing his very ambitious work to create a new Human Science was key to sustaining my own parallel effort.

The literature reviewed so far has had a direct impact on the development of the AIC concepts and practice. As part of the writing process for this book I have become aware of yet more relevant work. For example, from writers such as Winograd and Flores (1986) who link philosophical concepts from postmodernism to the understanding of the "whole." They base their work on ideas from Heidegger and the traditions of hermeneutics (the study of interpretation) and phenomenology (the study of experience and action) to challenge the belief that formal analytical understanding of reality is possible at all. They emphasize those areas of experience in which individual interpretation and intuitive understanding plays a central role. They emphasize the role of language in understanding and creating reality. They point to the role of the listener in the active generation of language and language as an act of social creation. Such thinking contributed to the "social constructionist" view; that we play an active role in constructing and enacting our realities (Weick 1979).

David Cooperider as part of his dissertation published in 1986 introduced the concept of Appreciative Inquiry, which has since become very popular:

> Appreciative Inquiry is the cooperative search for the best in people, their organizations, and the world around them. It involves systematic discovery of what gives a system "life" when it is most effective and capable in economic, ecological, and human terms. AI involves the art and practice of asking questions that strengthen a system's capacity to heighten positive potential. It mobilizes inquiry through crafting an "unconditional positive question" often involving hundreds or sometimes thousands of people.
>
> (Cooperider and Whitney 1999: 245–63)

The major difference between AI and AIC lies in David's emphasis on the positive. I have interpreted appreciation as the relationship to the whole, which in its highest manifestation (fifth dimension) is beyond the positive or negative, even beyond time. David's concept of appreciation, in the AIC framework, provides only a part of the whole; the positive valuation which would place it as appreciation in the influence-centered level or (I-a) (the fourth dimension). This levels deals with positive and negative values. At this level and in terms of concepts beyond the positive limitation there is a great deal in common between the AIC philosophy and the AI approach.

Gareth Morgan (1986, 1997), following in the tradition of Boulding, uses metaphor and images as vehicles for understanding the whole. In *Imagini-zation* (1997) he combines the concept of image and organization to symbolize the relationship between the creative potential of images and the transformational potential of organization. He shows

> how traditional concepts of organization can be radically transformed through imaginative processes whereby new images and metaphors are used to create evocative and energizing patterns of shared meaning.
>
> (1997: 263)

He points to a key characteristic of the appreciated world of metaphors and images, that it "rings true" it is a "chord" it "resonates":

> The process has self regulating quality; there has to be a resonance and authenticity to create energy and involvement.
>
> (Ibid.: 290)

He builds on concepts of power emerging from the postmodern school. Postmodernists reacted against structured power, the idea that our power is determined by the state, the structure of the world we find ourselves in. They want to reclaim each person's unique place and power in the world.

Foucault, for example, argued that people do not "have power," power is a process that people engage in. In that process the exercise and resistance to power are part of the same process. Morgan refers to the potential creation part of the process in the following way:

> *Imaginization* starts with ourselves and in its broadest sense invites us to assume our personal power in rethinking and reshaping the world around us.
>
> (Ibid: 292)

People in this power process are both, as he illustrates, "writing" and "reading" their lives at the same time.

Joseph S. Nye Jr, a political scientist interested in international relationship clearly identified what we call appreciative power under the label of *Soft Power*. He refers to what for us is a familiar progression from control though influence to appreciation:

- You can coerce them with threats (c).
- You can induce them with payments (i).
- Or you can attract or co-opt them (a).

(Nye 2004)

He equally attributes the key force behind soft power as "attraction"—what we have referred to as the gravity of appreciation.

Lyotard (1984) makes an argument for "generative conversation" as an approach that can be transformative and bring new ideas, images, and concepts to the process. Ulrich (1983), following Kant, argues that Newtonian science provides an adequate basis for understanding the technical but social science has to add another dimension that will allow us to deal with human purposiveness. The principles he developed are organized under three headings:

- Systems—the need for comprehensive mappings of social reality (a).
- Moral—the need to improve the human conditions for all (i).
- Guarantor—the needs to verify as much as possible of the information, feedback, and views of experts (c).

Again we have added the (a), (i), and (c) to indicate the underlying power relationship and have used the small letters, according to our convention, to reflect power as means rather than intention. . . .

Peter Senge in his 2004 book, *Presence, Human Purpose and the Field of the Future*, enters into a dialogue with three of his colleagues—Otto Scharmer, Joseph Jaworski, and Betty Sue Flowers—about the nature of wholeness and purpose. The book is essentially a dialogue on what we call appreciation, the relations to the whole, and purpose, but the word appreciation doesn't appear in the text or index, nor is any special relationship established between purpose and wholeness. They agree that "seeing from the whole" requires suspension of current "mental models."

They see the field of the "whole" as an emerging future that allows for redirection and has spiritual properties. They allow that the whole is not something out there but includes the very center of the self, the point where *we enter into a Dialogue with the Universe* and end up finding the universe in our very center.

The group several times picks up the theme of purpose, and appears to agree that life is intentional:

> "So, Joseph, coming back to this issue of intentionality, it sounds to me as if you're very comfortable with the idea that life has an intention," said Peter.
>
> "I believe that everyone is born with a destiny or a purpose, and the journey is to find it. That's the way I read Robert Greenleaf's work on servant leadership: the ultimate aim of the servant leader, the quest. . . ."
>
> (Senge 2004: 228)

However, later when Betty Sue wonders:

> "if what we've been exploring is really all about purpose in some sense . . . do you think a collective sense of purpose might be developing?"
>
> (Ibid.: 242)

Peter replies:

> "It's possible. But I think the question of human purpose is almost impossible for us to ponder in our present state."

The dialog that follows implies that we won't really be able to understand purpose until we can as humanity transcend our view as humans separate from nature to see ourselves at one with all species, even the universe itself.

From Jackson's (2003) *Creative Holism* we can extract some of the main themes that describe the postmodernist ideas about the nature of the whole, or our appreciated world:

> They deny that science can provide access to objective knowledge and so insist in the steering of organizations and societies in the face of complexity . . . Postmodernists emphasize instead that we have to learn

to live with the incommensurable, accepting multiple interpretations of the world and being tolerant of differences. Indeed they want to ensure diversity and encourage creativity by reclaiming conflict and bringing marginalized voices to be heard.

(p. 256)

Postmodernist thinking then brings to the concept of the appreciated world a greater sense of:

- purpose, especially, the purposes of all those non-participants affected by the organizations;
- the almost infinite diversity that makes this level less subject to understanding through rational systems thinking;
- the inclusion of the disadvantaged and underrepresented as part of the whole that makes power relationships an essential component for understanding wholeness.

In a world of multiple truths competing for prominence, even soft and emancipatory systems thinkers are left impotent unless they recognize the importance of power and engage with (rather than seek to avoid) the social and political context of their work.

(Ibid.: 261)

In 2006, Clegg *et al.* made a courageous contribution of reviewing and enlarging the framework within which power is viewed. They relate power to political performance, and hence to democracy. They point to emerging hybrid forms of organization that contain elements of hierarchy (c), oligarchy (i), and polyarchy (a).

They argue that these hybrids "shift the focus of organizational power from analysis of struggles themselves to that of social creation of political performance. Such political performance determines the perpetuation of the organizations through resolution of elitist and pluralist governance philosophies and practices." His point here parallels our point that our current state of evolution in theory overemphasizes influence for control rather than equally for appreciation.

They enter the "level of the whole" through the concept of institutionalization and recognize that power structures appear to be the result of institutionalization of the reciprocal influence of individual life histories and of established cultural frameworks shaping what it means to be and not to be part of elite groups.

They rely heavily on the work of Foucault, the modern French philosopher, as an influence on the direction of new thinking on power. Yet Foucault declares that he never conceived of his thinking in terms of power concepts. He struggles with a larger framework of power by focusing on institutions and the conditions of history and circumstance that create power structures, yet at the same time he says that you can't really understand power through analyzing the structures; you must look at the specific exercises of power at the level of action.

Summary

The key difficulty remains that power is in everything and is central to the understanding and practice of organization. The field of organizational sciences seems to be emerging from a period of denial of its importance and usefulness, which included a very negative view of power.

Our review of the mainstream literature does not reveal key insights into some of the themes that proved so useful in practice, particularly the nature of purpose and its relationship to power. In particular, no concept of purpose can lay claim to legitimacy unless it shows how it deals with unconscious purpose. Nor can any concept of power be viable without an understanding of fields and dimensions. One of the surprises and disappointments of this review of the mainstream literature has been the lack of pursuit of the concept of fields, especially given the success of its principal founder Kurt Lewin. Lewin, who developed the famous field equation $B = f (P, E)$—behavior is a function of the person and the environment.

Similarly, we cannot integrate all of these ideas into a philosophy and practice of organization, unless we understand the opportunities and constraints provided by the basic processor of all of this information—our individual and collectively embodied brains and minds—which in turn link back to a better understanding of the role and management of the unconscious.

For these reasons, and taking our cue from Max Weber, Mary Parker Follett, and Meg Wheatley, in the next three chapters we move outside the field of organization to the fields that represent the highest possible levels of power—religion, science, and philosophy, the mothers of all other disciplines—to search for fundamental insights. We synthesize these new insights on purpose and power into our best current understanding in the form of a new philosophy of organization in Chapter 5; a new theory and model of power in Chapter 6; and an organizing process that contains within it the wisdom gained from the philosophy and the model and several decades of experience in Chapter 7.

Part II

The Philosophy, Theory, Model, and Process

The four chapters of Part I describe the emergence of a new synthesis of experience, intuitive insight, and organization theory referred to as *Appreciation, Influence and Control* (AIC). Our review indicates that we are entering a new phase of theory and practice that is transcending the current open-systems emphasis. We are adding a new emphasis that centers on our relationship to wholes and the quality of wholeness itself.

The intuitive and experiential insights that have informed the framework of AIC concepts and practice reveal that a reformulation of our concept of purpose and power provides the key to understanding this new phase of evolution and its integration with previous phases. The reformulation provides a way to transcend the limits of the current open-systems phase that we synthesize as an overemphasis on control and on influence for control. However, to provide the basis for this new understanding we have had to widen our search to include fields of knowledge that are most concerned with understanding the whole of the human condition—its sense of purpose and its power to pursue purpose. A review of religion, philosophy, and science as the mothers and fathers of all other disciplines fulfills this function for us. Religion, in the broadest possible sense of the word, has, since the beginning of human culture, the task of helping us to understand our ultimate origin and purpose as a guide to how we can pursue a fuller life. As there is much in this relationship that we cannot understand with our conscious minds religion draws on our faith, on our intuition and sensing capacities as valid sources of information. Natural science, on the other hand, attempts to explain to us what we can know for sure with our conscious minds, what we can test and verify, about ourselves and the universe we inhabit. It relies much more on what we can count and measure objectively. Science, at least in recent history has been the most respected source of knowledge about how the whole works, how all forces combine to produce the world we live in. Its technical accomplishments have literally changed the face of the world we know. Historically, though, science is the child of philosophy, which in turn is the child of religion. Philosophy comes somewhere in between. It uses reason to bridge the gaps between what we know by faith and intuition through religion, spiritual traditions, or cultural wisdom and what we can know by experimentation through science. The following quote from the very first page of Bertrand Russell's *History of Western Civilization* sums this definition very nicely:

> Philosophy, as I shall understand the word, is something intermediate between theology and science. Like theology, it consists of specula-tions on matters as to which definite knowledge has, so far, been unascertainable; but like science, it appeals to human reason rather than to authority, whether that of tradition or that of revelation. All definite knowledge—so I should contend—belongs to science; all dogma as to what surpasses definite knowledge belongs to theology. But between theology and science there is a No Man's Land, exposed to attack from both sides; this No Man's Land is philosophy.
>
> (1945: 4)

Taken together an integration of religious, philosophic, and scientific thought provides us with our best current understanding of our culturally institutionalized concepts of wholeness. After reviewing the three fields we can see that each system of thought can be seen as an A, I, C contribution to the whole:

1   Religion or spiritual traditions provide us with *an appreciation* of our relationship to the *whole*, the universe in all its aspects. Religion addresses our relationship to the ultimate, however our faith inter-prets that relationship, as the Absolute, God, the Supreme Force, or agnostically as natural forces that we do not yet understand. Our religious or spiritual relationships are like our relationship to art. It is intensely personal and subjective. The common appreciative base of the relationship helps explain why religion and art have always developed hand-in-hand since the beginning of time.

2   Philosophy is a dance between science and religion, a set of "reason-able" explanations that bridge the objective world of science and the subjective world of religion. Philosophy helps us understand how the parts of the whole relate to each other: as such it is the ultimate *influence-centered* system.

3   Science explains to us the ultimate *form* of the world in a way that its explanation can be verified factually. It gives us information about how the material world and the forces that connect the physical elements of the world connect together to produce the world we can see, feel, touch, and measure, and therefore is the ultimate source of the *control-centered* perspective.

A full review of the three fields would take a lifetime's work in itself; however, I use the intuition that purpose is the source of power to provide a pathway through. If purpose manifests power as three distinct fields, then this pattern should appear in our earliest attempt to understand purpose and our earliest attempts to move purpose into action. This pattern should also be evident in each successive phase of evolution and still be recognizable using the basic properties of the relationship between purpose and power. I show in all three chapters that such patterns do exist and can be used to describe any purposeful system. Just as I have illustrated with the pattern in the relationship between religion, philosophy, and science, we will also see in this part of the book how the pattern exists even in the phases of human and organizational evolution themselves.

I use this understanding of purpose and its three fields of power to formulate a philosophy of organization in **Chapter 5**. In **Chapter 6**, I translate the philosophy into a theory of power and organization. **Chapter 7** translates the philosophy into a model that links purpose, power, and organization. In **Chapter 8**, I translate the model into organizing processes that enable purposeful systems to use more of the power available to them than do traditional models. In providing this philosophy, theory model, and process my long search from Rome is finally completed—I develop a framework of concepts and practice within which we can enable ourselves, our organizations, and our worlds to use much more of the power available to us in pursuing our purposes—to become more "power-full."

5 The Emerging Philosophy

The Nature of Purpose

Insights From Religion, Philosophy, and Science

The review of religion proved extremely helpful by enabling the broadest possible evolutionary sense of organization. It shows humanity struggling to understand its origins and its destiny and to find ways to use this understanding to improve its quality of life. It forces us to think about how our mental, spiritual, and cultural capacities developed. It gives us a sense of the role religion and spirituality play in giving us a sense of purpose as well as an understanding of the power available to us in pursuing that purpose.

The idea of God as an explanation of ultimate purpose and ultimate power accounting for all known and unknown causes and all seen and unseen forces affecting life probably originated about 14,000 years ago, according to Wilhelm Schmidt. Writing in 1912, he suggested that man was originally monotheistic. Humans imagined a Sky God who caused everything to happen. Over time this God in the Sky became too remote. He was a God that people could only *appreciate* at a great psychic and emotional distance. People wanted a closer, more personal God that they could talk to and *influence*. They began to associate gods with the mysteries of the sun, stars, sea, wind, and rain, gave them names and spoke to them. Gods became associated with tribes and favored their special people. People called on them to influence the outcome of battles and other conflicts. This relationship to the gods was highly emotional and could produce feelings from the extremes of wild bacchanalian excitement, to the most sublime sense of awe and dread.

Julian Jaynes (1976) links the development of the idea of God directly to the development of our brains and mind. He believes that this kind of human relationship with the gods actually began before humans had developed consciousness. He argues, from archeological evidence and research on the human brain that prior to 1000 BC humans could not think self-consciously. They had a bi-cameral mind. Our one mind operated just as our unconscious minds operates today when we do things mechanically. The second mind produced voices that told humans what to do when they were faced with decisions, especially under stress. The second mind was the repository of collective wisdom and fulfilled the function that later was externalized as gods and kings.

The bi-cameral human, when operating far from home and faced with a decision would hear the voice of his internalized king. Jaynes uses the Iliad as an example to show how the protagonists attributed every one of their decisions to the gods. Using the original texts, Jaynes also demonstrates that there were no words in the language for mental processes (appreciations), every word referred to physical action (control). This is not so obvious from current translations because the translators, unaware of this distinction used modern concepts to translate the original text. In this bi-cameral phase we could say that the voices, the precursor to God, gave mankind the power to extend the voice of the leader or king. It provided a mechanism of evolution for improved social functioning. By hearing these voices humans could live and develop in larger more specialized communities, which increased the power of the group and its chances for survival in competition with other groups and the elements.

Gradually these internal voices become externalized and built into socio-cultural institutions: we developed our tribal gods and our kingdoms. This evolutionary process continues in the Axial age (800 BC–200 BC). Changes in economic and social conditions; the rise of a merchant class, greater cultural and intellectual activity, all gave rise to shifts in power away from the all-powerful kings and priests and gave rise to more individualized power. Humanity needed a mental spiritual framework that could express and enhance this shift in social cultural power and its enormous increase in complexity. This latent need of the whole was manifest in the evolution of major religions, all of which had their origin in this time frame.

Humanity, as a whole, was working out a new relationship between individuals, social organizations, and the divine. There was much in common in the religions that emerged and that helps us understand the fundamental universal nature of purpose and its manifest powers. The essence of religion when experienced is very powerful and very difficult to explain, so we owe a great deal to the Greeks for their attempts to provide such explanations through philosophy. They provide the basis of an explanation of the relationship between purpose and power and they provide a rational for the threeness that appears in all major religious and hence in power relationships.

The Greeks introduced two concepts: *ousia*, essence and *energiaia*, manifest power, which are key to this explanation. The essence of God is the ultimate unknowable quality of God that exceeds the capacity of the human mind to understand. The manifest powers are the means by which the essence is revealed in the world. We can, then, take ultimate purpose to be a property of this essence. In other words ultimate purpose is unknowable, how it is made manifest in the world as the powers of God, however, is knowable. So, using this Greek-based explanatory power, if we look to the religions for an understanding of "wholeness," for explanation of ultimate purpose and its manifest powers what does it tell us?

The Common Message from Religions

First, there is surprising similarity across religions about the essence of the divine and how it is accessed. All major religions see a transcendent force operating in the universe that seeks to reveal itself through humankind and in the world. All major religions imagine the essence as a power that is unknowable and indescribable in human terms. The Eastern religions see the essence as a power that informs all things, for example, Brahma or the Tao. All of the major religions make some distinction between the nature or essence, the wholeness, of God, the source of all purpose and power, and the manifestation of that power in the world.

Second, the Western religions, while recognizing the unknowable indescribable nature of the ultimate essence do personalize it and refer to it as a God; the King of Kings. Third, the means of accessing divine purpose is also very similar. It asks us to express ourselves to the fullest in the light of its essence. We can only experience this essence, it cannot be explained or taught. The most common means of experience is meditation or prayer. In the West, though, there is also a tradition of experiencing God's purpose through revelation.

When we examine the expression of essence as manifest powers there is also a surprising agreement on the number of powers and their fundamental qualities. In all the major religions there is an expression of threeness either in the being of God himself or in his manifest powers. The threeness in all cases have AIC relationships; one dealing with the whole concept of God, one dealing with relationships to God and humans, and one dealing with the God in the individual.

The earliest expression of threeness in religion is found in Hindu and Brahmin explanations:

1   Brahma is the Supreme God; the control equivalent to the Christian Father.
2   Vishnu is the incarnate Word and Creator; the product of the Supreme God, the equivalent of the Son in Christianity that embodies God's Word and mediates between man and God.
3   Shiva is the Spirit of God, the appreciative whole in every part, the equivalent of the Christian Holy Spirit or Ghost.

The two major branches of Buddhism also have divisions of three in their manifest powers. The oldest branch, Theravada, literally "the Way of the Elders" has been the predominant in Sri Lanka, Cambodia, Laos, Myanmar,

Thailand, and parts of southwest China, Vietnam, and Bangladesh. Nibbana, the highest goal of Theravada Buddhism, is attained through three practices:

1   Meditation, sila (what we can do ourselves—control).
2   Morality, samadhi (how we relate to others—influence).
3   Wisdom, panna (how we relate to the whole—appreciation).

Its fundamental scriptural canon is taught in the Tipitaka, "Three Baskets":

- The Vinaya Pitaka, which lays out the rules. The Vinaya Pitaka contains the rules of conduct for Buddhist monks and nuns, obviously serving a control-centered function.
- The Sutta Pitaka contains the actual discourses of the Buddha, supplemented by extensive commentaries, with stories that convey the associated myths and legends, so it is not too difficult to see that it is influence-centered.
- The Abhidhamma Pitaka contains some of the most important doctrinal statements of Theravada, such as anatman, the absence of a permanent soul, no self; and pratityasamutpada, dependent origination, the many becoming one. It includes poems, hymns of praise by monks and nuns, popular doctrinal statements and stories of former lives of the Buddha. It is clearly the most appreciative of the three parts.

The second major branch of Buddhism, Mahayana, is regarded by its adherents as a more advanced form. Its main practitioners today are in China, Taiwan, Korea, and Vietnam. They would say that Buddha's early teachings on suffering, impermanence, and non-self were given in doses suited to a more childlike people. They claim to elevate the Buddha to an eternal, immutable, inconceivable, omnipresent God-like being. Buddha is seen as an idealized man-god, present in all times and in all places.

The Mahayana Buddhists developed a Trikaya doctrine—the three bodies, or personalities of the Buddha—at about the same time that the Christian church was formalizing the doctrine of the Trinity in the fourth century. Buddha has three "bodies":

1   The Dharmakaya is the un-manifest, transcendental part of the Buddha from which all things both arise and to which all return. It "embodies" the principle of enlightenment and is omnipresent and boundless. It is the equivalent of the ultimate appreciated world.
2   The Sambhogakaya is the interface with the Dharmakaya. It brings the transcendental into the realm of humanity and makes it accessible. It is regarded as the body of mutual enjoyment. It is the ultimate form of

the field of influence relationships; that between the divine and the human.

3   The Nirmanakaya is the created body carrying the Dharmakaya; informed by Sambhogakaya it is the physical body that is manifest in time and space; it represents the field of control.

In the Western world, H.P. Blavatsky (1877) reveals that threeness originated in Babylon:

> We find it northeast of the Indus; and tracing it to Asia Minor and Europe, recognize it among every people who had anything like an established religion. It was taught in the oldest Chaldaean, Egyptian, and Mithraicism schools. The Chaldaean Sun-god, Mithra, was called "Triple," and the Trinitarian idea of the Chaldaeans was a doctrine of the Akkadians, who themselves belonged to a race which was the first to conceive a metaphysical trinity.
>
> (pp. 45, 46)

The idea of the Trinity was not explicitly taught in the Christian Church until the fourth century; though scholars insist that it is implicit in the New Testament. Similarly, the Jewish faith does not overtly express God as a Trinity but the facets that are represented by the Trinity can easily be found implicit in Judaism. Jahweh is God the creator of heaven and earth, the Torah is the word that is God's presence on earth and treated as Christ in the Christian faith. And finally, the spirit of God in all people is the equivalent of the Holy Ghost.

The choice of three manifest powers is so ubiquitous that it must have a natural origin that affects the individual and collective mind and spirit beyond the bi-cameral mind of Jaynes. It appears to be a collective evolution applicable to all humankind. It is linked to the evolution of individual consciousness as the source of influence between the ineffable unknowable nature of the divine and the reality of the life and the world we live in.

In this Axial Age, no longer was this internal voice in humankind produced by simple stress of individual decision-making in the bi-cameral mind. It was the voice of God that spoke for all people. The translation was no longer for individual action but for all people; the whole. Unlike the Hindus and Buddhists who refused to allow the divine to be explained in human terms, the psalms of the Jews and Christians imagined God enthroned in his temple as a King. The purpose of the prophet, unlike in Buddhism was not to impart knowledge, to provide mystical illumination, but to take action, to obey.

The essential difference for Christianity was that Christ's followers, even though Jesus himself did not consider himself a divine being, eventually decided that he was not just a prophet but also the Son of God. The fact that in the year AD 320 sailors and travelers in Egypt, Syria, and Asia Minor were singing popular ditties about the nature of the Father, the Son, and the Holy Spirit attests to the fact that the debate was not a purely theoretical phenomenon. People need to be able to relate to the divine in a personal way, and these three distinctions resonated at a very deep unconscious level. A deeply felt spiritual need was at the heart of this intense popular debate. The controversy became so heated that the Emperor Constantine himself called a synod at Nicea (modern Turkey). The synod, against all predictions to the contrary, voted for the divinity of Christ and the acceptance of the Trinity.[1]

Though Christian theologians have debated and continue to debate the divine nature of Christ, emotionally, it is Christians' relationship to the humanity of Christ that enabled the Christian faith to survive and become a message of hope for the poor and oppressed all over the world. Christ as a middle ground between God and people met an enormous human need. Christ provided both a divine and human guide to life that people could identify with and talk to.

Figure 5.1 summarizes the relative AIC emphasis of the major religions. The Eastern religions emphasize the appreciative-centered power. They are more open and free from dogma. They do not deny other Gods and in some cases include the worship of other gods. The Hindu/Buddhist tradition avoided personalizing God. Easterners were not interested in explaining their religion as much as using it to live a good life. Religion was to be experienced not explained. So in some ways the Hindus and Buddhists continued with the view that the purpose of the divine presence was to help humankind lead a good life. In the Tao Te Ching, Lao Tzu gives leaders advice on how to conduct themselves by understanding the Tao—the way the Universe works, the essence—and the Te—the power that comes to the leader when he aligns himself with the Tao, the manifest powers (Wing 1986).

Islam emphasizes influence-centered power. Mohammed was both a prophet and a very successful politician; he did not regard himself as a God but a prophet. The moral imperative to build a just and equitable society is an integral part of the Koran. The Muslims voraciously opposed the worship of multiple gods but, in the beginning, were open to other religions believing that, particularly the Jews, Christians and Muslims served the same one God.

The Jewish and Christian faiths are the most control-centered. Theirs is the God on the throne, the God of command who must be obeyed. They too are very adamant about not worshipping other gods. Karen Armstrong in *A History of God* (1993) explains that the Jewish experience of God was very different. God came to the Jewish prophets out of the blue and told them what to do. For the prophet the experience was unexpected and terrifying. There was no Buddha or Yogi-type meditation or preparation. Isaiah, for example, felt the temple shake and one of the Seraphs flew with a burning coal to purify his lips to prepare him to speak the word of God. This explanation, though metaphorical, does convey the terrifying significance of the experience for the prophet. The prophets were humbled and felt inadequate to translate the words to their people. The strain of the translation from experience to words was almost unbearable.

There is not too much difficulty in understanding, and there is a great deal of agreement, on the nature of the divine in the appreciative-centered dimension. God is all knowing, all powerful and beyond the capacity of human description. God exists in a dimension beyond the capacity of our four-dimensional world of time–space to understand. It is also easy to understand the holographic nature of God or divine spirit, the resonance of a God or natural force felt in each of us. At the control level we can feel this; we can know it with our senses and complete our religious rituals, prayer, meditation, good works, and duties. There is also much agreement on this between the religions.

The problem is the middle level. How does God's power relate to us and the God in each of us? In God's light how should we relate to each other

	Religion	Essence of God (Ultimate Purpose) (*Ousia*)	---- Manifest (a)	Power (*Energiai*) (i)	--------- (c)
A	Buddhist	The Tao	------------ Yin	-----The Te------- Yin/Yang	-------- Yang
	Theravada	Vibhajjavada Wisdom of Experience	----------- Doctrine	The Pitakas -------- Discourse	--------- Rules
	Mahayana	Un-manifest Buddha	Dharmakaya Transcendent	Sambhogakaya Interface	Nirmanakaya Body
A	Hindu	Brahma	Brahma Supreme God	Vishnu Creator/Intermediary	Siva Embodied Spirit
I	Islam	Al-Lah	Transcendent Indescribable	The Koran Word of God	The word manifest in the world
C	Christian	God	Holy Ghost (The Spirit)	Son (The intermediary)	The Father (The Creator)
C	Jewish	Yahweh	The Spirit Of God	The Torah Word of God	The King of Kings

Figure 5.1 The AIC pattern in the major religions

and the world around us? There is violent disagreement at this level that contributes to the religious wars and unresolved ethnic conflicts that have existed for hundreds and even thousands of years. Perhaps the biggest challenge of our times still remains how we make manifest an appreciation of wholes, of human ideals, and create the means to transcend such difference of values and means.

Not only are the three AIC relationships apparent within each of the major religions it is apparent between them. Together they make up a whole, with the Eastern providing the appreciative part, Islam providing the influence part, and Judaism and Christianity providing the control part.

Science Demurs

Science makes no attempt at understanding this essence or ultimate source or purpose of the universe and has serious questions about the validity of the concept of purpose in nature. As Guiseppe Sermonti (1998) notes:

> the concept of "purpose" was barred from Science in order to purify it from imprecise metaphysical or anthropomorphic implications.

In science the closest we can get to the essence of all things is to acknowledge that the first nanoseconds of the big bang is the big "unknown."

Science, especially physics, does attempt to understand the field of forces, the manifest powers that transformed the big bang from a singularity to the world we know today. This understanding will contribute greatly to our attempt in the next chapter to model the manifest powers. Philosophers, however, are unconstrained by the limits of science and they do add considerably to the discourse on power and purpose.

Philosophy, Purpose, and Manifest Power

Philosophy, especially in the Classical period, reduced the manifest powers to a duality, for example the sensible world vs. the intelligible, idealism vs. realism. This is the duality that we see between the appreciative and the controlling domains. The middle domain of influence is omitted.

It is not until the time of Kant that we are encouraged to look at purpose and power in a way that does not require God of some other First Cause to be the ultimate source of purpose. He sees purpose not as imposed by a supernatural God but inherent in the natural fabric of relationships. It emanates from the center of every substance as inner purpose (its set of all possibilities) and progresses through what he termed a process of "outwrapping"—from primal forces to cosmic structure.

It is interesting that for philosophers the reliance on God for the essence of power, and the duality of the manifest powers—idealism versus materialism—lasted until we were able to conceive of the world in dynamic rather than static terms. It is doubly interesting that this process should begin with Leibnitz (1646–1716) who, as a mathematician found ways to make sense of the dynamics of the sensible, or material world that for Plato was too difficult to understand with all its imperfections. Leibniz's method of integral and differential calculus gave us a way not only to understand dynamics but also to calculate change and rates of change.

Kant initially worked in the tradition of Leibnitz, but then in his Inaugural Dissertation of 1770 he made an extraordinary leap of thought that pre-configured much of what would later become Einsteinian and even quantum science. He made an enormous leap by centering his philosophy on the middle realm between materialism and idealism, which strangely enough he called "community." With our modern interpretation of this word we might think that this was his explanation of "the whole," our appreciated world, but we believe that his use of the term "community" reflected recognition that this middle realm was a distinct realm within itself that was contained in a bigger whole; the "plenum" of space.

Kant was trying to develop nothing less than a full understanding of the powers of nature. For him the three levels of manifest power were substance, force, and space (Kant 1770).

In the case of substance he accepted Leibnitz's view that substances were independent entities "that can exist as a subject but never as a mere predicate" so are permanent—in AIC terms the ultimate of control as form.

Kant felt that the middle ground consisted of communities of reciprocal interaction of forces between the substances. The forces consist simply of attraction, repulsion or a balance between the two. He argued that the forces that move things do not lie in the body of the substance but in the relationship of the forces between them. Substances affect the outer world not by their motion but their reciprocal influence, their effects *in* other substances (in AIC terms, relationships of influence).

Space, then, for Kant was no longer emptiness or some aether, it was a "plenum" or container for all the communities of reciprocal actions. He had great difficulty in describing the relationship between those communities and the whole of space but he does recognize space, the plenum, as a transcendental ideality—beyond the communities of interaction (the AIC world of appreciation).

In summary, Kant also identifies three manifest powers and supports the notion of purpose as being part of the essence of all things. He is the first philosopher to develop the concept of the middle ground of influence as a power field in its own right, not just a mixture of Substance (control field) and the Plenum (appreciative field).

Heidegger focused particularly on the essence, which he conceived as being. He argued that the approach of classical philosophy produced an emphasis on beings as subjects opposed to being, i.e. being as a process. From this emphasis came the split between the essence and the manifest powers. He was trying to understand the essence as a whole un-separated from the manifest powers.

The term "being" in philosophical tradition was meant to be a base element one that could not be explained in terms of others. The truth of the essence, of "being" for Heidegger was its openness, so its meaning could never be fixed. Wherever historically we find ourselves being, we have to be open beyond the limitations of that state in order to capture the fullness of being (i.e. to capture the potentialities that have not been made manifest in that historical state). Consciousness is not our beginning or the beginning of philosophy, "being" is the beginning. Heidegger's primordial sense of being or essence also has its own triune manifest powers, which he describes in somewhat ungainly words, in terms of time (Korab-Karpowicz 2007).

1   **Existence**—which is future oriented and full of the potential for being; it is projected onto possibilities (appreciative field)
2   **Throwness**—the world of the past—is the reality into which the being is "thrown." Reality is always restricted in terms of its spiritual, material, and culturally determined possibilities (control field).
3   **Fallenness**—the world of the present—is the "being with," which includes being with those who appreciate existence and those who live in fallenness (influence field).

It was Heidegger, then, who first introduced the idea that it is time that causes the split of the essence into the three manifest powers. But he, too, explains that the time he is talking about is not the linear time (of the control phase) that we most commonly associate with time, it is what we call today holonomic time, a process unifying past, present, and future (of the appreciative phase), which only becomes experienced time (influence phase) through our "being here." He uses the German word *dasein*, which includes *da-* for here now, and *sein* for being.

This link of the basis for the division of the whole into threeness based on time is also supported in Arthur Young's *The Geometry of Meaning* (1976). He tries the ultimate act of synthesis by trying to "regain the whole by knowing how the parts fit together." Working from an ancient Egyptian insight that "All meaning is an angle," he uses a circle to represent the whole and derives all the base terms of physical science, and their corresponding meaning for a human science from the angular relationships between the radians of a circle. He describes three very different kinds of relationship based on fourfold, threefold, and twofold divisions of the whole circle. He begins with the fourfold, based on Aristotle's four causes, and generates a cycle of action that relates the basic elements of physics together—length, mass, and time. From these he deduces the fourfold cycle of action consisting of position, velocity, acceleration, and control. From a human perspective he notes:

1   position is observed
2   velocity is computed, and
3   acceleration is felt
4   control he left "indeterminate."

He found it too difficult to name the human action associated with control. However, with our understanding of purpose and power it is not hard to see that control produces a perspective on what is observed, computed, and felt: that perspective, as we will show later, is called a goal perspective.

He observes that there are two ways of going around this circle—clockwise gives action and anti-clockwise gives learning and demonstrates that the fourfold division can describe the aspects of a whole but is inadequate to express its experience. It is, therefore, inadequate to create a complete model of process.

The threefold is the "active" element, the process of action that has to be experienced. It consists of a cycle of act, relationship, and state. If analyzed it becomes separated from experience and moved back into the fourfold description of aspects.

The threefold operation is an entirely different way of cutting the cake. It is much more fundamental and cannot be analyzed—the threefold is the natural way we move in life. We see something, buy it, and enjoy it: food, eating, satisfaction, stimulus, response, result.

> To implement description it is helpful to correlate the three categories to past present and future. We could go further, for the threefold may even be more basic than time, in the sense that it gives to time not only its customary divisions (past, present and future) but its directionality. The direction of time, like other aspects of the threefold is not objective, and it cannot be communicated as we communicate comparative measures. Immersed in time's flow we have no opportunity to get outside of it.
>
> (pp. 99–102)

In terms of directionality he referred to the twofold flow of clockwise and anti-clockwise, from past present to future, and from future to present to past. We will revisit this issue of time more in the next chapter as we build a model of purpose, power, and organization.

The most significant example of the shift from the *twoness* of analysis to the *threeness* of experience in this work is the shift described

(a)
EVOLUTION FROM TWO TO THREE DIMENSIONS
Trist and Emery's Organizational Environments

	Organization	Environment
Organization	$L_{1,1}$ Internal	$L_{1,2}$ Transactional
Environment	$L_{2,1}$ Transactional	$L_{2,2}$ Contextual

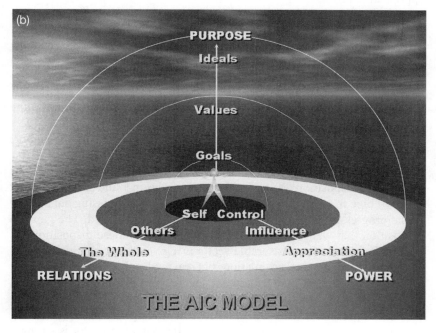

Figure 5.2a,b From two to three dimensions

in Chapter 2 from Emery and Trist's analytical concepts of environmental relationships shown analytically as a set of four, two-dimensional $L_{1,0}$ to $L_{2,2}$, translated into the three-dimensional set of nine relationships' presentation of AIC by placing an actor in the center. My experience with these concepts stimulated by the Guss Shumacher challenge converted the insight into a threefold field centered in the actor's purpose.

A key exception to the mainstream literature and a gem of discovery is the work of R.J. Rummel, a political scientist who works on global conflict reduction. He introduces the work of the philosopher Paul Ushenko (1969) who developed some key insights on the nature of power fields that Rummel then made the basis of his work on power. Ushenko was most interested in how we derive meaning from objects, in particular from the building block of our communication; a single sentence. He was particularly interested in the dispositional properties of objects. By this he meant the potential of an object to become manifest. This led him to the concept of power as a potential for manifestation, the same concept that we derived from the study of religion. In *The Dynamics of Art* he actually states that "Power is the capacity to exert influence and control." It is ironic that he actually develops most of his key ideas on power fields in this same book on art. What he describes is what I take to be a description of the appreciative process.

A work of art for Ushenko is an imaginative transformation of sense data that is a resolution of the tensions within the data, the artist, and the viewer. The rules of transformation are the rules of power that transcend the aesthetic field. Actuality, as with an act of appreciation of art, is a momentary cancelling out of these tensions:

> The physical world is a power, or potentiality, to be realized, on the scale of human perception [a] and transaction [i].
>
> (p. 21, [a] and [i] added by the author)

Rummel (1975) quotes the following example of Ushenko's power as potential or disposition. If we arrange a set of tiles in a line each a different shade of blue from light to dark, but we create a gap by missing out a shade in the progression our mind sees the gap and wants it filled. The gap is a disposition that wants to be filled. Ushenko regards these dispositions as potential power with a measurable vector in a given direction. Such vectors are not just mathematical calculations but real tendencies having real impact on mental processes and behavior. The vectors go in both directions outwards from the individual and inwards from the environment to the individual. It is the difference in strength between the outgoing and the incoming vectors that give meaning. For example, if the outgoing vector is stronger that the incoming vector then the actor has more faith in the outgoing proposition. If the incoming is stronger then he develops more doubt.

Rummel reviews the development of the concept of fields in natural science and in the social sciences, particularly psychology. Not surprisingly, the evolution follows the familiar pattern we have seen in religion and philosophy; that which we first noted in the field of organization. The concept of fields evolved from:

1   A physical spatial extension in which forces operate. It is a medium for those forces: e.g. the table for a game of billiards (i.e. control phase).

2   A set of conditions that activates the energy in the field: e.g. the electromagnetic field (i.e. the influence phase).
3   A set of latent functions that create conditions for 1 and 2: e.g. the human mind, a design or a gestalt that is greater than the sum of its parts (i.e. the appreciative phase).

Rummel sums his definition of power very simply as "a capability to produce effects" the forms that power takes he concludes depend on whether it is:

1   intentionally directed or not;
2   oriented towards the environment, another's body, or another self;
3   against another's will or not (force or not);
4   directed towards manifesting another's negative or positive interests;
5   based on threats, promises, persuasion, love, legitimacy, or controlling the situation and opportunities.

He sums his concept of power in the equation:

$$P_g = C_g \times I_g \times W_g,$$

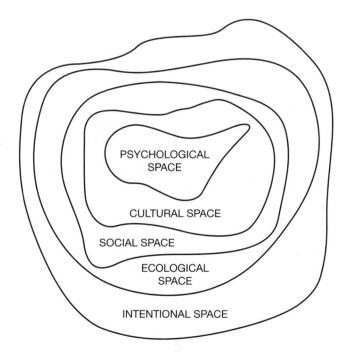

Figure 5.3 Rummel's five spaces

C_g = a person's capabilities to achieve goal g, I_g = his interest in achieving g, and W_g = his willpower to achieve g. The relationship among these terms is multiplicative. If any of these three aspects of power is zero, then a person's power to achieve his goal g is zero.

(Rummel 1975: Vol. 2, Ch. 26, Part 1)

Rummel also develops very similar thinking to our own about the nature of purpose. Although his graphical representation of the concepts appears to be quite distinct, his language in describing his concept is very similar. He creates an intentional space (field) that contains psychological, cultural, social, and ecological space. He wants us to understand that these spaces are separated for analytical purposes only:

There is, in fact, one space, the space of humankind and its intentions in their manifold dimensionality.

(Ibid.)

He refers to the ecological space as four-dimensional:

This is our four-dimensional ecology extending beyond the psycho socio cultural domain that is purely our sovereign subjective space. This is the outer world that we share with other living creatures; it is here that the diverse biospheres of all living creatures intersect.

(Ibid.)

He comes very close to acknowledging purpose as the center of this space:

At the center of this space are our dynamic motives, attitudes, and sentiments; our superordinate striving for self-esteem and self-actualization; our phenomenal dependency and practical freedom. This dynamic space shades into that defining our meanings and values, and our organized and semi-organized groups, such as universities, governments, and states; that is, into the space defining our cultural and supercultural systems.

(Ibid.)

His description of the intentional field is very close to our description of the appreciative field:

This is in total the field generated by our fundamental motives, sentiments and goals as the substance and direction through culture and society and confront each other in an ever moving configuration of opposing interests, attitudes, and capabilities.

(Ibid.)

Later philosophers have elaborated on these thoughts but we gained no major new insight that helped us understand the relationship between purpose and power. In summary, our very broad sweep through philosophy added the following to our ideas from religion and science:

1 It gave us ways to conceive of the purposeful properties of essence without recourse to an all-powerful external God.
2 It reaffirms that it is time that is the basis for the split of essence into three manifest powers.
3 It adds support to the insight that the many different triune descriptions of manifest power can be conceived in terms of:

    a Appreciation—openness, wholeness, or possibilities.
    b Influence—relatedness and dynamics, or probabilities.
    c Control—closedness, form, and certainties or determinism.

4 That this triadic division of the whole has its origin in experience while the tetradic or dualistic divisions of the whole have their origin in analysis.
5 It adds support for the concept that the middle ground, the influence field, can be conceived as a mediating domain equal in its own right to the appreciative and control fields rather than just a mixture of them. It supports the view that the basic function of this middle ground, influence field, is to sort out the positive and negative forces that come into play between the appreciative and the control fields.
6 Through the work of Ushenko and Rummel it leads to a greater ability to specify the nature of power fields.

The Emergent Philosophy of Organization: Purpose → Time → Power

We finally, then, have a philosophically reasonable answer to the ubiquity of the three manifest powers, the origin of AIC. The three powers appear under different names wherever there is a system built on an experience, an intuition, a sensing of the whole. There is an answer to the ubiquity of three faces of God, that Pagan, spiritual leaders, Greek scholars, and all major religions intuited and it lies in the nature of time. It should no longer surprise us that all purposeful holonomic systems based on mental, emotional, or physical experience tend to develop this threeness of relationships, the threeness of experience to be open, to relate, and to act. These are correlates of our time orientation to future, present, and past.

It is now possible for us to an attempt an explication of this implicate order as a philosophy of organization. Its essence is purpose and the three manifest powers that its purpose creates are produced by three very distinct orientations of time:

1   A holonomic orientation of timelessness that produces that part of purpose that is always open to new possibilities, to emergence from the whole—the appreciative field.
2   A present orientation based on timing, the equivalent of Beamish's RBT (Rhythm Based Time) the relationships between parts of a cycle that determine on time and off time—the influence field. As in music or dance or the political process it harmonizes relationships between parts within a time cycle.
3   A linear orientation that closes time to specific durations on a vector from past to present to future—a control field.

In Figure 5.4 we summarize this time orientation of purpose and its power manifestations.

When we understand that purpose is an inseparable whole, a trinity of three-in-one and one-in-three, we can begin to overcome deterministic views of purpose that provide many scientific objections to the use of the concept of purpose. The infinite openness of purpose at the appreciative level provides for emergence, serendipity, and creativity. Determinism can only apply at the control level of purpose—goals. Our highest levels of purpose are not specifiable or describable in an analytical way or in control time. They give us meaning and a sense of direction beyond time t hat can be experienced but not analyzed.

The highest level of open purpose is an ideal, which by definition is an end that can be successfully approximated but never achieved (Ackoff 1974). We can understand how real this ideal level is when we understand that it is ideals that humans willingly die for, not pragmatic goals.

At the other extreme our goals are closed in time and space: we want to achieve certain tasks in the office by Tuesday at 5.00 p.m. The form of expression and the space and time constraints are defined and closed. Control gives form to the conditions that exist and decisions that are made as part of the appreciative and influence processes.

In the middle ground we have purposes that are oriented to, or co-relative with, other purposes. These are purposes that we use like a sieve to reduce the more amorphous possibilities and ideals from the appreciative phase into something that can be shaped. They are the values we use to help us sort out what is important given future potential and past reality. After we have imagined that beautiful future of our ideals—the villa in Saint Tropez and the beautiful relaxed Mediterranean life-style—we have to face the existing constraints; for example, economic—Social Security income won't quite cut it and how often will see our children and friends? We have to deal with those factors that will both support us and oppose our dreams.

The three levels of purpose are always present even if we are only working at one level. Much of our short sightedness and lack of attention to the long-term implications of our actions comes from our focus on the goal orientation of purpose and the neglect of its relationship to others' values or the impact on the whole that is reached though consideration of our dreams and ideals. When we become aware of the three levels of purpose involved in everything we automatically begin to use appreciative, influence, and control power as a holonomic process. This shift in attitude provides one of the least costly and most effective adjustments we can make in becoming more "power-full."

The Essence and Manifestation of Purpose

PURPOSE	Essence (Ousia)	Time	Manifest Power (Energiai)	Prototypical Expressions
Open	Emergent Wholeness Possibility	Infinite Transcendental Timelessness	Appreciation	**Potential** **Ideals** **Meaning**
Permeable	Relatedness Dynamic Probability	The Ever Present Now Transformative Rhythmic Cyclical Timing	Influence	**Intent** **Values** **Relationships**
Closed	Form Structured Certainty	Past, Present and Future Formative Linear Time Duration	Control	**End** **Goals** **Form**

Figure 5.4 The essence and manifestation of purpose

The idea of three-in-one nature of purpose helps us to sort though the common vocabulary of purpose, the difference between "ends," "intentions," and "purpose":

1   End becomes a destination that has no connotation of means or connection with the actor—it stands free.
2   Intention includes the concept of an end but also, linguistically, includes the concept of "bending" a valence that is within the actor but is not definite about a commitment of means to sense of completion.
3   Purpose has the three-in-one connotation of an end and the concept of an inner tendency to that end and a commitment to use current or potential resources towards that end. The purpose then is:

   a   an ideal if it is infinitely emergent;
   b   a value if its existence depends on its relationship to other purposes; and
   c   a goal if it is definable in terms of space, time, and resources.

The three-in-one approach to purpose was the key to the design used in the Colombia case described in Chapter 1. We involved three levels: the decision-makers (control goals), the stakeholders (influence values), and members of the whole community (appreciation ideals). We asked the Columbians to design the best possible electricity sector for their grandchildren. We thus transcended their self-interest (values) to invoke their imagination towards the highest level of purpose (an ideal)—the best possible sector. The time span invoked by referring to grandchildren enlarged the influence and appreciative fields and added an emotive and personal tone to the mindset and deliberations.

Unconscious Purpose

If purpose, then, is the source of power with its triune manifestation of powers we have to acknowledge that much of that purpose is unconscious. We have to account for the role of unconscious purpose both in theory and practice. Once the explanation of a "God" providing for all levels of purpose was deemed unacceptable we had to look for other sources of unconscious purpose. This, of course, was the role of psychology.

This opening to awareness of the unconscious was Freud's major contribution to the social sciences. He helped us understand the emotional nature of unconscious motives. From his study of the individual he "analyzed" and discovered how unresolved emotional issues from childhood created neuroses later in life. His cure was to allow patients to free associate till they found the source of the emotional trauma and by expressing it gain emotional release from it.

FREUD'S MODEL OF CONSCIOUSNESS				
	AWARENESS			
STRUCTURE	**Subconscious** (a)	**Pre-conscious** (i)	**Conscious** (c)	
Id	Pleasure Principle	Under stress could surface	Enters our Awareness	**A**
Ego	Repressed by Ego	Aware but no attention	Being attended	**I**
Super- **ego**	In conflict with Super-ego	Pressure for Attention	Governing Attention	**C**
	a	i	c	

Figure 5.5 Freud's model of consciousness

In formulating a theory based on his insights from practice he saw the mind as a complex energy system that obeys the laws of conservation. The essence, the ultimate source of power in humans, for Freud, was the instinctive drive for pleasure in which sexuality played the most controlling role.

The essence of human drive or motivations was made manifest, according to Freud, through the manifest powers in the now familiar triune AIC pattern of relationship between the id, ego, and super-ego. In Figure 5.5 the id provides the base for our primal instincts and energizes our wishful thinking. It operates without any checks or reference to the reality of the situation. The ego interacts with the reality of the situation and is capable of mediating a solution that takes the likely consequences of action into account. The ego also mediates the demands of the super-ego, the part of our psyche that conveys our moral sense of what we should do—like a parent it tells us what we should do.

Figure 5.5 shows this three-level structure operating with three levels of awareness:

1   our conscious mind that includes everything we are currently paying attention to;
2   our preconscious mind that consists of things that we are aware of but are not paying attention to;.
3   the subconscious mind that includes those processes that affect our functioning but which we are not aware of.

The basic idea underlying Freud's structure of the psyche and its emotional base has basically stood the tests of time. However, Freud's narrow interpretation of the essence, or ultimate purpose, based in the pleasure principle centered on sexuality has been severely challenged. The challenge began with Freud's own chosen successor Carl Jung (1875–1961). Jung's own patients taught him that their repressions came from many sources; problems of social adaptation, oppression, tragic circumstance, status, loss of prestige, and so on. This challenge is worth illustrating because it demonstrates the extreme difficulty of communicating the products of the appreciative domain that can only be experienced to the domain of explanation and analysis.

Jung had a very rich childhood experience of the country. He knew that animals could sense storms and earthquakes, that clocks stopped at moments of death and he had personal experience of objects shattering at highly emotional or stressful moments. As a child his mother read to him and showed pictures of exotic religions and strange Gods. His own religious beliefs led him to see Jesus as a man prone to all human strengths and weaknesses. If he were a manifestation of God it was as all men are "manifestations of the inconceivable God." He took comfort in knowing that his friends had no appreciation of these country worlds that provided him with a much richer source for exploration and insight into the nature of the psyche.

He contemplated careers in theology and archeology but in the end chose medicine. At medical school, psychiatry was held in such low regard that he left that course at the end of the program. With the attitude of "let's see what psychiatry has to say for itself," he opened his first text. When he read that "psychoses were diseases of the personality" his heart leapt and he had to stand and draw deep breaths. This was the empirical field that combined spiritual and biological facts:

> It had become clear to me in a flash of illumination that for me there was no other possible goal but psychiatry.
>
> (Campbell 1971: xi)

It was this passion and this combination of interest that caused his famous clash with Freud. As Joseph Campbell narrates, in 1909 Freud had planned to anoint Jung as his successor. When the annointee Jung asked his views on precognition and parapsychology, Freud answered very sharply that it was sheer nonsense. Jung felt the answer was delivered

> with such a shallow positivism that I had difficulty in checking the sharp retort on the tip of my tongue. I had a curious sensation. It was as if my diaphragm were made of iron and were becoming red-hot glowing vault. And at that moment there was a huge, such a loud report in the

bookcase . . . that we started up in alarm fearing that the thing was going to topple over on us. I said to Freud: "There—that is an example of a so-called catalytic exteriorization phenomenon."

"Oh come!" Freud exclaimed, "That is sheer bosh."

"You are mistaken Herr Professor. And to prove my point I now predict that in a moment there will be another such loud report."

A few moments later a sharp report emanated from a nearby cupboard and they found the shattered blade of a knife.

Freud with his *idée fixe* about the Oedipus complex was sure that Jung saw him as a father figure and had a death wish against him. The end of their relationship came in 1910 when Freud insisted against considerable opposition that Jung be made Permanent President of the Association of Psycho-Analysis. In return he tried to extract from Jung a promise that he would never abandon the sexual theory:

"You see we must make a dogma of it, an unshakable bulwark."
Startled Jung asked him, "A bulwark against what?"
Freud replied, "Against the black tide of mud . . . of occultism."

Jung was alarmed by the words bulwark and dogma but equally dis-heartened that Freud wanted to deny everything Jung had learned about philosophy, religion, and parapsychology and their contributions to under-standing the psyche.

So it was left to Jung to flesh out a fuller picture of the conscious and unconscious mind and in this his contributions are enormous. The contri-bution, most related to our quest for understanding of wholeness and its associated processes, was the discovery of the collective unconscious.

In 1902, he completed his doctoral dissertation "On the Psychology and Pathology of So-Called Occult Phenomena" (*Collected Works*, Vol. 1). He took the results of his own 2-year review of mediums and séances and combined it with previous studies of altered states of consciousness pro-duced by such phenomena as hypnotism, somnambulism, hystero-epilepsy, amnesia, and other twilight states.

His dissertation foreshadowed all the themes that would make up the body of his future work:

1   The autonomy of the unconscious part of the psyche. Parts of the unconscious literarily take over the body of the person, as in sleepwalking.
2   That such action by the unconscious is purposeful and is designed to bring to awareness matters that require attention for the individuals well-being.

3   That the unconscious has intuitive capacities that are far more acute, in the order of fifty times more, than those of the conscious mind.
4   The unconscious has access to a second level—a collective unconscious that contains the traces of all human experience.

Jung continued his studies of mythology and by 1909 had completed a frenzy of reading in everything vaguely mythological. His effort was so broad and intense that he was left in total confusion.

By chance he came across a series of fantasies of a Miss Miller published in the *Archives de Psychologie*. He was immediately taken by the mythological correspondences of the fantasies. They instantly served as a catalyst between the two worlds of collective myth and individual fantasy:

> It was written at top speed, amid the rush and press of my medical practice, without regard to time or method. I had to fling my material hastily together, just as I found it. There was no opportunity to let my thoughts mature. The whole thing came upon me like a landslide that cannot be stopped.
>
> (Campbell 1971)

Jung's whole perspective was transformed in the process. Myth provided the purposive connection to the whole beyond the path of reason. We see in this intuitive insight a capturing of a whole perspective—an all at once phenomenon that seems to characterize the creation of appreciative insight:

> "Myth, is what is believed always, everywhere, by everybody"; hence the man who thinks he can live without myth, or outside it, is an exception. He is like one uprooted, having no true link either with the past, or with the ancestral life which continues within him, or yet with contemporary human society.
>
> (Campbell 1971)

We also see the reaction to the transformed perspective—the forces of orthodoxy, in this case Freudian orthodoxy, which took their toll.

So it appears that the conscious mind is prepared by long periods of reflection and experience and a transformation occurs when the products of this conscious process are linked to mythic patterns drawn from the whole of human experience contained in the unconscious. This linking of the conscious and unconscious processes seems to happen all at once. This "all at once phenomenon" was later recorded by Kuhn in relationship to paradigm shifts:

> Though each may hope to convert the other to his way of seeing his science and its problems, neither may hope to prove his case. The competition between paradigms is not the sort of battle that can be

resolved by proofs . . . Before they can hope to communicate fully, one group or the other must experience the conversion that we have been calling a paradigm shift. Just because it is a transition between incommensurables, the transition between competing paradigms cannot be made a step at a time, forced by logic and neutral experience. Like a gestalt switch it must occur all at once or not at all.

(Kuhn 1962)

Life, then, for Jung in both its conscious and unconscious manifestations, is fundamentally purposeful. The essence, the central purpose, is the ultimate unity of the self or individuation thorough incorporation of the unconscious into consciousness. The manifest powers, the translation of this essence into powers or capacities, for Jung was carried out by five primary functions. Two of the functions, intuition and sensing are opposing functions that enable us to develop two complementary perspectives of the whole:

- Intuition is a form of perception that has the power to process masses of information about the whole and integrate it very quickly. So, for example, it enables us to abstract images of the world very parsimoniously.

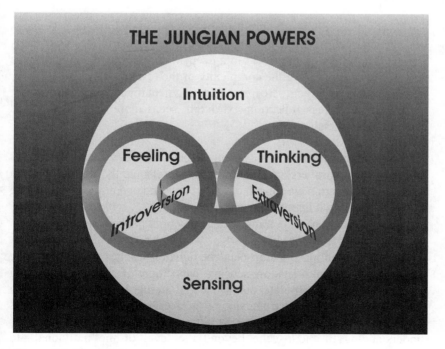

Figure 5.6 The Jungian powers

- Sensing is its opposite, complimentary function; it has the power to perceive and assemble data from the five senses so is able to produce very concrete realistic images of the whole.

Because these two functions allow us to perceive the whole we accept them as the human capacities associated with appreciation. The opposition of the potential revealed by our intuition and the realities perceived by our senses produces the energy necessary to invoke the next level of mental processing. The information we receive from our perceptive (appreciative) function is then transformed as it is processed through two opposing judgmental (influence) functions; thinking and feeling:

- thinking allows us to abstract what is important on the basis of reason and logic;
- feeling allows us to make subjective choices based on our knowledge about how we and others will react to such selection.

Again, it is the opposition between these two complements that produces the energy, the motivation towards the next level of resolution. In addition to these functions Jung recognizes two attitudes in which the previous perceptions and judgments are addressed to the world:

- Introversion directs the products of perception and judgment towards the inner world before turning them to the outer world. Thus introverts tend to reflect on the world in a deeper way than extraverts but have difficulty expressing the complexity of the results.
- Extroversion directs perception and judgment towards the outer world. As there is less reflection extroverts seem more spontaneous and therefore sociable.

The final solution of the opposing complementarities lies in action and reflection. Through extraversion we commit to and change the world. Through introverted reflection we consult our conscious and unconscious to imagine how we might do it better next time.

The fifth function is the transcendent function, our mindset that is open to appreciate the unconscious part of whichever function we are using. If we prefer intuition our transcendent function teaches us to appreciate and incorporate our shadow-sensing capacities. If we prefer feeling it teaches us to incorporate our shadow thinking and if extraverted to incorporate our shadow introversion. This emerging field maintains Jung's links with traditional wisdom and the more scientific approach and extends understanding of the psyche beyond the level of the individual—to organizations, life, and even the cosmos.

Practical Synthesis of Conscious and Unconscious Purpose

Figure 5.7 (plate 9) provides a practical integration of the concepts of conscious and unconscious purpose. The outer (yellow) circle represents the appreciative field, our conscious and unconscious relationship to the whole.

We have already seen how ideals are the most "open" expression of purpose at the conscious level. Purpose at the unconscious appreciative level is Jung's collective unconscious—the drives that derive from our being human animals. It is our collective history as a repository of our collective experience necessary for our survival. It is also key, as Jung shows, to our ability to transcend existing relationships and conditions. The information from this collective unconscious when married to our own experience provides our appreciation of the whole, a sense of what constitutes wholeness for us. In other words, it provides for us a sense of spiritual direction that is expressed in our *ideals*. This marriage of the collective unconscious and our current conscious experience is not an easy one. As in all marriages it is a marriage of opposites. Whatever ideals are evoked in our conscious state they have to deal with the aggregate of the whole that is left in the unconscious. So the conscious and unconscious together make a whole.

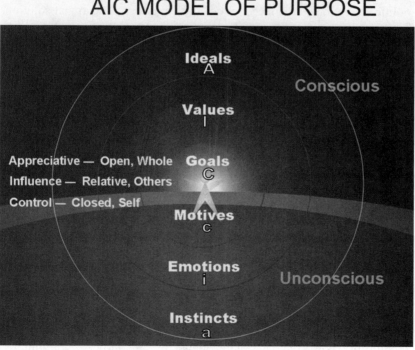

Figure 5.7 The model of Purpose

They have to carry the oppositional forces in the unselected part of the whole that constitutes our appreciated world. Our ideals of love compete with the aggregate of everything that is not love, which becomes manifest. As for lust, a complement, just as a complementary color, is the sum of all colors except the chosen one. Our ideal of truth produces the complement of pain avoidance, which makes lying so easy and natural. Our ideals of beauty create the complement of our need for plenty.

The marriage of conscious experience with our collective unconscious takes place in our dreams—both day-dreams and night-dreams. The opposition of ideals and instincts presents itself as patterns of images and feelings. The opposition, in terms of Jung's thinking, is that between intuition and sensing. The most common of these patterns derive from the most common human experiences and so their organization is recognizable as universal archetypes—the ideal mother, the wise man, the devil, or the fool.

As we move down to the red (center) circle we encounter a similar opposition. Conscious purpose at this influence-centered level, as we have seen, is "values" or relative purpose, the purpose we use to sift out what is important from the whole appreciated field. This opposition invokes the human capacities of thinking and feeling. Stakeholders may agree that the ideal direction for their program is to provide universal healthcare but they disagree about the priorities necessary to bring it about. Some favor political solutions, others economic, and yet others educational solutions. The unconscious reaction invokes the social animal in us; emotional fight or flight reactions, territoriality, submissiveness, and so on. For example, it was lack of awareness of this level and ways to cope with its effects that led to my difficulties with the Area Manager for Italy, recounted in Chapter 1. The thinking about the best means to pursue ideals invokes feeling of fear, anger, and frustration in those who disagree with the priority; and joy, satisfaction, and elation in those who agree. The essence then of this influence field is the sorting out of the positive and negative valences that result from the possibilities created by the appreciative future orientation and the realities deriving from past decisions, relationships, and conditions.

Finally, as we move down to the inner control circle with its conscious closed purpose of goals we encounter the unconscious opposition of "motives." We may know perfectly what we should do. That whole set of unfinished tasks needs to be completed but the detailed unrewarding nature of the task for us leaves us unmotivated. We just do not like doing this kind of work even though we are fully able, we know its importance and are aware of the consequences if we don't do it. We still find it very hard to do it and may end up rationalizing why we did not do it.

So open, timeless purpose, with its opposition between ideals and instincts creates the appreciative field, our relationship to the set of all possibilities that affect the achievement of our purpose. Our intuition invokes possibilities from the whole that create our potential. Our senses, especially our sixth sense, put us in touch with the set of all possibilities that constitute our perception of reality. Our appreciative field consists of the set of all possibilities that create potential for the achievement of our purpose and the set of all elements we perceive as part of our reality that must be faced in achieving such potential. The identification of these two halves of the appreciative field—potential and reality—are both acts of creation drawing on our human capacities for intuition and sensing.

Similarly, our relative, present-oriented purpose depends on the opposition between values and emotions. Once we use our values to choose priorities we have to realize that our choice will have an emotional impact on others affected (stakeholders). This opposition draws on our human thinking capacities to extract logical priorities from the appreciated world but equally on our feeling capacities to deal with the emotional results.

At the closed, control level of purpose goals, the conscious and unconscious opposition is between the goal and its intra-psychic cost. We may with our introverted capacities understand our motive resistances but still have to find extraverted energy to overcome them.

Our conscious purpose is manifest as intent—as a large A, I, and C is our intent—but does not become purpose until it is married with our unconscious reaction from the aggregate of our *being*—represented with a small a, i, and c. It is this unconscious aggregate of instincts, emotions, and motives that gives voice to our collective wisdom; Surowiecki's, *The Wisdom of Crowds* (2005).

Summary

Our philosophy, then, is based on a concept of purpose that includes three inseparable dimensions that operate holonomically:

1 Openness: a *timeless* orientation to the environment that enables the discovery of new possibilities—appreciation.
2 Permeable: being either open or closed depending on the *timing* of relationships with other purposes and information arriving from the future and past—influence.
3 Closedness: which allows energy to be focused and directed in known increments of linear time to create the form of purpose—control.

Purpose in all three manifestations exists as potential power that is enacted as kinetic power by the actors choice of orientation—A, I, or C—and is reacted to by the aggregate of the field not chosen—(a), (i), or (c). The enactment of purpose creates new possibilities, new relationships, and new forms that in turn change the orientation of purpose and gives rise to create new manifestations, and the process begins again. In the next chapter we will further develop the theory of power that evolves from this philosophy.

6 Building the Theory

Purpose and Power Fields

From the previous chapter a surprisingly simple view of power is beginning to emerge. Power is the means by which purpose is translated into action. Stated the other way around power is the "power to" achieve purpose and in turn to re-create purpose. It is this circular link between purpose and power that will allow us to take the next step in building a theory of power that is inseparably linked with the concept of organization.

We begin by summarizing the current understanding of power and purpose in organizations and social systems. Chapter 1 shows how the narrow concept of power as authority contained within an organizational hierarchy was prevalent in the early classical period. It was what Mary Parker Follett called "power over." The concept was so deeply embedded and accepted that power was hardly discussed as an issue. The source of power was not in purpose but in the structure of hierarchical control. Discussions of power outside of this base did not fit with the purpose of the scientific management establishment so were regarded as illegitimate or at best aberrant. They belonged to the personal domain, which was not relevant to the organizational domain. Our very understanding of power was being unconsciously limited by the exercise of power.

In Chapter 2, we showed how an open-systems philosophy made evident that the reigning concept of power and organization need enlarging. By opening up the study of organization to include environmental factors theorists and practitioners were faced with factors outside of the control of the organizational hierarchy. We noted James D. Thompson's seminal contribution in conceptualizing this insight. Consideration of power had to add concepts of power outside those of control, the kind of power necessary to engage with external actors outside the boundaries of the organization, the external stakeholders who were not subject to the mandates and constraints of the hierarchy. It was from this idea that I developed the key idea for my thesis that environmental relationships are power relationships (Smith 1983). The concept of power had to be enlarged from control through structures to include influence through processes. The study of both power and organization became exponentially more complex and intertwined.

The central goal of organization was still to increase control but now the whole new area of influence could be brought into that effort—it was "power with" in order to obtain "power over." This belief in the organizational goal of control led to many attempts to create models of power that would allow the kind of measurement that could be used for prediction in order to control. However, so many factors and so many intervening variables had to be taken into account that no general models of power emerged that were both theoretically sound and practically useful. As Pfeffer (1981) showed there were at least eight different power models that could be tweaked for application in different limited situations.

As we noted in Chapter 4, by the 1990s many writers were sensing the limits to our ability to explain power: something more fundamental, more encompassing was required. The concept of "power to" began to emerge as a more all-encompassing umbrella that would include both "power over" and "power with." This umbrella fit more appropriately with the concepts that were evolving out of experience with the AIC organizing process. It is, in effect, "power to" achieve and create purpose.

The previous chapters described the creation of three key insights necessary to build a new theory of purpose and power from experience with the AIC organizing process:

1   purpose is the source of power;
2   purpose creates three power fields; and
3   purpose is in turn recreated by the three power fields, thus producing the essential circular process of power/purpose generation.

(Smith 1980, 1983)

An organization's boundary, its internal environment, defines the boundary of its field of control. Those elements inside the boundary of the organization are its area of control. Everything outside that area, the organizations environment, is not subject to control. This does not mean that the organization is powerless relative to its environment. Chapter 4 noted, building on Emery and Trist's concept of transactional and contextual environments, that the boundary of the organization's transactional environment defines its field of influence and the boundary of its contextual environment defines its field of appreciation. By extension all system environment relationships are power relationships (Smith 1980, 1983). The following pages add and test a key new insight that was developed as part of the process of writing this book; that the three AIC power fields are organized dimensionally.

Power Fields Are Organized Dimensionally

This insight arose from the attempt to learn from science the nature and organization of the manifest powers that give form to the physical universe as we understand it today. What emerged was an extremely helpful insight. For scientists to create the current theories that link the major forces of gravity, the electromagnetic field, and the nuclear forces they had to think in progressively higher dimensions. The history of development of theory in science becomes a history of the evolution of human capacity to think in higher dimensions. Before we can explain and design social systems on the basis of dimensional thinking we have to satisfy ourselves that such dimensionally organized systems actually exist in the natural world. We found such evidence in the design of our brains, our visual system, and our color perception systems.

A Natural Example

In Chapter 3, we looked for a natural explanation for the threeness of the power fields produced by purpose and found an explanation in concepts of time. The search for a similar natural explanation for a five-dimensional model discovered that the five-dimensional structure of the physics of light was translated into a five-dimensional structure of our visual system that in turn created a five-dimensional structure in our color-perception process. From light to the perception of color we have three nested five-dimensional systems. This finding coincided with research that suggests that our whole brain is organized dimensionally, and links to David Bohm's views that our brains mirror the organization of the "implicate order" of the universe. Our journey through the field of dimension adds insight to this concept of "implicate order" with "explicate order" and enables us to link purpose and power to organization as one holonomic process.

Science and Fields

Faraday first introduced the concept of power fields in the nineteenth century. He visualized a field as a space filled with lines of force. In the case of magnetism and electricity he measured the strength and direction of those lines of force at any point in the space. A collection of numbers can be calculated for every point in space that completely describes force at that point. He demonstrated that all the forces of nature could be expressed as a field.

Faradays' field calculations worked fine in the three-dimensional space of Euclidean geometry but were not adequate for the natural world of curved space and non-linear relationships. It was Riemann in the 1850s who, through sheer brilliance, found a way to measure the force at any point, in any space with any number of dimensions. Single-handed he created the organizational equivalent of open systems when he broke the limitations of Euclidean three-dimensional geometry and paved the way for the break from Newtonian Science to Einstein's four-dimensional relativity.

Riemann also objected to Euclid's declaration on dimensions. Euclid, echoing Aristotle, had said that there could be no dimensions beyond the third. A point had zero dimensions; a line had one, length; a plane had two, length and breadth; and a solid three. There were only three dimensions in our world: length, breadth, and height. Riemann felt this statement came from common sense rather than any scientific logic. Riemann began very simply by extending the Pythagoras theorem that applied to the two-dimensional triangle to figures in multi-dimensional space. The theorem states that the sum of the squares of the smaller sides of a triangle equal the square of the longest side, the hypotenuse; $a^2 + b^2 = c^2$. He discovered that if we wish to add another spatial dimension all we have to do is to add another term to the equation. For example, in three-dimensional space the equation becomes:

$$a^2 + b^2 + c^2 = d^2$$

The figure is no longer a two-dimensional triangle but a three-dimensional cube: c is the third side and d is the diagonal inside the cube (Figure 6.1). For N-dimensional space the equation becomes:

$$a^2 + b^2 + c^2 + d^2 + \ldots = z^2$$

where d + adds sides of figures in hyperspace. It is almost impossible for us to represent these multi-dimensional figures in the two-dimensional space of a page but it is very easy for mathematicians to manipulate the properties of such multi-dimensional spaces with mathematical models. Riemann, in fact, had to create a new form of mathematics to do exactly that. He created a form of matrix, a metric tensor, consisting of a number of rows and columns equal to the number of spatial dimensions he wanted to calculate. His matrix produced a new geometry that could work in multi-dimensional curved space. For example, in the Euclidian geometry of two dimensions we know that the sum of the interior angles of any triangle add up to 180 degrees, never more or less. This is not true in three-dimensional curved space. To demonstrate this all we have to do is draw a large enough triangle on any sphere. We see that the angles of a triangle add up to more than 180 degrees. If the surface were convex, i.e. with negative curvature, the sum of the angles of a triangle would add up to less than 180 degrees (see Figure 6.2).

Riemann's discovery completely changed our concept of what a force is. Up until then scientists believed a force was a relationship between two

Three dimensions a, b, c with hypotenuse d

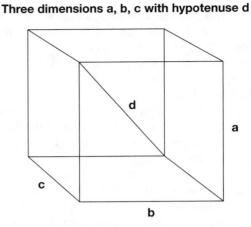

Figure 6.1 Cube three dimensions

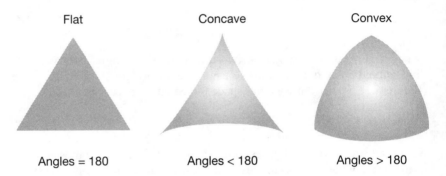

Flat	Concave	Convex
Angles = 180	Angles < 180	Angles > 180

Figure 6.2 Concave and convex surfaces

objects. They had to accept the notion of action at a distance. For example, planets influenced each other's orbits without touching each other. Riemann made the first major break with Newtonian science by declaring that "force" was a function of geometry, not action at a distance. Force had no independent qualities of its own. The apparent effect of a force came from the surrounding geometry. This meant that the curving, bending, and crumpling of our three-dimensional universe in an unseen fourth dimension causes all electricity, magnetism, and gravity. From this insight Riemann went even further to intuit that light itself was not a force but a series of vibrations in five-dimensional space (M. Kaku 2004, Ch. 4).

Einstein used Riemann's work to produce the elegant simplicity of the light and matter in the second half, the "mc^2" part, of his famous $E = mc^2$ equation. The "E," the energy side of his equation had no such elegance.

To complete that work he had to include gravity in his equations. The current knowledge summed up as the Standard Model, is a mess of sub-atomic particles that seemed to keep multiplying the more they were studied.

It took till 1915 when Einstein created field equations for gravity to make the discovery that if space and time could be unified into a single entity then so should matter and energy. The measure of energy depends on both time and mass and all three are interchangeable. As a spaceship approaches the speed of light its mass increases and time slows down. The increase in mass comes from the conversion of energy. The equation reveals that because the speed of light squared is such a huge number then small amounts of mass contain enormous amounts of energy. The nuclear age was born.

It was not Einstein himself who saw that his observation, that space turns into time and time into space, created a fourth dimension. H.G. Wells had conjectured that time could be a fourth dimension. Minkowski's mathematics revealed the simplicity and beauty of the four-dimensional structure underlying the theory of relativity. Einstein was not particularly impressed. He preferred to see physical images that reflected physical principles; mathematics for him was superfluous erudition, and he jested:

> "Since mathematicians have attacked the relativity theory, I myself no longer understand it anymore."

With time, however, he did begin to appreciate the full power of Minkowski's work, but not before he had a similar experience with another mathematician in moving from his special theory of relativity to his general theory, an attempt at uniting all the forces in a single theory including gravity that had been omitted from his first or special theory of relativity.

His breakthrough was to understand that the laws of gravity are the same as those in an accelerating field. In his famous thought experiment he illustrates how an elevator falling at a high enough speed produces the effect of zero gravity. While ascending the elevator produces the equivalent of gravitational forces, i.e. travel fast enough that you will feel the equivalent of twice the force of gravity—2G. This led him, inexorably, to the conclusion that light would be bent by gravity from a straight line to a curve and therefore that space itself must be curved. He made the same discovery as Riemann, but now he could answer Riemann's question . . . what caused the curvature of space-time was "e/m": energy/mass.

It is ironic that Einstein having twice turned to the concept of higher dimensions to produce his theories of special and general relativity should fail to produce the field calculations for gravity because he did not move to a higher dimension. He had to re-learn his own lesson that the laws of nature are simplified in higher dimensions. In April 1919 he received a letter from an obscure German mathematician, Thodr Kaluza. Kaluza demonstrated how to combine Einstein's theory of gravity with Maxwell's theory of light by moving to the fifth dimension.

Kaluza used Riemann's tensor to write down Einstein's field equations for gravity in five rather than four dimensions Then he demonstrated that these five-dimensional equations contained within them not only Einstein's earlier four-dimensional theory but an additional piece that reproduced exactly Maxwell's theory of light. Astonishingly, Kaluza had combined two of the greatest field theories ever known into one simple, powerful, and beautiful geometry. Einstein was so shocked that it took him more than two years to reply and eventually send the article for publication.

The last major step in the story of the role of dimensions in our scientific exploration leads us to string theory. String theory came into being by accident in 1968 when two young physicists (Venetian and Suzuki), quite independently, were looking for mathematical functions to help them describe particle interactions. They stumbled on one of Leonard Euler's functions developed in the nineteenth century that by some quirk of good fortune exactly described the strong interactions of elementary particles.

String theory holds that if we were able to examine particles at a small enough size we would find that they are not points of matter at all but tiny one-dimensional vibrating, oscillating strings. Some of them would be formed into closed loops and some would be open. There are many string theories but, in general, they rest on the basic assumptions of whether they include closed and open loops and whether or not they incorporate both bosons, the carriers of energy, and fermions, the carriers of mass. Here again at the very origin of physics we find the three fundamental concepts of openness, relatedness, and closedness and the relationship between open and closed strings; the AIC relationships in string theory.

String theory is still a theory; no one has yet been able to develop a set of field equations to express its functioning. Nor do we have the technology to prove it experimentally. For the first time, however, there is a theory that unites all the forces of nature with the same symmetries. Edward Witten, the current leading physicist who has contributed greatly through his astounding mathematical skills to superstring theory, acknowledges the simple power and beauty of string theory:

> Apart from the general predictions that I have stressed, string theory also leads in a simple way to elegant and qualitatively correct models that combine quantum gravity and the other known forces in nature, covering the main features of the standard model.
>
> (Witten 1988)

Not only, as we have noted, does Einstein's theory of gravity fall out of super string theory from the sheer demands of self-consistency, but the graviton (the quantum unit or "particle" of gravity) emerges as the smallest vibration of the closed string.

These symmetries exist in either ten or twenty-six dimensions depending on the assumptions used. In physics, theory has, for the first time, outstripped experience or experimental data. However, it is the only theory that finally unites all of the natural forces with a single set of symmetries.

Dimensions, then, in physics are fields that have greater degrees of freedom. They are not just additional factors or different types of variables. Each dimension is an actual quantum shift in power or capacity to achieve purpose, it is increased "power to." This power is expressed numerically as an exponent a^0, a to the zero power; b^2, b to the power of 2; and c^5, c to the power of 5. The increase in power is a real increase in potential to operate in ways that are not possible in lower dimensions. It is in this same sense that we use the concept of power and dimensions applied to organization and social systems. Each system from control-centered, through influence-centered to appreciative-centered involves a quantum shift in "power to," a quantum shift in capacity to achieve purpose at higher levels.

The classical view of hierarchical control in organizational theory equates with Newtonian science governing our three-dimensional world, the "power over." The open systems phase is concerned with relationships or relativity and addresses a fluid, dynamic, four-dimensional world represented by Einsteinian science, the "power with." Since the 1990s the writers, philosophers, and scientists exploring what we have termed appreciative-centered mind space, our relationship to the whole, the fifth-dimensional field, are drawing on the quantum sciences, the "power to."

A key advantage of the dimensional view is that it allows us to keep multiple perspectives at the same time. Our three-dimensional practical world still exists inside of the larger dynamic time-space of four-dimensional influence, which is in turn encompassed within the even larger five-dimensional mind space of appreciation.

The next section shows that this five-dimensional thinking capacity, which helped the evolution of science, is a direct reflection of the structure of our brain. It uses the example of the nested systems of our brain, its visual system and its color-perception system to describe the organization of natures five + dimensional systems. It then shows how this organization can also be inferred in social systems and enables us to take the next step in Chapter 7 to create purpose—power-organizing models that include 'power to,' 'power with,' and 'power to.'

The Brain and Five-Dimensional Organization

The continued study of patterns of purpose and power led to an extension of the search for roots and fundamental insights, but the more extensive the research the more prevalent the AIC pattern seemed to appear in all fields.

Given the starting intuition that purpose is the source of power, this, of course, is not surprising. If purpose is the source of power then we should find our purpose pattern in all things. It could also be that the discovery of a hammer was now turning everything into a nail. So it was important to discover a non-abstract, natural system that actually operated in the five+ dimensional way that has evolved as the AIC concept.

Some PhD work with personality and color, led me to speculate that an organization based on threeness existed in the brain and in our color-perception system. However, it did not prepare me for the almost unbelievable precision, beauty, and elegance of the actuality of that three-ness. Three nested sets of five-dimensionally organized triune relationships link the physics of light to our brains, our visual system, and color perception systems

Very early studies of the brain identified the same "threeness" that we found in religion, philosophy, and science. Greco-Armenian philosopher mystic George Ivanovitch Gurdjieff, writing in the early 1900s, had been exposed at a very early age to folkloristic and mythological tales recited by his father. The experience influenced his search for a way to reconcile the spirituality of the East with the scientific approach of the West.

He taught that the mind had three brain centers: an intellectual thinking, an emotional feeling, and an instinctive center. His work taught that all three centers had to be developed equally. He believed that because these centers are not yet fully developed we exist in a state akin to sleep. His work involved creating the processes to waken these centers to a fuller potential (Gurdjieff 1950, 1973).

The idea of three brains was further developed by Paul MacLean. In 1949 he joined the faculty of the Yale Medical School with an appointment in both physiology and psychiatry. It was during this time that he developed his theory of the triune brain. He proposed that our brain actually consists of three brains that reflect our evolution from reptiles, through mammals to modern homo-sapiens. Each new brain is built on top of the older one and provides some degree of regulation of it. But each brain is also capable of operating autonomously (see Figure 6.3).

The Reptilian Brain

Developed some 200 million years ago it is our oldest brain and consists of the structures of the brain stem, the globus pallidus, and the olfactory bulb. This brain controls muscles, balance, and our autonomic functions such as breathing and heartbeat. It expresses itself though the rigid repetitive patterns of behavior we associate with snakes and lizards. Their world is bounded by their skin. They are capable of relating to external environment stimuli with gross muscle motions but have not developed a fine enough nervous system to give them a sense of their internal state or

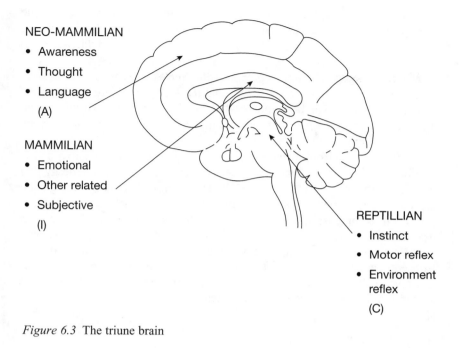

NEO-MAMMILIAN
- Awareness
- Thought
- Language
  (A)

MAMMILIAN
- Emotional
- Other related
- Subjective
  (I)

REPTILLIAN
- Instinct
- Motor reflex
- Environment reflex
  (C)

Figure 6.3 The triune brain

to carry out fine motor actions—hence the reason why frogs left in heating water do not sense the gradual increase in temperature and allow themselves to boil. The central stimulus response model of the reptilian brain we associate with control and three-dimensional powers.

The Mammalian Brain

MacLean (1978) called this middle brain the "limbic" system. It includes the hypothalamus, hippocampus, and amygdale. It evolved to serve the needs of most mammals but its characteristics are most clearly evident in the earlier mammals and are governed by the positive and negative opposition of pleasure and pain. It produces the emotions necessary for fight and flight and sexual behavior and so later evolves to produce the tensions we call social values.

> Whereas the reptilian brain is reactive to the external world the mammalian brain creates an inner world that process the effects felt from the outer world. The first brain developed the primarily neural connection to the outside world while the second brain developed both neural and chemical formation that created connections to form an inner

world. These chemicals, neuron peptides, report the inner state of the body to the brain. They are the chemicals of emotion.

(MacLean 1978)

MacLean sees in the development of the limbic systems the emergence of a sense of self. It is also the center that marks the first appearance of the *cingulated gyrus*, which produces what MacLean calls the *Family Triad*, the capacity to *nurture*, to produce the *vocal communication* between parent and child and to *play*.

It is this second brain that produces a resonant image of the world; a preformed view of the world that economizes on the time and energy that it takes us to view the actual world. We can focus only on those things that have changed or become more salient. This is very much like the process we use in compressing digital video; only the pixels that change between frames are actually processed. The mammalian brains' capacity to compare a self and environment over time and compute negative and positive consequence relative to different situations moves it from a three-dimensional or pure control stimulus and response power to the more dynamic relational powers in four dimensions.

The Neocortex

The third brain is the largest, filling most of both hemispheres. It is made up of the most recent development of the cortex, hence "neocortex," and some of the sub-cortical neuronal groups. It is the brain we share with the primates. The higher cognitive functions that distinguish humans from primates are found in the cortex. MacLean calls it "the mother of inventions and the father of abstract thought." It is the cortex that is divided into two halves and account for the popular distinctions between left and right brain functioning—the left half controls the right side of the body and in general is better at looking at the relationship between the parts of the whole—it is more logical, sequential, analytical, and objective. The right cortex controls the left side of the body and in general is more holistic, intuitive, synthetic, and subjective.

It is the third brain that produces curiosity for its own sake rather than for food or survival. In its higher forms it enables us to create the abstraction of languages and images numbers and symbols. It allows us to develop the mental capacities to compare and calculate, create logical sequences, tell stories, and play with color to produce art and with sound to produce music.

In very broad terms the first brain is involved with direct *sensing* (C) of the external environment and the second brain adds the capacity to process and *model* (I) that environment and process its reactions to it, the third brain gives a *perspective* (A) on both the reptilian and the mammalian brains. It gives an opportunity to put inputs from both into a more abstract framework and relate the past to the present and future. The third brain gives us our five- or more dimensional ability of intuition and imagination to link any part of our real or imagined world to any other part—to see the whole in every part.

There is in increasing amount of evidence, for example, that the neural function for memory is equally responsible for past memory and future imagining. Addis *et al.* (2008) worked with a set of young and old participants, asking them to remember past happenings and future imaginings and found that in older participants the amount of detailed information recalled or created was less detailed in the case of older participants. The researchers noted that both past memory and future imagining rely heavily on relational processing, leading them to speculate that the role of human memory may not be to remember the past but to imagine and prepare for the future.

To see how this broad interpretation is translated into operation we move to the actual operation of the most studied parts of the brain: our visual system.

Our Visual System

In the 1950s and 1960s, at the same time as the open-systems revolution was taking place in organization theory there was a similar revolution in the neurosciences brought about by the improvement in computers, graphical processing, magnetic-resonance scanning and the entry of new disciplines into the field: cognitive science and psychology, computer science, neuroscience, anthropology, and more: all helped develop a more robust visual science

Our process of vision is much more complex and unconscious than is generally thought and it still has some very fundamental theoretical and practical gaps to close before we can understand it completely. Although vision begins at the retina it weaves deep connections through most of the cortex. Our direct visual experience involves competitive separation by different visual systems and a recombination in which differences are sometimes accentuated and similarities smoothed out.

The visual process consists of the following five steps, which are adapted from Stephen Palmer's 1999 work. The details have been simplified to exclude information not relevant to concepts of organization and the emphasis on the dimensional element of organization has been added:

1   The first step is a primitive mapping of the image and a very rough shaping: 120 million cells map parts of the image as small as a single photon. This is akin to a one-dimensional listing of all the groups of "pixels" that are present in the image.
2   This retinal image is then filtered by sets of complex cells to eliminate noise and to increase contrast. These cells, arranged in columns 2 mm

wide and 10 mm deep, perform the two-dimensional line rendering of the edges of continuous areas for each eye.

3   Shading and texture and color information is then added to the outlines. Cues are added that aid depth and volume perception to give three-dimensional properties. They provide perspective.

4   This part of the brain contains some of the most specialized cells in the whole visual system. For example, some columns will fire only when there is movement in one particular direction while another column starts firing when the direction changes. In this fourth step information about that motion is added to our visual perception of depth and volume to give us our dynamic four-dimensional perspective

5   The object and its movement are then linked to categories and functional possibilities by linking to past memories. In this way features that are possible based on past experience rather than from current experience are connected to the image. For example, the hidden teeth of a predator are imagined, and feelings form as the possibility of harm causes the modulating cells to send bursts of emotionally charged information to our awareness center. This construction of present, past, and future gives meaning to the object and scene relationships in a five-dimensional process of imaginative seeing beyond which the linear process of past, present, and future is transcended.

It is this organization that is of most interest to us. How does our visual system take the complex dynamic information from the environment and our own memory of everything to select and construct the cohesive integrated view of our conscious experience? To discover this we will examine one of the most complex and controversial parts of the visual system—our color perception.

Color as a Five-Dimensional Language of Power

Color Perception

To understand how color is created we have to go back to the very basics of physics and begin the story of the extraordinary set of triune structures and processes that produce the five-dimensional phenomenon of light and the colors derived from it. We begin with the triune structure of atoms, electrons, and photons. Color versions of Figures 6.4 and 6.5 are provided on Plate 1.

Light, as we know, is the visible part of the electromagnetic spectrum. Its origin begins with yet another set of triune structures and processes that produce light and color—energy, matter, and light from Einstein's $e = mc^2$ (Figure 6.4).

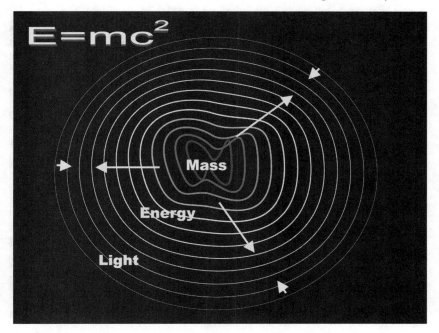

Figure 6.4 The triune production of light as photons within an atom

According to the type of atom, hydrogen, helium, and so on, electrons swarm around its nucleus in specific orbits called electron shells, which are symbolized in Figure 6.4 by the array of circles. The number of these shells is determined by the number of positively charged protons in the nucleus and the number of electrons occupying each shell at the same time. These orbits or shells constrain the movement of electrons within the atom. As the electrons become excited or energized they jump to specific levels of the shell determined by the atom's type. As the atom de-energizes the excess energy is released as photons, the massless energy of light, as the electron returns to lower level shells. The photons released from the movement from higher level shells produce high energy of light with shorter wavelengths, e.g. violet wavelengths—400 nanometers (nms). Similarly, photons produced by the electron moving between lower levels of shell orbits produce low energy—red light but longer wavelengths—700 nms. The light emitted from this energy exchange gives each different type of atom its unique spectral color structure.

This reference to color is a convenience: the wavelengths are not actually colored, as we will see below. The color is produced in our visual system stimulated by colorless electromagnetic waves. So color is a co-creation of external physical forces and internal processing of our brain. Although most literature discusses the origin of color in terms of wavelength its atomic

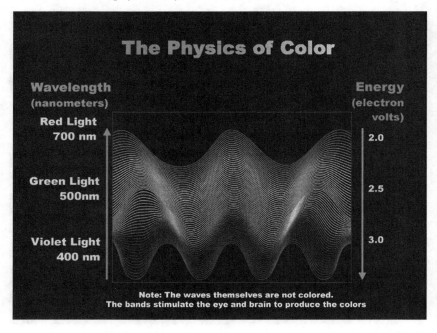

Figure 6.5 The physics of color

properties really derive from the second triune structure—the combination of *wavelength*, *frequency*, and *energy* (Figure 6.5).

Light, as we saw above is a series of vibrations in five-dimensional space. The question is how are these five-dimensional vibrations received by our brain's visual system and broken down into single colors and reconstructed as images that have tremendous stability (color constancy) in spite of all the different environmental conditions that affect the color of objects—the different color of the sun over the daily cycle, artificial versus daylight, differences of reflective properties of objects from surface texture to degrees of transparency?

If light is a vibration then our eyes are its perfect counterpart, they are much more dynamic than we generally realize. Our eyes vibrate at 30 to 80 times a second with amplitude that begins at 10 to 30 seconds of an arc and slowly increases to 6 minutes while making corrective movements at intervals of 3 to 5 seconds. Our retina is the extension of our brain that achieves this multi-dimensional magic.

Our retina is as thin as a sheet of paper yet contains within that thickness *three layers* that together hold more than 200 million specialized nerve cells. About 106 million of these are photoreceptor cells; the others filter and process the information before sending it on to other appropriate brain systems. One hundred million of the cells, called rods, concentrate on low light vision and motion and have almost no color sensitivity. The remaining 6 million, called cones do have daylight color sensitivity and higher powers of resolution than the cones.

The organization of these rods and cones on the surface of the retina is the third of the triune structures. Close to the center of the retina there is a 2 mm indentation, the fovea, which produces very high resolution images by focusing on the contrast between edges (the control part). The fovea has no rods and its cones are much thinner and longer and much denser than those in the rest of the retina. The middle circle surrounding the fovea consists of a mixture of rods and cones less densely packed (the influence part). In the third peripheral circle of the eye the cones become fatter and less densely packed. The reduction, far from being a disadvantage, actually helps overcome potential problems, for example, focusing aberrations due to the curvature of the retina. These peripheral cells provide information only about light, color contrast, and movement and our brain fills in the information about space and shape (the appreciative part).

The three layers of the retina also enable an organization of color information that is tremendously efficient. Our optic nerves have only 1 to 2 million fibers yet they have to process changing information from 126 million rods and cones. They do this by using a four-dimensional analogue strategy. They reduce incoming wave information to three overlapping wavelengths: short (S), medium (M), and long (L):

- (L) Long wavelength, which stimulates a "red" response (centered around 565 nm).
- (M) Medium wavelength, which stimulates a "green" response (centered around 540 nm).
- (S) Short wavelength, which stimulates a "blue" response (around 445 nm).

The photoreceptor cells calculate their response in an ingeniously simple *opponent process*. A group of cells, organized into a center periphery circular field structure, convert S, L, and M wavelengths into binary response positives and negatives, i.e. excitation or inhibition (Figure 6.6).

At deeper levels these single responses are averaged out with the effect of blocking out unnecessary detail of noise and accentuating important information such as sharpening outlines and keeping color perception consistent. It is the process of opponent contrasting that produces individual colors. Hardin (1997) produced a table that shows the simple power of this dimensional reduction:

$L + M > 0$ WHITE
$L + M < 0$ BLACK
$L + M = 0$ BRAIN GRAY

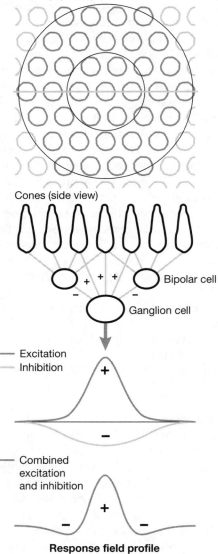

THE OPPONENT PROCESS
In colour perceptions

Retina (top view)

Cones (side view)

Bipolar cell

Ganglion cell

Excitation
Inhibition

Combined
excitation
and inhibition

Response field profile

Figure 6.6 Color opponency
Reproduced with permission from MacEvoy 2005

L – M > 0 RED
L – M < 0 GREEN
L + M – S > 0 YELLOW
L + M – S <0 BLUE.

However, our perception of color, as we indicated above, is not determined solely by production of isolated color areas. It depends also on context. The most recent color theories demonstrate how much our color is a response to color context:

> Color is not an illusion that is factually false, but a form of judgment in which sensory qualities is evaluated in context and transformed to provide a coherent image of the world.
>
> (MacEvoy 2005)

In summary, we describe our visual experience using three very different visual languages that are organized dimensionally:

1   color is the five-dimensional *appreciative language* of our visual system;
2   movement is the visual system's four-dimensional *influence language*;
3   shape is its three-dimensional *control language* or manifestation of control as form.

The five dimensions of triune power relationships of the color perception system are:

1   the production of photons from *energy* and *mass* to *light;*
2   the division of light into three fields: *Short, Medium* and *Long* wavelengths;
3   the different functions of the mixtures of rods and cones in *the three horizontal field*s of the retina around the fovea;.
4   the *three vertical field*s of the retina that distribute information to visual and non-visual parts of the brain affecting, for example, emotions and memory;
5   the *interpretation of the meaning* that the whole brain gives to the color effects, which include the juxtaposition of colors and the color context.

This description is the minimal possible to illustrate the color process. The dimensional interpretation, however, is my own contribution and is not directly stated in the referenced materials. For further excellent summaries of the current understanding of color theories see Hardin 1988 and Riley 1995.

If our whole brain operates in a similar way to our visual system we can understand how we produce the constancy of our sense of self as we move through the infinitely complex and dynamically interactive forces around us. Karl Pribrams's (1991) theory of the "holonomic" brain, developed with David Bohm, does provide support for this multi-dimensional view.

Pribram uses the pattern recognition properties of quantum theory to account for the brain's capacity to store and retrieve information while maximizing information and minimizing entropy. Each of the brain's senses is conceived as a lens that focuses wave patterns received from the environment. The interference patterns are a very economic way of storing information. They operate in the same way that three-dimensional images are reduced to two-dimensional interference patterns on holographic plates. Just as any part of the plate contains information about the whole picture so information about the external environment is distributed in many parts of the brain. In this fashion the brain can withstand damage, stress, and competing stimuli and still be able to process the whole of any event that needs processing.

Whereas a holograph is three-dimensional a holon is a dynamic version of a holograph and hence four-dimensional. Pribram uses the mathematics of Fourier transforms and their inverse, which are the same models that are used to capture the wave energy of light and sound and translate them into two- and three-dimensional images or wave forms that we are used to seeing on oscilloscopes, for example:

> But the advantage of holonomy, that is quantum holography, is that it windows the holographic space providing a "cellular" phase space structure, in patches of dendritic fields thus enhancing the alternatives and speed with which the process can operate. In short, though the information within a patch is entangled, cooperative processing between patches can continue to cohere or de-coherence can "localize" the process.
>
> (Pribram 1991)

He notes that this holonomic theory requires a higher dimensional form of mathematics. The Euclidian group operating in three dimensions has to be replaced with the Poincaré group that can operate in as many as ten dimensions.

The scientist who has best captured this idea of wholeness and its link between individual organism and the universe is Mae-Wan Ho, Director and Co-Founder of the Institute of Science in Society (ISIS). The resonance of her approach with the materials presented here is succinctly reflected in the abstract of her paper "Is there a Purpose in Nature":

> Purpose belongs to the realm of organisms. A purposive being is an autonomous whole. The wholeness of organisms not only entails perfect coordination of the parts, but the mutual implication of part and

whole such that a "self" emerges to guide the organism towards specific ends. An organism is a domain of coherent energy storage tending towards quantum coherence.

(1998: 1)

She goes on to identify the "irrepressible tendency towards the whole":

To be an organism is to be possessed of the irrepressible tendency towards being whole. In biological development, the most character-istic feature of the embryo is not so much that it is directed towards producing an adult organism of a specific form. Rather it has a tendency to maintain and develop into an organized whole, however it is disturbed.

(Ibid.)

She, in a very different way, also discovered color as a natural language. She describes, in her book *The Rainbow and the Worm* (1993) how she and her colleagues had discovered a way to use the polarized light microscope that scientists use to identify rock crystals to reveal the brilliant colors that emerge from the trillions of "molecular machines" that are involved in the internal processes of organisms, for example, in processing food and transferring energy to all parts of an organism. As light moves so much

Figure 6.7 Larvae of the fruit-fly magnified × 100, as viewed under a polarized microscope

Reproduced with permission

faster than molecules the polarized light has the same effect as the frame of a film stopping movement for an instant. As long as all the molecules in the muscle and tissue move coherently the view of a static order is obtained. Just as our visual color system is organized around a central pole (control) that moves from light to darkness so the organism has a global axis that moves from mouth to tail and its most coherent activities are expressed in bright colors and its least in dark colors (Figure 6.7; Plate 14).

It is also highly significant that in all live organisms examined so far

> the anterior-posterior body axis invariably corresponds to the major polarizing axis of all the tissues in the entire organism. This is a further indication that some global orienting field is indeed responsible for polarizing liquid crystalline phase alignment, and hence, in determining the major body axis.
>
> (Ho 1993: 166)

When the organism dies the colors fade away. Ho concludes that nature's language of colors tells us

> that the living organism is coherent and whole to a remarkable degree; that all the parts are co-ordinated at every moment and every level, down to the motion of individual molecules, of which there are at least trillions in an organism the size of millimeters. In a human being, there would be a billion times more!
>
> (Ho 1998b: 4)

She reflects with awe the transformative effect that this insight and experience has had on her:

> I can only give a flavour of how profoundly it changes life for me. Above all, it allowed me to see life in terms of spontaneity and freedom as opposed to mechanistic control.
>
> (Ibid.)

Summary: the Contribution of the Dimensional Perspective

What we have learned from our excursion into the example of the organization of the brain adds to and helps clarify the role of dimensions in the organization of natural systems. In summary, the theory states that purpose is made manifest through three fields of power organized in at least five dimensions, each containing an oppositional tension that causes energy to move up or down between the dimensions (e.g. the quantum leaps of electrons in atoms that produce light). The process of opposition and reduction serves to cancel out irrelevant information and smooth out disturbance in relevant information thus allowing us to establish what seems to us to be a stable image from a peripatetically dynamic environment (e.g. the production of color constancy in our visual system, which equates with the production of values in human systems). Each field, in each dimension, provides a unique capacity, a "power to" that contributes to the achievement of purpose. The same processes inside organizations allow for similar "consistency" in spite of all the different purposes and perspectives of internal and external stakeholders.

Power is an "essential," inherent, part of the whole. Purpose is potential power. The manifest powers, kinetic power, and the power fields are the expression of that potential reflected in three different time orientations. They become the means for organizing and producing the final form, the closedness of the purpose. How purpose is made manifest as form is a question of organization. We now, then, have everything we need to build the model.

7 Building the AIC Model

In this chapter we use the three nested systems of: our brain, its contained visual system, and its contained color perception system to illustrate the naturally occurring pinciples of five-demensional organizing. The chapter illustrates how nature uses all of the dimensions of power available to achieve its purposes. We will then use this ideal to create a practical model of organization that can be applied to any purpose from micro-problem solving to addressing the major issue of our times. The whole process is reviewed in the sequence of color plates from 1–15, between pp. 155 and 156.

The Dimensional Perspective

Although our study of science shows us that the manifest powers of nature are organized dimensionally and that in theoretical physics it takes from ten to twenty-six dimensions to come up with a full explanation of the world of physics, we note that organizational scientists operate explicitly with two- and three-dimensional models, but are struggling implicitly with conditions that cry out for at least four- to five-dimensional capacities. Our implicit four-dimensional models require the development of five-dimensional concepts and processes before they can be made more explicit and useful. Many scholars and practitioners are working under very different labels at this level but common concepts and models that fully exploit an understanding of five-dimensional properties have not yet been developed. The following paragraphs take a step in this direction and introduce color as a five-dimensional language capable of helping us to explain and build the model.

Purpose, Zero Dimensions, and the Complementarity Link to Wholeness

We are generally introduced to dimensions in geometry. Our teacher asks us to draw a box, such as that in Figure 6.1 on p. 138 with a line representing height as the first dimension, a line representing breadth the second, and a line representing depth the third dimension. However, forms in nature are not made up of straight lines, right angles, squares, and cubes. Nature's forms are made from curves, circles, spheres, and tori and their fractal parts. The vortex in our bathtub drain, tornados, the pattern of most plants and trees, the circular forms of planets to galaxies and atoms to universes, mirror nature's basic form as the three-dimensional sphere and its dynamic dimensional version: the torus. So when we think of natural organization it helps to think curvilinearly using circles, spheres, and tori.

To build our model of organization we begin with a thought experiment in which we use curves and their dimensional derivatives to design the ideal organization. Our definition of the ideal organization is one that takes into account all the factors that affect the achievement of its purpose and draws on all of the power potential created by that purpose. Performance is also defined as the total effect of the organization on its internal and external stakeholders and the world in which they are embedded.

In this thought experiment white light represents the highest possible level of purpose, the ideal, and its component colors represent its manifest powers. Our challenge is to show how we can so organize that any color can be generated and have an equal opportunity to combine with any other color to create any color and have equal opportunity to create white light.

One-Dimensional Organization

The simplest possible form of organization we know from kindergarten when we learned to form lines. We use it in our daily lives when we make lists of things to do. In adult life we become familiar with one-dimensional organization as the organizational hierarchy, the line from top to bottom of our classical organization chart. There is only one degree of freedom, to move up and down, to have more or less power. Height seems to be universally associated with power or control, the original God was a Sky God, the powerful ones are always "up there," the masters are "upstairs." The president is always at the top of the hierarchy and the worker at the bottom. Height then is the dimension associated with control. The line is split at its center, the zero dimensional point of its origin, its purpose, marks the separation between the powerful (+) and the powerless (–). The powerful have control and the powerless have no control. The contribution, then, of the first dimension is to provide the hierarchy of "ends." It has one purpose: to reach the "end" of the line specified by the "top," to have more control over the achievement of the purpose. The color of control is blue because it is the darkest of the three light primaries—green, red, and blue—being the farthest away from the light (see Figure 7.1; Plate 3).

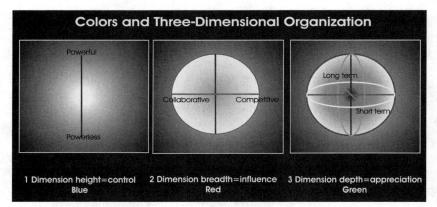

Figure 7.1 Color and three-dimensional organization

Two-Dimensional Organization

The line of horizontal relationships "breadth" completes the classic organizational chart. Boxes at the same vertical level have the same degree of control but their relationship to each other is one of coordination or influence. Each point on the line, by definition, has an equal degree of control. Its power difference lies in its influence on *ends* through its use of *means*.

The zero-dimensional point represents the division, for example, between collaborative use of means and competitive use of means. At the highest level this difference becomes the difference between Love and War. Red is the color for Valentine's Day as well as the uniforms of the British Redcoats. In Plate 3 the same two-dimensional field is shown as two concentric circles with blue, the first dimension, in the center, surrounded by the second dimension, the field of red.

Three-Dimensional Organization

The third dimension is the "depth" that gives the perspective for choosing ends and means. In our natural world it is our brain that gives perspective to the two different views of each of our eyes to produce our three-dimensional vision. In our organization charts that perspective is given by the title of the chart, e.g. "Organization of the Production Department." Ends (positions in the hierarchy) and means (the boxes at the same level) are selected on the basis of controlling and coordinating the resource of the production department. The appreciative perspective in our organization chart is the white paper, the whole, the context from which our production department's organization is extracted. The white paper represents the implicit or "implicate" order that lies in the whole field, inside, behind, in front of, below, above to the left and to the right of all the boxes.

The origin splits the depth perspective, for example, into long- or short-term, soft or hard, local or global perspectives. The three-dimensional perspective encompasses all this spatial perspective and the dimensions of ends and means. Not surprisingly, the color of the three-dimensional appreciative perspective is the lightest remaining primary—green. Green in nature also fulfills this function of representing the whole and is now used to symbolize the new emphasis on consideration for our "whole" environment. It is for this reason that green is chosen as the overall color tone for the paperback cover of this book.

Although Figure 7.1 is a good way to illustrate the simplest possible single-purpose, one- to three-dimensional organization we need to add the complexity of multiple purposes to our model. For this we create Figure 7.2 (see also Plate 4). Relying on our philosophy and theory we divide the world of purpose into three fundamentally different types of purpose—perspective (A), coordination (I), and control (C). We let a radian rotate through all the frequencies from the highest red to the lowest indigo and produce the color sequences in Plate 4. Every color represents a different combination of powers, a different proportion of control, coordination, and perspective. In practice, we could give a unique name to every combination. Each combination, each color, represents a different means, a different capacity or power for accomplishing the end.

Our organization now has many means (colors) by which it can achieve its ends. However, the range of means is still limited. The addition of the three primary colors in two-dimensional space is not enough to produce colors lighter than yellow or darker than indigo (dark blue). The third dimension is present in the "quality" of the color green but it is treated no differently from the one-dimensional blue and the two-dimensional red. Similarly, there are colors lighter than green that belong to higher dimensions and colors darker than blue that belong in lower dimensions. Our circular organization equates, in practice, to a flat, single-level organization with everyone earning the same pay and being given exactly the same working conditions even though their contributions produce very different values.

We need another dimension to allow more movement within the hierarchy, to add more values and to better utilize their differences. We achieve this by rotating our two-dimensional circle on its east/west axis and allowing lighter colors to be created by moving towards the North Pole and darker colors to be created by moving towards the South Pole (Figure 7.2; Plate 5). We now have an organization, in which everyone can have a space equal to their degree of control (contribution to ends—lightness and darkness) and their degree of influence (contribution to means—their color hue).

However, this sphere is still a pretty authoritarian organization. All the colors and their shades are serving one "end": the one at the top. Even then not all colors have equal access to the top. The light colors are in a privileged position closer to the top and the dark colors are at a disadvantage at the bottom. Any color at the equator occupies more space than colors above and below the equator so have more opportunity to be chosen or to

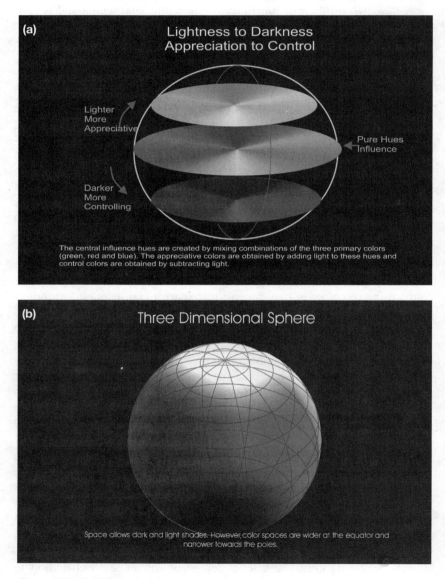

Figure 7.2a,b Lightness to darkness

Origin of Our Color Perception

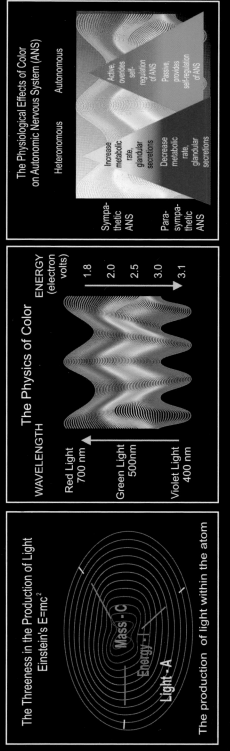

The Threeness in the Production of Light
Einstein's $E=mc^2$

Mass - C
Energy - E
Light - A

The production of light within the atom

The Physics of Color

WAVELENGTH		ENERGY (electron volts)
Red Light 700 nm		1.8
		2.0
Green Light 500nm		2.5
		3.0
Violet Light 400 nm		3.1

The Physiological Effects of Color on Autonomic Nervous System (ANS)

Heteronomous   Autonomous

Active, overrides self-regulation of ANS

Passive, provides self-regulation of ANS

Increase metabolic rate, glandular secretions

Decrease metabolic rate, glandular secretions

Sympa-thetic ANS

Para-sympa-thetic ANS

These orbits or shells around the atom constrain the movement of electrons within the atom. As the electrons become excited or energized, they jump to specific levels of the shell determined by the atom's type. As the atom de-energizes, the excess energy is released as photons, the massless energy of light, as the electron returns to lower-level shells.

The photons released from the movement from higher level shells produce high energy of light with shorter wavelengths. Similarly photons produced by the electron moving between lower levels of shell orbits produce low energy red light but longer wavelengths. The light emitted from this energy exchange gives each different type of atom its unique spectral color.

The rods in our eyes first distinguish between degree of lightness. Some cones then subtract from the spectrum, which if above a certain level registers as yellow, and below a certain level as blue. Another subset of cones takes the yellow portion of the spectrum and breaks it down into red and green parts.

Purpose as the Source of Power
The Five-Dimensional Language of Color

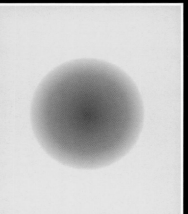

White light represents purpose, the source of power

Our visual system first sees difference between light and dark. Cones in our retina then separate white light into its blue and yellow components. Others separate yellow light into its red and green components.

Using this model we represent purpose as white light. The three primary colors (green, red, and blue) then represent the three powers manifested by purpose, appreciation, influence, and control.

Blue is subtracted from the white light and creates a yellow field the complement of blue

When red light is subtracted from the yellow field it creates green light.

The colors themselves do not exist in nature but are co-produced by light and our visual system. These four physiological

Colors and Three-Dimensional Organization

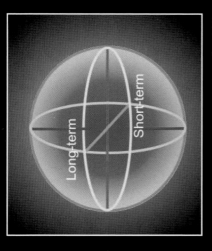

1 Dimension height=control

The three primary light colors (blue, red, and green) combine to make white light. As lightness is associated with appreciation and darkness with control, blue, the darkest color, represents control; red, the intermediate degree of lightness, represents influence; and green, the lightest, represents appreciation.

The first dimension is height—a vertical blue line. It is the line in organizational charts that goes from top to bottom, from the powerful to the powerless. In its simplest form it consists of making lists of priorities.

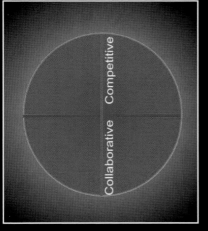

2 Dimension breadth=influence

The second dimension is width—relationships of equal height or control. In an organizational chart horizontal relationships are literally coordinative relationships of influence. They are the means used for control. The color red symbolizes the extremes of coordinative relationships—those of collaboration and competition.

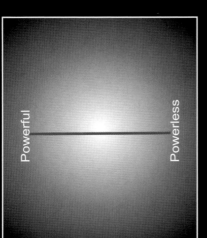

3 Dimension depth=appreciation

The third dimension is depth—that which gives perspective to the use of control and influence. Depth provides the appreciative perspective as goals for the use of control and influence (for example, short- or long-term goals). The color green symbolizes the holism of this perspective.

Color Complementarity—Opponency and Wholeness

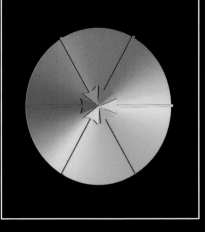

The blue vector creates its complement, the sum of all colors other than blue=yellow. Similarly, blue is the complement of yellow.

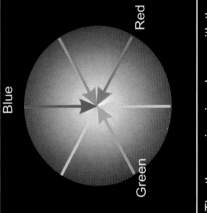

The three primaries shown with their complements. Each primary and its complement add up to white light.

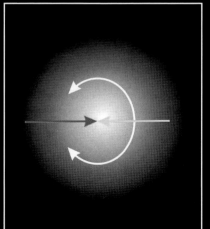

The mixing of the primaries with adjacent colors produces all color hues.

Color complementarity gives us a very easy way to gain insight into the nature of wholeness, as represented by white light. Every power vector, every act of power, is a separation from the whole. However the reaction, the complementary vector always represents what remains of the whole. It is this aggregate of wholeness that, in practice, produces the requirement for appreciation.

The limits of two dimensions do not allow us to show color hues lighter than yellow or darker than blue. For this we require another dimension.

The Three-Dimensional Perspective: Dark to Light

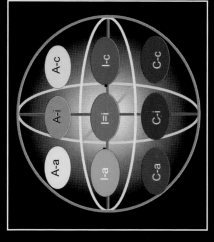

The 3-D sphere can now show the colors that correlate with all nine basic power relationships.

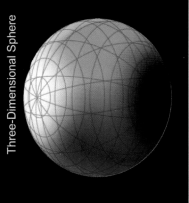

Three-Dimensional Sphere

The 3-D sphere is able to show light and dark variations of all the hues.

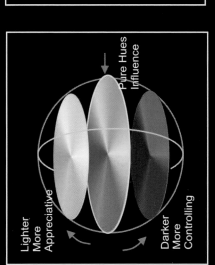

Lighter
More
Appreciative

Pure Hues
Influence

Darker
More
Controlling

The influence hues are converted to appreciative colors by adding light and to control by subtracting light.

Although the 3-D sphere allows us to see all variants of hues from dark to light, the color placement is static and the size of segments of color at the equator is greater than segments placed closer to both poles. This arrangement is typical of single-purpose organizations with reliable and predictable sources of means and a stable environment. They are not, however, well able to deal with changes in their environment.

The Four-Dimensional Perspective: Dynamic Cycles

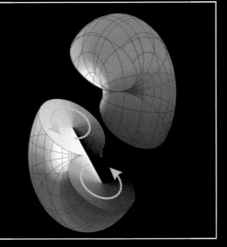

To enable all colors to have equal opportunity to occupy any space, top, bottom, and latitude or longitude, we rotate the sphere around a virtual torus tracing its colors on the torus's surface.

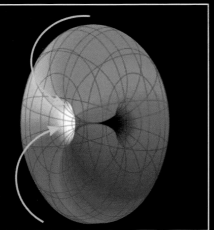

All colors can now rotate from the equator to the center of the torus, contracting as they mix with other colors to produce white light. At the zero degree point they become black and spread out again into their unique hues.

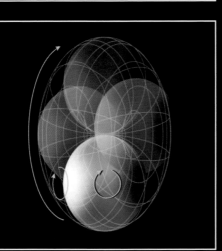

If we slice the torus at any diameter we see complementary circles of color. Each circle consists of all shades from light to dark of those colors. As the spheres rotate, each shade of each complement comes in contact with each other.

By rotating our sphere around the torus over time, and by rotating the sphere as it moves around the torus, we created the capacity for our organization to use all its resources equitably. Each color has equal opportunity to occupy any point on the surface of the torus. However, each color is limited by its sequence around the sphere. It is not free to step out of this sequence and mix with any other color at any time. For this additional creative power we need another dimension.

Plate 6

The Five-Dimensional Perspective: Infolding and Outfolding

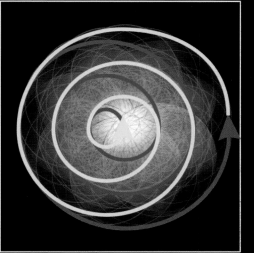

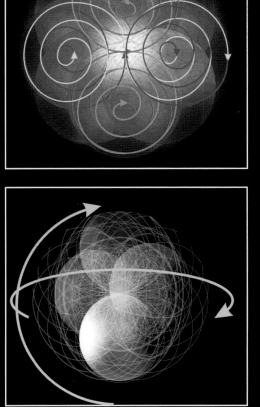

Now the torus is rotated 360° in all directions so that all colors have an equal opportunity to connect to any other color to form any possible combinations in any sequence.

Internal colors of light and dark shades inside all of the spheres rotating within the multiple tori infold and outfold, ensuring equal opportunity to occupy internal and surface space.

The union of wholeness and oneness is captured by the yellow spiral of 'implicate order moving inwards from five dimensions and beyond, descending through the fourth to the third and finally through zero dimensions to emerge as the blue spiral outwards of 'explicate' order.

Interpreting white light as purpose and all colors as individual powers, we illustrate that it takes at least five dimensions of organization to use the full power of human purpose. Our task, then, is to make ourselves, our organizations, and our world more 'power-full' by designing organizing processes that use all five dimensions of the power of human purpose.

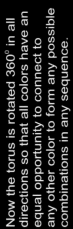

Plate 7

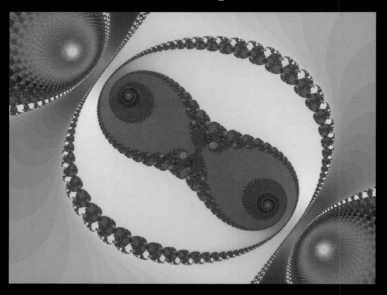

A Fractal Dimensional view of multiple interacting AIC fields

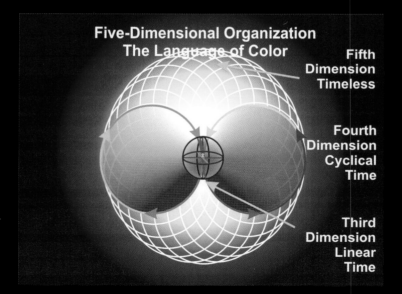

Schematic symbolizing the different nature and substance of
the five dimensions: the pure open, timeless quality of the fifth
dimension; the cyclical timing, relative nature of the fourth
dimension; and the closed, linear nature of the third dimension.

Plate 8

Purpose and Power

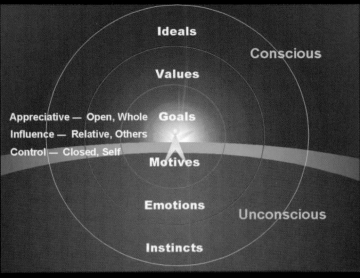

Purpose is manifest in three orientations: (i) open, timeless, (ii) relatively open, depending on the phase of the time cycle, and (iii) closed, with a fixed time orientation. The conscious A, I, and C purpose projects power onto the world and the unconscious a, i, and c purpose provides internal complementar feedback.

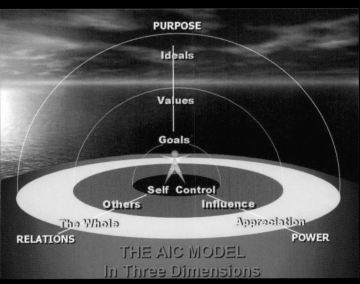

The three time orientations produce three power fields in which appreciation is the field open to the whole, everything that affects purpose, but which we cannot influence or control. Influence is our relationship to others and control our relationship to ourselves.

Plate 9

Power and Fields

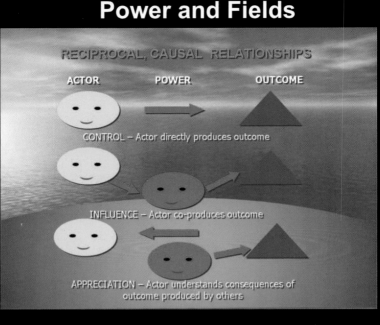

Power is the means by which we achieve outcomes in our world. When we can produce outcomes directly we have control, when through others influence. However, we also have power from appreciating the outcomes of others.

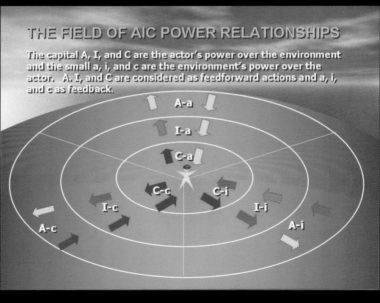

Our power field consists of reciprocal relationships with our world. We approach our world with A, I, or C and the world reciprocates with a, i, or c.

The fifth dimension allows the whole to resonate in every part and every part to relate to the whole. Creating appreciative conditions requires encouragement of oneness, and non-judgement. In practice it means avoiding opportunities for influence or control.

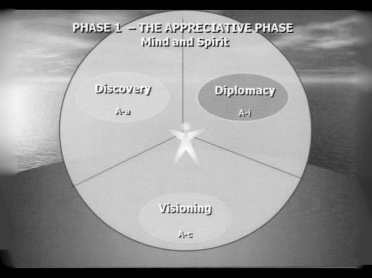

PHASE 1 – THE APPRECIATIVE PHASE
Mind and Spirit

Discovery
A-a

Diplomacy
A-i

Visioning
A-c

Successful projection of appreciation (A) onto our world requires the use of all three (a), (i) and (c) means. The three types of appreciative power that result are built into the organizing process as three phases (A-a) Discovery, (A-i) Diplomacy and (A-c) Visioning. The three phase set the tone for everything that happens afterwards.

The Four-Dimensional Cycle

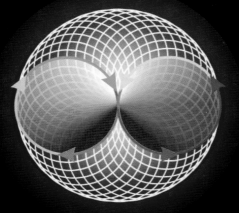

A cross section through a single torus shows the feed-forward of A, I, and C phases (green, red, and blue) and the complementary feedback of (a), (i), and (c) phases (yellow, magenta, and cyan). The white circles represent multiple rotating tori of the fifth dimension.

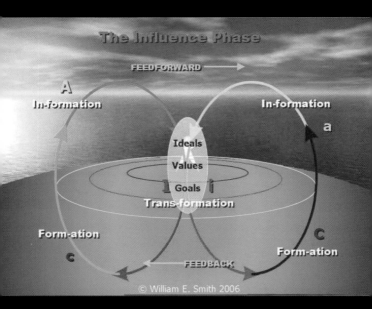

A more schematic view emphasizes the transformational role of influence in the organizing process. (A), (I), and (C) make the feedforward wave of a cycle of organizing, while (a), (i), and (c) make the feedback wave. The crossover point at (I-i) is the center of transformation.

Plate 12

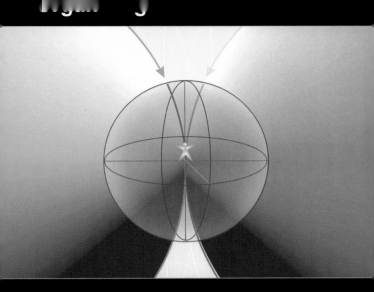

The schematic illustrates the closed, linear nature of control and its dimensions. However, we can still see how it is fed by the fourth and fifth dimensions.

What I Will Do	The Means I Will Use		
	(c) Action	(I)Relations	(a) Learning
Control	Operations	Agreements	Appraisal
Influence	Strategy	Negotiation	Evaluation
Appreciation	Policy	Diplomacy	Discovery

The three dimensions are reduced to a goal but for each goal we see how the three perspectives of action (C), (I), and (A) are achieved through the three different (c), (i), and

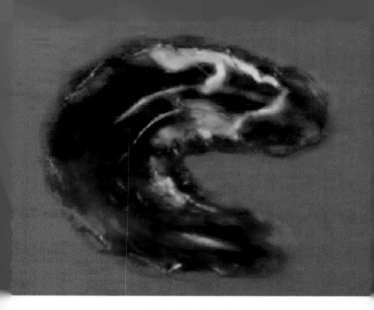

**Larvae of Fruit Fly Magnaified x 100
as viewed under polarized microscope
(Reproduced with permission)**

Mae Wan Ho's images show how the same principles
of color are inherent in the very life process itself.

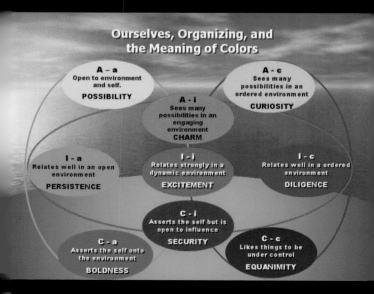

Ourselves, Organizing, and
the Meaning of Colors

A – a
Open to environment
and self.
POSSIBILITY

A - c
Sees many
possibilities in an
ordered environment
CURIOSITY

A - i
Sees many
possibilities in an
engaging
environment
CHARM

I - a
Relates well in an open
environment
PERSISTENCE

I - i
Relates strongly in a
dynamic environment
EXCITEMENT

I - c
Relates well in a ordered
environment
DILIGENCE

C - i
Asserts the self but is
open to influence
SECURITY

C - a
Asserts the self onto
the environment
BOLDNESS

C - c
Likes things to be
under control
EQUANIMITY

The Power Map interprets the nine organizing powers as
personal ways of engaging our world.

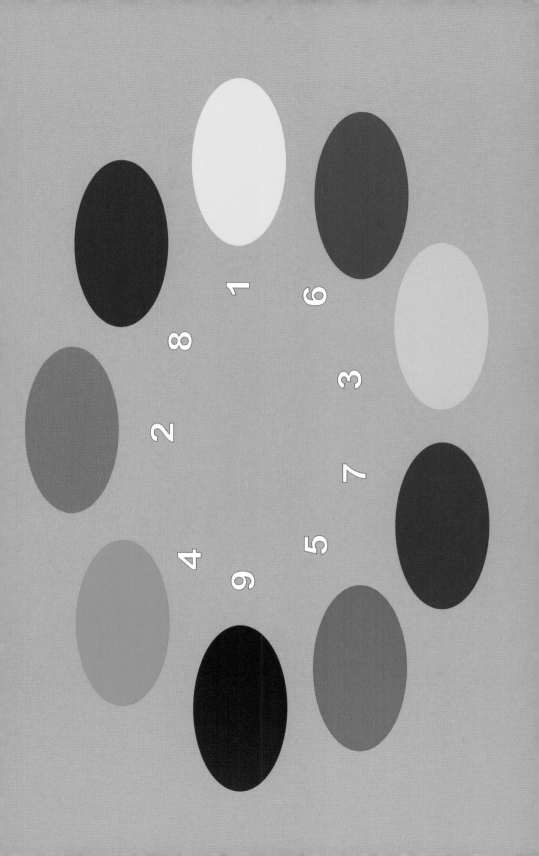

come into play. In addition we can only see the colors on one side of the sphere. Either we have to move around it to see all colors, which add another dimension of movement or the sphere has to rotate over time, which adds the same dimension of motion but the motion is coming from the sphere itself. To overcome these inequities or lack of potential we add another degree of freedom to allow for this movement of our colors.

Four-Dimensional Organization

To achieve this extra degree of freedom we rotate our sphere of colors around both its north/south and its east/west axes as it moves around a circle to create the torus in Figure 7.3 (Plate 6). If we take a vertical slice through our torus at any point in time we create two circles of complementary colors. Each circle contains all the possible shading of that color from light to dark. In this case the two complements are yellow and blue.

Our organization now has the potential to use any of its resources at any level and the purpose of the organization can shift to match that of any color occupying a top position. However, the four-dimensional torus changes our

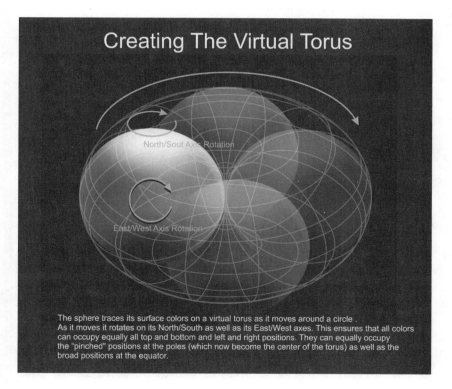

Figure 7.3 Creating the virtual torus

thinking about "the top." There are now many top positions traced around the topmost circle of the torus. The single point of focus is no longer a "top" position but a "central" point. This point is the zero-dimensional point, the hole in the center. It is the point of transformation where, literally, black can become white and all colors have the opportunity to become any other color (see Figures 7.4 and 7.5; Plate 6). The center of organization in this fourth dimension is the point of interchange and transformation for all colors. It is the point at which it is possible to cycle to a higher dimension, move to a lower dimension or remain cycling in the same dimension.

The organization is now as democratic as it can be and as adaptive as it is possible to be. It has many semi-autonomous parts with equal control and can coordinate the use of all means of all units. However, it is still not as creative as it can be. The relationship of the colors to each other is fixed even though their movement around the torus is very fluid. To access the organizations full creative power we need to add one more degree of freedom that will allow any color to mix with any other color to produce any color combination including white light.

Five-Dimensional Organization

If the third dimension adds the degree of freedom provided by a goal perspective, and the fourth dimension adds the degree of freedom that comes from the cyclical interchange and transformation of values, the fifth dimension adds the degree of freedom that comes from an infusion of

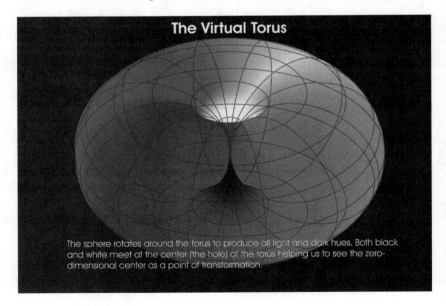

Figure 7.4 The virtual torus

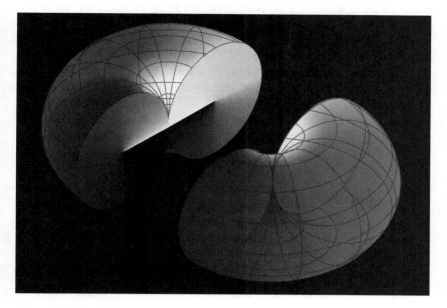

Figure 7.5 Cross section of torus

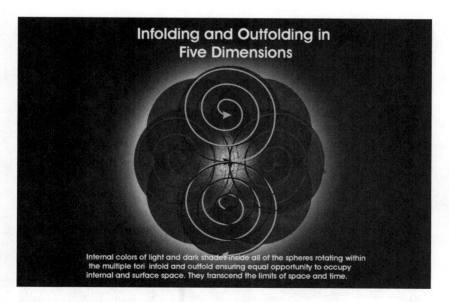

Figure 7.6 Infolding and outfolding in five dimensions

meaning that folds inwards and outwards through every aspect of the organization's internal and external functioning. To see this dynamic process of in-folding and out-folding we have to imagine that our torus consists of wrapped layers. If we cut a cross section to see inside it looks like the spirals made by the layers of a Swiss cake. From the surface of the torus we see the top layer moving into the center, say the left side, and disappearing down the hole in the center only to emerge on the right side after spiraling though the inside of the left side. The feedforward blue (dark) spiral of one sphere of any torus becomes the yellow (light) spiral of the sphere that makes up its second half. When the layer is at the equator, which is easier to see when looking at a single torus (Figure 7.4), it is as wide as it can possibly be, that is as differentiated as it can be, but as it moves to the center it becomes compressed, combining colors into lighter hues. When the surface reaches maximum compression at the center of the torus it becomes pure white, the combination of all colors. It is as integrated as it can possibly be. In the ideal it is then completely transformed into its opposite; the complete absence of light or blackness. It is at its height of life and the depth of death as it enters the next higher dimension or falls to the next lower dimension. The center, zero-dimensional point, is the French "le petit mort" with the same human intimations of the orgasmic ecstasy of pleasure and pain.

As all the layers of colors fold inwards and outwards to and from the center it is possible for all colors to combine with each other. Every color

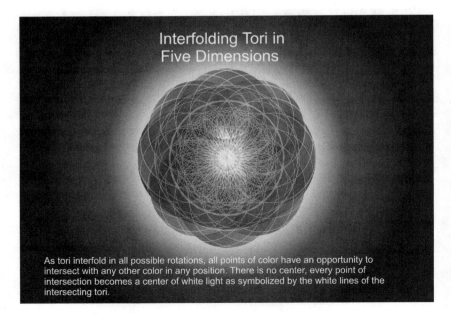

Interfolding Tori in
Five Dimensions

As tori interfold in all possible rotations, all points of color have an opportunity to intersect with any other color in any position. There is no center, every point of intersection becomes a center of white light as symbolized by the white lines of the intersecting tori.

Figure 7.7 Interfolding tori

now, through compression and rotation between layers has the ability to blend equally with any color to produce any other color. Every point in every sphere that makes up the tori becomes a center. Each is, at the same time, a single dimensionless point of light and the whole five-dimensional set of all possible colors and their combinations. We have created our ideal organization capable of drawing on all the power and all the levels of purpose of all constituents. We enable all to reach their spiritual ideal; the highest possible level of purpose and power.

Our most common experience of this fifth-dimensional infolding and outfolding is life itself. Every breath we take is an infolding and every breath we exhale is an outfolding. The oxygen from every breath in-forms every cell of our bodies and every exhalation of our breath transforms our world. The word breath itself, at its origin, means spirit. We know spirit's resonance in the heights and depths of feelings from the sense of oneness with the successes and failures in our personal lives, of our work's groups and organizations. We experience this dimension through our culture in the stories, the myths and legends, and other artifacts of our group and organizational cultures.

Fractal Dimensions

If our organizations and their worlds were really constructed of multiples of three, in whole numbers in five whole dimensions, then everything would be perfectly round, or at least elliptical. The fact that we have such odd shapes as eyebrows, bee's knees, swing dancing moves or the Federal Government arises because the generations of evolution that produce them do not iterate with perfectly whole numbers but with fractions of those whole numbers. However, there is in nature considerable order behind the myriad Byzantine shapes, movements, and evolutions, as revealed by Benoit's Fractal Geometry.

The fractal nature of the AIC pattern became evident during the thought experiment when creating the color circle. For example, we begin with a radian, a line that has one dimension. By the time we rotated it through all 360 degrees it had created a two-dimensional circle. However, in between every color is a fractal (partial) dimension from 1.10 to 1.90. For example, when the radian reaches three o'clock it is 1.25 dimensions and at half-past the hour it is at 1.50 dimensions. Similarly, our two-dimensional plane when rotated through light and dark versions of the colors moves from 2.00 to 3.00 dimensions. So degrees of lightness and darkness can be expressed as fractal dimensions. In the fourth dimension phases of the whole cycle of movement can be described as fractal dimensions, as phases between 3.00 and 4.00 dimensions just as degrees of infolding and outfolding in the fifth dimension can be expressed as fractal dimension between 4.00 and 5.00 dimensions. So although three powers in five dimensions give us 243

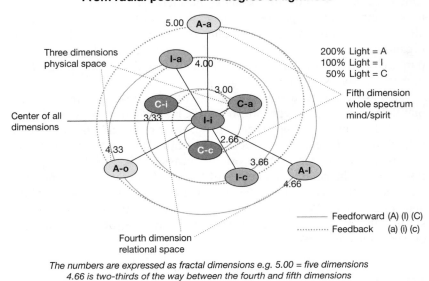

COLORS AND DIMENSIONS
From radial position and degree of lightness

The numbers are expressed as fractal dimensions e.g. 5.00 = five dimensions
4.66 is two-thirds of the way between the fourth and fifth dimensions

Figure 7.8 Colors and dimensions

powers or colors, of which we name only twenty-seven, there are thousands of fractal powers in between the twenty-seven we have selected. The infinite variety of our daily experience results from these fractal difference. However, underlying these difference are simple forms and relationships that can be more easily seen when expressed as whole numbers.

The practical impact of the ability to create fractals is that shapes and patterns of power relationships do not come in neat circles, spheres, and tori, they come as messy and beautiful asymmetrical trees, eyebrows, complaints, appeals, love, war, and life. The paperback cover of this book shows a seedling as a fractal shape emerging from the three-dimensional world of earth and depending on its five-dimensional context for air and water. Figure 7.9 shows how a simple Y shape, such as that seedling, can be represented by the three radians of our color circle. Used as a fractal part the radians can be iterated to produce a rudimentary tree. A slightly more complex asymmetrical fractal can produce lifelike trees that can be recognized as oaks or maples.

In the fourth dimension we move from the simple Y *structure* to phase *relationships*, which we have shown can be expressed as colors. Figure 7.10 shows one possible rendering of a fractal image produced by iterating these AIC *relationships*. The colors then represent the five-dimensional *field* relationships. It is easier in this fractal rendering to see the spiraling that we were at pains to imagine and describe in our torus imagery above.

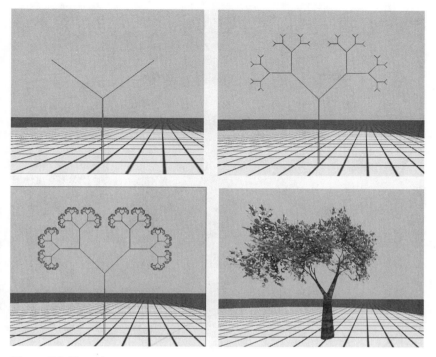

Figure 7.9 Fractal trees

Equally, the importance of fractal dimensions lies in their tremendous power to create rich complex wholes from the very small amounts of information contained in their fractal seeds. Computer images, for example, created from fractal algorithms use hundreds of times less space than traditional pixel-based images. Similarly, the AIC fractal has the same parsimonious power to convey information about wholes across multiple scales from individual parts to global. We explore the practical implication of this for the leadership, organizational, and institutional design in Part III.

The simple beauty and effectiveness of color as a language of power relationships can be gleaned even from these primitive representations of the five dimensions of light illustrated in the color plate section (Plates 1 to 8). Even in the limited two dimensions of Plate 4, colors opposite each other are complements, but any number from two to the more than 2,000 or more colors we can discriminate, when spaced equally around a two-dimensional circle, add up to white light. As we move into the third, fourth, and fifth dimensions of our model, there is, literally, an exponential increase in the possible *manifest power* relationships and their complements that the color language can express. The whole field can be represented numerically,

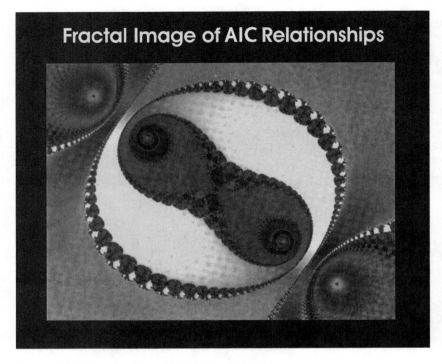

Fractal Image of AIC Relationships

Figure 7.10 Fractal image of AIC field relationships

relationally, and conatively by two color vectors—the feedforward color of green (A), red (I), or blue (C) and their complement (a) magenta, (i) cyan, and (c) yellow when organized dimensionally.

Goethe, the first color theorist, intuitively recognized this complementarity and wholeness and called it "universality":

> When the eye sees a colour it is immediately excited, and it is its nature, spontaneously and of necessity, at once to produce another, which with the original colour comprehends the whole chromatic scale. A single colour excites, by a specific sensation, the tendency to universality. In this resides the fundamental law of all harmony of colours.
>
> (Goethe 1982: 317)

Color enables us to meet the requirements of Humpty Dumpty's law as described by Russ Ackoff:

> If you never separate the whole from the parts you never have the cost of putting them back together again.
>
> (1999)

It enables us to keep action and aggregate together as one whole, the exercise of power creates its own feedback from its mathematical prime or complement—the whole.

Keeping this wholeness is something that natural language and our mathematics, and even our common-sense thinking finds very difficult to accomplish. Lere Shakunle's *Transfigural Mathematics* (1996) is a brilliant exception.[1] He has developed a mathematics that like color keeps the wholeness of numbers in their relationship to all other numbers, i.e. their aggregate. I believe that he has developed the mathematics of purpose and that in his work we can substitute his mathematical concept of the "*itson*" for purpose. For example, if our mathematical focus (purpose) is number 7 it is always seen in context of all the numbers to the right from 8 to infinity after it, and all the numbers from 6 to minus infinity before it. All his numbers, then, have the threeness of the whole. The number in the foreground, 7, is treated as the center or 0, for him the *itson* relationship (influence). All numbers after it are for him the *alpha*, in our language the appreciative. The numbers before the 0 *itson* relationship, the *omega*, are in our language the control. Lere's mathematics, like color, is able to express quantities, relationships, and qualities.

Color and complementarity, then, help us to see the whole in every part and every part as a whole—a key characteristic of five-dimensional field space. We can see every organizational choice, every use of power, as containing its relevant whole through its complement. By relevant complement we mean everything (the whole) that affects purpose but which cannot be controlled or influenced, for example the action that was not taken, the choice not made. It is this complementarity and wholeness that is captured in Eliot's poem:

> Where is the life we have lost in living?
> Where is the wisdom we have lost in knowledge?
> Where is the knowledge we have lost in information?
> (T.S. Eliot "The Rock" 1934)

The aggregate of the field of our choice or action remains and is felt as an unconscious complement, a form of residual energy that produces opponency. The tension and its harmonization between the chosen and its aggregate is the essence of every power relationship in every dimension. An understanding of the enormous potential of this hidden power and practical ways to use it goes a long way in making our models of the organizing process more "power-full": i.e. they take advantage of all the power available for purpose, both conscious and unconscious, both select and aggregate, the implicate and the explicate order. It is this capacity that is accessed though the appreciative field, transformed by the influence field, and formed by the control field.

The Nine Basic Manifest Powers

We will now use this dimensional organizing ideal and its color language to create a practical counterpart; a model of organization that incorporates the capability of transforming ideals into values and then goals and back to ideals, while using all of the power that each of them uniquely creates.

We again take white light with its five-dimensional properties to represent the purpose of the relevant whole (Plate 10). Just as in nature we divide this whole into three parts with an (A, I, and C) orientation and we center ourselves at the middle level with an (I) orientation. We differ from traditional organization models in that we have a *center* of influence rather than a base or *end* of control. The three primary light colors represent the three different powers in this center of influence. Organized by degree of lightness they are green, red, and blue. The primary light colors become our primary power relationships:

Green = Appreciation
Red   = Influence
Blue   = Control.

As adding colors together creates more light, and more light means a higher dimension, we create the three colors of the appreciative level by adding together the primary colors representing the influence level. When we add the primaries to each other we create the three appreciative colors:

1   100% green + 100% red = yellow   > (A-a) is appreciation in the appreciative level
2   100% red + 100% blue = magenta   > (A-i) is influence in the appreciative level
3   100% blue + 100% green = cyan   > (A-c) is control in the appreciative level.

We use the three primaries, pure green, red, and blue as the center from which we build our model of organization. So the three influence colors at the central level are the three primary colors:

4   100% green > (I-a), is appreciation in the influence level
5   100% red   > (I-i) influence in the influence level
6   100% blue > (I-c) control in the influence level.

Just as we add light to produce more appreciative colors so we subtract light to produce more controlling colors (see Plate 5). We doubled the light to produce the appreciative colors so we halve the light to make the three control colors from the following combinations. We actually subtract the appreciative colors from the influence colors, i.e. G − Y but as yellow consists of R + G we gain our color by adding half as much blue as green to make a total of 50 percent light, which produces a green/blue or teal color. In the same way, we derive the proportions of color for the two other control colors to produce brown and indigo:

7 33% green + 17% blue (50% light) = teal > (C-a) appreciation in
    the control level
8 33% red + 17% green (50% light) = brown > (C-i) influence in
    the control level
9 33% blue + 17% red (50% light) = indigo > (C-c) control in the
    control level.

Adding and subtracting light is the same as rotating upwards and downwards through the five dimensions of power. Each level has the same amount of light, i.e. the (A) level has 200 percent, the (I) level has 100 percent and the (C) level has 50 percent. We noted, for example when we examined one- and two-dimensional organization that the second dimension, breadth, represents equal levels of control; all boxes at any given level have the same amount of control but different levels of influence. The same calculation can be made from the radial position, the colors on three plates representing the natural hues (see Plate 4):

1 the center plate, the Influence level, contains the combinations of green, red, and blue;
2 the upper plate contains the lighter shades of these hues, the Appreciative level;
3 The lower plate contains the darker shades, Control level.

Figure 7.11 (see also Plate 7) summarizes the color model as the "Religio," the feedforward and feedback of power relationships in at least five dimensions. The figure shows a blue spiral (dark) of *feedforward* (A, I, and C) moving from center to periphery and upward through the dimensions from control-centeredness though influence to appreciative-centeredness. The yellow (light) appreciative spiral of *feedback* (a), (i), and (c), moves from periphery to the center, from appreciative-centeredness through influence to control-centeredness. The spirals represent the essential *active* feedforward power process of *organizational planning* and the *reactive* feedback power process, e.g. of *organizational learning*. The color red, the highest frequency, is the point of transformation where both spirals meet and can continue to cycle at the same rate or move to higher regimes (lighter colors) or downwards to lower regimes (darker colors).

Figure 7.11 The religio: power relationships in five dimensions

Every selection of purpose, every selection of color, is a reduction from the whole or advancement to the whole So just as each color consists of an internal tension within itself between conscious intent and unconscious reaction so does each color have a complementary relationship, for example (C-c) power, indigo, creates an unconscious complement of yellow, an (A-a) energy.

The Power Relationships as Holons

There are nine combinations of (A, I, and C) and (a, i, and c) and each is a holon consisting of three parts: an end, a preference for means, and a power process. Each holon is also organized in all five dimensions:

1   The large letter A,I, or C is the end, the first dimension.
2   The small letter (a, i, or c) is the feedback influencing choice of means, the second dimension.
3   The name is the type of resolution that emerges from the tension—the third-dimension goal perspective.
4   The relationship, the in-flow and out-flow of energy between ends and means, for example, the relationship between (I-c) that creates a value, is the fourth dimension.

5   The color gives the fifth dimensional resonant, emotive quality that permeates the whole, the ideal perspective.

The dimensions provide different contexts that derive from the different orientation to purpose in each dimension. The fifth dimension deals with the most open, future orientation to purpose; ideals. The fourth deals with an orientation that is sometimes open and sometimes closed. Its degree of openness is related to the phase (a, i, or c) of resolution in the current time cycle. The third dimension has a closed orientation, relying very much on realities that have been created from past events.

Appreciative-Centered Organization, Five-Dimensional Mind Space

A practical way to conceive of this fifth dimension of our model is as "mind-space." Our minds have enough degrees of freedom to combine all possibilities (colors) into purposes, manifest them as powers, and organize them to affect our environment, which then feeds back to reorganize our purpose. Our minds have the capacity to move beyond *time* duration, and *timing* to *timelessness* to transcend past, present, and future, daily cycles, the seasons, and life's own cycle to create images and ideas, even imaginary universes with their own galactic cycles that have never existed before and that will never exist in physical time.

In this appreciative-centered field there is no center, or more accurately every part is a zero-dimensional center that contains the whole, just as our universe is expanding equally from every point making every point a center of the universe, so in reverse the appreciative field is attracted equally to every point and every possibility within it.

It is this holonomic quality that carries the spiritual properties of the appreciative-centered field. Spirit is infused in every part of the whole and gives each part its identity with the whole. It is this spiritual yearning for wholeness that provides our highest level of purpose. It is the ultimate source of tension—separate unique individuals searching for identity and meaning by becoming one with the whole.

In Figure 7.12 and Plate 8 we present the dynamic in-folding and out-folding of five-dimensional powers as a two-dimensional slice through the set of interacting tori we described above. When in this appreciative-centered space we are our whole beings—spiritual, emotional, and physical—and so our interpretation of our power vectors (A, I, and C) in this dimension is different than when in the others. We also interpret our small (a, i, and c) as feedback from our whole world, not just from the elements we are directly dealing with at the time. Our feedback in this appreciative-centered dimension is from the whole of our conscious and unconscious

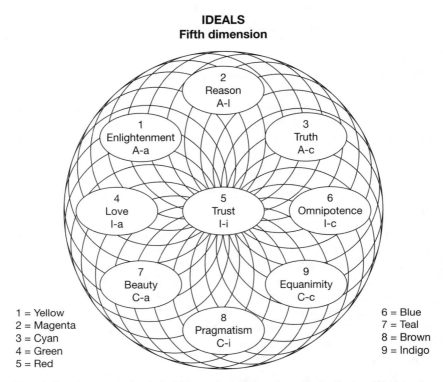

IDEALS
Fifth dimension

The spiralling circles symbolize the in-folding and out-folding of power in the timeless fifth dimension
Every color, symbolizing possibilities, passes through all points equally and combines equally with
all other colors.

Figure 7.12 Ideals: fifth dimension

expectation from our genetic make-up, our cultural shaping and or own experience.

Purpose, in this dimension, is an *ideal* that can never be achieved, it *is timeless*, always open to the emergence of new possibilities. Time, in this sense, is infinite beyond our control or influence. In Figures 7.13, 7.14, and 7.15 we give names to these ideals, but the names are illustrative only. They can only truly be named in a specific context, because naming is in itself a major act of control. In giving an idea, a relationship, or form a name we separate it from its context and give it a distinct existence to bring it back into context requires an exercise of appreciation. The names I choose reflect a mix of Greek and Eastern philosophy tempered by an understanding of the power relationships involved.

The interpretation of these ideals and their implications are dealt with more fully in Chapter 11.

The Manifestation of Purpose, Power and Process as Holons in Five Dimensions		
PURPOSE **Ideals**	**POWER** **Relations**	**PROCESS** **Meaning**
Enlightenment	**A-a**	We are totally open to our world (A) and believe the world will to be equally open to us (a)
Reason	**A-i**	We are totally open to our world (A) and understand that we must be influenced by it
Truth	**A-c**	We are totally open to the world (A) and see the need to bound its possibilities (c)
Love	**I-a**	We fully express our thoughts and feelings in our world (I) and are unconditionally open to the ideals of our world (a)
Trust	**I-i**	We fully express our thoughts and feelings in our world (I) and understand that we must allow our world to do so equally
Omnipotence	**I-c**	We fully express our thoughts and feelings in our world (I) but know that the world wants things to be under control (c)
Beauty	**C-a**	We know ideally what we must do (C) and believe that our ideal must be attractive to our world (a)
Pragmatism	**C-i**	We know ideally what we must do (C) and understand: we must be influenced by our world (i)
Equanimity	**C-c**	We are confident in our ideals (C) and know that our world is equally confident in theirs

Figure 7.13 Manifestation of purpose in five dimensions

Influence-Centered Organization: Four-Dimensional Timing

The appreciative-centered dimension, being our relationship to the whole, pervades all dimensions with its spirit and so sets the context for what is possible in the influence-centered fourth dimension. In the influence-centered dimension we extract from the appreciative field what we *think* and *feel* are the most important ideas, relationships, and resources for advancing the purpose in our current situation. The large (A, I, and C) are no longer our ends as whole human beings. They represent our ends in our roles as stakeholders with an interest in particular ideas, people, and resources (a, i, and c). The oneness and wholeness of the appreciative dimension now breaks down into clusters of related purposes, which we interpret as values. Values are the sieve we use to reduce the appreciated world into something more manageable. While the oppositional differences in the appreciative domain became a source of creativity now these differences become a source of support and opposition. Part of the job of the appreciative phase is to prepare the ground for us to deal with these differences by creating trust and emphasizing the higher level purpose that transcends these differences.

The time orientation in this dimension shifts from the timelessness of appreciation to the cyclical timing of the dance of influence. That the process is a dance is aptly illustrated, as I write, in the influence process labeled national politics. Hillary Clinton and Barrack Obama have taken part in a dance that decided who best represents the Democratic Party (appreciators). Obama has entered a new dance with John McCain, the surviving candidate representing the Republican Party (controllers), awaits his turn to dance with the winner. Meanwhile, the electorate (the influencers) is convinced that the cycle of our times requires a major shift, and they are turning out in record numbers to become themselves engaged in the dance to have their voice

VALUES
Fourth dimension

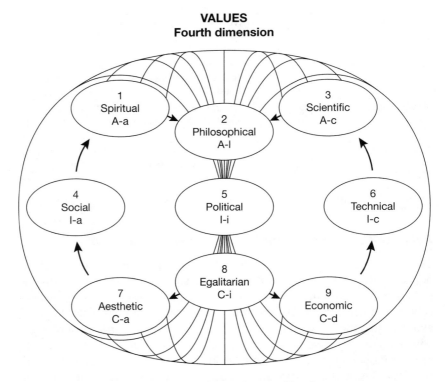

Values seen as clusters of dynamic oppositional purposes.
The cross-section of the torus symbolizes four-dimensional cycles of time-space

Figure 7.14 Values

heard in resolution of current value differences. Barrack Obama himself illustrates the use of five-dimensional appreciative power—his search for solutions that transcend current frameworks of thinking, his ability to have people resonate in emotional and spiritual way to his message. It also accounts for the criticism he receives—of not focusing on the solution to specific problems, i.e. not being control-centered.

The cyclical quality of time that governs this dimension is described by Peter Beamish (1996) as Rhythm Based Time (RBT). He contrasts RBT with Signal Based Time (SBT), the conventional control-centered concept that sees time moving linearly from Future → Present →. In other words, conventional (control) time is distance traveled on a line from future to past divided by the speed traveled. Just as influence is a reduction, intensification, and transformation of energy from the appreciative dimension so our values are reductions, intensifications, and transformations of our ideals. We all have value differences that can't be solved in this cycle of organization so we have to employ a political process that enables us to resolve for now our differences in the most constructive way possible. We have to be open to others' influence (a) and be willing to take their values into account (i), even though we know there is no final solution to our difference in this particular time cycle. We have to find a way to place a boundary, to create an arbiter to resolve the issues for now. Often it is the technical constraints

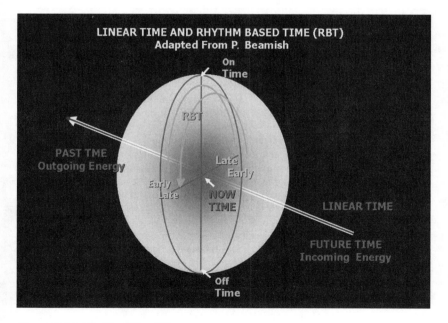

Figure 7.15 Rhythm Based Time
Adapted from Beamish (1996)

and the demands of technical processes with their resource constraints (c) that provide relatively objective bases that help convince the parties that enough is enough and it is time to *agree to a resolution.*

The implication of these values for institutions and organization is dealt with more fully in Chapter 10.

The Manifestation of Purpose, Power and Process as Holons in Four Dimensions		
PURPOSE Values	**POWER** Relations	**PROCESS** Meaning
Spiritual	A-a	We transform enlightenment and its supportive appreciative powers into values affecting all stakeholders. Practically, we will be open to all values (A) and expect others to be open to ours (a).
Philosophical	A-i	We transform *reason* and its supportive appreciative powers into a particular philosophical approach. We have insight into the different values that our stakeholders have (A) and we understand that there can never be a final solution. We are able to accept our gains and losses philosophically (i) without under or over reaction.
Scientific	A-c	We transform our ideal of *truth* and its supportive appreciative powers(A) into a search for insight into our differences in values that relies as much as possible on objective information (c).
Social	I-a	We transform our ideal of *love* into a willingness to engage with others from our value perspective (I) and are open to gain insight into their values (a).
Political	I-i	We transform our ideal for *trust* into engagement with others from the perspective of our values (I) while we expect our stakeholders do the same (i).
Technical	I-c	We transform our ideal for *omnipotence* into a value for technical control. We engage with our stakeholders (i) to find technical boundaries (c) that will form the basis of our resolution.
Aesthetic	C-a	We now know what we are committed to do (C) but are concerned that others understand and believe that what we are doing is good (a) This qualitative value, a concern for the final form and its resonance with the whole purpose (a) suggests an aesthetic that measures wholeness.
Egalitarian	C-i	We know what the final form should be (C) but we want to be sure that all others have an equal chance to influence implementation (i). We are in control but are willing to listen to be influenced by others equally.
Economic	C- c	We know what our options are (C) and we expect others to know theirs (c). This makes for the best choice of options, in terms of time and resources and so is the most economic way to get things done.

Figure 7.16 Manifestation of purpose in four dimensions

Control-Centered Organization: Three-Dimensional Physical Space

Control-centered space provides another reduction and subtraction—this time from influence values to control goals. The consideration of options and priorities, relations, support and opposition give way to action and reflection. In this dimension we create and commit to our goals, we establish specific linear time frames for implementation.

The implication of these goals and power relationships for organizations is dealt with more fully in Chapter 8, which spells out the details an organizing process using these distinctions. Chapter 10 shows how these distinctions are linked to institutional values and cultural ideals.

Third dimension

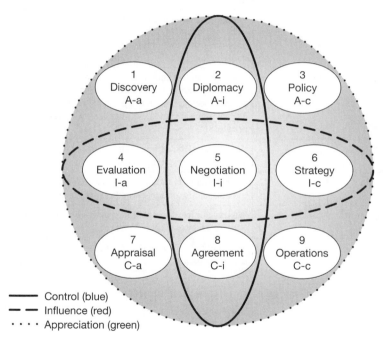

Goals (3D) seen as perspective on ends (1D) and means (2D).
The sphere symbolizes the classic spacial dimensions of height (1D),
breadth (2D), and depth (3D)

Figure 7.17 Goals

The Manifestation of Purpose, Power and Process in Three Dimensions		
PURPOSE Values	POWER Relationships	PROCESS Meaning
Discovery	A-a	We suspend our judgment about our particular commitment and listen to others' commitments (A). We also expect everyone else involved to be able to suspend their judgment too (a).
Diplomacy	A-i	Our new insights from discovery (A) could well have far-reaching effects on current commitments, so its products have to be handled with the gentlest form of influence (i) possible.
Policy	A-c	Safe boundaries (c) must be found to enclose the discoveries and possibilities that pass this diplomatic test. (A)
Evaluation	I-a	We use our values to subtract relevant "*in-formation*" from the "*whole*"(I) but remain open to identify potential positive and negative factors relevant to our strategy (a).
Negotiation	I-i	We negotiate agreements for more policy and operational commitments with internal and external stakeholders (I) and in the process transform as many negative options into opportunities for mutual gain as possible (i).
Strategy	I-c	We influence the selection of options (I) and give them form (c) as strategic priorities.
Appraisal	C-a	We commit to our choices as goals (C) and appraise the conditions for achieving those goals (a).
Agreement	C-i	We use our joint goals (C) to create working agreements (i) between lateral operational units.
Operations	C- c	We carry out our work (C) and expect out work teams to do the same (c).

Figure 7.18 Manifestation of purpose in three dimensions

Summary

1   The focus of the model is on purpose in its inseparable trinity of manifestation as open, timeless ideals; relative, cyclically changing values; and closed goals in linear time.

2   It shows that it is both the manifest (*explicate*) powers and the un-manifest (*implicate*) powers that make up the whole to be appreciated. It is feedback from both that recreates purpose.

3 The manifest and un-manifest powers are organized in at least five dimensions.

4 Each dimension, each phase, and each power relationship contains within itself an opposition that results from appreciative and control tensions from both within the manifest powers and between the manifest and un-manifest powers. It is the resolution or failure to obtain resolution of these tensions through influence that moves power up and down between the dimensions, just as light is produced by electrons making their quantum leaps between levels of the atom as energy fluctuates.

5 The model demonstrates that purpose, power, and the organizing processes that give form to purpose are inseparable and complementary aspects of each other and are themselves a meta-level expression of the AIC fractal pattern. Purpose provides potential power as (A), the three manifest powers provide the kinetic reciprocal energy (I), and organizational process gives form to that energy (C).

6 Quite appropriately, this holonomic model of purpose, power, and organization fits with the intuitive insight of the first writer on administration to attach central importance to purpose and power, a woman, Mary Parker Follett. She wrote, as we saw in Chapter 2, that people do not seek power for specific ends, they seek reciprocal power. People don't like to receive without giving. They want to restore balance in their power relationships. She saw that we cannot conceive of power as something one person or group has. She saw that power was not just "power over" but "power with." Since then the concept of "power to" has been added and further developed in this work. She also saw the circular nature of power, which we have just illustrated. Her comments, quoted in Chapter 1, are eminently worth repeating:

> "Total behavior" brings us back again to our formula: the will or purpose of a man or group is to be found in that activity which is a constant function, or a combination of such functions, of some aspect of his environment . . . this formula, with its implied definition of behavior as a function of the interweaving between the activity of organism and activity of environment, gives us a new approach to the social sciences
>
> (Follett 1945: 64)

She also elegantly captures the five-dimensional nature of purpose in power:

Purpose is always the appearing of the power of unifying, the ranging of multiplicity into that which is both means and ends, the One holding Many.

(Ibid.)

Through understanding the dimensional nature of the holonomic model we are able to add explanation to her insights. Once we have this dimensional construct it becomes easier to see how power is in everything and, therefore, we have the "power to" accomplish any purpose; we are limited only by our imagination. Only in five dimensions is the whole in every part, "One holding Many" with the "power to" create purpose. In four dimensions, we begin to understand the basis of the multiple dynamic circular relationships of "power with." In three dimensions we finally catch up with control-centered organization and "power over." However, it is now tempered by *in-formation* from the whole and has been *trans-formed* by multiple sources of influence so that its intense power is *formed* into results that reflect the full-power, the white light of the purpose of the individual, the organization, its stakeholders and their worlds.

8 The Process in Practice

It was the practical discovery, described in the Introduction and in Chapter 1 that drove my search for new concepts and practice of organization. Intuitive experience inspired by some of the early writers on organization indicated that it is possible for us as individuals, organizations, and social institutions to achieve much higher levels of purpose than we currently do at much lower cost and in much less time, while at the same time making our engagement with the organizing process a much more constructive and fulfilling one. In the following pages we pull together what we have learned so far about the design and implementation governed by this ideal.

The premise that drives the new concepts and practice is the philosophical premise that purpose is the source of power. This means that the principles behind the organizing process provide a meta-framework that applies to any purpose from 15-minute problem-solving sessions to the greatest issues of our times. The process works by drawing on more of the power created by purpose than do more traditional approaches. For example, the addition of a phase of conscious appreciation enables actors to become aware of possibilities that enable them to transcend their original concept of the outcomes that were achievable. This was the case in all of the examples reported in Part I. The outcome I was seeking in Rome was improved technical operations, but what resulted was an improvement in all operations so that Fiumicino became the best-performing airport on BOAC's network. Similar results were obtained in the corporate sector with National Silicates, and G.D. Searle. The Colombia project began with the purpose of facilitating one workshop. The project ended up producing a series of self-organizing events that transformed the sector and spread to other sectors. The cost of the workshop and its follow up was approximately $500,000 yet it achieved the result of more than five typical World Bank projects costing on average $3 million each. The official outcome of the Thai project was to teach thirty people in one NGO how to do rural development. It ended with a nationwide process in all sectors of the economy and caused a change in the Thai Constitution.

Application at the opposite end of the spectrum to individuals rather than large systems in workshops and academic classes has similar multiplicative or transformational impact:

> My emerging realization now knows that others have purposes, desires, goals, dreams and values. My new self is genuinely concerned with others. Some of the words may stay the same for any given conversation . . . "How are you?", but now I will actually care because I want to hear how the other person is in relation to themselves and how they feel they are in relation to the environment.
>
> (*Nate Vogel Journal*, June 2006)

A young woman, Diane, after experiencing the appreciative phase of a course in organizational sciences at George Washington University made the following revelation:

> This class has come at the best time of my life. I was diagnosed with stage 1 breast cancer in April and I did nothing about it. I ignored it. The first class here really got me doing something to help myself. I learned to appreciate what I have and not to ignore it. I did a kind of circle chart about what I can do to make myself better and not to ignore it: to realize that this is something I have to deal with (see three circle exercise in Chapter 9, pp. 212–13). The whole process really changed my life and my values about how I am going to handle this.
>
> (Quoted with permission from video of Class Review, July 2007)

So how do we build such transformational potential into our organizing process for all our major purposes? We have seen in the last chapter through our thought experiment that it takes at least five dimensions of organizational capacities to approximate the ideal of using all the power created by purpose. In practice, we have discovered that for an organizing process to spread, to self-organizing and self-multiplying, its principles have to be built into the process itself. Participants then learn by doing. Combining the intellectual and the practical we conclude that each phase of every organizing process has to be a fractal that contains the wisdom of the whole. The following sections capture the key principles as we understand them so far and then describe how they incorporate this fractal concept into the organizing process itself.

Principles in Process

1   The first principle requires *faith* or *wisdom*. It asks us to accept the infinite potential of purpose. The practical implication is that we incorporate

consideration of purpose at the level of ideals and let it infuse the whole organizing process. Purpose, then, is treated not just as a specified end to be achieved (control orientation) it lies in the infinite possibilities that are invoked by ideals (appreciative orientation). It also lies in the values by which we choose our course of action when we consider who will support and oppose the pursuit of our ideals (influence orientation).

2   The second principle requires *understanding* to help us transcend the limits of our current models of power. Purpose creates power and in return is re-created by power. Our traditional understanding of power is based on a one-way view of "power over" the imposition of our purposes on others and our world. We have much less understanding of the reciprocal role of power in re-creating our purpose and increasing our "power to." The process addresses this gap by paying equal attention to feedforward and feedback at every level of process. (Every step of the process consists of an element of feedforward, an act of (A), (I), or (C) and an element of feedback (a), (i), or (c); see Chapter 7.)

3   The third principle requires *knowledge*. While nature, nurture, or the demands of the situation may require an emphasis on A, I, or C feedforward, successful implementation requires an equal use of (a), (i), and (c) feedback, which we have seen translates in practice as our choice of means. In this sense the organizing process does not attempt to change people or even organizations but rather to develop them. It asks us not only to honor their A, I, or C essence, but also to transcend it by incorporating an equal use of (a), (i), and (c) means into their organizing processes. To develop the capacity to use (a), (i), and (c) equally we need to have knowledge through experience of each of the appreciative, influence, and control fields. In practice we have found it takes three iteration of the use of the AIC organizing process to accomplish this.

The statement of these principles is an example in itself; a fractal that contains all five dimensions of whole (see Dimensions in Chapter 7):

1   faith and wisdom require five-dimensional capacities;
2   understanding requires four-dimensional capacities; and
3   knowledge requires three-dimensional capacities .

The principles are enacted by using seven questions that act as A, I, and C power vectors and create the three corresponding power fields. The seven questions, naturally, are modified to meet the unique circumstance of each case. They begin with one question on purpose then two each for each of the A, I, and C fields. The two questions within each field are our way of invoking the complementary or oppositional process between the A, I, and C vectors of power and their feedback vectors (a), (i), and (c).

Purpose

The first step, then, of the organizing process is to ask:

Question 1: "What is the Purpose?"

In large-scale organizational or community-wide transformational programs the presenting purpose is often worked out in a design workshop that contains a small group of seven to fifteen people, a cross-section of the program's stakeholders. The design workshop is a mini AIC process that takes from 3 hours to a day and a half. Its objective is not to solve the problem but to go though the process to gain a better appreciation of the orientation and depth of purpose and to discover which stakeholders to involve in the full process. In essence the design team creates the invitation and decides who it should be sent to. This mini (fractal) process is the first cycle of the appreciative phase. It is ideal-seeking in that it is searching for the latencies for higher level purpose that exists in the world surrounding the leaders initiating the organizing process. The presenting purpose serves as an attractor for other purposes that may better express the latencies in the environment. This is why the highest levels of openness or appreciation are so necessary at this stage.

The more controlling the environment the more difficult it is to create this appreciative environment. This difficulty was evident after completion of the very first full-scale application of the AIC concepts in Colombia (Chapter 4). The Minister of Transportation for Colombia wanted to replicate the success of the energy project and asked ODII for help. The ODII team assumed he wanted the same policy-level intervention that would require the participation of all sectors of the economy so we began to identify the national and international stakeholders that would be involved. He looked perplexed and then clarified:

> "Oh no, I don't want to involve all of those people I just want to do it with us, the top people in the Ministry" (read "best and brightest").

After much discussion he wouldn't budge from including outsiders so we offered:

> "Perhaps it was not a new policy that you really want but a new strategy for implementing the policies you already have? You are willing to accept the external constraints placed on transportation and within those constraints you just want to do a better job."

This insight resolved the problem for a while till we explained that the reason the process worked is that we always included three levels of organization (to capture the three levels of purpose) and this involves one or two system levels outside of the organization. Since he did not see the need to involve external stakeholders we would not really be creating new policy but rather revisiting strategic premises and examining how they had been implemented. For this we would still need three levels. The top decision makers within the Ministry would form the appreciative-centered level. They would be open to, i.e. appreciative of, new implications for policy change but this would not be the focus of the effort. The second and central level would be the directors of the various subdivisions who would actively look at new strategies for implementing the existing polices. Helping them develop a strategic focus on existing policies would be the central focus of the workshop. However, we would have to add a third level that was not present in the electricity program—the operational managers—the control-centered level. The operational mangers would give the directors feedback on the likely consequences of different strategic options for their operations. Again the Minister's staff objected:

> "These people don't really have anything to offer the high level dialogue that would take place. Besides they were from very different backgrounds [read class] and it would be very difficult to have them work with very senior people."

The Minister eventually accepted our point of view and we completed the process. It was no surprise that it was the reluctantly included lower managers that were the source of most energy and ideas for the improvement of such a strategically and operationally focused intervention.

The opposite situation existed in Thailand. In Chapter 4 we explain how we had chosen to work in Thailand in order to learn about natural appreciation from an appreciative culture. It was Paiboon's and Pravit Wasi's realization of the resonance between the appreciative process and Buddhist philosophy that enabled them to trust the AIC process and to develop it "Thai Style." From the beginning the orientation was towards appreciation, its range was to be the whole country, and the participants really did involve their "whole" selves in the process.

If our purpose is to create a new policy, new culture, or new vision for an organization we have to reach outward to the external stakeholders and into the whole community to discover what latent potential, what possibilities exist that will help our purpose become an attractor for all that latent power. The higher our level of purpose the more latent power will be available to us.

In the Rome story of Chapter 1, unlike the situation in Trinidad, the airport had all the necessary control elements, equipment, and procedures present.

The Italian staff were also very good at work relationships; able to deal with their colleagues well, able to inform each other when things went well or badly. The latency was for some meaning in the work. My being an appreciative type unwittingly brought that appreciative field into the work place through the newsletter. The latency was so huge that it took less than six months to completely change the performance levels from mediocre to the best. No amount of the kind of analysis I knew how to do could have revealed that latent power. A similar latency for change seems to be present as I write in the climate within the United States, and Barack Obama, the democratic candidate, seems to be tapping into it.

The question of purpose sets up the parameters for the whole organizing process and selects the stakeholders to become involved. In cases where workshops are used as part of the organizing process issues of purpose are resolved through the selection and invitation to attend the workshop and become involved in the process. The most critical decisions are made before the workshop process even begins. Finding the right stakeholders to be involved in the process, those who are likely to be in tune with a wider set of potential to raise the level of purpose and engagement, provides the first and most critical step in that first cycle of influence.

So the first step of the process is to ask the question "What is our purpose." We then have to set up the conditions to uncover the three levels of that purpose. What do we have to learn that we currently don't know, even those things that we don't know that we don't know? Who will support and oppose us? What are their purposes and how can we enlarge our purpose to include theirs? Enlarging our purpose both increases our power field and enables us to transcend differences of purpose of those who would oppose us. If we have a very large purpose we may have to iterate through this process many times each time widening our circle of influence till we arrive at a circle capable of addressing the whole issue. We may, for example, have an ideal to solve the problem of world hunger, but we may only have enough influence to begin with a group of friends who can help design an approach to feeding the homeless in our local area. Our success here will help us build a larger influence circle that could tackle the problem in a district and so on till we develop an influence circle large enough to tackle world hunger.

This may sound utopic, but in a recent class a young African American woman shows how the process works. Corrine Marr, a young African American student saw a video, *Invisible Children*, on the effects of the civil war in Northern Uganda—it shows children being kidnapped, forced to fight and kill, tortured, and turned into sex slaves. She had just taken the class on the appreciative process so as an exercise she made a list of potential and realities she saw for improvement in the situation.

She realized then that the plight of the Ugandan children had now been brought into her appreciated world, so action for her had been brought from the impossible to the possible.

Not only did I appreciate from this standpoint, but also from the point of appreciating my personal situation. There is never a day where I have to seriously worry about being kidnapped, being murdered or watching my loved ones murdered, not having food, not having clean water, not having a safe place to sleep. These are all things that I take for granted, things that these children would see as pure luxuries. It's funny to think that as a kid, I thought that my immediate family and I were the most important people in the world. Then as you grow up, you began to realize that there are other people—other countries, cultures, and issues. I think that just now I'm starting to realize that we as individuals take up such a tiny space of the world and if we're smart enough and lucky enough, we can find a way to impact the people around us.

(Class Paper on the Practice of Appreciation)

She discussed the issues with her friends and organizers of the forum presenting the film. She realized that she could do two things to raise awareness of the plight of the children (*appreciation*) and also raise money (*control*) to directly help buy food, but also to *influence* American and Ugandan stakeholders to take action. She was not at all experienced in fund raising so thought one thing she could do was to begin with a fundraiser for her friends and work colleagues. As part of her listing of potential for improving the situation she had listed Oprah Winfrey's rally in Washington DC, "Global Commute" that raised awareness of the issue. She discovered that on the same day as her fundraiser Oprah was airing a special about the issue. Excited, she succeeded in getting her company to air the show in the lobby that got most traffic. She was able to interest people in the issue and get more people to sign up for the fundraiser at the local pub. The fundraiser was a success.

Matt, the person who had presented the film to the forum Corrine attended, came to see her and told her what an inspiration she had been. He had used her as an example to tell people about the forum. Her example so affected him and the people he told about it that he became more successful and as a result was promoted to the board. Corrine now sits with a map of Africa posted above her desk. Her example is in this book, which hopefully will affect many people around the world. She has been changed forever and she is changing the world.

Corrine showed in a small arena the same principal that happened in the larger arena in Thailand—the power of very ordinary people to tap into higher level purposes latent in the whole and with relatively few resources and relatively quickly to achieve results that most people would think impossible.

The key to this multiplicative power is to organize AIC relationships outward from one's area of control rather than inward. If Corrine had just looked inward to appreciate her own resources, relationships, and ideas she would have concluded there was almost nothing that she could do. The problem was just too large. It was when she looked outward to external relationships, to discover new possibilities that serendipities started to happen. The possibilities for the connections she made were always there. What had changed was her attitude of openness. Without this openness to see new possibilities she would never have seen the connection between Oprah's show and her fundraiser.

The organizing process is the control part of the AIC philosophy in action. Intuiting and sensing purpose is the appreciative part; discovering and engaging the stakeholders is the influence part. So in describing the process we will use the naming of the AIC powers from the control-centered level form taken from Figures 7.17 and 7.18 as the base for describing the more formal part of the organizing process in action.

Making the Impossible Possible: The Appreciative Field

The statement of purpose included in the invitation provides the first part of the power equation, the power vector that expresses the A, I, or C orientation of the purpose, the aggregate field (a, i, and c) lies unconsciously in our built-in expectation of what the invitation might bring into being. In practice this relationship is not consummated until there is a joint experience with some representation of the whole field. We typically evoke this resonance at the beginning of the full workshop or program meeting. Participants introduce themselves and give their own views of what they want to achieve through the transformational process. Apart from recording brief notes on everyone's contribution no effort is made to summarize or give meaning to this contribution from the participants. Much more than their conscious words create this "implicate order" that becomes the appreciative field. Each individual, as a center of purpose, has their own relationship to this field. This is why no leader or facilitator should attempt to summarize or synthesize the results of this phase. Each participant may say what the experience means for them but cannot speak for anyone else or the whole: to do so would invoke attempts at influence and control.

In essence, these introductions begin the appreciative process by providing the source of power; the open-ended expression of purpose. The process continues by striving to build on this openness.

The two questions, or opponent power vectors, designed to achieve this are:

Question 2: "What is the *potential* for achieving the purpose?"

Question 3: "What are the *realities* we must face if we are to harness this potential."

The tension between *potential* and *realities* provides the energy that drives the field. To be effective invoking the appreciative field we need to exclude as much as possible the exercise of powers that pull us to lower dimensions of consciousness. (Using our light analogy this is the point at which the white light of purpose is separated into its yellow and blue complements.) In practice we do this by minimizing opportunities for influence and control; we limit the use of the thinking and feeling capacities that characterize influence power and the need for action and reflection that characterize control power. There are many ways that help achieve this:

1   **Choice of Location**: for example, in a workshop on National Creativity in Norway we chose a modern art museum as the venue. Taking advantage of the venue, participants were able to point out a sculpture that epitomized three-dimensional organization, another showed the essential creative dynamic of the four-dimensional influence phase, the ultimate creative centering of male and female forces—a statue of a man and woman making love. A third sculpture provided an excellent illustration of the appreciative fifth dimension—a man and a dog transcending the physical limits of a gate by just passing through the wooden material.
2   **Random Grouping**: organize sub-groups in ways that minimize social or business influences. For example, ask people to call off in sequence numbers equivalent to the number of groups. So all those who called out "one" go to group one, and so on.
3   **Constraining Dialogue**: participants give their views on potential for achieving the purpose and for the realities that have to be faced in achieving that potential, but other participants receive this information in silence, which reduces their opportunity for influencing or controlling.
4   **Using Appreciative Methodologies**: art to capture the wholeness of participants' discoveries is a favorite. Others are sculpture, stories, games, anything that will stimulate imagination and help participants broaden the set of possibilities they generate and try to connect with.

In order to set up the appropriate conditions we have to use all three means: (a), (i), and (c). To accomplish this we allocate a phase to each means. For the Appreciative dimension the three phases are illustrated in Figure 8.1. For each phase we also have a mini (a), (i), and (c) in the design of the process. Individuals must complete the task on their own (c) then join a small group to work on the phase (i) and then present their results to the whole group (a). The tendency in most group-planning efforts is to skip or undervalue the first step—individual work. We find that all three should be given equal weight.

(A-a) Discovery

Discovery is the prime function at the appreciative level. It is designed to help participants transcend the limits of current frames, to be open to new sets of possibilities. As each participant presents their view of potential and the realities to be faced the others receive the comments in silence. The openness of feedforward (A) and feedback (a) is maintained by not allowing opportunity for influence or control.

(A-i) Diplomacy

Diplomacy is the gentlest form of influence. It serves discovery by setting up conditions where very different and possibly dangerous ideas that emerge from the A-a process can be tested safely and be given enough space to be heard. This gentle influence enables the diplomat to infer likely effects and outcomes as he uses his charm to tease out and test new ideas, new possibilities.

(A-c) Visioning

Visioning serves the discovery process by giving its results a name, an image, some form of meaning, direction, or boundary. The visioning

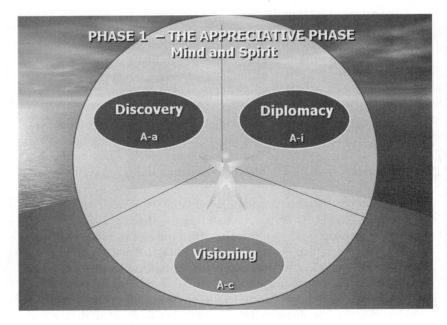

Figure 8.1 Appreciating the whole

Decimated Thai Village

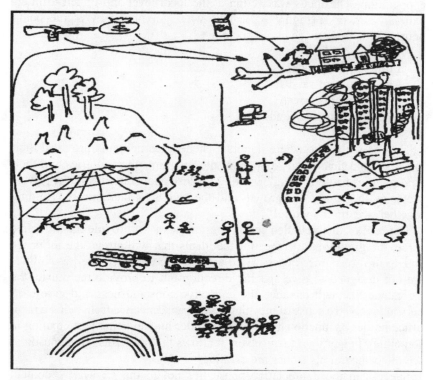

New Development Paradigm Workshop
Appreciative Phase – Realities

Figure 8.2 Thai village decimation

process presents an artistic set of possibilities rather than a definitive vision. Its task is to attract like minds rather than give a specific direction. In practice, asking people to draw their image of the ideal helps this process of visioning.

Two such images from "The New Development Paradigm" workshop are attached below. For the realities exercise a Thai drew a powerful illustration depicting the decimation of village life in his country, showing an empty hut surrounded by a denuded forest, a river carrying nothing but dead fish, and inhabitants migrating to a polluted, traffic-clogged city.

For the potential exercise one group dreamt of creating an on-going democratic process, where people would participate and work together to achieve astonishing results where all the creative energies of the grass roots, the institutions at local and central levels in the countries would work in cooperation. The focus was action at the local level and linked to international networks (Figure 8.3). This was symbolized by a tree being nourished with water as in the poem:

> Little drops of water . . .
> Little grains of sand . . .
> Make a mighty ocean . . .
> And the beauteous land.

They saw a future where donors "listened, learned, and provided their expertise and finances in support of the programs the countries and their communities had prepared," working in close cooperation with the private sector as the engine for growth and the NGOs as facilitators. "Holding together, we are the world!"

The role of this bounded set of possibilities is to provide the attractive force, the gravity and trigger for the ideals that will attract the influence and control resources necessary to achieve the purpose. The possibilities are not designed to give specific direction but to provide the music, the resonance that will enhance the collective consciousness and give each person involved a sense of meaning, even transcendence from being a mere office holder or functionary to being a fuller human being participating in something bigger than themselves. It allows the proverbial stonemason to see the cathedral his stones are creating.

Success in the appreciative phase lies not in the *knowledge* content created by the responses to these questions but in the *wisdom* involved in creating and resonating with the field of relationships that is created by the process of answering the questions.

Leadership role: the role of the leader in facilitating the three phases of appreciation provides another example of opponent processing. The leader's process goes counter to that of the participants. In the appreciative phase (A) the leader uses control (C). In order to facilitate the (A-a) process of discovery she operates in the (C-c) mode. What she is controlling is the boundaries that ensure the space within them is appreciative. She uses her control to set up the boundaries and then to ensure that people stay within that space. For example, she insists on some form of random group participation and enforces the rules limiting the amount of influence and control by the participant. For the (A-i) part of the process she operates in (C-i) coaching the group in ways to maximize their appreciative experience and keeping them safe from undue attempts at influence or control. At the end of the appreciative process in (A-c) she adopts a (C-a) role still controlling the process but appreciating the result. The control provided by the leader is protective. During the appreciative process the participants are very vulnerable, they are revealing themselves at the deepest personal level of spirit and some of their revelations can have far-reaching and threatening consequences for themselves, others, and their world as we saw in the World Bank case in Chapter 3.

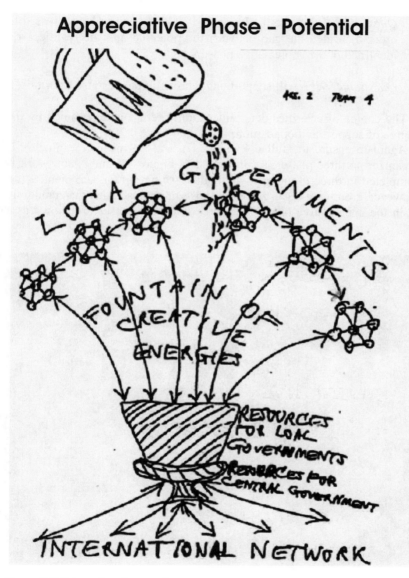

Figure 8.3 International network

Orchestrating the Dance of Influence

The purpose of the influence phase is to reduce the holistic image of the whole to more manageable parts and to harmonize the power field of the multiple stakeholders affected by these parts.

The two oppositional questions or power vectors that invoke the influence field are:

> *Question 3*: What are the key priorities that need to be addressed in order to bridge the gap between the potential and the realities you identified in the appreciative phase?

> *Question 4*: Who will support and who will oppose those priorities?

The choice of priorities determines and in return is determined by the degree of support and opposition.

Again to ensure the full use of (a), (i), and (c) means the process is organized in three phases, as illustrated in Figure 8.4 and again, work is completed in three groupings—individual (c), group (i), and plenary (c). However, groups are organized on the basis of interest rather than randomly as in the appreciative phase. The three influence phases are shown as a

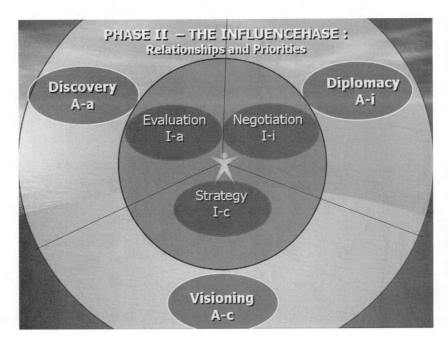

Figure 8.4 Functions of influence

reduction of appreciative space not separated from it but operating within it and conditioned by it. Successful influence depends on successful appreciation, which prevents many problems arising in the influence field. For example, the creation of trust makes the oppositional nature of the influence phase much more manageable.

(I-a) Evaluation

In presenting the essence of this phase as purpose at the value level, we often heighten the central importance of value and value multiplication by hyphenating the word as follows. E-VALUE-ATION, in other words the phase is about drawing value out of the process. The (I-a) function is designed to ensure that as many relevant values as possible are brought into the process. This includes not only human values but intellectual, social, technical, and economic values. The (I-a) phase is responsible for producing this extensiveness.

In practice we accomplish this extensiveness by extending the pool of people normally involved in such strategic organizing efforts. We encourage participation based on interest rather than responsibility. If we are working with a large enough group we often use a version of Harrison Owen's *Open Space* (1997).

Participants self-select into groups based on the priorities that they believe are most important for bridging the gap between potential and realities. We stress that they can form and join any group they are interested in. They don't have to be qualified or have responsibilities in that area. We dramatize the use of influence by asking each individual as soon as she or he has decided on a key priority area to announce it and start recruiting people for their group. Following Owen we make a market place, a model of the influence process, in which people trade their ideas, and mix and match them to form "priority" teams. By using this interest-based approach we increase the number of ideas, the number of relationships engaged, and the number and quality of options considered.

(I-i) Negotiation

Just as (A-a) *discovery* is the key appreciative process, so I-i *negotiation* is the key influence process. It is not only the central function of the influence cycle it becomes the central function, the heart, of the whole organizing process. Not only are the (I-a) and (I-c) the functions of *evaluation* and *strategy* in service of (I-i,), but the whole of the appreciative and the whole of the control level service this central point of the organizing process. Influence is amplified as each stakeholder engages other stakeholders in a process of influence that spirals both upward and outwards towards greater appreciation of each other's worlds as well as downward and inward to negotiate for the resources needed for successful implementation in their respective control phases.

The (I-i) process is the dance that brings together the whole appreciated world, represented by the spirals in Figures 7.6 through 7.8 in the last chapter and also on Plate 8. It is the dance of the ultimate feminine and the ultimate masculine forces offering the possibilities for further engagement. It is both an affirmation of life-giving forces and an opportunity to recreate life (purpose) itself. Its rhythms can shift from the romance of a waltz to the staccato challenge of the flamenco, from a dance of love to the drums of war. Imagine our surprise, then, when we discovered that this feminine/masculine imagery was not only a metaphoric help in capturing the spirit of the influence phase, but also that its masculine and feminine imagery proved to be literally true.

During the influence phase of a workshop in Bath, Maine—designed to cope with the effect of the decline of shipbuilding due to the end of the Cold War—we noticed that in the (I-i) phase heated discussions were being carried out almost exclusively by male–female pairs. They were not flirting but the issues, which were whole community issues, organized themselves into the opposition of appreciation and control. That might have been an amusing story good for making a point except that this has happened many times since. It happens unconsciously, and physically demonstrates the existence of the "implicate order" of the complementary aggregate fields. The more broad and intense the issues the clearer such fields manifest themselves. During the "New Development Paradigm" workshop attended by ten different countries the film crew came up to us excited that they had captured a wonderful "dance of influence" between two people—they happened to be an African man and woman from two different African countries. We asked the crew to look around. There for all to see were animated conversations almost exclusively between males and females. Again, this is another manifestation of the unconscious flow of the appreciative and control oppositions in every issue that become manifest in physical and social and mental form as male and female, control and appreciative perspectives.

(I-c) Strategy

The (I-c) process consists of discovering the commonalties and differences in all of the priority maps generated. In workshops this process is carried out after each interest or priority team has presented its results. Participants also discover that no matter where they started with their ideas for priorities, as they map out related priorities, they discover similar patterns of relationship to other groups. It is the patterns of relationship that provide a constancy of perspective that makes collaborative effort possible. It removes the noise left over from the appreciative phase and it harmonizes the flow of the aggregated field. We have seen in Chapter 7 how nature uses this same process to provide color constancy in our visual system.

I personally became aware of this noise reduction, stabilizing function of the influence phase when reflecting on the results of our programs. I had observed many teams operating at different levels of effectiveness and with different degrees of commitment to their tasks. Yet in no circumstance had anyone ever complained about the results of programs by going back to this strategic part of the process and pointing out the shortcomings of one of the teams in order to challenge the results. It was then I realized that something more than rational information processing was going on in this phase. Its function is one of harmonizing and stabilizing the results of many interactive purpose operating in different cycles. People can sense the strength of the emerging flows as they begin to coalesce into a single cycle and can see how they relate to those flows. They still feel part of the flow even when they have major differences with their direction.

Leadership Role

The role of leader or facilitator in the influence phase is also one of influence but the order of the phase is the reverse of that of the participants. In the (I-a) evaluation phase the facilitator carries out an (I-c) role. He allows participants to choose their own groups of interest but still specifies exactly how the exercise is to be accomplished. In the (I-i) phase, the plenary discussion between groups, both he and the participants adopt (I-i) roles. His job is to facilitate debate and negotiation. If he senses, for example, that teams are not really debating or fully engaging opposing viewpoints he may ask them to reverse their assumptions and see what other options and consequences emerge. Group techniques such as the *fishbowl* from organization development can be used. A representative from each interest group sits in a circle with one empty seat. They debate with each other the options they chose. Any member from the audience can come into the *fishbowl* and to bring or debate one issue and then leave the seat for someone else.

The influence phase closes with a set of options that seem to gain the most positive valuation and the least negative consequences. But they do not become the fixed elements of a strategic plan. They are the options that are considered by those with the responsibility for action in the next control phase. The leader's role is (I-a). She influences participants to stay open and not move to premature control. The unconscious emotions evoked by difference of priorities that have their roots in different values must allow the aggregate field to uncover the consequences that actors both fear and hope for. As the groups at this stage are interest groups not responsibility groups they cannot be allowed to make decisions in areas for which they have no responsibility, this is exactly why we organize them this way. It is only those responsible in the control phase that, consulting their conscious and unconscious purposes, can actually make decisions.

The product we ask participants to produce is a map showing priorities and stakeholders' support and opposition for each priority area, because the aim is to dramatize the *relationship* aspect of influence; whereas in the appreciative phase the aim is to dramatize *imagination*. A typical chart from the same "New Paradigm" workshop is reproduced below. Within each of the groups, once formed, the members practice appreciation by listening first to everyone's ideas without comments, and then they enter into a discussion and debate over the priorities and likely support and opposition they will receive.

Each of these priorities is then examined for stakeholders and stakeholder effects. The generation of positive and negative consequences of selected priorities is the key part of the exercise (Figure 8.5). The process encourages the development of other options to reduce negatives and increase positives thereby increasing the value of the options selected. There is no attempt to come to closure in the choice of a single option. The product is a map or set of maps that show the priorities and their combination of positives and negative consequences.

It is difficult to convey the energy that such processes generate. In the few cases where the process does not produce a wide variety of highly

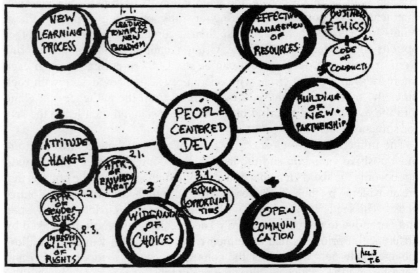

Figure 8.5 Priority maps

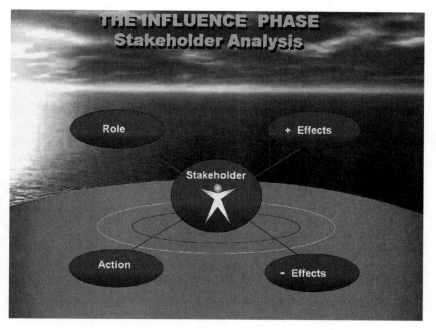

Figure 8.6 Stakeholder analysis

valued options the leaders or facilitators directly challenge participants to generate more telling options. One method is to have groups reverse their assumptions and follow through the resulting options generated.

The success of the influence phase can be judged by how much participants are able to say what they really think and feel. This expression of thoughts and feeling brings into the process real felt power from the aggregate field rather than the political correctness of the consciously controlled field. This is why control *solutions* cannot be the outcome of this phase, e.g. a strategic plan that determines or specifies action in the control phase. People would act too defensively or too aggressively to defend a particular *solution*. This production of a specific solution is not the goal of the influence phase. What we are looking for here are options where the "in-flow" of energy becomes harmonized, the places that reflect consistent patterns of power oppositions that are subject to *re-solution* rather than *solution*, which is left to the domain of control phase.

The individual, the organizational and the global transformations we address as the theme of this book are born in this space. It is this space that we ask actors and stakeholders to accept as their new home, their new center of activity. This is the space to explore the elemental opposition of appreciative and control forces of attraction and repulsion. This is the space from which we learn equally to fly in the air, swim in the water, and walk on the earth.

The Control Phase: Action as Feedback

When the control phase is carried out in a workshop setting a new grouping of participants is required. Whereas the appreciative phase groups people at random and the influence phase groups people by interest, the control phase forms groups by area of responsibility. If the operational groups are large enough the process feels as though it is beginning the process all over again. However, this time it is in a much more bounded area.

The two questions the responsibility groups have to answer are:

> *Question 6*: What do we have to control, influence, and appreciate in order to contribute to our part to the purpose?

> *Question 7*: If all of us meet these commitments will it achieve the purpose?

The tension between these two vectors lies in the opponency of action and reflection. Again we ensure equal use of all three (a), (i), and (c) means to create and resolve this tension by allocating a phase to each.

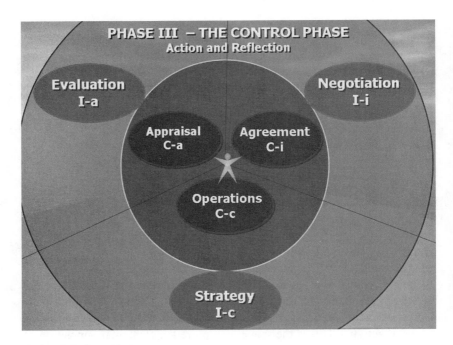

Figure 8.7 Control phase

(C-a) Appraisal, Reflection

The participants are divided into groups that have actual responsibility for implementation of operations. Their task is to appraise the information that has emerged from the previous phase, summarized as strategic priorities and stakeholder effects, as they impact the realities of current operations. Often the organization has a monitoring, appraisal, or evaluation system that provides useful information for this purpose.

When this process is not part of a workshop in which participants have participated in all phases, this control process is carried out by the operational level of staff. From their perspective the whole organizing process is just beginning. They would be carrying out exactly the same steps as the appreciative-centered phase described above. However, their scope or field of appreciation is more limited:

1   the controlled entity is now an operational unit rather than a whole company;
2   the potential is very much conditioned by the strategic priorities and stakeholder relationships developed in the influence-centered phase;
3   the realities are those derived from their appraisal of the current state of operations;
4   the stakeholders are external to the unit but most will be internal to the organization.

(C-i) Working Agreements

Whether in a workshop or at the operational level of an organizational process the participants negotiate working agreements not only within their team but also with any external stakeholders' support—or opposition—they have to minimize.

(C-c) Operations, Action

Finally, they detail the steps of implementation in some form of action plan. In simplest form such action plans specify:

1   what the operational unit can control without input or support from any other stakeholders;
2   what they can influence, i.e. what support they need from other stakeholders;
3   what they want others to appreciate about their situation.

Summary: Back to the Center

In a workshop setting these lines of action are carried back to the whole group as part of the final exercise of reflection. This is a final illustration of the centering of the process in (I-i). The plenary presentations represent the appreciative whole, each task group is a source of influence on other groups, but is also a source of control of its own operations. All meet to exercise their influence on the whole and on the individual parts, and in turn to be influenced by them. The goal is to use the full spectrum of influence both upwards to create new appreciations and downwards to create better-informed control. In practice the process generally unfolds as follows:

1   each unit presents its action plan;
2   the group as a whole reflects on how well implementation of all the units' operational plans will advance the purposes of the whole;
3   task forces are set up to work on the areas of joint influence;
4   the areas requiring appreciation are discussed and converted to action plans if necessary.

At this stage of the process each control entity now has full appreciation of both the dreams of the whole and the operational realities from each individual unit. It is this (I-i) process that then becomes the core of an ongoing strategic organizing process and the center for transforming the organization.

The AIC process is designed so that only the actor, the operational group, organization, or institution that is responsible can exercise control. In simple terms this understanding incorporates the principle derived from the Trinidad story in Chapter 1:

> We must organize so that we don't have to tell people what to do.

However, this principle can only be truly applied if control is seen within a context that progresses from appreciation to influence and then control. For example, a new employee has to be told what to do because he doesn't yet appreciate the situation, nor has he built up the influence relationships to understand the consequence of his choices. Similarly, in crises when we see someone unaware of an approaching danger we tell them as forcefully as we can to get out of the way. There is no time for explanation or discussion, i.e. no time for appreciation or influence.

It is this central point of the whole organizing process (I-i) in which all three system levels, the large (A), (I), and (C), policy, strategy, and operations come together to engage in a process of discovery, negotiation, and improvement of operations that is the heart of the strategic organizing process. This feedforward from all three levels engages the (a), (i), (c) feedback from the operational levels to negotiate the next round of the process to enlarge the scope of appreciation and to make operations more effective.

After this (I-i) review operational managers have all the feedback information that it is possible to obtain from both their internal and external stakeholders and they must commit to action. It is then that they decide, based on both their conscious and unconscious purpose, what they must do. It is never certain that the control actor will make a theoretically "right decision."

What matters for the process is that it draws on all the power available, both conscious and unconscious. Once we have set up the conditions for each actor to appreciate the whole to understand the complex process of choosing and plotting the interaction between priorities, we have to trust that the actors are the best people to make the decision about what they and their unit can best contribute to the common purpose. They must also shoulder that responsibility. Each operational actor is then asserting their large (C), (I), and (A) onto the situation given the (a), (i), and (c) information and feedback they have received. Not all their decisions will have the full support of other stakeholders but all stakeholders will understand and have the information to be able to adjust their own operations to accommodate the effects of the decisions made by their colleagues. As we discovered in the management planning process developed in the Canadian National Silicates program described in Chapter 1, the process is only partially participative. At the critical control stage it relies on an individual to make the final choice. Participants take part in the appreciative and influence phase but at the end of the control phase it is the person with responsibility that makes the decision. The possibility for group think is minimized.

The person with responsibility needs to use all their power to be effective. Much of that power is unconscious, but as we have seen we have access to this knowledge through intuition and our sixth sense. The decision-maker must be allowed to bring this knowledge into the situation. After the actors have been fully informed through appreciation, and their values transformed through the exercise of influence they must decide their course of action even though they may be unable to fully explain it. They must still, however, be held accountable for the results.

Part III

Implications for Ourselves, Our Organizations, and the World

Part I set out to fill in some of the gaps in our understanding of power and purpose and their relationship to organization theory and practice, and called for a more comprehensive approach. As there are many partial theories I decided to follow the learning—famously illustrated by Einstein—that the solution to problems doesn't lie at the level at which they are presented but beyond. We looked, then, beyond the field of organization to the highest level possible for sources of insight, knowledge, and experience about purpose and power. Chapters 2, 3, and 4 culled the fields of religion, science, and philosophy for fundamental insights. We hoped to gain a better perspective on which to build a more holistic view of purpose and its relationship to power.

Part II took the insights gained from this research and combined them with the results of our several decades of action research to spell out the current state of our understanding of a new philosophy, theory model, and process of organization, based on purpose as the source of power. In the process I found that the AIC pattern of power relationships was so ubiquitous that it must have some common origin. I found correlative matches of the process in the design of our own brains. In particular I found an analogue of the five+ dimensional processes built on a base of threeness in our visual and color perception processes—the most studied parts of our brains. It is more than likely that this pattern, as Pribram suggests, exists in our whole or holonomic brain.

Chapter 8 took this new level of understanding and incorporated it into a holonomic organizing process that represents our best understanding of what it takes to lead organizations to achieve higher levels of purpose, using less time and resources than more traditional control-centered approaches while making participation in the process more constructive and fulfilling for all stakeholders

Part III uses our understanding of the philosophy, theory model, and our experience with the process to draw out implications that might stimulate the reader to extend, deepen, and apply both the ideas and the practice. What would happen if we obeyed the Humpty Dumpty law and never separated the parts, ourselves, and others, from the whole? What is the potential if at every level of purpose we added the influence and appreciative levels? What would happen if we treated the appreciative influence and control fields equally? What are the realities we would have to face in order to achieve that potential? To explore these questions we use the logic of the philosophy, model, and process developed in Part II.

Chapter 9 invites the readers into a virtual exercise to experience the creation of the three AIC fields around their own purposes. It shows how we can gain insight into our pattern of purposes and power though a process of "power mapping." The chapter uses the case of Bill Graham, the mayor of a small town in Southern Indiana to illustrate this process. It reveals his inner power pattern and shows how it has been the creative power in the transformation he has made in himself, his organization in Scottsburg, and in his world. The chapter shows how you as a reader, can generate a brief version of your own power map. You will be able to see the particular pattern that your creative power takes and that illustrates the path you are taking in transforming yourself, your organization, and your world.

In **Chapter 10** we take you into the world of organization to illustrate how to both think of and make the best use of your creative power. We view organization as the middle ground of relationships that links our mental and spiritual world with outcomes we seek in the material world. At this level we see the central task of organization as harmonizing the different values of internal and external stakeholders

Chapter 11 moves to the level of our world and considers humanity as the actor. It explores what we can do to affect our world by creating conditions for the success of our organizations and ourselves. We deal with the most difficult problem of any whole: how do we create a mindset in the whole that can suspend judgment, the wish to influence and control based on preconceived notions so that we can access new levels of imagination, new possibilities and creativity? Even when we succeed in this how can we protect the innovators and keep their "wild" ideas floating long enough for them to seek supportive connections? How can we make mindset strategies to deal with the paradox of being open yet reducing the infinite possibility of the whole to a manageable set that still represents the whole? We will, in essence be taking an appreciative-centered approach to the organization of our own minds as part of the collective human mind. What are the implications for both us and our institutions as we strive to incorporate a conscious concept of the impact of whole into our collective mindset?

9 Implications for Ourselves

After assembling the materials for this chapter I was concerned that something of the spirit of the message would be lost if they were presented as description. To sense the resonance of the appreciative field requires an experience with some whole, to grasp the dynamics of influence requires an engagement with others, that is why stakeholder analysis is such an inadequate means for understanding stakeholders, only with engagement can we create the influence, the harmonization of multiple "in-flows" that provide the basis for collaborative action. I was struggling with this issue when I met a friend I had not seen in more than 5 years, Jessica Lipnack, who's husband's work on *Holonomy* some 20 years earlier (Stamps 1980) had had a great impact on my own work, as mentioned in Chapter 3. Being an excellent writer and an enthusiastic advocate she leveraged the public impact of their joint work (see, for example, Lipnack and Stamps 2000). In this sense it was a very serendipitous meeting.

Jessica was trying to publish her first fictional work that had a great deal of deep personal history at its origin. I shared with her the basic story of AIC, which also had deep personal origins. We looked at the alternative ways that our work was complementary and different and some of the difficulties we were experiencing, including the writing of this chapter. Using her writing acumen she challenged me to focus on the reader and on the essence of the message. In response to her challenge I found myself saying:

> "The book is about our personal transformation enabling organizational transformation and the transformation of our world. The center of that transformation is the influence phase, the ever present now. The moment we are in now is the sum of everything that has past and has the potential to influence everything we do in the future. So organizing is really about creating the conditions for us to take full advantage of that potential in the present."

As we were about to conclude the meeting I realized I had just lived the answer to my question. In 45 minutes as two very different people, we had just met, shared our worlds, and then focused on some areas of common interest in our work. We supported and challenged each other. We were going away more energized to carry on our work. We had created the conditions for our meeting to leave us more "power-full" than before.

The challenge, then, is to use the materials for this chapter to create for the both of us such an experience. So, come with me on an imaginary journey and let us create those conditions. We will draw on several decades of experience of workshops and classes that have attempted to create such transformational experiences. As I haven't attempted this before in writing, hopefully, this will contribute to our joint potential for transforming ourselves, our organizations and our world and will leave us both feeling more *power-full*.

Phase 1: Discovering Our World

1   Imagine we are part of a group that has come together to learn about and practice transformation using an AIC approach.
2   We form a circle around the room facing outwards. You are close to the people on either side of you but you cannot see them. You are on your own facing outward to your world.
3   You are about to take a trip to anywhere in that world you want to, at any time period—past, present, or future—and you can go with anyone you want, from the past, present, or future.
4   You are free to go to as many places and times and change the people you are with as often as you like. Note what it is you see and do and how you feel.
5   When we get to the end I will let you know we are at the end and you will have a few moments to say your farewells and bring yourself back to our world.
6   Show us that you have returned by turning around and facing the group.
7   Now close your eyes and spend about 10 minutes on this journey.

Phase 2: Telling the Story

When you have finished, imagine yourself turning around to face the other people in the room. I ask each of you to share the highlights of your trip. Each listens but does not comment on what they hear. The following are typical accounts that you might hear before you present yours:

> *Sarah*: I went to multiple places, but travelled with the same person, my husband. I first went and visited him where he is living, Spokane, WA, then we traveled to where I am from, Foster, RI, where I saw my friends and family.

I pictured the people that I love, recalled the things we have done, and the things that I dream about doing with them. Since I am fresh out of college, a lot of those faces were the people that I had lived with for the past two years. They were the first girl friends that I had that truly stuck.

With my family I thought of the recent time that I spent with them in the summer and the plans that I have to visit them more often than I did when I was across the continent.

My husband and I travelled to different countries, I don't know what many of them are truly like, but we have both wanted to go to Japan, I have been to Italy (and would like to go with him) and other countries in Europe, specifically Ireland or England. I spent a lot of time in Ireland in my mind, viewing the lush green and the stark gray cliffs. Ireland reminds me of peace and my foster home.

By the time the signal was given, I had gone to everywhere I wanted to go and saw everyone I wanted to see. So I fixed myself in Ireland and concentrated on the green colors that I have seen in movies and imagined what it would be like to stand in the wind with an Irish-wool sweater and a warm mug of tea, looking out at the ocean and hearing the crashing of the waves

Mike: My journey led me through our global village . . . from Europe, to Africa and Asia, from Australia to South and North America. I saw the rich tapestry of race, culture, and sovereign nations. Simultaneously, I was struck by the paradox that connected all persons in the human tapestry. A desire for peace was the common thread among all people . . . peace with self, with others and among nations. Innocent children cried for peace in violent areas of the world. Mothers prayed for peace within their families. Fathers hoped for the day when peace will reign in the hearts of civic leaders and among communities. Throughout the world there was a hope for peace.

Lauren: My name is Lauren. I travelled extensively to Russia, Spain, Bangladesh, Australia, Taiwan, and Brazil, but everywhere I went, I saw the same thing: people moving together through the universal motions of life. It was as if I had the eye of an omniscient being who could strip away the barriers of discovery, and who could see behind walls, under housetops, and through doors. I could see people moving in the early light out of bed, looking at their faces in mirrors. The laughter of the thief rang like the laughter of an innocent child; the tears of hatred felt as wet as tears of joy. Then, slowly, I began to feel a kind of contentment, mixed with appreciation and awe at the universality of the human condition, from old to young, north to south, rich to poor, evil to saintly. It was a sense of Oneness, Inclusiveness, Totalness, Completeness—peace and freedom—children, fighting and fretting, and laughing until they cried. I could see elderly kings and beggars alike struggling to stand up; I could see people who hated each other having the same dreams at night. Oddly enough, I could see our president, target of controversy and ridicule, whistling in the shower. I saw ugly things—thieves breaking into houses, children bullying other children, hate crimes against the persecuted. I saw beautiful things—the birth of a child, a sailor enjoying a sunset, people coming to terms with grief, an old woman laughing with a child.

Now imagine the others in the room and recount the highlights of your journey to them, what you saw, what you did and what you felt. Take a piece of paper and record your highlights now.

Phase 3: Committing to Action

When everybody has finished their stories I ask you all to return to your seats and I provide you with a large sheet of flip-chart paper:

On this sheet draw three circles that represent three spaces. The outer circle represents the world you went out into in the first part of the exercise. In that space record some bullet points of what you would like to see happen in that world. There aren't any good or bad answers; anything at all that comes to your mind is OK.

In the second circle list the people who would support the things you would like to see happen and those who would oppose them. In the last inner circle write what you would like to do about all you have written in the next year.

When everybody has finished I ask you to present your chart in the following way:

1   Think of the three parts of the exercise. In each you were operating in a very different kind of space. In the first you were on your own exploring the whole of the world with your imagination. In the second, when you turned around, you were in this circle facing other people who you could now see and interact with through your stories. In the third you went back to your seats and on your own you completed the task on the flip chart.
2   When you report out I would like you to tell us which of the three circles you preferred to be in and why.
3   I would then like you to begin with the center circle and tell us what it is you would like to do in the next year, and then explain with reference to what you wrote in the other two circles.

You, the reader, should now imagine that you are at your seat in the room with others and complete your chart before reading on.

Some typical results are presented below.

> *Sarah (1-a)*: I, like most other people, would love to see a harmonious world. International peace, global understanding, and widespread environmentalism are my essentials. In many ways, I see globalization as the pathway to this future, so it is something that I would like to see occur. In reality, I do not only see this as something I would "like" to see happen, but something that I find to be necessary for the continuation of the homo branch of the evolutionary tree. I don't think anyone wants to be remembered like the Neanderthals are remembered.
>
> The people who would react negatively or positively often overlap in my mind. There are similar groups on each side. My father would be one of those standing in the way of my perfect vision of the future, along with the many other things that he supports like the Republicans and the administration headed by George Bush. There are probably other "conservative" countries, groups, or people that would oppose or react negatively. Conversely, Democrats and many of my friends and

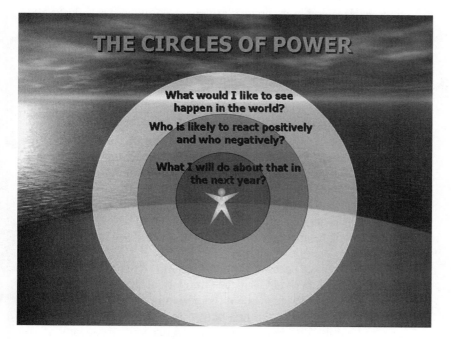

Figure 9.1 The three circles of power

family would react positively to these types of change. Also, some of the same "conservative" countries, groups, or people may react positively! Many governments would be in favor of these changes; the European Union is a very strong example of this. Religious groups could react both positively and negatively.

The best thing that I could do was to adjust my living habits and set an example of what I would like to see in the world within a year. Gandhi and I seem to be on the same page! So, I could set an example by eating healthier, taking better care of myself, working at a non-profit organization and to discuss things with people and not shying away from an intense conversation.

Mike (A-i): It is clear I lean toward the realm of possibilities. A wise mentor observed some years ago, "Mike, where others see only problems you see possibilities." True. I feel most comfortable at the place where possibilities are conceived. This exercise confirmed the way I'm hard wired . . . an A-i orientation.

For the past 20 years it's been my honor to serve in the U.S. military. Two weeks ago my family and I returned to the States after 4 years in Okinawa, Japan. Last night my 15-year-old son changed the TV channel to the local news. He was shocked to hear about four murders in DC. He noted, "Dad, during our four years in Okinawa there were no violent crimes." Deployed to Iraq, I witnessed the devastation of ethnic hatreds and interpersonal violence. Hatred and self-destruction do not have to be our collective destiny. Over the next year my life will echo the words of the song "let peace begin with me." As peace exudes outward, my hope is to see new life breathed into a couple of contentious relationships with family members. I also plan to begin to participate in the process of peace building among nations . . . specifically the war-torn regions of Iraq, Afghanistan, and growing conflict between the U.S and Iran.

Those who support peace building recognize our global interdependence. They will recognize it is not only a matter of survival but about the individual pursuit to discover meaning and purpose in life. Those who support peace building will seek to overcome biases and hatred. Those who oppose peace building will resist the change it brings in order to maintain the status quo. They will choose the comfort of familiar prejudice and hatred over a new life of peaceful existence.

The goal is to see peace as the dominant thread in our human tapestry . . . peace within individuals, peace in relationships, and peace among nations. My outer circle is about the possibility of PEACE.

Lauren (A-a): I liked the first part of the exercise best. I found my story to be quite different from some of your journeys. Many of you visited exotic places, traveled back in time, and met famous people. You visited deceased loved ones, tasted new foods, and smelled new things. In my journey I did not so much go out into the world, but I let the world come and show itself to me.

Although we had the unique opportunity in our appreciative journeys to be anything we wanted to be and to go anywhere we wanted to go, I found that almost as soon as my journey began, I lost myself. I don't mean that I didn't know where I was, but rather that there was no meaningful "I" anymore; the concept of self became so unimportant to me that it ceased to exist. I also realized partway through my journey that time and place didn't seem to matter very much either. It was as if I had the eye of an omniscient being who could strip away the barriers of discovery, and who could see behind walls, under housetops, and through doors.

But the ugly and beautiful appeared the same to my omniscient eyes; trying to fit infinite ideas into the bounded meanings of words left me nearly speechless. I could describe what I saw as individual and finite observations, but how could I communicate the impact of sensing all of these actions when time and space are collapsed?

The exercise, which takes about 45 minutes to an hour, is a fractal summary of the whole AIC philosophy, model, and process, all the major elements of the concepts and practice are included even if not immediately visible.

1   The outer circle, when you turned outwards, represents the appreciative field, your relationship to the whole. You were in a circle of the whole yet you were on your own as an individual part of that whole. You faced the same world as the others yet you had a different angle, a different attitude, than any of the others. You had no limits of resources, space, or time in making your journey and no one could influence or control what you did or how you went about it. Only your imagination and your inner resources limited you.

Those who prefer this space like its openness, its freedom, the wonder and awe at all that we can do and see in so short a time: on a whim we can move from America to Africa, Europe or Asia. We use words like idealistic, miracle, wonder, and awesome to describe the space. It is the space of openness, of possibilities, and ideals, it is both awesome and awful. It is our appreciative circle, our relationship to everything that affects our purpose but which is outside our area of control or influence. You felt the timelessness, the selflessness, the beyond, the multi-dimensionality of the appreciative world.

2   The second circle in which you turned around and faced your colleagues represents our relationship to other people, parts of the whole, the influence circle. Your space is now limited to the circle of colleagues and there is a time cycle. Someone must speak first and someone last. What one person says has some influence on what others say or don't say and how they say it. You find it a challenge to reduce the fullness and multi-dimensional nature of your experience to words.

Those who prefer this space like its collegiality. They like sharing experiences with others and feel even more energized in so doing. Others feel constrained not knowing how their colleagues might judge them. This is the space in which we have to choose which aspects of our appreciations we want to deal with. This is the space in which purpose, which was previously expressed in open, idealistic terms, sifted and reduced through our values relative to others in our space. It is the space where people who share the same ideals differ about priorities and the roles people should play in implementation. There is no escape from these differences of value; they provide the source of energy and power for this phase.

3   The third circle in which you returned to your seats and produced the flip chart was your relationship to yourself. You and you alone had the responsibility for deciding what to do based on what you appreciated, how you were influenced by the group, and the support and opposition you felt you would receive from others. Those who like this space best feel that now there is something concrete they can do, something they can get their teeth into. Those who dislike this space feel it is too constraining. There is so much to do but almost everything falls short of what we experienced in the open, ideal world of appreciation. Others feel they did not have enough time to think through how they would overcome all the opposition and build the necessary support. This world of control is the most constrained and intense space. Resources are limited to what you can control. Time is a fixed duration tied to the achievement of a specific goal.

The results of the exercise are quite profound in practice. After the initial world exploration when the first people share there is a little nervousness and some protective joking, but gradually the sharing begins to flow more easily and goes deeper, with people feeling freer to express what they experienced and felt. Freed from the responsibility of commenting the quality of listening changes as people are able to resonate with the music that is emerging.

It is the group's first conscious experience of appreciative power. Even though we experienced all three powers, this exercise is appreciative-centered. Our purpose is to create the appreciative field for this whole, the group. By convention, as we have seen in previous chapters, we designate an appreciative-centered orientation with a big (A) and then show its three parts; the means by which (A) is achieved with a small (a), (i), and (c). The three parts of this exercise are these (a), (i), and (c) parts of a big (A) phase. You choose these means based on your unconscious inner expectation of how the world reacts to you. The three parts or phases of appreciative-centeredness are:

1 (A-a): the first phase of the exercise, in which you went out in the world on a voyage of *discovery* (a generic label we gave to this process in previous chapters). The process requires you, as the actor, to be open (A), and you in turn expect the world, the reactor, the others in the environment, to also be open to you (a). Both you and the world you discover contribute to the creation of the appreciated whole.
2 (A-i): in the second phase of the exercise, as you turn around and begin to share your appreciation (A) you are aware of the others in the room and they have an influence (i) on what and how you choose to share your appreciation. This is the gentlest form of influence that comes from just being. The others did not say anything but they were there and you had some inner sense of how they might react. We call this (A-i) process *diplomacy* to express the very light appreciative form of influence.
3 (A-c): In this third phase everyone takes their appreciation of all the participants' stories (the whole) and passes them as *in-formation* through their own sense of purpose (*ideals*, *values* and *goals*) and give *form* (c) to that purpose as a statement or *visioning* of what they want to see in the world and what they want to do about it.

As well as introducing participants to the three spaces as three power fields the exercise shows them how the three-in-one property of purpose manifests as the three power fields:

1 Open, emerging, timeless, purpose; a dream, a sense of direction or a vision creates the appreciative field.
2 Relative purpose; that is, purpose as influenced by the cyclical, rhythmic, changing dynamics of support and opposition of others over time creates the field of influence.
3 Closed purpose; that which is committed to achievement within specific space and time constraints produces the controlled field.

All three purposes form a three-in-one unity. All three exist at the same time no matter which level is the center of focus; the ideal (A), the values (I), or the goals (C).

When everyone reveals their own experience of the three fields the group has an appreciation of the *potential* and *realities* of working with this group, *the whole* in this case. This appreciation is as much implicit as explicit because much of the interpretation of what people say, write, and how they present themselves is unconscious. Our appreciation of the participants' contribution goes beyond what they say. It includes an interpretation, an intuition and sixth sense about the whole person in the situation and what we feel they really meant beyond the words they used and how they presented themselves; it is this unconscious part that our small (a), (i), and (c) captures. We resonate with the part of them that is in us and they become part of us (they become part of our internalized world our "*a, i,* and *c* "). Through this resonance we create the oneness of the whole—we create or enhance the spirit of this group.

Because people are sharing something of their *essence*, their *purpose* at all three levels, they diffuse the space with their spirit. This accounts for the depth of feeling and the emotion to the point of tears that is often evoked (see Colombia story in Chapter 3). It is the resonance of the spirit of the whole with the spirit within each person that provides the essence of the experience of appreciation. It is this experience that generates respectively meaning, trust, and hope. No amount of description or analysis can substitute for this experience.

The Power Map

The exercise above gives us a way to experience how we impact our world, so its focus is on our conscious attempts to affect others and our "explicate" world. We also have a way to tap into our unconscious purpose and the pattern it produces. We can say that the previous exercise traces the blue spiral (solid spiral) of Figure 9.2 (see Plate 7). The power map we are about to discuss traces the green (dotted) spiral. The two together provide the opponent forces that govern creation and feedback of our purpose and power. It reveals how purpose and the three-in-one-fields are manifest in our "implicate" world. We can do this because AIC relationships, as we showed in Chapter 7, exist in nature and are reflected in the way our brain, visual and color systems react to our world. We can tap into this pattern by using our preference for colors. As color is a five-dimensional, holonomic phenomenon, we can use our preference for colors as a fractal pattern that represents our relationship to our whole world. To do this well requires the use of a computer to process the amount of information that has to be processed. I have included an abbreviated version in the Appendix. It is a little complex to do by hand. However, together with the example we will give below and some patience we can glimpse the origins and manifestation of our purpose and power and derive from that an image of our capacity to transform ourselves, our organization, and our world.

The personal profile we will use belongs to Bill Graham, the mayor of a small town in Scottsburg, Indiana, who is the major force behind the transformation of the town after the devastation of the rust belt era of the late 1970s when Scottsburg lost much of its manufacturing employment.

Bill Graham has achieved exceptional performance as mayor through a natural, intuitive use of principles of AIC. He illustrates perfectly our power to transform ourselves, our organizations, and our world.

I met the mayor in late 2003 at the Renaissance Hotel in Washington DC when I was helping a colleague to make a proposal for a project for Scottsburg's Technology Center. During the course of the meeting Mayor Graham gave a 10-minute resume of the history of Scottsburg and his 17 years as mayor. He focused on the ways in which he and the town's leaders went about the transformation of Scottsburg. Bill Graham, a republican in a predominantly democratic area, was re-elected for the fifth time as mayor during the writing of this chapter.

His story fascinated me by how much it mirrored the AIC process. It was so succinct and yet covered all the main points of organizing process. His story is recreated below using supportive quotes from a recent history of Scottsburg during the mayor's tenure (Scottsburg 2006).

Mayor Graham had been an entrepreneur in housing, realty, oil distribution, and banking. After spending a few years away he noted:

> The quality of life kept drawing me back to Scottsburg. I liked the fact that everyone knew my children, that I didn't have to lock my door.
>
> (Ibid.: 17)

So when he returned and won the election as mayor he was particularly concerned that the town's children were not staying in or returning to Scottsburg. The real unemployment rate was as much as 25 percent. Many people had just given up and were not counted on the official unemployed roles:

> We saw family businesses that were the wealth of the community closing their doors. Half the buildings around the square were vacant. I had no positive comment to make as I drove through downtown.
>
> (Ibid.: 18)

Mayor Graham's approach is so classic in terms of the AIC approach that we are able to organize it by just adding the names of the AIC organizing phases and sub-phases.

Implementing Appreciation

1   **Purpose**: He found that the town had lost any sense of purpose, it was dispirited and could not see beyond the negative. He gathered some community leaders around to better *appreciate* the situation. They began to look at the potential that already existed in Scottsburg.

2   **The Potential**: The mayor and his colleagues saw the transformation of Scottsburg in the same terms as we noted in the introduction to this book; an evolution of spatial relationships. He saw Scottsburg's transformation in terms of traversing ever larger spaces. Scottsburg's founding was based on the transit of the railroad. Their industrial transformation added transit brought about by the increased density of roads and the wider international reach of airports. Scottsburg was located in the space known as the "automotive alley," 90 miles south of Indianapolis, with heavily concentrated automobile and auto-related manufacturing, 30 miles north of Louisville, Kentucky, and 110 miles west of Cincinnati, Ohio. The I-65 and U.S. 31, major north–south routes were power vectors that brought potential to Scottsburg. They had international potential through access to the airports at those three cities.

The mayor saw that the next transformation would take them beyond the international potential of the space reached by road, rail, and air to that of the "information highway," the global mind. If they were suffering the consequence of globalization in low wages and out-sourcing, they could tap that same global potential through the Internet. His team also saw the huge internal potential represented by large amounts of inexpensive land and their large pool of underemployed people that could be harnessed to realize that potential. The only limit to this new global space was that of human imagination:

> We were unbeatable when you really looked at it. But if we didn't recognize it, who would?
>
> (Ibid.: 20)

3   **The Realities**: In order to become unbeatable in the new global economy they had to face some harsh realities. Not only had they lost most of their workforce but the community was not equipped to train people with the higher level skills required by new markets. They lacked the social service support and the educational resources necessary to support such a transformation. Their economic planning was disjointed and ineffective and unsuited to generating any momentum.

Implementing Influence

4   **The Priorities**: in determining their priorities they opened up to the three levels that the AIC process requires for effective organization:

a   at the center they created their own flexible leadership team;
b   this team engaged members of the whole community in contributing to the process;

c   they also made a concerted effort to go outside the boundary of Scottsburg to the state and national levels as well as other communities and external institutes:

> People seek outside help for community needs, and many compete for government grants and contracts for economic and social programs. Scottsburg's network is more fitting of a large city than that of a small town of 6,000 people. The city's leaders are extremely tuned-in to what resources are available at the state and federal levels, and the strong entrepreneurial and business base of other community leaders ensures that the network between private firms remains strong.
>
> (Ibid.: 18)

5 **Stakeholder Interests**: This emphasis is central to the whole organizing effort. It is the key difference that the mayor personally provided to the transformation and still provides. He personally engages all the stakeholders involved one by one. At every moment on the street and in meeting breaks we can see his delight in contacting and renewing contacts with people. He is modest, unassuming but vitally interested and encouraging. It is easy to see that he is very much loved and he reciprocates that love. People know that in his eyes and in his huge embrace they are equal parts of the whole. This is the seed that resonates and keeps feeding and regenerating the purpose, the power, and the progress:

> One remarkable aspect of Scottsburg's momentum building efforts has been the community's ability to leverage existing assets, such as a strong volunteer base and a high level of commitment to caring for community members, with appropriate partnership building. Where other communities may have succumbed to turfism and sector loyalty, Scottsburg was able to bring competing groups together to transcend limitations and engage in productive dialogue.
>
> (Ibid.: 21)

His power map, which we use below as our example, shows perfectly how these capacities are manifest in him.

Implementing Control

Action: A bias to action is reflected in the conviction that, in the long run, you have to do it yourself. The principle is illustrated in the town's insistence on developing its own wireless network in spite of state and national opposition from the IT industry and from government. For the mayor the issue was very simple. He had three businesses—a Chrysler dealer, a defense contractor, and a plastics company—that could not continue in Scottsburg without better broadband communication. There were no more T1 lines left for Scottsburg. Even if they could be provided they would cost each user more than $1,300 per month, almost $1,000 a month more than the service in neighboring Louisville.

The mayor called in six contractors to make proposals. Each proposed roughly the same solution. There would be an initial study costing between $50,000–60,000 and then the installation of cable connection would cost 5–6 million dollars for the town's 6,000 residents—an impossible burden. The mayor had discovered another town in Kentucky that had provided service to its citizens but the cable stopped at the perimeter and the businesses and households were connected wirelessly. The mayor and his team asked whether the whole system could be operated wirelessly and was surprised to learn that it could. He ended up linking most of the county, a much wider area than the contractors had bid for, for $385,000. However, every year he still has to battle the IT industry, the State and Federal Governments to maintain the right for his municipality to run its own service.

Reflection: The story also includes the final point of the process—constant reflection and learning. The mayor himself acknowledged on national TV that he knew very little about information technology. However, he and his team constantly asked, listened, and reflected and in the end they made their own decisions:

> Scottsburg's leaders don't think just about tomorrow—they think about five years from now, and a hundred years from now. The Mayor called this "strategic visioning," in which he takes a holistic look at a project 21 and asks how it will affect the quality of life in Scott County in the future.
>
> (Ibid.: 20)

Creating the Power Map

This portrait of the Mayor of Scottsburg and his leadership role gives the necessary background for interpreting his power map, which in turn will help you interpret your own map should you choose to do so.

The map is based on our preference for the nine colors reproduced as Plate 15. Each color is assigned a number from one to nine.

To complete the map we choose the colors in pairs, the one we like best and the one we like least. We then go on to the remaining seven colors and choose and do the same, till we have chosen all nine colors. We have the opportunity to repeat the process and make a second set of choices if we were not sure the first time around. The Appendix tells us how to record our results and obtain interpretations.

To interpret the colors we use single words to represent ideals, values, and goals. Each color has a different interpretation according to its location in five-dimensional space. That location is determined by our preference for the colors:

1 When we choose the first color pair, the one we like best and worst (cell 1 and cell 9 in the chart) we span the whole spectrum of all nine colors. In Chapter 5 we showed that light consists of five- dimensional vibrations. The reduction from white light to darkness occurs through a subtraction or reduction of colors. The reduction in light corresponds to a movement down the power spiral from five to three dimensions. That chapter also gives the rationale for the choice of the nine colors.

2 When we choose the second set of colors in cells 2 and 8 we are selecting from a reduced set of seven colors. Referring to Figure 9.2 we can imagine our choice as a power vector rotating around our center in cell 5 and downwards through the spiral from the fifth to the fourth dimension.

3 When we make our third set of choices we do so from a reduced set of only five colors. Our choices entered in cell 3 and 7 represent a power vector rotated downwards through the spiral into the third dimension. The choices we enter in cell 4 and 6 are made from only three colors. They take us into the second and first dimensions. The color left over and entered by default into cell 5 has special significance.

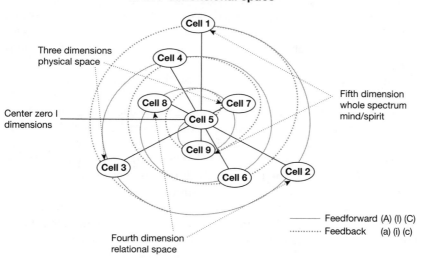

LOCATION OF COLOR CHOICES
In five-dimensional space

Figure 9.2 Color choices in five-dimensional space

It is the zero-dimensional center of the power field. Because it appears as the center in all dimensions we will interpret it first.

4   Whichever color we place in cell 5 becomes the center of our power field. This is the hole in the torus, the center-point for all dimensions. It is the point we mark in Figure 9.2 as the *origin* of the feedforward spiral and the destination of the feedback spiral of power.

How to Interpret the Power Map

Although the Power Map is a two-dimensional matrix, each row, column, and diagonal of that matrix is a vector through five-dimensional space. Each part, each cell is a fractal, a holon that has a dynamic, dimensional relationship with every other cell. The rows, columns, and diagonals of the matrix all have meaning as indicated by the lines of relationship in Figure 9.2. As these relationships are multi-dimensional they require the help of our imagination to visualize. For example, the solid blue spiral moving outwards from the center represents the feedforward of the large A, I, and C, the positive (+) power vector moving through five-dimensional space. It signifies the self, the individual or collective control entity, moving from the third dimension to the whole that affects and is affected by its purpose. The green dotted spiral moves as negative (-) power, feedback (a), (i), and (c), from the outside to the inside, from the fifth to the third dimension. The double spiral, like the double helix of DNA, is the carrier of information, the force for transformation and the creation of form in the multi-dimensional power field created by our purpose. The interaction of feedforward and feedback spirals, in all five dimensions, produces all possible power relationships of which we choose only nine to represent that whole. These points are based on A, I, and C as whole dimensions, 5.00, 4.00, and 3.00. There are thousands of fractal dimensions, their corresponding powers and colors in between these whole dimensions (see Fractal Dimensions in Chapter 7).

The two spirals create the opposing forces that require resolution in every dimension and in every phase of organizing in every cell of our matrix of power. The process of resolution can increase or decrease energy. When energy is increased it drives power upwards into a higher dimension. When energy is reduced in power it moves downwards into a lower dimension. The process functions in the same way that the application of energy moves electrons up and down the levels of an atom to produce light (Figure 6.4, p. 147). When we move upwards we *transcend* the current power modes or capacities to achieve our purpose; when we move downwards we *transform* our power modes into *forms* that define action in the controllable third dimension. To help translate the choice of colors into power relationships and into words I have summarized the three charts of ideals, values, and goals from Chapter 7, Figures 7–11, 13, and 15, as Figure 9.3. If you

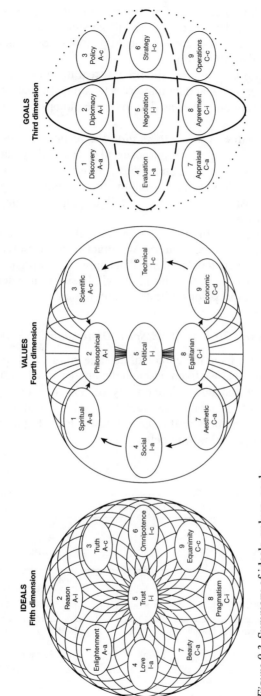

Figure 9.3 Summary of ideals, values, goals

are tracking the interpretation of your own power map as you read, it would help you to make a copy of the full version of these three charts. This information is also available in the Appendix—"Scoring Forms and Interpretation for the Power Map."

As we interpret our results we should not treat them as personality test or typing but rather as a mandala that gives us a pattern that enables us to focus on appreciating ourselves as five- or more dimensional beings.

1   The primary value is the *appreciation* we receive of the interactive multi-dimensional aspects of purpose and power as they play out in us, and between us and our organizations and our world.
2   The secondary value lies in passing the most important aspects of our life, our purposes and our "power to" accomplish them, through a holonomic process.
3   Thirdly we gain useful information from the whole process about ourselves and our power pattern. We practice on ourselves the same kind of multi-dimensional thinking that applies to our organizations and our world. This information lies in the whole experience not just in the mechanical interpretations of entries in our chart.

Interpretation of the Fifth or Mind/Spirit Dimension

In the first round we have the choice of all nine colors. Out of this whole we selected the one that we liked best and the one we liked least. This span represents the first and largest opponency of power in our appreciative world, our whole life situation, the state of our mind and spirit. If we look at Mayor Graham's choices in the sample power map, Figure 9.4, we see that he placed indigo, color 9, in cell 1.

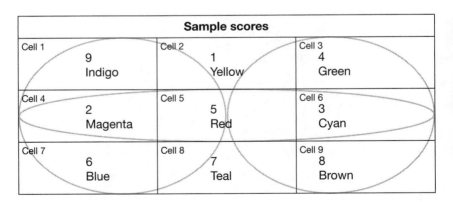

Sample scores		
Cell 1 9 Indigo	Cell 2 1 Yellow	Cell 3 4 Green
Cell 4 2 Magenta	Cell 5 5 Red	Cell 6 3 Cyan
Cell 7 6 Blue	Cell 8 7 Teal	Cell 9 8 Brown

Figure 9.4 Sample scores

The interpretation of this color from the ideals section of Figure 7.13 1 is Equanimity, the (C-c) power. This ideal represents the mayor's strong desire to create the conditions in which everyone knows what they have to do (C) and expects that everyone else will do the same (c). This desire is opposed by the reality represented by the color he placed in cell 9, brown, color 8. The color meaning extracted from the "Goals" section of Figure 9.3 is Agreement, the power relationship (C-i). The interpretation of this reaction is that the mayor unconsciously fears that in pursuing his ideal for Equanimity people will fail because they will be unable at the practical level of action (C) to come to working agreements with others (i). This opponency between the best and the least of the whole set of colors influences all other selections and their interpretation. This is the tension of the whole that lies in every part. It is our life's spiritual tension.

In the mayor's case he mediates this tension between the potential of his ideal and the reality of his unconscious fear by the color he places in cell 5, the color red, number 5 meaning *political* values. He obtains this from the "values" section of Figure 9.3. He resolves the dilemma between potential and reality through the use of *political* values, that is, he gains the *trust* of people through pursuit of his ideals at the appreciative level. He helps people to *negotiate* their differences and then, he hopes, they will be able to reach *agreements* on their own. The power in cell 5 is the zero-dimensional power that is at the center of all dimensions and its role in mediation is the center of all transformational power.

Interpretation of the Fourth or Relational Dimension

To obtain the four-dimensional, relational, or political interpretations we rotate our two-dimensional power vector clockwise through five-dimensional space and spiral down to the fourth dimension where cells 2 and 8 represent opposing values. In Mayor Graham's case he chose color 1, (A-a) *enlightenment* in cell 2. This means that his ideal for *relationships* is for people to be the most open possible (A). He expects people not only to be open to themselves, but also to allow other people to be open (a). This ideal invokes the unconscious fear in him that this might not have the right *qualities* (a better interpretation of the word *appraisal* (C) in this situation). In practice, he fears that the everyday situations in which people find themselves may not allow them to appreciate (a) what is needed. The tension between this opposition is mediated again by his *political* values as above. He wants people to create more *trust* to be better able to *negotiate* and come to better *agreements*.

Interpretation of the Third Dimension

To arrive at the third dimension we rotate our power vector down the feed-forward spiral to cells 3 and 7. The mayor chose green, color 4, the (I-a) power at the ideal level interpreted as *Love*. The form of closure he seeks is that people relate to each other (I) in such a way that they truly accept each other as equal human beings (a), the ideal of loving our neighbour. The unconscious fear created by this ideal in the mayor is expressed in cell 7 as the color 6, blue, the (I-c) power relationship, *Omnipotence*. He fears that peoples' desire for relationships (I) is to have people under control (c). Again, this opponent tension between the potential he hopes for and the unconscious reality he must face is mediated through *political values*, i.e. creating *trust*, *negotiating*, and forming working *agreements*.

Preferred Ends and Means—Second and First Dimension

As we saw in earlier chapters the large letters (A), (I), and (C) refer to the power we project onto our world, our conscious intent, which we refer to as our ends. The small letters (a), (i), and (c) indicate what our unconscious tells us about how the world will react to that action. This feedback from our unconscious greatly influences the means we choose to implement our chosen (A), (I), or (C). The Appendix shows how to calculate our preference for both ends and means, and Table A.2 in the Appendix gives a thumbnail interpretation of the resulting pattern.

We noted in the more theoretical Part II of the book that the natural cause of the split of purpose into three is time orientation. The power of purpose is oriented to: (i) *timelessness*, which in our everyday world we experience as the *future*; (ii) *timing*, the rhythm of support and opposition, which we experience as in the *present*; and (iii) *linear time*, which expresses duration between past, present, and future. The rows are an expression of our manifestation of power in these three time orientations. They reveal our priority of intent for (A), (I), or (C), our conscious feedforward attempts to affect others and our world. The columns give the unconscious priority we give to how the world will react to our (a), (i), or (c):

1   The first row shows how we project ourselves into the future. The mayor's profile shows someone whose future ideal is *Equanimity*. He would like to achieve this ideal through *Enlightenment* and he bounds this future in a vision of *Love*.
2   The second row suggests how we currently narrow our ideals to values based on our perception of support and opposition. Mayor Graham's profile shows that in his present situation he is tackling these ideals by being *philosophical*, i.e. using reason to sort out priorities. He handles relationships through the give and take of *politics* and tries to make approaches to strategy that are sound or *scientific*.
3   The third row indicates what we are moving away from or avoiding based on our past experience. The mayor's case shows that he avoids using strategy based on power; he resists *appraising* others and does

not rely on making personal *agreements* at the operational or detail level.

The columns give us additional information about our priorities for our unconscious choice of means, based on the image of our world contained in our sub-conscious (our a, i, and c):

1   The first column gives us information about how we learn in appreciative influence and control conditions. For example, the mayor sets up (C-c) expectations that the highest level of learning will enable each to control his own destiny and allow others to do the same. Such learning is obtained by managing relationships diplomatically (A-i), but he understands that in the end people will only be influenced to learn options that they care about or will have some control over (I-c).

2   The second column, we have already seen, coincides with the fourth dimension and reveals the three powers that form the basis of our political system.

3   The third column gives us insight into our being, executive, doing self. For example, Love (I-a) is essential to the mayor's sense of *being* who he is. In action he complements his appreciative perspective by ensuring that he translates his ideal into *scientifically* or theoretically sound solutions (A-c). The end goal of his executive power is to overcome his fear and obtain working agreements (C-i) that ensure his ideal of everyone knowing what to do and expecting everyone else to know equally what they have to do.

Interpreting Zero-Dimensions

The point representing zero dimensions lies exactly in the middle between the two opponent powers that we entered in cell 5. The power relationship that surrounds this point is our habitual way of resolving tension between our world, our organizations, and ourselves in all dimensions. For example, the mayor placed (I-i) in cell 5:

1   In control-centered situations, three dimensions, the mayor uses *negotiation* to resolve difference.

2   In influence-centered, four-dimensional situations he is guided by his *political* values.

3   In appreciative-centered, five-dimensional situations he relies on Trust.

Interpreting our own results, our political style consists of the power we entered in cells 3, 5, and 8 and is implemented by what we place in cells 4 and 6. What we have to watch for is how we balance the amount of appreciation and control. Ideally in these cells we want as much of a balance between A, I, and C, and a, i, and c that we can get.

The Power Map and Leadership

The holonomic nature of these slices through multi-dimensional space allows us another layer of interpretation by viewing the three maps in Figure 9.3 as functions to be carried out. The "Ideals" map represents nine functions that cover the organizational spectrum of functions in appreciative-centered fields. The "Values" map from this perspective represents nine functions that cover the whole spectrum of functions in influence-centered fields. The "Goals" map represents the whole spectrum of nine functions in control-centred fields.

Each cell then represents an organizational "function." Those people who carry out the functions that fit the needs of the situation best are leaders. It is possible to read our map in terms of the type of leadership we exercise based on the priority we give to different functions. Our first three choices in cells 1 to 3 represent our ideal or future-oriented functions—the ones we are moving toward. Our second three choices on row 2 represent the functions we call on in the present, and our last three choices represent the functions we are moving away from.

Figure 9.5 summarizes the nine pure leadership types that emerge from this preference for functions.

Leading Appreciative-Centered Organizations

The ideal leader for someone in an appreciative-centered organization is one who operates with the broadest bandwidth of functions from cells 1 to 9. The three functions that best cover this bandwidth are (A-a), (I-i), and (C-c) taken from the fifth-dimensional, ideals section of Figure 9.3:

1   this means that if we placed these three functions in the first three cells of our Power Map we are trying to become that kind of leader in the future;
2   if we placed them in the second row we are already that kind of leader influenced by the situation as much as by our ideals;
3   if we placed them in the third row, because of past experience, we either don't wish to be or have transcended that kind of leader.

According to the order in which we place these three functions in cells 1 to 3 the interpretations change slightly. For example:

The mayor's future orientation in Row 1 (C-c), (A-a), and (I-a) comes very close to that of a spiritual leader, ideal for an appreciative-centered organization. In terms of bandwidth he has all three (A), (I), and (C) feedforward components. In terms of means or feedback he has two (a) and

Power and Leadership Functions

Category	Functions			Sum	Type of Leadership
Holistic leaders have equal access to all levels of ends and means: (A), (I), (C) ends and (a), (i), (c) means	A-a	I-i	C-c	15	Spiritual (Appreciative-Centered)
	8 Possibilities	All have I-i in the center	See Note 2 Chapter 8	15	Charismatic (Influence-Centered)
	C-a	I-i	A-a	15	Executive (Control-Centered)
Specialists at one level A, I, or C but using all means (a), (i), and (c)	A-a	A-i	A-c	6	Philosopher
	I-a	I-i	I-c	15	Strategist
	C-a	C-i	C-c	24	Pragmatist
Leaders who specialize in means but operate at all levels, i.e. specialize in Learning (a), Politics (i), Execution (c)	A-a	I-a	C-a	12	Guru
	A-i	I-i	C-i	15	Politician
	A-c	I-c	C-c	18	Manager

Figure 9.5 Power and leadership functions

one (c). So, for the ideal appreciative level he is missing one (i) of the feedback components. Interpreting this order of choice, the mayor's desired leadership is based on his ideal, *Equanimity*, that people be in control of their own destiny and that they allow others to do the same. The kind of relationship he would like to create to achieve this is the spiritual ideal of *enlightenment* in which each is open to discovering the world and themselves. He differs from the ideal profile only in his choice of (I-a), the social ideal of *Love*, rather than (I-i), the political ideal of *Trust*.

Leading Influence-Centered Organizations

Pure influence requires a perfect balance between (A), (I), and (C) and (a), (i), and (c). This means that every row, column, and diagonal would have to have the same amount of (AIC) and (aic). In the last chapter we showed how we can create this balance through a magic square, a matrix of numbers in which the rows, columns, and diagonals all add up to the same number. (Note 2 of Chapter 10 shows the eight patterns that achieve this.) All columns, rows, and diagonals add up to 15, the magic number for a 3×3 matrix. Of the hundreds of profiles I have seen over more than two decades I have not found one person with any of these 8 pure patterns. Many people however, do have perfect balance in a row or a column. We see, for example, that the mayor's third column, the *being–doing* column scores 15, indicating a perfect balance in this executive function. He also comes very close, as we noted, to a perfect balance in his top row; his future orientation as a *spiritual* leader in which he scores 14. In effect the closer the sums of our columns and rows come to 15 the closer we are to being a charismatic leader.

Leading Control-Centered Organizations

The ideal executive in a controlling environment would have some combination of the third-dimensional diagonal functions, (A-c), (I-i), and (C-a) on his first or second rows. The mayor has two of these executive functions—(A-c) and (I-i)—on his second row, but he also shares two of the political functions as we saw above. This means that although, at the ideal level, he is striving to be a more appreciative-centered leader in the future he is actually operating with a strong component of executive and political leadership. His difference from the more pure executive leaders and political leaders is in the direction of his ideal, his choice of (A-i) rather than (C-a) or (C-i). This choice shows his preference for the more appreciative level of leadership.

If we take Mayor Graham's leadership relationship to time then:

1   In his Future Orientation (row 1) he most resembles the *Spiritual* leader.
2   In his Present Orientation (row 2) he shares two functions with both the *Politician* and the *Guru*.
3   In his Past Orientation (row 3) he most resembles the *Pragmatist*.

Figure 9.5 shows that there are three fundamentally different types of leader:

1   Holistic leaders who make broad and balanced use of all three levels, (A), (I), and (C), of ends, and all three means (a), (i), and (c). Notice that such holistic leaders can be control-, influence-, or appreciative-centered. What determines their relative effectiveness is the environment they are operating in.

2 Level-specific leaders, that is:

    a   leaders who operate particularly well at the appreciative level (A) relating to the whole, especially the external world;

    b   leaders who operate well at the influence level (I) by developing and maintaining relationships between all stakeholders;

    c   executive leaders who are particularly good at the control level (C), focusing on the goals of the organization and internal operations.

3 Means-specific leaders, often staff or functional leaders:

    a   leaders who specialize in the appreciative (a) function of learning, leaders of research, human and organizational development, and knowledge management;.

    b   leaders who specialize in relationships (i), the political functions of developing and maintaining relationships with stakeholders, e.g. leaders of marketing and public relations;

    c   leaders who specialize in the functional operations (c), they manage the production of the organizations, products, and services, e.g. leaders of production, sales and service, and finance.

Through the power map, then, we can create information about our potential for transforming ourselves, our organizations, and our world. Our preference for the large A, I, or C and a small (a), (i), or (c) describe our typical power relationship with our organizations and our world. Our large letter is the conscious power vector we project or feedforward onto others and our world. The small letter represents our unconscious view of how the world will react to us.

Our potential for transformation is indicated by our interpretation of row 1, the future orientation, compared to row 2, our present orientation, and row 3 that indicates what we must face up to from the past. Recall that the real value of this mapping is to help us understand the interactive, multi-dimensional nature of purpose and powers. It is this understanding that will improve our power to transform ourselves, our organization and our world by becoming more "purpose-full" and more "power-full."

It is the *in-flow* of these two power vectors that create the energy of life in the moment. This in-*flow* of power provides the essential opposition of attraction and repulsion, liking and disliking that is the essence of influence power. It is at the zero point that we have the opportunity for transformation and we can take our interaction to a new level by focusing equally on appreciation with the other (I-a) and translating those options into strategies (I-c).

Summary

We exist in the here and now centered in fields of influence. The world of the past, the world of control, for good and bad constrains our current potential. The good gives us stability and security the bad constrains us from seeing new possibilities and potential. The timeless world we experience as the future contains infinite possibilities and infinite interpretations of reality. These offer our imagination, our intuition and sixth sense the most powerful resource for transformation that exists.

Once we appreciate ourselves, others, and our world from that center of influence we are able to use our manifest power of appreciation, influence, and control (a), (i), and (c) equally. From our center of influence we move upwards to free ourselves from current constraints and become open to possibilities and realities that transcend those encapsulated in the current situation. We then use our influence to engage with others to explore our joint worlds to discover new possibilities and new interpretations of the realities we face. How well we carry out this central (I-i) relationship for every purpose determines the degree of our leverage, our transformational potential.

10 Implications for Cultures, Institutions, and Organizations

In Chapter 9 we explored purpose and power within ourselves and illustrated how the AIC pattern of multi-dimensional power relationships exists within us and can be used to understand our relationships to ourselves, our organizations, and our world.

We are now becoming familiar with the basics of the generic AIC organizing process. It begins with sense of purpose, which comes from some latency in ourselves and our world. Our purpose then produces potential power, an A, I, or C orientation, our intention to move to an end. However, we have contained within ourselves an unconscious view of our world that influences us to adapt (a, i, or c) means to implement then combines with our intent to produce our actual purpose, which now contains a large unconscious component. Although this aggregate field, this unconscious component, is a source of feedback and great potential power it can both help and hurt us to the extent that it is based on the actual potential and realities of the situation. Our development of the AIC organizing process shows how we can tap into this hidden power through the use of appreciation and overcome its biases by equal use of (a), (i), and (c) means in our organizing process.

In this chapter we build on these insights and illustrate their fractal nature to draw out their implication for whole organizations operating in their institutional and cultural environments.

We take the organization as the field of control and following our model we center our organizing perspective one level above—the influence level. For an organization, this level consists of its stakeholders. It is the level that consciously or unconsciously mediates value difference between the organization and its community or world at large. In organizational terms we can think of these clusters of value as formal and informal institutions. The formal institutions are those that represent societies core values; those we have identified in Figure 7.14. We have, for example, religious, scientific, social, and political and economic institutions. But the organization also has to deal with informal organizations such as family, charity, entertainment. The third level, the one above our center of influence, consists of all those factors that affect the organization but which it cannot control or influence, at least within the time cycle in which its performance is evaluated. We treat this appreciated world as culture and will begin to draw our implications of viewing organization though our AIC lens from that perspective.

Cultures as Context

Looking at culture as an appreciative field implies that its substance is mental and spiritual. At the highest level it is humanity's collective conscious and unconscious awareness of everything that affects its purpose. It sets the conditions for the creation and continuing existence of institutions and organizations.

As we look at global human culture as the appreciative level for all humanity we should be able to apply our organizing concepts and identify its natural division into three parts and their opponent processes. Our work in Part II has already laid this groundwork for us. If we revisit Chapter 3 we find that religion or spirituality is the reflection of humanity's highest level of purpose and therefore the creator of our appreciative field or culture. The chapter shows the breakdown of religion into three major divisions.

1   (A-a): the more open, appreciative attitudes to the whole, as illustrated in Buddhist and Hindu religions;
2   (A-i): the more relative, influence-oriented attitudes to the whole, as illustrated in religions such as Islam;
3   (A-c): the more closed, control-oriented attitudes, as illustrated in the Jewish and Christian religions.

These three basic orientations, which are the (a), (i), and (c) means for the whole of humanity, now become (A), (I), and (C) ends for three regional cultural subdivisions of the whole, which in turn have great impact on our institutions and organizations. That the pattern is refracted to the next level is shown in a remarkable but little-known piece of work by Edwin Nichols (1976). of the U.S. Department of Health. He has identified the cultures that adopt these three regional perspectives—Asian, African, and European. He also identifies the means by which the three perspectives are made manifest—epistemologies, logics, and processes. The resulting matrix of ends (AIC) and means (aic) are reproduced as Figure 10.1.

He argues that the three major orientations arose from the initial conditions in which the three cultures were created. Europeans moved from Africa to the northern cold climates. These northerners in order to survive had to learn to conquer nature, to plan ahead, to count and measure supplies to survive winters—in the process they developed white skins and the embryo of a control-centered orientation to life and nature. For Africans

CULTURE		**Purpose** **Axiology** Value orientation	***(a)*** **Epistemology** Knowledge orientation	***(i)*** **Logic** System of relating	***(c)*** **Process** Way of living
A	**Asian** **Asian-** **American** **Polynesian** **Native** **American**	Member- Group The highest value lies in the cohesiveness of the group	Conative One knows through striving toward the transcendence	Nyaya The objective world is conceived independent of thought and mind	Cosmology All sets are independently interrelated in the harmony of the universe
I	**African** **African-** **American** **Hispanics** **Arabs**	Member- Member The highest value lies in the interpersonal relationships between persons	Affective One knows through symbolic imagery and rhythm	Diunital The union of opposites	Ntuology All sets are interrelated through human and spiritual networks
C	**European** **Euro-** **American**	Member- Object The highest value lies in the object or the acquisition of the object	Cognitive One knows through counting and measuring	Dichotomous Either/Or	Technology All sets are repeatable and reproducible

Figure 10.1 The philosophical aspects of cultural difference

Developed by Edwin J. Nichols PhD
AIC orientation by W.E. Smith

who stayed behind the major problem for survival was not nature but the tribes over the hill. Developing relations to create friendships and deal with hostilities was key to survival—the embryo of an influence-centered approach. The embryo of Asian culture was most likely created by the long trek east. Cohesion of the group to adapt to changing conditions and support each other to ensure survival was crucial to ensure that everything necessary for each trek was completed. Failure by any individual to do their part on the trek would affect progress of the whole—the embryo of an appreciative-centered culture.

Figure 10.1 re-orders Nichol's original sequence to maintain the format of the AIC generic organizing process and has added AIC sub-headings to help relate Nichol's work to AIC. Otherwise all the text is original Nichols. Some of the terms used as sub-headings in his chart are more fully explained by Phillips (1990).

Each culture has its own particular ordering and weighting of values and ways in which it manifests them. Figure 10.1 uses the label Purpose, believing that an ideal is for Nichols a higher level value, and a goal is a lower level value. It is this axiology or "level of purpose" that is then manifest as the three different (a), (i), and (c) means or "power to" for achievement of the culture's purpose:

1   Epistemology, *our ways of knowing* (a) appreciative means.
2   Logic, the rationale for our *way of relating to others* (i) influence means.
3   Process, *our ways of living* (c) control means.

Six of these values—religious, scientific, social, political, aesthetic, and economic—were identified as long ago as 1928 by Edward Spranger in *Types of Men*.[1] Allport (1937) used these values to discriminate personality differences and in (1960) with Vernon and Gardner translated them into a widely used scale for measuring dominant personality interests.

Cultures, then, provide the appreciative level of organization that covers the field between humanity and the individual human. They provide the "religio" between the ideals of humanity and how they are transformed into

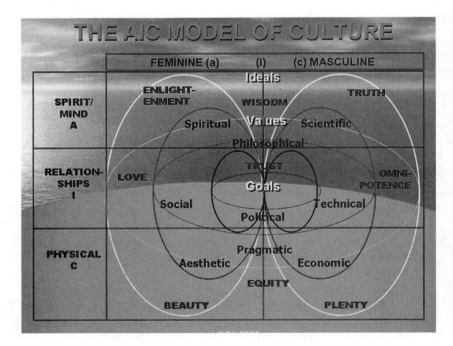

Figure 10.2 The AIC model of culture

values by people from different geographic regions of the world (space) and with different histories (time).

Figure 10.2 links these cultural values back to the power map of ideals developed in Chapter 7, Figures 7.10 and 7.11. It illustrates the transformation from the fifth-dimensional process created by the ideals of humanity into the fourth-dimensional process of dynamic relationships governed by values. The next step in the organizing process is to find out how the values selected by a specific culture are prioritized and related to each other.

Institutions and Long-Term Values

Over time the values initially selected because of the unique needs for survival in the specific conditions of geography, relationship with surrounding people, and state of development become embedded in the way cultures influence thinking, organizing, and practical ways of living. The starting values become the default values, which are only changed very gradually and then only in times of great stress or unusual opportunity. This process of institutionalization of values produces the formal and informal institutes that stabilize, defend, and promote the culture's core values. They are the institutionalization of (a), (i), and (c) feedback, which greatly influence the culture's choice of means for implementing its ends.

Each core value creates a latency that provides the energy and source of legitimacy for the creation of an actual institute. For example, churches are created to tap into our latent need for wholeness or spirituality. Universities and other scientific institutions tap into our latent need for truth. Social institutions and associations tap into our need for love. Defense and the military tap into our need for omnipotence. Political institutions tap into our need for trust: that this connection proves to be humorous shows us how far off current political systems are from their ideal. Art institutions tap into our need for beauty, while economic institutions tap into our ideal for plenty.

The process for organizing values follows norms of influence and is very different from that for organizing ideals. Ideals are forever attractive, and timeless. There is no trading off of ideals; they are there and exist forever, they are neither positive nor negative. This is why conflicts of ideals are so difficult to deal with—there is nothing to transcend them, we can't go beyond the ultimate whole to transcend differences.

Figure 10.3 shows the range of nine values that govern influence-centered organization. Consistent with the fractal nature of the model they are recursively divided into their own three A, I, and C levels. Each provides a very different tone, process, and outcome than when applied to the appreciative-centered level.

The influence phase moves equally up to the appreciative level and down to the control level, the goal of the excursion into the appreciative level is to "dissolve" value differences, at the core influence level its goal is to "resolve" those difference that can't be dissolved, and finally to set the parameters for a "solution": at the control level.

> **Dissolution**: The three appreciative values—spiritual, philosophical, and scientific are (a, i, and c) means to access the *timeless* level of ideals. They move the actors outside of the current time cycle, to invoke larger purposes that can transcend current values differences, and current frames of operation. In the Colombia case in Chapter 4, for example, we asked the workshop participants to design an electricity sector for their grandchildren. It is this excursion into the appreciative realm through these three values that is most often missed out in strategic planning processes.
>
> **Resolution**: The influence phase then uses the three social, political, and technical values to work out the best possible "resolution" for this cycle only. That is, it works out the best combination of ideas (a), relationships (i), and resources (c) that will have most benefit for the organization (C), its stakeholders (I), and society (A). This is the core of the whole organizing process.
>
> **Solution**: The three control values—aesthetic, egalitarian, and economic —help balance the distribution of resources that will go into the solution. The actual solution is not provided until the control-centered phase, but the controlling values are surfaced and brought into play through the process of resolution.

(These distinctions between "solution, resolution, and dissolution" were introduced by Ackoff (1978) in relationship to levels of problem solving. He also added *absolution*, ignoring the problem, as another mode of problem solving.)

Organizations as Individuals

Organizations are for cultures, the instrumental means for translating institutional values derived from humanity's ideals into specific goals. They provide the control centered level in the space between humanity and the individual. For example, there is a permanent institutional need for defense giving rise to the institution the Department of Defense. However, there is only a relatively short-term need to produce a particular kind of weapon, which gives rise to specific weapons-producing organizations that may go out of business when that weapon is no longer needed. The Department of Defense, however, never goes out of business because it is meeting a permanent need. Organizations, of course, can become so adept at meeting such needs that they acquire institutional status.

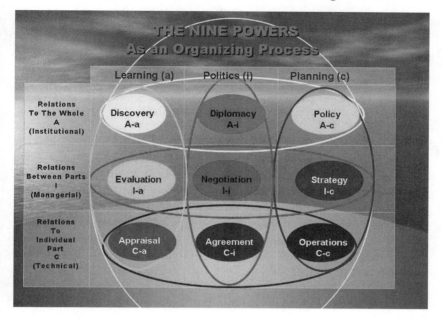

Figure 10.3 The nine powers
© William E. Smith 2005

Many organizations consciously pursue this strategy by linking to them-selves through advertising to higher social needs e.g. McDonald's attempts to link itself to the institution of family (see story in Chapter 1 on Victorian values).

Organizations at the control level, then, transform the long-term values into organizational goals or functions. Just as for each ideal there is a corres-ponding value, Figure 10.3 shows the goals or organizational functions that corresponds to each value.

At the appreciative level (A)—which Parsons in Chapter 3 called institutional—spiritual (a), philosophical (i), and scientific (c) values trans-late into the function of discovery (a) such as research, diplomacy (i) and policy-making (c).

At the influence level (I)—Parson's managerial-level—social(a), political (i), and technical (c) values become such functions as evaluation, negotia-tion, and strategy.

At the control level (C)—Parson's technical level—aesthetic (a), egalitari-an (i), and economic (c) values translate into appraisal, working agreements, and practical operation.

The actual naming of such functions depends very much on the specific situation. The names chosen here are designed to be as generic as possible.

In our examples, for example in the Virginia Beach police example below, we show how they are adapted to better suit the situation.

Similarly the names of the columns and rows adjust to the context. At this functional level we chose Parson's descriptors for the A, I, and C levels. Just as we interpret the columns as the learning system (a), politics (i), and planning (c).

Power Patterns for Organizational Effectiveness

As summarized by the template in Figure 10.3 all organizations need to "relate to the whole" (A)—the relevant context that they cannot control or influence (in the time cycle that governs their purpose). All organizations need to relate to "others"—their internal and external stakeholders (I)—and all organizations have to manage the resources they control—ideas, people, and things, their individual parts (C).

In terms of means all organizations have to keep open at all three levels, i.e. to have a *learning process* (a). They also have to have a *political process* (i) to sort out differences of value. All organization also need some form of *planning process* (c) to give form to their ideals, value resolutions, and control of resources

However, as we have just seen some organizations or levels of organization through their purpose need to focus primarily on appreciation, (cultural values); influence (institutional or core values); or control (resource values). By understanding the priority and sequence of values in these three pure types of organization we create the basis for understanding all organizations that are some fractal combination of these pure types. For a discussion in practical terms of the centrality and ubiquity of power and the political process see Eldred (1999).

Effective Appreciative-Centered Organization

Appreciative-centered organization is ideal for organizations that serve the whole community without distinction between members, for example, churches, governments, associations, and even universities. Appreciative-centered organization also applies to that part or phase of any organizing process that deals with relationships to the whole, the larger context that the organization cannot influence or control. The principles and processes are the same in both cases.

Successful appreciation results in increased legitimacy for the organization's purpose and increased opportunities for mutual influence. For a whole organization, this role, ideally, is the role of the Board. Members should be selected on the basis of their capacity to influence and be influenced by segments of society most affected by the purposes of the organization. Board members, in effect, become a group of stakeholders that represent the two-way power of society and the organization. This is not the perspective that most Boards take today: they generally adopt an internally directed posture emphasizing its control-centered role as a watchdog and safeguard of shareholder values. They have an unrealized potential to both co-create and safeguard the culture of the organization, all its stakeholders, and contribute more effectively to society.

There is only one pattern of values for pure appreciation, as illustrated in Figure 10.4. The ends are ordered precisely as rows of (A), then (I), and then (C) values. The columns, representing means are also ordered in the precise sequence of (a) then (i), and then (c):

1   The primary function of an appreciative–centered organization or of any appreciative process is (A-a)—to be equally open to all constituents and to society. We have described this as a *spiritual* value that translates practically into the organizing process as *discovery* and learning in order to better harmonize constituents' ideals with those of society and vice versa. (This is an example where our generic word *spiritual* may not be the best fit and particular organizations might substitute words such as *cultural* or *societal*.)

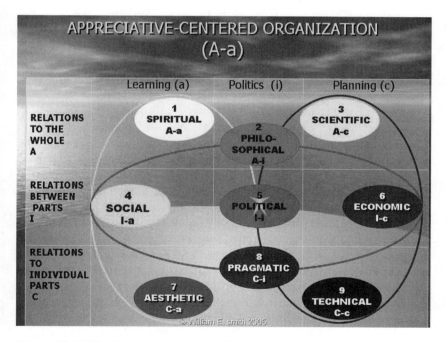

Figure 10.4 Effective appreciative organization

© William E. Smith 2005

2   This openness to society and its members is supported by *philosophical* values (A-i) that translate into an emphasis on *diplomacy*, which derives in turn from the wisdom built into its *philosophy*. Discoveries are quite likely to come up with new views that affect everything and so depend heavily on diplomatic skills to safeguard relationships to the whole.

3   The openness of discovery is then bounded by *scientific* or well-reasoned theories to produce the most acceptable and attractive *policies* that will satisfy the whole constituency and society (A-c).

The criterion for effectiveness of the appreciative-centered organization is legitimacy—the alignment of society and organizational values.

Effective Influence-Centered Organization

Influence-centered organization applies both to whole organizations, e.g. political and issue-oriented organizations and to the influence level within an organization. Political organizations, NGOs, lobbying firms, and management consulting firms are examples of influence-centered organization.

When we look at influence as a phase of organization, the emphasis is on engagement in a *political* (I-i) process that is enacted through some form of *negotiation*. This process is supported by being open to the others, a *social* value (I-a) through some means of *evaluation* to bring to some *technical* closure as options in the form of (I-c) *strategy*.

However, when we come to patterns for the whole organization the prioritization and sequencing of values is more difficult than for appreciative or control-centered organizations because there are many more pure sequences. The ideal for influence-centered organization is to have all sources of influence—ideas (a), people (i), and resources (c)—interact so that all possible means of implementation, with their likely positive and negative consequences can be *evaluated*. To implement this we need to have the most varied possible pattern of (AIC) ends and (aic) means in every row and column, there should be no bias to appreciation or control. This means that power is balanced at every level.

Conceptually, the solution to this complex problem is surprisingly simple. We find it in the concept of magic squares. A magic square is a matrix with an equal number of columns and rows in which the numbers in all columns, rows, and diagonals add up to the same number. For the numbers 1–9, arranged in a 3×3 matrix, that number is 15. To find influence patterns we have to find the magic square in which all columns, rows, and diagonals add up to 15. Our numbers represent degrees of power from pure appreciation to pure control. So these relative numbers can be used to designate valid power relationships and their differences.

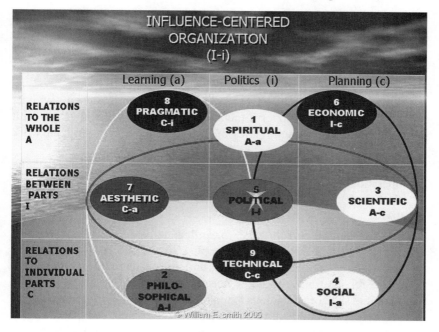

Figure 10.5 Effective influence organization
© William E. Smith 2005

The solution is provided in Figure 10.5. However, because order matters in AIC there are eight different orders for this set of numbers. We obtain these combinations by rotating the magic square in all four directions and also reversing it horizontally in both directions. The full eight combinations are shown in Note 2.[2] Two of the combinations are for use in appreciative conditions, i.e. when the levels above the organization have an appreciative culture, so we label them I-a patterns. Four of the combinations are for use in influence conditions, i.e. they operate in an influence-centered culture. Figure 10.4 is one of the four (I-i) patterns. Two options are for use in control conditions, or control culture and so are labeled (I-c) patterns.

All eight pure influence patterns achieve the perfect balance between (AIC) and (aic) by having one (A), (I), or (C) in every row and one (a), (i), and (c) in every column. Figure 10.5 demonstrates clearly the essence of influence-centered organization as the balance of opposites, the dance of the "masculine" (C) and (c) and the "feminine" (A) and (a). The dance between ends (vertical) is that between the most controlling end possible (C-c) *technical* and the most appreciative ends possible (A-a) *spiritual*. Its strategic level (horizontal) is a dance between opposite choice of means; the (a) in the aesthetic value (C-a) and the (c) means in the scientific value (A-c).

The profile in Figure 10.5 might belong to a well rounded NGO:

1   **Appreciative level**: The firms' highest value is social. However, it wants to spread its message through access to technology (C-c) which is guided b a well-developed philosophy (A-i) or mission.
2   **Influenced Level**: The NGO is adept at creating relationships with its stakeholders and supports them by maintaining relationships with the scientific community (A-c) and by producing quality strategic work (C-a).
3   **Controlled Level**: The NGO is economically effective at the operational level (I-c) and supports this with a very pragmatic (C-i) and open (A-a) approach to its workers.

The criterion of performance for influence-centered organization is effectiveness, i.e. the effectiveness applies to the choice of priorities of the parts—ideas, people, and resources and the means for their harmonization. The recognition and adherence to a core set of values becomes paramount in such organizations to maintaining their identity and providing internal coherence and loyalty of its members. The most effective strategy is the one that allows all levels of ends to mix with all possible means to foresee likely consequences. This is why having the greatest possible mix of (AIC) and (aic) at every level, as illustrated in Figure 10.5 is so important.

Effective Control-Centered Organization

Control-centered organizations are those that are dedicated to the production of products and services above all else. When we talk of organization this is our default image and most of organization theory is built around this model. Just as for appreciative-centered organization, there is only one pure pattern and it is exactly the reverse of the appreciative pattern (Figure 10.6). Its orientation to its world in order of priority is (C) then (I) then (A) and the order of use of means is also (c) then (i) then (a) at every level. In both ends and means it provides an inexorable march from the highly valued certain or closed values to the least certain or most open values.

The primary value of the pure control-centered organization is the assurance produced by the certainty that every person and every process does what it is meant to do; that ends and means are under control (C-c). This value is supported by a very pragmatic view of relationships focused on achieving that end, (C-i). It is also supported by an appraisal process

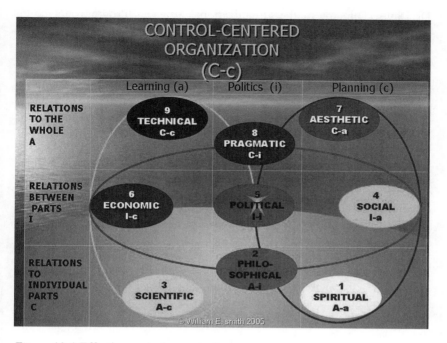

Figure 10.6 Effective control organization
© William E. Smith 2005

—the control part of the learning process—that monitors progress to that end (C-a).

At the influenced level, the control-centered organization has the same values as an appreciative-centered organization but the order is reversed. It gives primacy to economic (I-c) rather than to social values (I-a), but both types of organization and all our pure influence organizations have political values (I-i) in the center.

Pure control-centered organizations give less value to the *scientific* (A-c) favoring *pragmatism* in operations. They are even less concerned with *philosophical* values (A-i), rationalizations of their activities or their relationship to the community as a whole (A-a).

Illustration of Practical Use of Value Priorities and Sequence

The practical use of these insights into values for different types and levels of organization is illustrated in the following case. Working through ODII,

Dr Davis, Director of the Organizational Sciences Program at George Washington University and the author, helped design a program for "Building a Culture of Integrity" with the Virginia Beach Police Department headed by Chief A.M. "Jake" Jacocks, Jr. (Chief Jacocks kindly gave permission for the use of the following material in this book.)

The case will also show how the labels used to describe the powers have to be adapted to the situation. Each real case is an actual fractal combination of the pure relationships identified in our illustrative figures. Very few organizations are pure control-, influence-, or appreciative-centered organizations.

We interpreted the concept of *integrity* not just in its ethical sense but also in its organizational sense as described here, i.e. designing an integrated process that would incorporate all the powers (values) created by the purpose. The program would help ensure that the full range of values was used to *integrate* both internal and external leadership capacity in a way that would benefit the department, its stakeholders, and the community at large. Such integrity of organization would lead to the more traditional concept of ethical integrity by providing transparency, common ideals, values, and goals. The approach used was an AIC action learning process as illustrated in Figure 10.7.

Figure 10.7 Integration of action learning

The figure shows the three levels of actors who represent the "whole system," the appreciated world that impacted the performance of the police department:

a   the police department itself (control);
b   its stakeholders—those who had a direct part in providing or receiving services from the department (influence);
c   the community at large who were beneficiaries but had no direct control or influence over the force (appreciation).

The integrated process was designed to ensure that the goals of the department addressed the values of its stakeholders and the ideals of the community in its operations, its strategies, and overall policies. To achieve this, the department, the stakeholders, and the community were involved in an action learning process that:

1   evaluated policies (appreciation);
2   appraised strategies (influence); and
3   monitored goal performance (control).

The reader will note how we changed the names of the axes of the model to fit the unique assignment. In the case of the appreciative means, the *learning* column (a) we kept the same title, the learning process, but because of the emphasis on *evaluation* we made evaluation rather than "*discovery*" the prime value and divided its levels into *evaluation (A-a)*, *appraisal (I-a)*, and *monitoring (C-a)*.

The Action/Learning/Organizing Process

The process was organized by using the AIC phases:

1   The purpose of this first phase was to gain an appreciation of community ideals and values as they impact the policies, roles, and performance of the police department. This phase establishes the degree of legitimacy of the policies in the eyes of the stakeholders and the community. The design team headed by Deputy Chief Greg Mullen and Sergeant Mark Bowman selected sixty-five people who represented the major stakeholders who affected and were affected by the performance of the police department. The list included stakeholders from the hotel industry, conventions, the Sheriff's Office, legal services, victims, social services, and the NAACP. Initially, while the process was new, stakeholders from the judicial, political, and media systems did not attend but once they understood the new approach they began to attend.

2   The second, influence, phase was designed to discover if the right
     priority areas and the right stakeholders were engaged in the process.
     (It was at this stage that the second level of stakeholders came in.)
     Answers to these questions determine the effectiveness of the program
     by ensuring that as wide as possible range of values are identified and
     utilized. Based on the results of the appreciative phase the design team
     selected sixteen of the stakeholders who they felt had most influence
     or who were most influenced by the departments programs. It was these
     sixteen stakeholders who became the quasi-Board.

3   A one-and-a-half-day workshop allowed each stakeholder to give their
     interpretation of the three major sources of information they had about
     the department:

     a   the community meetings;
     b   an internal departmental strategic planning process, which had
          identified key issues;
     c   external interviews that had listed a number of short-term issues.

Power maps or as they were called in this project, value maps, were used
to compare information from the three sources. We began with a template
that showed the typical range of values involved in any whole systems
approach to organizing. The labels used basically reflect the maps we have
drawn above but were adapted a little, as we recommend, to meet the
organization's own language and culture. The template is reproduced as
Figure 10.8:

a   appreciative-level values provide legitimacy for the organization
     within the whole community;
b   influence values contribute to the effectiveness of the organization's
     social and political process in engaging its stakeholders;
c   control-level values contribute to its efficiency in pursuing its goals.
     The columns were divided between the soft or open means (apprecia-
     tive with a small "a") for pursing ideals values and goals and the harder
     or closed means (control with a small "c").

This guide helped the stakeholders to compare different maps and notice
different areas of emphasis. Notice that the middle column that would be
(i) is missing. In practice we treated this as a living "column," this is what
the results of the *evaluation* were to provide. The strategy is to balance
the *spiritual* and *cultural*, the *social* and *political*, and the *aesthetic* and
economic. The values emphasized in the chart (the lighter gray labels) were
taken from the acronym PRIDE—the forces slogan—professionalism,

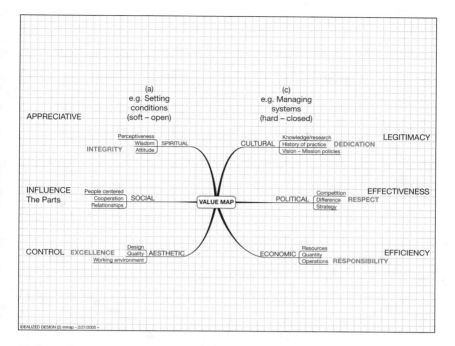

Figure 10.8 The template: AIC systems generic values map

respect, integrity, dedication, and excellence. We included them in the map to show that in fact those values taken together were holistic; they did cover most of the value segments of the map.

Consistent with Surowiecki's (2005) concept, *The Wisdom of Crowds*, it was the community that gave the most holistic view of priority issues. The appreciative community meetings feedback, as shown below, covered all value segments (Figure 10.9).

Priorities as Identified by the Community Meeting

Prior to the culture of integrity program the department had carried out a traditional internal strategic planning process. We mapped their list of issues on the value map. All except one of their issues fell in the (I-c) or (C-c) segments of the map (Figure 10.10). This distribution made it very clear to the department that this classical view of strategy, specifying action plans, could not possibly provide the bridge between all of the nine powers in all six segments of the map. It also made evident in a very dramatic way that

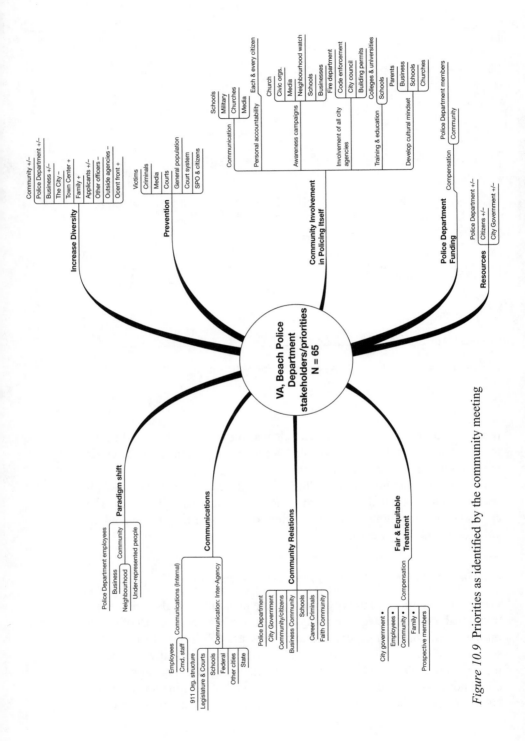

Figure 10.9 Priorities as identified by the community meeting

Remain cognizant of public
perception & demonstrate
core values to the public **Public Perception**

Virginia Beach Police Department Strategic Planning Sub-Committee Key Issues List 12/4

Organization/ Administration
- Timely, regular, accurate communications between all levels of the org., all bureaus, citizens
- Need to adopt & integrate the Nat'l. Incident Mgt. System and Incident Command System to bring into nat'l. standards
- Investigate, monitor, report on racial profiling (remains issue for members of minority community
- Evaluate resource requirements at all levels
- Ensure fair & consistent discipline by supervisors
- Continue to explore expansion/addition of specialized units as needed

Community/ Environment
- Residential/commercial/redevelopment in city requires reorganization, reallocation or staffing, additional staffing
- Better communications with all city departments at operational level daily (critical incidents/special events

Human Capital
- Retention: pay, compression, benefits
- Recruitment, retention, promotion, workforce planning for ease of employee transitions
- Workforce diversity reflective of the community
- Develop joint training and protocols with outside agencies
- Continue to explore expansion/addition of specialized units as needed
- Continue to place high emphasis on training

Equipment
- Need to prepare a long-term equipment replacement plan

Service Delivery
- Traffic congestion increases impacting police response time & services
- Increasing demand on Department police services from other city agencies (parks, libraries, public works, recreation, health
- Citizens express need for additional traffice enforcement

Financial/Budget
- Less federal funds for local law enforcement & tax reduction initiatives cold reduce potential for new programs/projects
- Overall reductions in mental/human services will heighten need for use of law enforcement
- Continually need to demonstrate value of our programs/specialized units to ensure continued funding

Technology
- Need to invest in technology resources (personnel/funds) to meed Depart. needs
- Use of technology to manage costs/reduce emphasis on employee staffing should be given priority
- Improve technology resources within the Department
- New automated system required (redundancy issues, simplify payroll

Facilities
- Some police facilities are in need of renovation/replacement

Figure 10.10 Internal strategic planning priority issues

a real strategic plan cannot be made internally; it has to involve external stakeholders.

The control phase consisted of the more traditional part of the evaluation process. Two sets of evaluation questionnaires were designed to gain feedback from internal and external stakeholders, both those who had attended workshops and those who had not.

Results from the evaluation were summed under five major headings, as shown in Figure 10.11; Culture, Communications, Community Relationships, Human Capital, and Management.

Those surveyed in descending order of power to affect the results of the process were:

1 Police who had attended the organizing workshops and had a direct hand in designing and implementing the program (C-c).
2 Police who had not attended the organizing process but through their role as police officers influenced the implementation of the outcomes (I-c).
3 Members of the community who attended the organizing process, so had some influence both on the design and also on their community (I-i).
4 Members of the community who were not part of the organizing process but who would have been affected by the community results (A-i).

The scores for each of these groups are shown for each issue (the human capital issue was an entirely internal one concerning salaries and terms and conditions of employment so was not rated by the external stakeholders). For example, the score 75, 8 in the outer circle is the score on culture for the community members who did not attend. The first score 75 is its positive percentage rating and the second score 8 is the negative percentage rating.

What is really interesting is that the highest scores describing the impact of the program for creating a "Culture of Integrity" came from the most appreciative group, the members of the community who had not participated

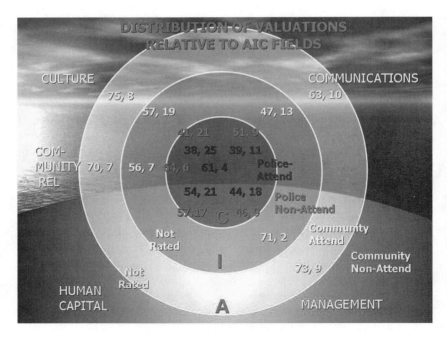

Figure 10.11 Distribution of valuations in AIC fields

in the process. This, of course, is the group that a cultural program, a program addressing the whole, should impact.

1   In general, those in the appreciative field, the community not attending the AIC workshops, had the most positive evaluation, averaging over all cluster 70 percent positive and 8 percent negative averaged over all value clusters.
2   Those in the influence field, the community members who did attend the AIC workshops, had less positive results 58 percent positive and 10 percent negative over all clusters.
3   The internal group straddling the control influence line, the police not attending the AIC workshops, had averages of 52 percent positive and 12 percent negative.
4   The internal group with most control over the culture of integrity program (those attending the AIC workshops) had the lowest valuations, with averages of 49 percent positive and 16 percent negative.

One possible interpretation of these results is that those with most organization-specific knowledge are more cognizant of the means used to enhance the culture of integrity program and are expressing the extent to which they fall short of ideals. It is often true that those closest to and who have intimate knowledge of their organizations can be the most critical of its performance. Because no previous study of this nature has been done we cannot know for sure whether this is a general pattern or not. Our AIC theory would suggest that the more one is placed in an appreciative role, i.e. the more one moves outward from an internal control role to a more external role the easier it is to take a more appreciative, less judgmental role. The more one is in an internal controlling role the more the climate encourages judgment and critique; it is easier to see and judge the specific errors and not appreciate the more general progress.

The result suggested that the creation of an advisory board of the most influential stakeholders who in turn engaged a wider set of stakeholders in an AIC process were able to improve the "legitimacy" of the police department and enhance the program for creating a Culture of Integrity. The same appreciative and influence approaches were not used within the internal organization of the police department. We took communications to be an indicator of the overall success of appreciation, that people trust each other when they have an opportunity to engage about things that are important to them and are able to say what they think and feel when they do engage. This information suggests that the police department was effective in conveying its culture/philosophy externally but had more work to do with its internal stakeholders.

The results of the internal surveys, however, suggested that such improvement is not made through the technical teaching of communication skills or stand-alone communication programs. Rather, communication is about all aspects of the work itself in the organization. The next step recommended was to start a new cycle of the organizing process with the feedback from this evaluation. However, this time the process should be continued downward within the police department.

Summary

What we find from this exercise is that the fractal AIC pattern can be applied to the whole represented by an organization, its institutional and cultural environments and to each of the parts. Each level—cultural, institutional, and organizational—uses all three major components of feedforward (A), (I), and (C) but in different orders. What we say about appreciative-centered organization applies to cultures and what we say about institutional organization applies to influence-centered organizations, and within this whole context organizations are control-centered entities.

Our profiling exercises and of practical examples reveal that whereas appreciative- and control-centered organization, for example, can have all three forms of (A) or all three forms of (I) or (C) at any one level this is not true for means. All forms of organization require the [use of] all three types of means, (a), (i), and (c) at each level. For example, in Figure 10.4, the appreciative-centered organization uses all three large (A)s at the top level as its primary power orientation for achieving its purpose, but it also uses all three means (a), (i), and (c) at that level. So it balances its feedforward power, an emphasis on (A) by making sure it uses all three different kinds of means, i.e. it uses one (a) in (A-a), one (i) in (A-i), and one c in (A-c). Similarly, the appreciative-centered organization uses all three types of (I) at the middle level and all three types of (C) at the bottom level, but each uses all three (a), (i), and (c) means.

What is extraordinary in terms of both theory and practice is that in all these ten ideal cases, the balance of the nine complementary powers is maintained by having the (I-i) process, number 5, in the center of the matrix. This centering on the (I-i) process becomes an essential characteristic of the AIC organizing process:

1   in appreciative-centered organization (I-i) translates as "Trust";
2   in all eight influence-centered organizations (I-i) translates as "Politics";
3   in control-centered organization (I-i) translates as "Negotiation".

The three together are the backbone of the organization's political system. As we saw in the last chapter *trust* (I-i) is the central resolution of all nine ideals. In this chapter we see that *politics* (I-i) is the central process of the nine power processes that transform the ideals into values and ultimately into goals. The operational result of political action at the control level is *negotiation* (I-i).

In practical terms we label organizations appreciative, influence, or control-centered (large A, I, or C) based on their purpose; the latency that they serve relative to society, the whole. This felt latency translates into their feedforward function, the push of their power onto their worlds. However, whichever orientation to purpose they have, the organization has to pay equal attention to appreciative (a), influence (i), and control (c) means. This requires them to place the influenced level in the center. They organize so that their center of focus is with their stakeholders. From this perspective they move upwards to appreciate the world of the levels above them and downwards to ensure that their internal stakeholders have control of all the resources necessary to achieve their goals. This centering of effective organization in influence explains why we often refer to the AIC organizing process as a strategic organizing process. It provides one of the most significant changes required in our current approach that uses influence primarily for control.

This emphasis on central values is what Art Kleiner (2003) believes happens in all organizations. Core groups who are not the official hierarchy but have similar values decide the direction the organization is going. Who they are and how they achieve what they do is not formally determined. However, when they are not connected to the whole, our appreciative dimension, they often function in ways that are counter to the long-term interest of the organization and its community. He concludes:

> In the end, perhaps it is not just a corporation or organization that is great because it has a great Core Group. Perhaps the quality of community or nation depends on the quality of the Core Groups within it— and their ability to maintain a respect for the global and local citizenry as a whole.
>
> (p. 227)

In this conclusion Kleiner has captured the essential role of influence: to "maintain equal respect for the global (our appreciative level) and local citizenry" (our control level). This is the critical evolutionary issue we identified in Chapter 2.

Even though the AIC model suggests that all organizations center themselves in influence the sequence of power/organizing process they use is quite distinct, as we saw above. Appreciative-centered organizations will be more "power-full" if they adopt appreciative patterns. Influence organizations such as political organizations, non-governmental organizations, interest groups, and many service, even consulting organizations will run better following the influence patterns. Finally, productive organizations— those producing goods and services will rely more on control-centered norms. This does not mean, of course, that our current control emphasis in corporate organizations is sufficient. Control-centered organizations still need to center themselves in influence (I-i) even though their goal is (C-c). For example, the ideal control type above still requires the organization to add the level of influence and appreciation but evaluates them for their contribution to (C-c).

This insight is supported by a recent study in which McKinsey, the consulting firm, shows how a similar three-level complementary process carried out internally within a business organization does account for exceptional performance. The study, covering some 400 discrete business units of some 231 global businesses over 4 years, discovered that a small number of complimentary practices provide the most stable base for high levels of performance (Leslie *et al.* 2006). It identified these as:

1   an inspiring Vision
2   an open and trusting culture
3   clear roles.

They emphasized that it is the complementarity between the three types of practices that accounts for excellence. Companies that used this "base three case" outperformed others in revenues and margins. Readers will readily recognize the appreciative function of 1, producing vision, the influence emphasis on relationships in 2, open culture, and the control emphasis in 3, clarity of roles. The article charts the direct relationship between performance and the use of the base organizational model. It also calculates the economic value of different degrees of application of the organizational model.

When presented with these ideas organizations believe that they would be very costly to implement. They view the suggestions as sharing *control* rather than sharing *power*. They have difficulty factoring in the tremendous extension in power that *power with* and *power to* grants. Resources spent to enhance influence or "power with" give hundreds of percent return, while investment in "power to" or appreciation has potential for infinite returns. What is at stake is the understanding and wisdom necessary to develop an appropriate balance between risk and certainty. The tens of percent return that come with control are very predictable, what you pay for is what you will get for the most part. The "for the most part" points to the unintended consequences from failure to appreciate the aggregate field produced by our actions. With influence strategies such as our new strategic partners and improved core group relations we can achieve probabilities of hundreds of percent return but they may be in areas or ways we had not predicted. The return from appreciation may revolutionize a product, a whole division, the company, or an industry but where and how that will happen is even more uncertain. As we have seen, to balance these risks and uncertainties appropriately requires a combination of faith or *wisdom* that comes from appreciative means (a), the *understanding* that comes from the use of influence means (i), and the *knowledge* that comes from control means and experience.

In control-centered organizations understanding and wisdom take a longer term, broader perspective or, as we would say, higher dimensions of organizing capacity than most are able to take. Engagement with stakeholders brings about both improved influence and improved appreciation, which come about as actors learn more about their stakeholders' world and enlarge the set of possibilities that becomes available for them to influence. This emerging, more holistic role for the institutional level is much more powerful and relevant to the long-term success of the organization and its legitimacy in society.

What the AIC theory and model is able to do is give the root explanation of the three base areas that McKinsey identified as those that most affect organizational performance and their complementary relationships. It is also able to show how they are applied differently for different purposes, different organizations, and in different contexts. The simplicity and parsimony of the process and its scalability across levels is drawn from nature's holonomic organizing processes. The process attempts to utilize all the power created by every purpose, every function, and every phase of organization at every level from individual, to organizational, to institutional and to cultural levels.

11 The Humpty Dumpty Rule

Exploring the Potential

We are at the beginning of a new phase of evolution in both our understanding and practice of how we organize to achieve our purposes. We are still experiencing the aftermath of the last great breakthrough stimulated by the effects of World War II and expressed as an open-systems approach. This shift affected not only the way we think about organizations but also the way we think about ourselves, our relationships to each other, and our worlds. Ironically, though, the shift stopped short of enlightening us about the nature of the "whole," as we showed in Chapter 1. Much of advanced thinking about organizational systems has focused on the dynamic relationship between the parts of organized entities and their environments with a view to obtaining more control over them. Only in recent years have we started to reach for a more inclusional view that transcends this control-oriented perspective to suggest that wholeness itself is an equal valid end of our organizing efforts.

Current organization theories and practice still stress control as the end we seek through organizing. Even though open-systems thinking has taken us beyond the use of control means to the use of influence means, both in theory and practice, we tend to use influence for control of behaviour and action rather than equally for appreciation of the conditions that make effective action possible. Current approaches stress the causal properties of feedforward without giving equal weight to feedback. This chapter will illustrate, at the highest possible level, the implications of bringing the "whole" into the conscious level of our organizing processes both as an end and a means.

The ultimate whole for us is everything that affects or is affected by human purpose. The highest appreciative field is everything that affects human purpose but which we cannot control or influence. We have treated religion (spirituality), philosophy, and science as repositories of this knowledge and understood that they are the mothers and fathers of the dozens of disciplines that contribute to our knowledge of organization.

Figure 11.1 The Humpty Dumpty rule

It is our highest possible level of purpose, our infinitely open, future-oriented ideals that create this appreciated world of mind and sprit. We understand that when we say this we also include the part of our mind and spirit that links inextricably to unconscious purpose at the level of the whole—our basic instincts and our collective unconscious (see Figure 5.7).

Our pursuit of ideals, which gives us our highest levels of potential, also invokes our highest level of constraint. We are human animals and still hold within us the vestiges of our animal evolutionary patterning in the form of our basic instincts. If we have any doubt about this we only have to look at our recent history to see what happens when leaders actually achieve a form of "Omnipotence"—the unaccountable power over life and death achieved by such leaders as Hitler, Stalin, Pol Pot, and Saddam Hussein. Such power invokes in their reptilian brain an equally enhanced fear for their own death and enables a total unfeeling instinctive, reptilian reaction to the remotest potential threat to that power. Such reaction eventually destroys all levels of trust so that even the most intimate of friends and family members become suspect. Such ideals as wisdom, love, and trust become negated or so distorted that the leaders become consumed by fear and react accordingly. We see the same effect in authoritarian leaders who end up serving their own survival more than the whole they claim to serve. We see the creations of a vicious circle in which control displaces both influence and appreciation. Fear increases the desire for control and distorts information, which begins to destroy relationships, and then loses the appreciative connection to reality, potential, and meaning.

As the AIC theory holds that every purpose, at all levels, recursively creates three power fields of feedforward and feedback relationships we were able to construct a map of nine human ideals (Chapter 7) that provide the poles that define the appreciative-centered field of potential for human development. Development that does not open itself to the whole field indicated by these poles is not as *power-full* as it could be.

When we use this nine-poled map of our mindset we practice the AIC organizing process at its highest possible level. We enter the five-dimensional world of mind and spirit, an infinite set of possibilities that can be connected in new ways beyond the constraints of time and space. We become free to conceive of combining possibilities in ways that enable us to address the most promising and the most difficult issues that humanity faces. We enter a world of infinite potential where the impossible becomes possible. At the same time the opponent side of this appreciated world calls us to be equally open to the reality that such potential evokes—the unconscious reaction of our species' basic instincts. There are no potentially *awesome* results without equally potential *awful* consequences.

Can ordinary people struggling to pay the mortgage and save for their children's education, or even worse, in the third world, struggling to earn $1 a day just to survive, take advantage of these insights? Can hard-headed businessmen, pressed to make next quarter's numbers, really believe that understanding this appreciative-centered world could make any difference? We believe, and will try to show, that not only is it relevant to ordinary people but it provides them with a way to put their struggles in perspective. It relieves a big part of their stress by freeing them of the unnecessary burden of control. More than that, however, it will show that they in their struggles are the ultimate providers of the solutions; the potential power of the whole resides equally in each of us.

In Chapter 7, we took our first step in making the appreciative quality of wholeness equal with control. By interpreting the nine appreciative powers as ideals we equated them as a level of purpose with values and goals. With minor modifications we reproduce the chart of ideals from that chapter here. As we see, the vertical dimension of the chart—the rows—represents the active or feedforward part of humanity's ideals, the mental or spiritual attitude or posture to the world (A,I, or C).

The horizontal dimension—the columns—represents humanity's expected reaction from the world, its feedback about the degree of attraction to the possibilities produced by this ultimate state of openness. In Chapter 7 we showed how we designate this reaction with a small (a), (i), and (c) and can interpret it as the means that humanity (the *actor*) chooses to uses to address (*interact with*) the world (the *reactor*).

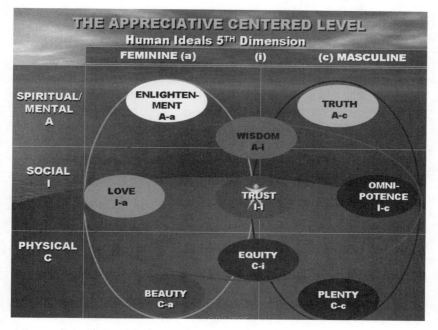

Figure 11.2 Appreciative-centered ideals

To help in both developing and understanding our choice of labels for the nine mental and spiritual powers, and to give them a human face, we have linked the word *feminine* with appreciative means (a), and the word *masculine* with control means (c), the *interaction* represents the flow of power (i), the dance that connects and resolves, at least for the cycle of the dance, the role of the masculine and feminine.

The primary purpose of the appreciative-centered fifth dimension is to become mentally and spiritually open to discover new possibilities (A). Once possibilities have been identified, secondarily, they need to be shared and explored for their consequence to those who might be affected (I) and then, thirdly, presented as a set within boundaries (C) that will be recognizable and attractive to the world. This is a very mundane reduction to explanation of one of the most marvelous mysteries of our existence: how our minds link to the infinite universe of the future and the realities of the past to formulate its most powerful insights and inspirations. Fortunately, Part I with examples from religion, science, and philosophy gives some more poetic descriptions of the process including my own personal experience.

The appreciative-centered dimension provides the gravity, the power of attraction for all future, thought, relationships, and action: it becomes the whole in every part. The attractiveness, the gravitational force, of the products of the appreciative-centered domain provides the latency for those products within the whole. Hence, the ultimate circularity of purpose that Mary Parker Follet observed (Chapter 1). The purpose of the whole is in every part and the purpose of every part co-creates the purpose of the whole. Individual differences of purpose and its expression co-create the evolution of the purpose of the whole.

A major implication of this way of looking at the world is a confirmation of pure or ideal democracy, the honoring of every individual as having a unique contribution to make to our evolution. Governance or control by the best and the brightest, the elite few, is therefore not as "power-full" as an ideal democracy that allows every individual freedom to express their power from purpose and participate in creating the conditions that affect the achievement of those purposes. As we have seen, every dictator, every authoritarian leader who is not acting in the interests of the whole, knows this and fears the power of the people, at least at the unconscious level of basic instincts.

Figure 11.2, then, provides a map, albeit a very minimalist one, of human potential. The names we have chosen for the ideals, as we have indicated in previous chapters, are suggestive rather than definitive and we invite readers to choose their own names to match their own purposes, culture, and field of endeavour.

1   (A-a) Enlightenment: Humanity reaches out to the universe in the most open, appreciative way possible (A) and has *faith* that the universe will respond in kind by being equally open to humanity (a). This reaching out is the basis of all religions and spiritual traditions. It is natural, then, that we should find the word for this ideal, *enlightenment*, in one of the most open of the major religions—Buddhism. I also like the word enlightenment because it includes the word "light" which helps us to link back to the highest levels of physics in which light is a set of five-dimensional vibrations (Chapter 5).

Such enlightenment, involving at least five dimensions of mental/ spiritual processing, has far-reaching implications for our whole world. It is the source of new religions, new philosophies, new sciences, and new ways of expressing them, such as art, language, mathematics, music, and dance, and yes—new theories of organization. The results of enlightenment at all levels from individual to global are so powerful that the actor often has great difficulty in expressing them

Appreciations come in the language of the whole, nature's energy. They are more like the language of dreams than English or Mathematics. We receive them as wholes that cover everything all at once. They may take a whole lifetime to unravel or their interpretation may be instant. It took Mohammed more than 23 years to unravel his revelations. It took Newton one instant of apple-shock to unravel a theory of gravity. Many innovators in all fields, including this author, claim that their major insights came from a single episode of intuition that took decades to work through.

2 (A-i) Wisdom: The products of enlightenment (A) have to be shared (i). As we saw in the Introduction and the chapters on religion and science, such appreciations can be very dangerous. They can change the basis and foundation of the existing appreciated order. Our religious leaders, scientists, philosophers, and artists have suffered greatly in receiving and processing their intuitions and revelations. We still see today that both major and minor innovators are often ignored, ridiculed, and punished. The Wright brothers' own father three months before the first flight, made his famous declaration:

"If God wanted us to fly he would have given us wings."

Thomas Watson in 1843 declared:

"I think there is a world market for maybe five computers."

Sir Harold Spencer Jones, the Astronomer Royal of Great Britain in 1957, declared that:

"Space travel is bunk."

We noted in the Introduction how the concepts of power and particularly those of appreciation received similar discounting, ridicule, and fear from both academic and professional colleagues.

Although it is possible to say that such examples represent just a few good ideas out of thousands of bad or crazy ideas that deserved to be discounted and ridiculed it is also clear that this process of identifying and nurturing new ideas is crucial to our creative ability to tackle the greatest issues of our time. Designing an ideal (A-i) process has huge implications for such creativity. It requires us to design safe conditions in which every actor at every level from individual to global can reach out to the world with their *enlightenment* or their *truth* to engage in a safe way with those who may not share their faith. The safety required is a space in which we can suspend our judgment during a phase of exploration. *It does not require us to accept the ideas or even be influenced by them.* It requires enough space, time, and suspension of judgment, especially destructive judgment, to give it an opportunity to connect with a wider set of possibilities. In this time the strange ideas can cross the horizon of our joint world of possibilities as a temporary shooting star that enjoys its moment of light then returns to the dark or creates fireworks by igniting other possibilities that illuminate and reveal latencies hidden in the mass of the universe of potential.

This is the kind of space David Bohm (1990) tried to invoke with his concept of "Dialogue." It is the kind of space David Cooperider and his colleagues (1987) provide in *Appreciative Inquiry*, Harrison Owen (1997) with *Open Space* and Marvin Weisbord (1992) in his descriptions of "Future Search." It is the Appreciative phase of our own practice of AIC. This suspension of judgment, influence, and control of the appreciative phase provides the least cost way to have the most possible impact in addressing the major issues of our times.

3 (A-c) Truth: The function of this ideal is to put boundaries (c) around the set of possibilities that emerges from the exercise of enlightenment and wisdom (A). The (A-c) power gives a name to this boundary: framing is a form of appreciative control. The name or boundary gives an identity that expresses its essence. Having an identity gives an implied legitimacy to the existence of the "Truth"; that these possibilities now exist as a generally (wholly) approved source of potential. The word "Truth" carries the connotation of science but also connotes the reason and enlightenment that surrounds it. It is what we mean when we speak of presenting or representing our "Truth." To maintain these connotations such truths are best expressed poetically as metaphors or symbols capable of awakening the unconscious powers of the whole carried as unconscious as myths and archetypes.

At this appreciative-centered level of mind/spirit the function of this resonant truth is not to direct action but to be a source of attraction to the power necessary for action. The truth may be in the form of a revelation, a myth, a theory, a vision, a story, or even a policy. Its task is to capture the latent power of both the conscious world and the unconscious by combining images from both our conscious appreciated world and our unconscious appreciated world of motives, emotions, and instincts.

Lao Tzu, the first philosopher of power based on threeness, identified naming with the beginnings of empowerment. The very first symbol of the Tao Te Ching has four solid lines, which for us is the ultimate form of control:

> *The Tao that can be expressed* (The manifest powers—our AIC)
> > *Is not the Tao of the Absolute* (The essence—our ultimate purpose)
> *The name that can be named*
> > *Is not the name of the Absolute.*

In the following lines he also notes the openness to perceive the subtlety— the double openness of (A-a)—and the boundary that marks the beginning of reality—indicated by the small (c) in (A-c).

Thus, without expectation, (A-a)
   One will always perceive the subtlety (a)
And with expectation, (A-c)
   One will always see the boundary (c).

As the achievement of all three ideals is a mental–spiritual process it costs nothing, yet it is the source of the greatest possible creativity for humanity. Successful development depends on tapping into this infinite source. The five-dimensional characteristics of the field tell us that this source of creativity is distributed equally in the whole. It explains Surowiecki's *Wisdom of Crowds* (2005). Surowiecki found the judgment of large crowds of people to be consistently better than even the best of their individual members. For this to be true he found that three conditions had to be met, and these turn out to be the conditions necessary to create an appreciative field:

1   Diversity, i.e. they represent the whole—appreciative means.
2   Decentralized, in that their organization had to have relationships in which they were free to disagree and contest rather than reach consensus or compromise—influence means.
3   Independent, they decided on the basis of their own perspective—control means.

What we have to learn is how to create this space by allowing the crowd, the whole, to have voice. We need to add this appreciative level to every purposeful process; from 15-minute problem-solving sessions to the resolution of humanity's most pressing problems of religious, political, and social conflict, philosophical, scientific, and economic differences.

The three Influence ideals respond to our need to engage with others and their "Truths" as we pursue our own ideals. They are secondary in this appreciative-centered domain in that they support the primary purpose of mental and spiritual openness.

4   (I-a) Love: in this context, represents Humanity reaching out to engage others (I) with its resonant truth while being willing to listen without judgment to the reaction (a), to influence while being the most open possible. This is the ideal of "Love." It is an ideal based on the belief that all people, at the level of being human, are equally worthy. Everybody should accept each other's humanity unconditionally. We accept all as brothers and sisters of one human family. It is an ideal shared by all major religions.

5   (I-i) Trust: is the central ideal of all nine. As the source of balance between the feminine ideals of love and the masculine ideals of power at the influence level it is also at the point of balance between "Wisdom" at appreciative level and "Equity" at the control level. It provides a balance vertically between wholeness and individuality, between mind and body, as well as horizontally between female and male, openness versus closedness. The sequence of ideals up to this point ((A-a) through (I-a)) sets up the conditions for trust, and the process after this ((I-c) through (C-c)) depends on trust for its success. The sequence confirms Ronald Regan's famous statement "Trust but verify." Trust is not blind, it takes all the work of appreciation to set up but then must be verified by action in the control phase:

- Appreciation builds Trust
- Control tests it, and
- Influence renews it.

6   (I-c) Omnipotence: Trust lies between Love, the ideal that acknowledges no difference between people, and the ideal of Omnipotence that is based on the difference between all people. If the actor's purpose is to prevail, ideally he must be able to overcome all differences: he must be "Omnipotent." We see the image of the all-powerful God in control-centered monotheistic religions and the God of Love more easily in the appreciative-centred religions. In Christianity Jesus (the influence level of the Trinity) is a God of Love (I-a). The Old Testament God (the control part of the Trinity) is the Omnipotent Father (C-a) and the Holy Spirit (A-a) is the God in all of us. When we want to make peace we seek the commonalities between us; when we seek war we point to the differences. When we do productive work we "trust" that both our commonalities and differences will be negotiated in a way that is beneficial for the whole.

In this five-dimensional field, as we have noted, influence is secondary and is in support of the primary appreciative-centered power of Enlightenment. Within this influence field the Center of Trust is prime, and Love and Power are equal and secondary or supportive of Trust.

The three control ideals imagine the form that products of enlightenment and trust will takes as:

- Ideas—e.g. theories, philosophies, art and inventions.
- Relationships—e.g. institutions, organizations, families, groups, and couples.
- The physical form of objects—e.g. habitats, infrastructure, tools, and adornments.

7   (C-a) Beauty: gives appreciative form (a) to the mental and spiritual products we have discovered, dialogued, and negotiated (C). The highest possible form is one of "Beauty." This beauty of form plays a significant role in the degree of attractiveness of the "Truth" revealed by enlightenment. The beauty of the manifestation of the purpose helps to amplify its resonance with the latent need the purpose addresses. The beauty of the Arabic that Mohammed wrestled from his revelations caused instant conversions to Islam. This is why art, stories, and films do a much better job of tapping into latencies, and evoking awareness, connection, and support for major issues than do studies, plans, or explanations. They are much better at creating "resonant" wholes. People can relate to them in their own way, they are a part of the hologram. There is now a growing literature on the importance of this aesthetic aspect of communication (Robert McKee (1997), Stephen Denning (2005), Janet Greco (1996)).

8   (C-i) Equity: ideally we would like everybody to enjoy such beautiful products but where this is not possible we at least want the means of their distribution to be fair. "Equity" becomes the ideal of relationships at this resource level. Ideally, we want fairness in opportunity to access, mental, relational, and physical products, i.e. access to knowledge, to people who affect our lives, to products and services that affect the quality of our lives.

9   (C-c) Plenty: Finally, the ideal of "Plenty" ensures that everyone has enough so that each of us can have autonomy over enough resources to ensure our well-being: you can be in control of your resources and I can be in control of mine. Under such ideal conditions of plenty we can imagine overcoming the problem of resource distribution. We can see humanity enjoying peace and harmony, which will increase our trust and create space for more enlightenment.

Again, in this appreciative-centered domain the control phase is in service of Influence, especially Trust, which is in service of appreciation, especially Enlightenment. However, within control the priority is on C-c or Plenty. Beauty and Equity are in the service of Plenty. Appreciative-centered organizations, churches, universities, associations, families, then, can most effectively achieve their purposes by concentrating on developing their own form of spirit or enlightenment, building trust, and then seek the wellbeing of their constituents.

The nine ideals operate as a whole. Together they model full power potential for humanity. Through the circular nature of purpose they become self-organizing and self-balancing.

Facing the Reality

As the opponent side of the *potential* of appreciation is *reality*, in this second half of the chapter we need a reality check to see how much these ideals and the use of appreciative power has anything to do with the major realities facing us as humanity today. Is there any evidence that the pursuit of nine ideals covers the "whole" of the major issues we experience? Is there any evidence that the pursuit of appreciative ends in contrast to solely control ends actually produces massive progress at much less cost than control ends and with much more constructive engagement than a reliance on processes that emphasize control ends? Do holistic organizing frameworks such as AIC help us to know what we might do more effectively to tackle those issues?

The American Forum for Global Education has been continuously keeping track of studies of global issues covering the last 50 years. The following is the list of the top nine issues taken from their list:

1   Conflict and Its Control: Violence/Terrorism/War.
2   Economic Systems: International Trade/Aid/Investment.
3   Global Belief Systems: Ideologies/Religions/Philosophies.
4   Human Rights and Social Justice.
5   Planet Management: Resources/Energy/Environment.
6   Political Systems: International Structures/Institutions/Actors/Procedures.
7   Population: Demographic Growth/Patterns/Movements/Trends.
8   Race and Ethnicity: Human Commonality and Diversity.
9   Sustainable Development: Political/Economic/Social.

(The American Forum for Global Education 2003)

The first task is to check whether all the ideals are covered. By comparing this list with our list of ideals we can tell how well our human community covers the spectrum of ideals. Is it seeing the whole picture?

It may seem a little surprising that give or take a little for the problems of interpreting such aggregated lists, Figure 11.3 shows that the nine issues are fairly well represented by the nine powers. This finding provides further support for Surowiecki's *Wisdom of Crowds* hypothesis—that the collective wisdom of the whole is better than that of any single individual or small group of experts. This list is a summation of all (the whole) global studies over the last 50 years. If the list had not shown coverage of all nine powers it would have revealed even more clearly the bias in the system, just as happened in the police example in Chapter 9.

The list also provides support for the basic thesis of this book that purpose is the creative source of power. If purpose is the source of power then our highest levels of yearning, our ideals, should match the greatest problems we face. We are yearning for a place where we transcend these issues. Our appreciated world is created by our highest levels of future purpose, our ideals, but the appreciative process also works by using the opponent process to ensure we face our major realities—in this case the nine highest priority issues facing humanity.

Power Map for Humanity		
	Learning	Politics	Planning
Relations to Whole	Conflict and its Control I-c	Science/ Economic Systems A-c	Global Belief Systems A-a
Relations to Others	Human Rights and Social Justice I-a	Technology/Planet Management C-c	Political Systems I-i
Relation to Resources	Population: Demographic C-a	Race and Ethnicity and Diversity A-i	Sustainable Development C-i

Figure 11.3 Power map for humanity

The next test is to see whether an AIC interpretation gives us any insight into our global condition and what needs to be done about it. For this purpose we use the power map we introduced in Chapter 9. We place the nine priorities in order into the 3 × 3 matrix of ends and means and interpret the results in the same way as we did for individuals. Figure 11.2 translates the issues into power relationships, ideals, and colors.

Fifth Dimension: Spiritual System

The fifth dimension covers the whole state of humanity. We derive our interpretation of this dimension of humanity exactly as we did in Chapter 9 for our individual maps. We compare the opposition between the ideal entered in cell 1 with the reality entered in cell 9. This tension gives us our "whole state" or spiritual dilemma, which is then mediated by the power place in cell 5:

- Cell 1—(I-c) from the ideal map, Figure 7.13—tells us that our current state is characterized by a desire for power *omnipotence*.
- Cell 9—(C-i) from the goal map, Figure 7.18—tells us we face the operational reality of lack of *agreement* on priorities. This reality in turn derives which derives a lack of value for egalitarianism.
- Cell 5—(C-c)from the values chart, Figure 7.16—tells us that we are trying to resolve this dilemma by applying *economic* solutions.

This insight fits with our diagnosis that we are in an age that is in a crisis of influence in which we have evolved from a belief in control as the only source of power to one in which we have learned to use influence, but we are using it only for control (I-c).

Fourth Dimension: Political System

Our entries in cell 2 and cell 8 give us our political dilemma, which is again mediated by what we have in cell 5:

- Cell 2—(A-c) from Figure 7.13 tells us that humanity's political system is driven by the ideal of *truth*.
- Cell 8—(A-i) from Figure 7.18 indicates that we are hampered in this search by our lack of *diplomatic* powers, which in turn derive from a lack of understanding and wisdom.
- Cell 5—(C-c) from Figure 7.16 again indicates that we try to solve this problem through economic processes.

Third Dimension: Executive System

Our entries in cells 3 and 7, again mediated by our entry in cell 5 indicate the state of the executive functions of our global system:

- Cell 3—(A-a) from Figure 7.13—tells us that we have very *enlightened* ideals.
- Cell 7—(C-a) from Figure 7.18—tells us we have no way of *appraising* our progress towards those ideals.
- Cell 5—(C-c) from Figure 7.16 again tells us that we use economic processes to solve the dilemma.

Our study of organizational profiles suggests that the power map for humanity reveals a state that is far from desirable. As humanity is an appreciative-centered system it should be powered by the opposition between *enlightenment* and *economics* (A-a and C-c) and mediated through *political* processes (I-i). To be viable any solution would have to have all three A, I, and C in some order and (a, i, and c) in some order. Our current situation is centered in control (C-c) in position five. It should have at least one (I) or (i), preferably both to carry out the appropriate mediation between the levels. To have C-c in this position guarantees premature closure of consideration of strategic options and is a likely cause of much distortion of information and even corruption.

Historical Test

Another test of reality is to see if these patterns can explain the major trends of modern history and if they suggest a path for evolution. Fortunately, this

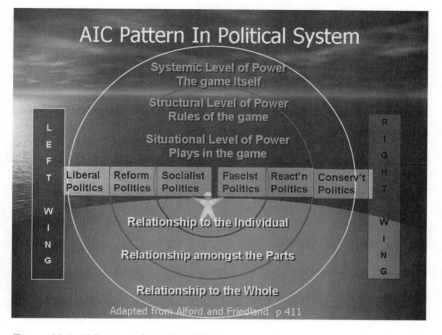

Figure 11.4 AIC pattern in political system
Adapted from Alford and Friedland (1985: 411)
Reprinted with permission from Cambridge University Press

work has already been done for us by Alford and Friedland (1985) who explain the current development of Capitalism, the State and Democracy and uses a model of development strikingly similar to AIC.

They illustrate the dimensions of struggle between the same three levels of power; the System, the Structure, and the Situation, and the same internal opposition between Left Wing (feminine, appreciative) and Right Wing (masculine, control). These oppositions were the cause of two world wars and the source of their resolution.

The three levels of power they describe are:

1 The Systemic level of power—the game itself: these appreciative boundaries define the political game and everything that affects or is affected by it. (A)
2 The Structural level of power—the rules of the game: these are the formal relationships of influence. (I)
3 The Situational level of power—the plays in the game. (C)

We can see from their chart that the whole political struggle that gave rise to the World Wars was a struggle between the left—(the feminine appreciative) and the right (the masculine control). When translated at the highest level of appreciation these invoke ideals of liberalism—all people are equal (Love I-a) and the ideals of conservatism—all people are individuals and, therefore, different so need to be controlled to prevent chaos (Omnipotence I-c).

When liberals have to translate their ideals of *equity* (C-i) into structures and rules of the game they favour intervention to make systems fairer. When conservatives translate their ideals of equity into structures and rules of the game they prefer non-intervention, except when things get out of hand and then they will *react*. They believe that, for the most part, if you leave people alone they will work out their differences (C-c) the *laissez-faire* doctrine.

If either the left or the right ignores the ideals and values of the other and tries to take control, what we get is the kind of socialism that is centrally controlled for the good of the whole—as in communism or the kind of control that tries to eliminate all difference, which we have experienced as fascism. The creation of the middle ground of democracy as influence has been the answer. It has been very successful in preventing participating countries from going to war, i.e. it has found a way to develop (I-i) relationships within and between democracies. However, modern democracies have not done well in terms of equity or love (treating all people as equals). The gaps between rich and poor are growing both within countries and between countries. Our major wars are based on these differences and are often justified by religious affiliation. Iraq is a good example. It is hard to imagine the war without considering oil and its wealth as a major factor. Democracy was put forward as the official aim, but it is the kind of representative democracy that does not ensure love or equity. In these circumstances it has created conditions that increased both inter-religious conflict—Christian versus Muslim—and intra religious conflict between Shia and Sunni sects. The initial strategy for intervention was control-centred, a military solution (C-c). It then moved into an influence strategy to involve regional actors more (I-c) and then into an appreciative strategy relying primarily on diplomacy (A-i).

The democracies have developed the process of solving problems through influence (the political or representative system) but most of that influence is geared to getting more control based on self-interest: too little is addressed towards appreciation—improving the system for everyone. It is this combination of excessive influence for control that accounts for the corruption that is endemic in modern democracies, the relationship to the whole is undervalued, hence problems with ethics, the environment, and a sense of meaning beyond possessions and status. The problem is no more paramount than in those countries that are by nature inclined to influence— African, Arab, and Latin American countries (see Nicholls model in Chapter 10, Figure 10.1). Such countries tend towards ideals that honor relationships more than rational logic-based principles. When linked with the strong control-centered values of the countries that colonized them or that brought strong cultural bias towards control in other ways the result has been influence for control—which lays a fertile ground for corruption. The greater success of Japan, S. Korea, and other Asian cultures may well be based on the more constructive combination of appreciation and control. The Asian value of sacrifice for the whole (group, family, country) works well with the combination of the control emphasis of individual responsibility. These countries, though, have still not produced influence systems that are strong enough to avoid corruption but their cultural bias towards appreciation gives them somewhat more trust in the whole. There is even a paradox in the fact that Asian countries that have more appreciative cultures than Western countries also have more authoritarian governments. A possible explanation for this is that the appreciative culture accepts more readily the need for governance of the whole and is willing to sacrifice personal freedom for it.

Arthur C. Brooks (2006) in his book *Who Really Cares* reveals a similar anomaly in the West. The common perception of the liberal (appreciative) left is that it is more compassionate than the conservative (controlling) right. Brooks, through careful research shows that the actual behaviour of people who adapt the two opposing political philosophies is exactly the opposite. Conservative States give 30 percent more income to charity than Liberal States. Republican States gave 3.5 percent while Democratic States gave 1.9 percent. A clue to the paradox lies in the four factors that predict who gives more:

1 religion
2 scepticism about the government's role in economic life
3 strong families, and
4 personal entrepreneurship.

The conservative does not see or want anyone to be "responsible" for the whole; he trusts only the individual and expects less of any government. He sees charity as a personal responsibility not a general one. The liberal, on the other hand sees poverty as a systemic characteristic of the whole so she looks for general rather than individual solutions and therefore does not give individually.

The *Economist* points to a similar economic paradox in which ethical food actually harms the planet. The article shows how individuals who buy organic food, shop for Fair Trade products and local rather than multi-national produce may be doing more harm to the environment than good. For example, organic food takes more space so will result in the cutting down of more forests to feed the world. Fairtrade products are sold at higher prices with the extra being passed on to the farmers. However, these subsidies lead to overproduction, which in turn leads to lower prices—defeating the original purpose. A British study found that the cost of transportation was much higher for local food because the number of individual trips to a local organic market was far more than the cost of highly efficient large trucks distributing to more local supermarkets. Again, the answer lies in a whole-systems perspective that takes into account all three levels:

> Real change will require action by governments, in the form of a global carbon tax; reform of the world trade system; and the abolition of agricultural tariffs and subsidies, notably Europe's monstrous common agricultural policy, which coddles rich farmers and prices those in the poor world out of the European market. Proper free trade would be by far the best way to help poor farmers . . . But these changes will come about only through difficult, international, political deals that the world's governments have so far failed to do.
>
> (*Economist*, December 12, 2006: 12)

An African Test

The same issues arose in practice at the global level when ten African countries used the AIC approach in 1995 to evaluate the role of the World Bank and the Multilateral Development Agencies (Smith and Sato 1996). The participants suggested a quiet revolution in which the World Bank redis-covered its purpose as a bank rather than a development agency. They felt it should focus on the design of financial institutes and mechanisms that would provide the equivalent of Mohammed Yunnus's micro-village-level lending to economic units at the town, provincial, and larger levels.

The key to their suggestion would enable the World Bank to tap into all the power of purpose of those directly affected by their projects. People would individually and collectively work on their own purposes and develop their own power. The role of regional and global financial and other agencies would be to help overcome abuses of power from those who for selfish reasons would constrain or distort the distribution of information and resources.

The planning unit from the World Bank's perspective would shift from projects to a more macro basis. The boundaries would be the largest possible that gave humans a sense of identity along with a recognizable economic base. Such local regions would have populations in the low millions. This would give the local regions or small nations an influenced environment about ten times larger than typical projects. Each region would then have the potential for global impact.

The Feminine–Masculine Test

It is ironic that the feminist movement, which we would expect to be a major cultural force for appreciative-centered solutions has the same difficulties as the control culture (see, for example, Gherardi 2003). The radical feminine movement historically has adopted a control (C-c) strategy:

> Radical feminism, therefore, attempts to create a discursive arena freed from the tyrannies of male-oriented political discourse.
>
> (Whelehan 1995: 67)

The modern liberal feminist seems to adapt an (I-a) stance but is unwilling to engage the existing system in an (I-i) relationship:

> When a woman in the United States or Western Europe first identifies herself as a feminist, it is often as a liberal feminist, asserting her claim to the equal rights and freedoms guaranteed to each individual in democratic society.
>
> (Nye 1988: 5)

> Because of liberalism's long history of links with industrial capitalism; liberal feminists tend to be reluctant to pose any direct challenge to capitalism, which effectively leaves the option of a limited intervention in the institutions which maintain it.
>
> (Whelehan 1995: 38)

The feminist movement has taken the perspective that at the appreciative human level men and women are equal, but it is only beginning to acknowledge that at the influence level, which deals with difference, there is all the difference in the world:

> Feminism needs to re-emerge from the mire of "identity politics" in order to fully engage with and interrogate the nature of subtle ideological and material shifts which have occurred since the beginnings of its second wave.
>
> (Whelehan 1995: 146

The world of influence is based on the different values of appreciation and control, love and power. We have to honor the difference between the feminine and masculine and not deny them but transcend them in the interest of the whole. Many women's programs, study groups, and institutes still focus only on women. The problem of the inequitable treatment of women, like all other problems cannot be treated at the level at which it is presented. Although women dialoguing with women and developing women's leadership skills is useful it does not contribute as much as it could to the bigger issue of the whole—how to transcend the differences between men and women for the good of the whole. Many such programs unconsciously undermine the message by adapting the control perspective that changing the self or the conditions one controls is the way to change the world. We need to go to a higher level purpose, that of all humanity, all men and women, to honor and transcend the problems of inequity.

To get to this level, however, the feminist movement needs to make the same shift as society. It needs to move up to a higher level of purpose to the level of the whole in order to shift the ideals and values that will influence mindsets, relationships, and behavior.

Jeannie Marshall, a Consultant in Human Resource Development, reflects these views when she says:

> It is an issue of the Spirit which intensifies the human experience of separation—separation from the whole, separation from each other, separation from the divine. The confusion about masculine and feminine encourages unhealthy competition (and not just *between* genders), dysfunctional comparisons, low self-esteem, and imbalances of many kinds.
>
> (Marshall 2006)

This was the stance that ODII took in its Thai project (see the Introduction). In that project our goal was to understand women's organizing ability in an appreciative culture. We would thus learn a double dose of appreciation: from feminine culture and from Thailand—one of the most appreciative cultures on earth. We transcended the difference by making the project about development for the whole of each village, which then became the whole of the province and then the whole of the country.

We dealt with the masculine and feminine by making a rule that participation in the development process must be 50–50 men and women. As recounted in Chapter 3, the project was so successful that it was replicated throughout Thailand and was even influential in changing the Constitution to better reflect these values. The results also had a dramatic effect on the career of the chief researcher involved in the program—a woman, Orapin Sopchokchai of the Thailand Development Research Institute (TDRI). The Institute, like most classical research institutes valued the masculine empirical; numbers-based research and looked down on the holistic, qualitative approaches such as action research, the approach we used on the women's project. Women who were not as valued as men in the Institute would get assigned much less important projects. The success of the project was not foreseen by TDRI nor was the international acclaim that later came to Ms Sopchokchai (Sopchokchai 1993).

Practical Impact of the Appreciative Level

The final reality is to look for evidence that the addition of the appreciative-centered level of mind/spirit is actually happening and making the huge "power-full" differences that we predict. The most dramatic of such evidence lies in the most significant human developmental of our time, the development of the Internet and the Web. The *Time* magazine cover for January 1, 2007, which identifies the person of the year, shows a computer with a mirror as its screen with the inscription underneath:

> YOU, Yes you. You control the Information Age. Welcome to your world.

Doug Engelbart, who invented the mouse, Windows, and hypertext, was a founding figure of Web technology, and has remained at the heart of this global transformational experience even though it took decades for his contribution to be appreciated. His story illustrates in practice the power of the appreciative perspective.

Doug is of Norwegian descent, with grandparents who survived the Depression on a small farm near Portland, Oregon. He carried out studies in electrical engineering and his experience in the Philippines as an electronic/radar technician laid the foundation for his later invention of the mouse.

After three years of working as an electrical engineer with Ames, the forerunner of NASA, he grew restless. It was then that he asked the big question: "What can an engineer do to help humanity." His answer was very simple and not at all in tune with the engineering and nascent computer world of his time:

> To use our technology to connect people to solve humanity's greatest problems.

As his daughter Christina notes in his web biography, he began to imagine:

> . . . people flying around his cathode-ray-tube display in information space where they could communicate and organize with incredible speed and flexibility.
>
> (Engelbart 2003)

He completed a PhD, picking up half-a-dozen patents in the process, and then stayed on at Berkeley to develop his "wild ideas." Predictably, they would not fit into the narrow expectations and constrained role prescriptions of what a university values and rewards in an acting assistant professor. He soon found himself out of the university and at the Stanford Research Institute (SRI) in 1957. He earned enough of a reputation to be allowed to follow his ideas for augmenting human intellect, improving information infrastructure, and co-evolution of technical artefacts with socio-cultural language practices:

His thinking prompted assessment of the infrastructure of capabilities that support the operation of organizations of collectively purposeful humans, capabilities developed atop their genetically endowed capabilities to provide their personal and collective operational effectiveness.

(Engelbart 2003)

His fundamental thinking follows the same three levels of A, I, and C, but he conceived of the three levels of *power relationships* as levels of *system improvement*. He referred to the A, B, and C levels, which are labelled in the opposite direction of A, I, and C:

- A is the system itself (our C).
- B is improvement of the system (our I).
- C is the improvement of the improvement process (our A).

Doug saw that we could get exponential improvements from working with the improvement of the improvement process. It was this appreciative level that took him into the realm of culture, language, and communities of practice.

In 1967 when ARPA decided to network its thirteen separate research labs, including Doug's, Doug was delighted. He now had a vehicle for building his collaborative networked system. His results were dramatically highlighted in a 1968 Joint Computer Conference when he and his staff delivered, to a standing ovation, what is now called the "mother of all demos:"

His lab harnessed some leased video links to the conference site, borrowed an unusual, new device that could project dynamic video brightly onto a 20-foot screen needed to provide readable NLS screens [Doug's computer software hypermedia—for oN Line System] in a space holding 1000-plus attendees. At a special session, Engelbart, operating NLS from the stage through a home-made modem, used NLS to outline and then concretely illustrate his ideas to the audience while members of his staff (with their faces shown on the screen) linked in from his lab at SRI.

(Engelbart 2003)

He had shown how three groups separated in space could now "fly around in information space," they could each occupy a separate "window" and the windows could be linked with a new small electronic device with four little wheels and an electronic tail which began magically, in a way no one remembers how, to be called a "mouse." Each of the three partners could add their own text and could modify the others text. The Web was born.

In 1989 McDonnell Douglas, who had purchased Tymeshare, the company that owned the commercial rights to NLS, could not see the usefulness of Doug's experiments with collaborative software. They closed his lab and he and thirteen of his staff moved to Xerox Parc.

Once again Doug Engelbart found himself out of step with the nascent computer information industry. Xerox's ideal for the computer was "aesthetic" (C-a)—produce the most beautiful documents possible on the screen so that they would look exactly as they do in real life. IBM—the only other major computer company at the time—had an ideal of "plenty" (C-c) for the computer. The purpose of the computer was to process infinitely more information faster and at less cost. Doug Engelbart's work to augment the human intellect had convinced him even more that the ideal purpose of the computer was connectivity (I-i) *Trust*. The computer, its software and its infrastructure should be designed to connect people to solve the greatest problems of our world

He had two of the three ideals necessary to influence his world, the ideal of *Love* (I-a)—to treat all people as equal in their right to take part in solving the world's problems—and the computer and software would provide the means for *Equity* (C-i). What he was missing was the power (*Omnipotence* I-c) to gain a hearing.

The power, however, eventually came from the person honored by *Time* magazine, from each of us, and from our story about what we have done with the gift of the Internet:

> It's a story about community and collaboration on a scale never seen before. It's about the cosmic compendium of knowledge Wikipedia and the million-channel peoples' network "YouTube" and the online metropolis MySpace. It's about the many wresting power from the few and helping one another for nothing and how that will not only change the world, but also change the way the world changes.
>
> (*Time*, December 13, 2006)

In the same issue of *Time* Stephen Johnson, comparing the second generation of the Web to the first, which ended with the dotcom bust about the year 2002, wrote:

> Web 1.0 was organized around pages web 2.0 is organized around people. And not just those special people who appear on TV screens and in Op-Ed columns. Web 2.0 is made up of ordinary people: hobbyists, diarists, armchair pundits, people adding their voice to the Web's great evolving conversation for the sheer love of it.

In other words the Web has empowered ordinary people to express their purpose. What we need now is the change in institutional and organizational mindset to allow this new power to find its full expression.

We are now living in the information space Doug Engelbart imagined. We fly around in a plasma or LCD screen rather than the cathode-ray tube and are beginning to use its power to solve the greatest problems on earth. It is still not easy. One of his strategies was to set up frontier outposts to scan for new ideas and test out ideas. Susan Turnball, Senior Program Advisor, Office of Intergovernmental Solutions, Office of Citizen Services and Communications and her colleagues lead one such outpost in the US Government Service Administration (GSA), a bastion of control-centered thinking. Government, of course, is one of the institutions that has most to gain by adjusting its mindset to a more appreciative-centered one. It is, after all responsible for the organization of the whole country and its relationships to the whole world.

She combined Doug Engelbart's philosophy and technology with the appreciative-phase concepts of AIC to produce a very unusual, for GSA, set of expedition workshops whose job was to bring all parties affected by technology together:

> The first workshop, in March 2001 was a simple brown bag lunch. George Brett shared with Susan Turnball and several colleagues his perspective about tools to help individuals work in community. As of April, 2004, all-day workshops draw 60–80 people together from multiple perspectives. Participants share a sense of purpose around societal challenges immune to tactics by single groups. The Expedition workshop story is being documented as a technological change process that goes beyond "technology-driven" change. By centering around people and the "whole system" challenges they organize around, IT design and development processes can mature with less risk and greater national yield of breakthrough performance innovations.
>
> (OIS website)

She would ask such simple questions as:

> How can we overcome unstable conventions of meaning that thwart information sharing?
>
> How can we create conducive conditions to be informed (not overwhelmed) by the combined complexity of our multiple forms of expertise?

The open appreciative workshops produced results so much faster and with such far-reaching impact, compared with the traditional organization in which select committees would deliberate and write papers that had to go through many levels of review. Her work put her at the nexus of conflicts of interest between purveyors of private software and open-source software, between meetings that were exclusionary or opposing, or worse: limited to special interests.

It is not surprising that Susan was moved to new positions at least four times in 6 years. However, because appreciation is a property of mind it cannot be controlled. If it is in tune with the latent needs of the whole it keeps popping back up. This is what happened to Susan, she just kept popping back up as she automatically addressed the latent needs of her field for more appreciation, more transparency, more openness for the good of all people. Susan and her many colleagues provide one of those frontier outposts that show the way while, unfortunately, in the process, having to absorb personally the shocks of the transformation.

Summary

Very simply the message from our survey of the *potential* and *realities* of humanity's global systems is that we try to resolve too much through control. An equal emphasis on appreciation dissolves many of the problems of control and influence and provides the means for this resolution. Control without supportive appreciation and influence produces stove-piped organizations that find it difficult to share information or resources. They are not capable of fully appreciating and evaluating the situation and alternative course(s) of action. They are unable to use all of the power that is available to them. The over-emphasis on control leads us to believe that the solution of our greatest problems depends on resources. Our power map profiles and all the experience and learning recounted in this book leads us to believe that this is not true. What we need is more wisdom, that wisdom is a property of the whole, the "crowd" that we are all part of. Our solution is for all of us to use our influence to develop our organizations so that they in turn use their influence to better link themselves to their appreciative world, which will give them their higher level ends that in turn will make it easier to achieve their ends in their world of control.

Our application of our power map to the design of humanity's global systems supports a major thesis of this book: that we are at a phase in our evolution of social organization in which we have transcended the limits of a pure control view of power (power over), and have learned to use influence (power with), but we continue to use its evolved power of influence for control. What we need to learn and to build into our organizing processes is an equal application of influence for appreciative ends (power to). The equal attention to appreciative ideals of the whole will provide the means for our organizations to transform their ability to serve themselves, their stakeholders, and their world.

12 Reflections

The Three Transformations

This book has now interwoven three stories of transformation. The first is a personal one in which a wonder at the potential of the field of organization is transformed into a career-long pursuit to unravel its secrets. The second is the story of the transformation of the field of organization itself, from a concern with design of structures for efficiency to a more organic concern with the organization of the conditions that make life rewarding and meaningful. The third and unanticipated story to emerge through the process of writing itself is our story, the story of the human spirit struggling to make the best of the conditions we find ourselves in. It is the story about how ultimately we find ways to transcend theory and practice to transform our world. This chapter reflects on the key points of insight and experience that contributed to these three joint transformations.

The seeds of the three transformations were planted at the moment of my introduction to the field by the three questions posed by J.A.C. Brown in his seminal work *The Social Psychology of Industry*:

1   What is the nature of man as an individual, and what if any are his basic needs?
2   What is the nature of man as a social animal and how does he relate himself to society?
3   What is the nature of industry, and how far does it fit in with what we know of man as a human being both socially and individually.

(Brown 1954: 21)

His first question leads to reflections on personal transformation. His second question is reflected in the lessons about organizational transformation and his last question points to perspectives that transform our world.

Transforming Ourselves

In Peru the airport manager taught me in a very practical way the essence of control. All elements of performance for both on-time departure and passenger service were related. It was his emphasis on those elements that *could have* created a delay or a failure of service that triggered the connection (Chapter 1). My interest in organization as structure, in methods analysis and systems thinking all stemmed from that initial experience and confirmed in me the prevailing image of organization as a machine to be controlled. He gave me a hint of the power of appreciation in ceremonies for flight departure but I regarded them as a quaint anachronisms.

It was the accident of high performance at Rome that shook the very foundation of this belief. The change could not be accounted for by the changes in structure, methods, systems, and procedures I introduced. The disquiet was strong enough and the search for answers so unsatisfying that it led me to leave BOAC and eventually my country in search for something I intuited was very powerful and very fundamental.

My failures in relationships in Trinidad and Rome as illustrated by the story of the area manager for Italy, and my experience in consulting and G.D. Searle were trying to show me the importance of the influence field, but I had no ears to hear or eyes to see. It would be many years before I could grasp the significance of those lessons. I was not looking in the right places.

It was the combination of my daughter, Michele, waking me up to my chauvinism and the McDonald's consulting assignment that opened me to feminine and masculine differences that led me to see the conceptual emerging influence field as a distinct and separate field whose primary function was to work out such fundamental value differences. The research I carried out for G.D. Searle added grist to this mill. My research showed the different phases of organization in the evolution of multinational companies. I applied the results to the pharmaceutical industry and G.D. Searle in particular (Smith and Charmoz 1976). It was the height of my progress in rational thinking applied to what were really political problems of organizational change. The research was very well received by all three major competing groups within the company—the corporate divisions, the international division, and the domestic organization. However, rather than enlightening them to transcend their differences each took from the research the parts that supported their viewpoint and carried on the battle with sharper tools. An understanding of power and politics from then on became central to my search. I knew that competing political parties had to develop their own solutions and this capacity to help interest groups transcend their difference had to be built into the organizing process. Even the best of classical research was not powerful enough to deal with the hidden drivers of choice and action that were buried in the political process.

It was the reaction of the factory workers in National Silicates in Canada that gave me my first experience of a design that created an appreciative field. The plant workers were asked, for the first time ever, to tell their own story of the plant in which their fathers and their grandfathers had lived their entire work lives. They had an opportunity to contribute to the design of their ideal plant. Within the three months that it took before my next trip to the plant they had literally transformed its appearance by getting rid of its rust-belt detritus by cleaning and painting the whole edifice and making its grounds into gardens. From then on I built what I would later call the appreciative field into everything I did, but I still saw it as just a logical step of consulting with and including everybody in the organizing process.

If there was a single point of transformation it was the jolt and subsequent revelation that came all at once from Gus Schumacher's well-meant opponency in the World Bank:

Why couldn't we find practical words for the concepts of internal, transaction and contextual environments?

The all-in-one insight that the philosopher Alfred North Whitehead calls a "prehensile unification," described in Chapter 3, was wonderful in that it gave a sense and feeling of being in tune with and knowing the connection between all things at some very deep level. However, at another level it was torture because the "unification," apparently, doesn't come in language or images but in nature's energy; some form of resonant knowing that can take decades to unravel. Some of the things I could translate were too fantastic to communicate in the logic of professional community and the accepted discourse of academia. How, for example, could I tell my colleagues that ultimately we would know that mass and purpose are the same thing and this was the major energy that was driving my intuitive sense of the nature of wholeness and connection?

I settled for the translation that the internal, transactional, and contextual environments were power relationships, which I labeled control, influence, and appreciation. I even had to downplay the key part of the translation that purpose is the source of power. The most difficult part of the translation was to explain appreciation. Every attempt to step beyond a logical systems explanation—that it is our relationship to the whole—got me into more trouble. Chapter 3 tells how my introduction of the concept of appreciation invoked the wrath of my professor, Russ Ackoff and of my professional colleagues. However, the effects in practice were calling out for something more and I wasn't finding it.

The transformation of perspective again, came just as gently as the answer to the question:

If A, I, and C are power fields where does the power come from?

In that case the question asked for a word. In the case of the nature of appreciation the transformation came from the use of a word. It happened when the Colombians explained the self-organizing process that had been triggered by our work in the energy sector. They said that many of the people who were part of that process were also part of helping to solve many of the country's other problems. So there was a national core group that would find their members in task groups contributing to the nation's major problems. They would say to each other:

Let us try to solve these problems in the spirit of Santa Marta.

Santa Marta was the location on Colombia's Caribbean coast where our first workshop was conducted. Just hearing that word "spirit" was the gentle trigger that coalesced my understanding of the field of appreciation. I knew then that spirit was the essence of the field. Something changed in me at that point such that since then I have never had a problem with the concept or practice of appreciation. Up until that point something in the way I related to, expressed, or practiced the appreciative phases as just one of three logical phases of organization was out of synch, an obstacle to creating and maintaining the presence of the field. I now know that we cannot explain the essence of appreciation; we have to experience it. Any explanation becomes a story about such experiences. When I give such story explanations now, even people who are still not satisfied go away more wistful than angry.

Transforming our Organizations

I am always surprised when I think about organization and I realize that it is not the concept of appreciation that has had the most impact on the transformation of our practice but the concept of influence. My best guess is that organization is the middle ground, the influence field, between purpose and action so middle-ground relational concepts best express the essence of the field. Classical thinking viewed organizations as entities of control in an environment that consisted of "everything out there" that wasn't under control. So implicitly the field has always been two-fold, the organization as the controlled part of our world and the environment, the uncontrolled part, was the appreciative part. So to add a third level, the influenced part of the environment that reduced the uncertainty of "no control" to "influence" was something new that had a major impact on organizational theory and practice. My master's degree mentor, James D. Thompson, had been instrumental in the intellectual development of this space as the "task environment" and my PhD. mentor Eric Trist and his colleague Fred Emery had added the concept as the "transactional environment." However, there were other key qualities that defined the space that were not being elicited by the practical use being made of these concepts. Again, it was practical experience that provided the stimulus for the missing insight.

In the period after the success of the Colombian experience we carried out dozens of workshops repeating the Santa Marta approach but had most difficulty with the conduct of the influence phase. We used the logic of the "task environment" and "stakeholder engagement" and brought them together to produce a strategic plan. However, the process always seemed to be complex and artificial and would run out of steam. We noticed, however, that the first part of the process when we divided people into interest groups to discover priorities the process was very animated and seemed to make great progress. It was only in the second half when we tried to close it down into the strategic plan that it became heavy and lifeless.

It was the graphics we had begun to use to explain the differences of the concept of time in the phases that triggered the answer. We showed time in the influence phase as "timing": a series of infinite loops that needed to be harmonized. The loops suggested that there was no beginning or end. Yet the way we were treating the phase as the production of a strategic plan that would drive the control phase was making a closure that felt unnatural. The energy in that phase was clearly not ready for closure or control, it wanted to continue the circular process of the in-flow, its influence.

We just stopped closing at that point and dropped the reference to a strategic plan. We moved from producing as many options as possible in the (I-a) phase to the most significant that emerged from the debates in the (I-i) phase but then left the (I-c) phase semi-open with a few major options. These few options were then used as appreciative "in-formation" for the control phase (C-a).

The graphic enabled us to honor the essence of the I-i relationship symbolized by the masculine and feminine dance. This was the point at which the spiral of "hard" realities from the past met the "soft" potential of the future in the present. In fun, we would occasionally show, as in Figure 12.1, a masculine and feminine figure at war for the purpose of love, the ideal of *omnipotence* versus the opposing influence ideal of *love*.

We realized that we had made the I-i process the center not only of the influence phase but of the whole organizing process. This was the point of transformation in our view of the field of organization. Organization is as much about improving the conditions for the effectiveness of this process as it is about the efficiency of the design for producing the products from the process. It requires centering in the dance of influence, in the I-i process. Organization is not just the inevitable linear march from appreciation to influence to the goal of control. Organization is centered in influence (I-i) in order to pay equal attention to appreciative purposes (ideals) and control purpose (goals). It achieves this by creating its own space with its own substance and norms that create the best possible conditions for the resolution of differences (values).

The over emphasis on control leads to extremely wasteful and harmful effects as we try to control that which is not controllable. The pressure is

Figure 12.1 Influence: engaging the issues

so strong that it creatures the culture of "the lie," which was made so evident, for example, when the executive of Tobacco Companies stood in front of a Congressional Committee to lie about their knowledge and collusion in concealing research on the enormous health damage and deaths caused by smoking. What was so compelling was that the executives knew they were lying, the Congress knew they were lying and just about everyone watching the hearings knew they were lying. They, however, felt that they had such a degree of control over massive resources that they could do so with impunity. So, many of us learn to live the lie "that we are in control" to survive organizational life, but as newer generations insist on meaningful work-life the pressure to change is equally great. The pathway is for us to learn to use our new-found sources of influence equally for appreciative purposes not just for control purposes.

Half of the effectiveness, economies, and constructive engagement that occurs from using such holistic organizing processes as AIC, which stress equal use of appreciative, influence, and control means comes from this reduction in wasted energy; the distortion, lies, and corruption that come from trying to control the uncontrollable. The other half of their effectiveness comes from taking that lost energy and applying it to appreciation, which multiplies its power exponentially by creating the conditions for more effective use of all three means—appreciative influence and control. Suddenly we see that the role of the organizing process is to create the conditions to improve the (I-i) relationship at all levels of purpose:

1   In the appreciative-centered dimension to govern conditions for creating *trust*.
2   In the influence-centered dimension to manage conditions so that the *political* system so uses its influence to improve both its appreciative relations to the world as well as to control the resources necessary for implementation.
3   In the control-centered dimension ground conditions for better *negotiation* processes for the use of scarce resources.

The organizing process is the middle ground between purpose and action. It helps create the ideas, engage relationships, and manage resources. We waste so much energy in trying to jump from potential to form in the forced march to control. The remedy is to learn to dance to improve the way we engage with ourselves, our organizational stakeholders, and our world. To create an idea, to improve a relationship, to produce a product or service is not the end point. Our products and services are feedback on the way to improved quality of life in all its aspects, including the process of deciding what to produce and the process of producing them.

The transformation we bring about, centered in influence, does not produce a world of pink bows and political correctness. It actually allows more difference and therefore more conflict to surface. By discovering the higher purposes we serve, by sensing the meaning people seek in their lives we create a spirit of trust that can help us better understand our differences and help us prevent them from spiraling out of control. The creation of more trust allows us to say more of what we really think and feel. The results are very often "not nice," just as in competitive sports we can end up with our nose in the mud. However, we are better able to deal with the hidden power, the elephants in the room, that everyone knows are there but the culture does not allow us to address.

In our influence-centered organizations we don't have to solve the problem of the elephant, we just have to acknowledge its existence and trace its likely consequences. It is not until we enter our own world of control that we have to face our own demons. Each of us is the only person who has access to our unconscious power and purpose. It is only at this point that the unconscious is directly addressed. Each of us makes a decision on the basis of everything we have appreciated, on all the options and positive and negative consequences revealed in our influence exchanges. This is our personal inner point of transformation, it is where our spiral of future potential meets our spiral of realities from the past and our conscious and unconscious minds have to coalesce. This is why we "sleep on it," we take nature's appreciative time to process what we should do. We wake up in the morning, make the decision and accept the responsibility for its consequences. In the end we have to make our own decisions and the welfare of the whole depends on that independence. The ideals of both the Republican and the Democrat are achieved. This is the way each of us access the whole of our power. It is only when the whole of our power is conjoined with the whole power of others who appreciate the whole that our organizations are transformed to become as 'power-full" as they can be.

Transforming Our World

Throughout the book the word "world" has been used as a translation of "whole" very much as we mean in such expressions as the "world of music' or the "world of the fortunate." The concept of appreciation is used to define the outer edges of that field of power we call a "world." These edges define the limits of our power relative to that world, they are the limits set by the field that affects our purpose or is affected by it. Yet if we take the basic premise of holistic systems thinking then the appreciated environment for any purpose consists of all past reality and all future potential. In effect, there are no bounds to the appreciative field; it is theoretically infinite. In practice, however, as we have shown, we carry within us an image of that world and it is that image that bounds our appreciated world. When we are trying to organize a lunch next Thursday with a group of friends, we don't carry out a five-year planning process or carry out a psychological study of each of our friends. We have within us an appreciative field about lunches that includes a sense of our friends' lunch worlds. The extent of our appreciative field in this case is determined by that inner world associated with the ideal lunch. It has its own space- and time-cycle determined in days or weeks not months or years, its physical space is several blocks or miles not whole countries and worlds. That is not to say that when we get to larger organizations one of the most useful things we can do is to uncover those implicit dimensions and question the appropriateness of these implicit constraints under new conditions.

To transform our world we extend our appreciative powers of intuition and sensing to move both deeper into our spiral of reality and higher into our spiral of potential. To make full use of the insight and discoveries that come from these appreciations we have to create a safe space where the products of this discovery can see the light of day and like a moth live long enough so that our light can connect with other lights. If enough of the lights find sources of attraction they can combine to create the fire of passion that creates new life in both old and new endeavors. The light of the spirit moves into the fire of passion and then into a shape forged by the heat that "transforms" our world.

The transformation of our world, then, comes from our collective journeys higher and deeper into the spiral of potential and reality that provide the "religio" between bounded and unbounded time. We have a natural orientation that makes us more at ease with the field of realities created by the past, the field of potential created by the future, or the field of the present that relates the two. Our job is not to change that; it is our gift, our difference. Our new world is calling on us to honor our differences, to acknowledge them as the ultimate source of our contribution and to collectively transcend them by making equal use of appreciative, influence, and control powers to accomplish our purposes.

It is the collective unsung stories of people such as those mentioned in this book—Francis Lethem, Ben Thoolen, Turid Sato, Gus Schumacher, Ken Murrell, Corrine Marr, Diane, Bill Graham, and Susan Turnbull—that are the stuff of which this transformation is made. It is our collective purpose and power that co-creates and recreates our world. It is up to us to stretch for our own higher purpose, it is up to us to use our influence equally for appreciation and control. What we co-create, the form we give to those ideals, transforms our world.

Appendix

Scoring forms and interpretation for the power map

Choosing your Colors

Examine each of the nine colors from the "Color Selection for Power Map" see Plate 15, at the end of the color section.

On the basis of how you react to those colors at this time only (i.e. not in reference to fashion preference or symbolic meanings) choose the colors you like best and those you like least.

It is important to follow the sequence outlined below in which you have three rounds of selection—choosing the color you like best and the color you like least. You enter the resulting color numbers in Table A.1. You can only use any of the nine colors just once.

You can then work out your power type by entering your selections into the boxes on Table A.2.

Table A.1 **Power map worksheet**

Round 1 Color choices

Cell 1	Cell 2	Cell 3
Cell 4	Cell 5	Cell 6
Cell 7	Cell 8	Cell 9

Round 2 Color choices

Cell 1	Cell 2	Cell 3
Cell 4	Cell 5	Cell 6
Cell 7	Cell 8	Cell 9

Round 1

Of all the nine colors, which do you like best and which do you like least? Enter the numbers corresponding to those colors below:

Like best ☐ enter # in Cell 1   like least ☐ enter in Cell 9

Round 2

Of the remaining seven colors, which do you like best and which do you like least? Enter the numbers corresponding to those colors below:

Like best ☐ enter # in Cell 2   like least ☐ enter in Cell 8

Round 3

Of the remaining five colors, which do you like best and which do you like least? Enter the numbers corresponding to those colors below:

Like best ☐ enter # in Cell 3   like least ☐ enter in Cell 7

Round 4

Of the remaining three colors, which do you like best and which do you like least? Enter the numbers corresponding to those colors below:

Like best ☐ enter in Cell 4   Like least ☐ enter in Cell 6

Enter remaining color # in Cell 5 ☐

If in doubt about any colors repeat the process again and enter results in Round 2 Cells.

Scoring Your Colors

Enter your color numbers from A.1 into the three sections of Table A.2.

The first section gives you your overall score of A, I, or C, which indicates that over all dimensions you are primarily an A type, I type, or C type. The second part gives you the sequence with which you use your large (A), (I), or C to impact your world.

The third part gives you your (a), (i), or (c) score: how you think your world is likely to respond to you. This strongly influences the means you choose to implement your ends.

1 Table A.3 gives you a thumbnail sketch of your particular combination of Ends and Means.
2 This general pattern, however, changes according to the environment that you are in. Each environment can be classified as appreciative-centered, influence-centered, or control-centered.
3 Table A.4 gives you a form on which to record your profile.
4 Tables A.5, A.6, and A.7 give you a sketch of what those environments look like.
5 Table A.8 interprets your color in Cell 5: as your zero-dimensional score the point of "Power Resolution and Transformation." You use this power to reduce tension between your ends in (A, I, or C) and the reaction you expect from your world (a), (i), or (c) in each dimension or environment.

You can use this information to build a profile of yourself that covers all five dimensions. Chapter 9 walks you through an example of how this is carried out.

Table A.2 **Scoring sheet for ends and means (first and second dimensions)**

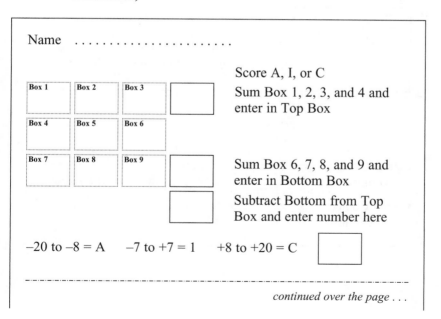

continued over the page . . .

. . . continued

Add rows to obtain score for ends (1st Dimension)

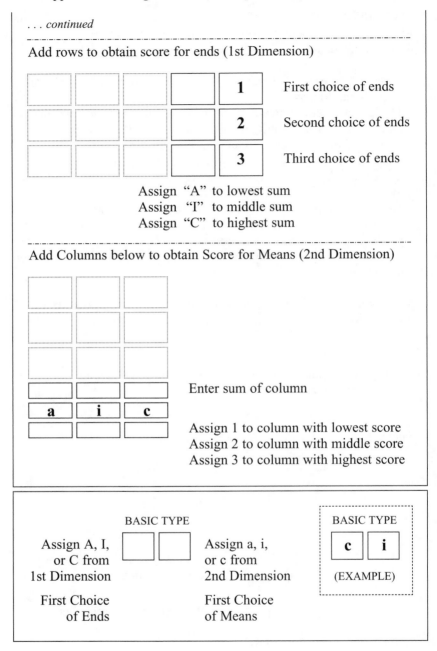

				1	First choice of ends
				2	Second choice of ends
				3	Third choice of ends

Assign "A" to lowest sum
Assign "I" to middle sum
Assign "C" to highest sum

Add Columns below to obtain Score for Means (2nd Dimension)

Enter sum of column

| a | i | c |

Assign 1 to column with lowest score
Assign 2 to column with middle score
Assign 3 to column with highest score

BASIC TYPE

Assign A, I, or C from 1st Dimension

Assign a, i, or c from 2nd Dimension

First Choice of Ends

First Choice of Means

BASIC TYPE

| c | i |

(EXAMPLE)

Power Map Interpretations

Table A.3 gives your basic power-posture; the way you typically address your world and the way you expect your world to react to you.

This reaction is modified by the environment you are in. Tables A.5 through A.8 give you the information about how you see the three worlds that represent the range of possible environments.

A.5 shows an appreciative-centered world, i.e. when the world expects you to be open to discovery and not use your influence or control. Your reaction to this world is shown in the colors you place in Cells 1–3.

A.6 shows an influence-centered world, i.e. when your world expects you to be focused on relationships. Your reaction to this world is shown by the colors you place in Cells 4–6.

A.7 shows a control-centered world, i.e. your reaction to this world is shown by the colors you choose in Cells 7–9.

A.8 gives the interpretation of the color at the center of your power chart, the zero-dimensional point that shows how you deal with the tensions and opposition that are inherent in all three appreciative-, influence-, and control-centered worlds. It provides clues to your core transformational power in all dimensions.

Table A.3 **Your power (ends and means in 1 and 2 dimensions)**

C O L O R	P O W E R	The Conscious Ends you seek (A, I, or C) and the Unconscious Means that constrain or enhance how you go about achieving them (a), (i), or (c) (This is your tendency, which is then altered by your actual environment (i.e. when you are in a control environment, 3rd dimension; in an influenced environment, 4th dimension; or in an appreciative environment, 5th dimension)
1	A-a	Your pattern is the most appreciative. You want to understand the world and inspire others with that understanding. You have special ease with the spiritual and artistic levels but may equally express yourself as a philosopher or scientist within your field.
2	A-i	Your pattern is highly appreciative. You use your power to explore the world and inspire, engage, and fascinate others. You have the reasoning powers of a philosopher but may be a missionary in your field and make great use of your diplomatic powers.
3	A-c	You lean towards use of appreciative power. You recognize the need for patterns and order in nature and your world. This gives you the power used by scientists but may also be expressed by being a philosopher or wise man in your field.
4	I-a	Your pattern is primarily one of influence. You typically use your influence to find others with whom you can share common goals. You are very open to challenge and tend to use your power to promote ideas.
5	I-i	Your pattern is the most influential. Your typical use of power is to be very active in engaging others in the pursuit of your passions. You use your power to compete and love the thrill of "love and war."
6	I-c	Your leaning is towards influence. You use your influence to collaborate with others on your goals. You tend to be very responsible and realistic in your expectations and your relationships.
7	C-a	You prefer control power. You use your power to lead others, and to create long-term strategies. You function well in situations calling for direct action where you are in charge.
8	C-i	You prefer control power. You use your control to coach and persuade others, to do what you know to be right. You are careful not to overstep your boundaries.
9	C-c	You prefer control power. Your use of control is to find others to collaborate with you on common goals. You have things under control and you expect others to be in control too.

Table A.4 **Your power map (interpretation of all five dimensions)**

	Learning	*Politics*	*Planning/executing*
Ideals Chart A-4 Enter results from this chart in this row	**Cell 1** Col # . . . Interpretation . . .	**Cell 2** Col # . . . Interpretation . . .	**Cell 3** Col # . . . Interpretation . . .
Values Chart A-5 Enter results from this chart in this row	**Cell 4** Col # . . . Interpretation . . .	**Cell 5** Col # . . . Interpretation . . .	**Cell 6** Col # . . . Interpretation . . .
Goals Chart A-6 Enter results from this chart in this row	**Cell 7** Col # . . . Interpretation . . .	**Cell 8** Col # . . . Interpretation . . .	**Cell 9** Col # . . . Interpretation . . .

Table A.5 **Appreciative-centered environments (fifth dimension)**

The manifestation of purpose, power and process in five dimensions

PURPOSE *Ideals*	POWER *Relations*	PROCESS *Meaning*
Enlightenment Color 1	A-a	You are totally open to our world (A) and believe the world will to be equally open to us (a)
Reason Color 2	A-i	You are totally open to our world (A) and understand that we must be influenced by it
Truth Color 3	A-c	You are totally open to the world (A) and see the need to bound its possibilities (c)
Love Color 4	I-a	You fully express our thoughts and feelings in our world (I) and are unconditionally open to the ideals of our world (a)
Trust Color 5	I-i	You fully express our thoughts and feelings in our world (I) and understand that we must allow our world to do so equally
Omnipotence Color 6	I-c	You fully express our thoughts and feelings in our world (I) but know that the world wants things to be under control (c)
Beauty Color 7	C-a	You know ideally what we must do (C) and believe that our ideal must be attractive to our world (a)
Pragmatism Color 8	C-i	You know ideally what we must do (C) and under-stand: we must be influenced by our world (i)
Equanimity Color 9	C-c	You are confident in our ideals (C) and know that our world is equally confident in theirs

***Table A.6* Influence-centered environments (fourth dimension)**

The manifestation of purpose, power and process as holons in four dimensions

PURPOSE Values	POWER Relations	PROCESS Meaning
Spiritual Color 1	A-a	You transform enlightenment and its supportive appreciative powers into values affecting all stakeholders. Practically, we will be open to all values (A) and expect others to be open to ours (a).
Philosophical Color 2	A-i	You transform *reason* and its supportive appreciative powers into a particular philosophical approach. You have insight into the different values that our stakeholders have (A) and we understand that there can be never be a final solution. You are able to accept our gains and losses philosophically (i) without under or over reaction.
Scientific Color 3	A-c	You transform our ideal of *truth* and its supportive appreciative powers *(*A) into a search for insight into our differences in values that relies as much as possible on objective information (c).
Social Color 4	I-a	You transform our ideal of *love* into a willingness to engage with others from our value perspective (I) and are open to gain insight into their values (a).
Political Color 5	I-i	You transform our ideal for *trust* reason into engagement with others from the perspective of our values (I) while we expect our stakeholders do the same (i).
Technical Color 6	I-c	You transform our ideal for *omnipotence* into a value for technical control. You engage with our stakeholders (i) to find technical boundaries (c) that will form the basis of our resolution.
Aesthetic Color 7	C-a	You now know what we are committed to do (C) but are concerned that others understand and believe that what we are doing is good (a). This qualitative value, a concern for the final form and its resonance with the whole purpose (a) suggests an aesthetic that measures wholeness.
Egalitarian Color 8	C-i	You know what the final form should be (C) but we want to be sure that all others have an equal chance to influence implementation (i). You are in control but are willing to listen to be influenced by others equally.
Economic Color 9	C- c	You know what our options are (C) and we expect others to know theirs (c). This makes for the best choice of options, in terms of time and resources and so is the most economic way to get things done.

Table A.7 **Control-centered environments (third dimension)**

The manifestation of purpose, power and process in three dimensions

PURPOSE Values	POWER Relation-ships	PROCESS Meaning
Discovery Color 1	A-a	You suspend our judgment about our particular commitment and listen to others' commitments (A). You also expect everyone else involved to be able to suspend their judgment too (a).
Diplomacy color 2	A-i	Our new insights from discovery (A) could well have far-reaching effects on current commitments so its products have to be handled with the gentlest form of influence (i) possible.
Policy Color 3	A-c	Safe boundaries (c) must be found to enclose the discoveries and possibilities that pass this diplomatic test (A).
Evaluation Color 4	I-a	You use our values to subtract relevant *"in-formation"* from the *"whole"* (I) but remain open to identify potential positive and negative factors relevant to our strategy (a).
Negotiation Color 5	I-i	You negotiate agreements for more policy and operational commitments with internal and external stakeholders (I) and in the process transform as many negative options into opportunities for mutual gain as possible (i).
Strategy Color 6	I-c	You influence the selection of options (I) and give them form (c) as strategic priorities.
Appraisal Color 7	C-a	We commit to our choices as goals (C) and appraise the conditions for achieving those goals (a).
Agreement Color 8	C-i	You use our joint goals (C) to create working agreements (i) between lateral operational units.
Operations Color 9	C-c	You carry out our work (C) and expect our work teams to do the same (c).

Table A.8 **Power resolution and transformation (zero dimensions)**

Your color in Cell 5: To reduce the tension between your ends in (A, I, or C) and the reaction you expect from your world (a), (i), or (c) in each dimension or environment

1 **Yellow**	A-a	You remain open but need encouragement. You try to introduce novel ideas but seek assurances against potential loss. You accept others ideas without imposing your own.
2 **Magenta**	A-i	You seek to gain appreciation from others through your charm and sensitivity. You need people to believe in you and you help them believe in themselves. You feel vulnerable but do not readily reveal this.
3 **Cyan**	A-c	You listen to people and give them objective feedback. However, if you don't get the recognition and respect you feel you deserve you begin to detach yourself. You become more principled.
4 **Green**	I-a	You step back from warm engagement to understand what is really going on. You become more measured as you relate what is going on to your own needs.
5 **Red**	I-i	You become very active and put a great deal of energy into recruiting those around you. You express yourself strongly and let other people know where you stand. You encourage others to do the same.
6 **Blue**	I-c	You put greater effort into communicating, and seeking common ground. You want to be able to rely on those around you and involve them in your vision for the future. In this you have to guard against flattery or deceit.
7 **Teal**	C-a	You become more assertive in maintaining your viewpoint and directing those around you. You take on the responsibility for making things right.
8 **Brown**	C-i	You persist in your path but seek less stressful, more comfortable ways of working. As you have a strong awareness of others needs you are able to arrange compromises.
9 **Indigo**	C-c	You become very calm and focused on your purpose. You are able to gather others around you who are willing to do their share. Your authority is readily accepted.

Notes

2 Learning to Dance: Experience of Influence

1 Jay Galbraith (1973), also a contemporary DBA student of Thompson's used both Simon's and Thompson's insights to begin to understand the demand of such an information-processing viewpoint for the design of complex organizations. One of the major outcomes was the understanding of the more subtle patterns of control and coordination that were required in modern organization. The single chief at the top of the hierarchy could not ensure high performance through control alone. Success was contingent on environmental actors who could not be controlled. Competing areas of organizations might even demand dual control, so the idea of the "matrix" organizations with two centers of control was born. In any case, from this point on the management of lateral relationship in organization became just as important as the management of hierarchical relationships. It was Galbraith and Nathanson who took the internal paper on "Coordinate Line Management" and published it in their 1978 book *Strategy and Structure*.

2 Jim Thompson died in the year I applied to join Eric Trist in his Wharton doctoral program in Social Systems Sciences, and it fell to me to inform Eric of his untimely death.

3 Learning to Fly: Experience of Appreciation

1 Fred Emery at that time was a visiting professor in the Social Systems Science Department.

4 International Development: Examples and Evolving Concepts of Wholeness

1 Turid and I by this time had become both work and life partners till her tragic and untimely death in October 1997.

5 The Emerging Philosophy: the Nature of Purpose

1 Note on Nicene Code:

At the time of the synod there was, as we indicated, no prevailing orthodoxy on the divine nature of Christ. There is no doubt that if a vote had been taken at the beginning of this synod it would have come out on the side of Christ as a human prophet with divine inspiration, not as a god with a human body.

As Karen Armstrong (1993) recounts, Arius, a popular and charismatic pres-byter from Alexandria, and Athanius, a very gifted assistant to Alexander, the Bishop of Alexandria, represented the two extreme points. Arius who was very wellread in the scriptures, argued passionately a well-documented case for belief that there was only one God. To dilute his essence by making Christ divine would be to weaken the message and power of the transcendent God the Father. He argued that it was precisely because Jesus was human that he could be a model for us. If he were divine how could we expect to be able to equal him? Athanius had a much less optimistic view about human capacity to incorporate the word of God through a mortal figure. He believed that Jesus came to earth as the word made flesh, that Christ was both of the same nature of God and the same nature as man. Through him we could become divine. Although most bishops before the conference did not share Athanius's views, by the end of the conference all but three had accepted the doctrine of the divine incarnation of God in Christ.

7   Building the AIC Model

1   Quoted with permission from Lere O. Shakunle (June 1996) "Organic System Design: the ITSON—Beyond Field and Particle," in the *Journal of American Computer Science.*

Features of itsons

Three of the fundamental features of itsons are:

    Ai.   Itsons are the alphabets of the language of Mind, Nature, and Being.

From this follows:

    Aii.   Itsons is the common language of Mind, Nature, and Being.

Two of the special features derived from the above fundamental features are:

    Bi.   No two itsons are the same.
    Bii.   Every itson is an indivisible unit of thought that is the carrier of idea and the seat of identity. Identity is in part cognitive-molecular, by which we mean part of identity is cognitive-genetic.

The itsons of this paper are based on this interpretation.

Structure of the Itson

Geometrically, itson is the indivisible unit of a lifeline. Lifelines are potential curves at every point. A lifeline line bends into a curve, which grows into a fold at infinity. Every point on the lifeline is a curve. Every curve is a potential fold. Both sides of a point are minus and plus domains whose summation is an inexhaustible zero. The minus and plus depict positive and negative infinities whose addition is the absolute zero. This means every point on the line is the summation of infinities. There are three types of infinity in a lifeline. These are:

    (i)   inner infinity
    (ii)   outer infinity
    (iii) absolute infinity.

Point in a lifeline unifies the features of points in Euclidean and non-Euclidean geometries. The life history of a lifeline is concentrated on the point.

    In what follows we shall present the itsons of a muson. Don't try to figure out what an itson or a muson is. The geometry of the lifeline that follows should help fire the imagination to the extent that by the time we get to the end of this first step in its introduction we will be able to say that we have some idea of what an itson is and how it relates to the muson, which is the local domain that harbors it.

As our first step in the introduction of this geometry, we shall explore together three axioms of the line of spiral geometry. Even though we have said it before we hasten to repeat that when we talk of the line in spiral geometry, which is the geometry of the physics of infinity, one of whose organs are the itrons, we mean the "lifeline."

Axioms of the Line

Axiom I: *Every straight line is a curve at infinity.*

Like we said, there are three types of infinities in the lifeline of spiral geometry.

[In the text of this document, we shall use the characters o-o to represent the symbol for "infinity" and the text /a, /t, /z and /w to represent the subscripted Greek mathematical symbols – Editor.]

These are:

i. inner infinity: o-o/t
    This is the nuclear domain of the non-vanishing zero It is the inward spiraling of the line at t which is the region of the nuclear domain.
ii. outer infinities: o-o/a, o-o/w
    This is outward spiraling of the line depicted by li and lj of the /a-domain and /w-domain which are the local domains of /t-domain.
iii. Absolute infinity o-o/z
    with z: zeroids. This is the coupling of the inner and outer infinities. The zeroids are the non-vanishing numbers of zero.

Before the second axiom, let's go to the geometric figures above. In the beginning [Fig. I] we have the lifeline. There is a point on this line [Fig. II]. At the end of the line are the outer infinities o-o/a, o-o/w. In [Fig.III] we have the phenomenon of the point. At this juncture, let's try to decode the metaphor of the point. We can draw our examples from our personal experience with ideas. Suddenly a bright idea occurs to you, brought as it were on the wings of thought. What you do under such circumstances is turning the idea around which is the same thing as looking at it from different perspectives. Let's say you are lucky to get the right perspective within a short interval. You then begin to work on this idea which leads to the expansion of your thoughts, like something taking on a definite shape. Your thought grows as the idea develops. This idea, still an embryo while you are thinking of it, is delivered as a baby when you put something about it on the paper. This done, you go back to it again in thought. There comes a stage when you feel you have to take a pause because either the whole thing is becoming an avalanche, which you have to dam, or it is thinning out and so you need to clear the canvas by doing something that does not relate at all to the idea. This is what is called the thinking pause or "Denkenpause". This denkenpause is the infinity of this moment.

To extend it you need to get away from it all. This we can liken to a ship disappearing from your gaze. The point at which you can no longer pursue a thought, because it is becoming a downpour or thinning out, is the place where infinity is placed on the line. In the case of a ship disappearing, it is the point where the line that connects you to the ship bends and comes back to you thus making you the center of the line. One of the peculiar features of this lifeline is that all you need to do is put a point on the paper, move it to the right and you get same length of the line on the left. Thus every point on the life line produces lines on both sides of it such that the point—any point at all—is always at the center of the lifeline. In the case of an idea whose thought requires a pause either to maintain your sanity or for a new input, the point of infinity is where you take the pause and go back to another state which has nothing to do with the idea. This time the line returns to the possessor of the idea who is, in this case, the center of the lifeline.

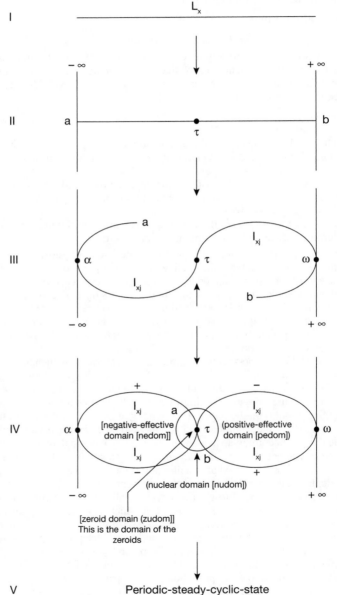

10 Implications for Cultures, Institutions, and Organizations

1 Gordon Allport and his colleagues developed a values instrument based on this work that was widely used in the 1960s and 1970s. The list is another example of the missing middle level of influence. From our discussion in the last chapter we added the middle (i) column of values—hilosophical and pragmatic. We also added technical as an (I-c) value. Our summary of the AIC model of culture as values is contained in Figure 10.2.

2 Magic Squares: all columns, rows, and diagonals add to 15.
The eight Balanced Influence-centered Types.

Table 10.1 Balanced towards Appreciation I-a

6	7	2
1	5	9
8	3	4
8	3	4
1	5	9
6	7	2

Arab Cultures

Table 10.2 Balanced towards Influence I-I

4	9	2
3	5	7
8	1	6
8	1	6
3	5	7
4	9	2

Northern African Cultures

Table 10.3 Balanced towards Influence I-I

2	9	4
7	5	3
6	1	8
6	1	8
7	5	3
2	9	4

Southern African Cultures

Table 10.4 Balanced towards Control I-c

2	7	6
9	5	1
4	3	8
4	3	8
9	5	1
2	7	6

Latin American Cultures

References

* Available on website www.odii.com.

Ackoff, R.L. (1974) *Redesigning the Future*, New York: John Wiley.
—— (1978) *The Art of Problem Solving*, New York: John Wiley.
—— (1999) *Ackoff's Best: Classic Writings on Management* (Ch. 1), New York: John Wiley.
—— and Emery, F. (1972) *On Purposeful Systems*, Chicago, IL: Aldine Atherton.
Addis, D.R., Wong, A.T., and Schacter, D.L. (2008) "Age-Related Changes in the Episodic Simulation of Future Events," *Psychological Science*, Blackwell Synergy, reported in Ker Than, *Nature*, doi:10.1038/news.2008.408, online Jan. 4, 2008 News.
Alford, Robert R. and Friedland, Roger (1985) *Powers of Theory: Capitalism, the State, and Democracy*, Cambridge: Cambridge University Press.
Allport, Gordon W. (1937) *Personality: A Psychological Interpretation*, New York: Henry Holt & Company.
——, Vernon, Philip E., and Gardner, Lindzey (1960) *A Study of Values, A Scale for Measuring the Dominant Interests in Personality: A Manual of Directions*, Boston, MA: Riverside Publishing.
The American Forum for Global Education (2003) *Global Issues, Problems and Challenges*, www.globaled.org/guidelines/page2.php (accessed January 22, 2008).
Armstrong, Karen (1993) *A History of God*, New York: Ballantine Books.
Barnard, C.I. (1938) *The Functions of the Executive*, Cambridge, MA: Harvard University Press.
Beamish, Peter (1993) *Dancing With Whales*, St John's, NF: Creative Book Publishers.
—— (1996) *Rhythm Based Communication*, The "Lanzarote" Paper, World Conference on Sustainable Ecosystems, Lanzarote, Spain, 1995.
Bertalanffy, L. (1950) "The Theory of Open Systems in Physics and Biology," *Science*, 111: 23–9.
Blavatsky H.P. and De Zirkoff, Boris (1877) *Isis Unveiled: Collected Writings*, Wheaton, IL, and London: Theosophical Publishing House.
Bohm, D. (1982) *The Enfolding-Unfolding Universe* (Ed. K. Wilber), Boston, MA: Shambhala.
—— (1985) *Beyond the Brain*, Albany, NY: State University of New York Press.

—— (1987) *Science, Order, and Creativity*, New York: Bantam.

—— (2002) *Wholeness and the Implicate Order*, reissue ed., July 4, New York: Routledge.

—— and Peat, D. (1990) *On Dialogue*, Ojai, CA: David Bohm Seminars (P.O. Box 1452).

Boulding, Kenneth E. (1961) *The Image: Knowledge in Life and Society*, Ann Arbor, MI: University of Michigan Press

Brooks, Arthur C. (2006) *Who Really Cares?*, New York: Basic Books.

Brown J.A.C. (1954) *The Social Psychology of Industry: Human Relations in the Factory*, Harmondsworth: Penguin Books.

Clegg, S.R. and Hardy, C. (Eds.) (1999) "Studying Organization: Theory and Method Assessment," *The Academy of Management Executive*, 12(3): 6–16.

——, Courpasson, D. and Phillips, N. (2006) *Power and Organizations*, London: Sage Publications, p. 2.

Cooperider, D.L. and Srivastva, S. (1987) "Appreciative Inquiry in Organizational Life," in W. Woodman and R. Pasmore (Eds.), *Research on Organizational Change and Development*, Vol. 1, Greenwich, CT: JAI Press, pp. 129–69.

—— (1999) "Appreciative Inquiry: A Positive Revolution in Change," in P. Holman and T. Devane (Eds.), *The Change Handbook*, San Francisco, CA: Berrett-Koehler Publishers, pp. 245–63.

Dahl, A.R. (1957) "The Concept of Power," *Behavioral Science* 2(3) (July): 201–15.

Dawkins, Richard (2006) *The God Delusion*, Boston, MA: Houghton Mifflin.

Denning, Stephen (2005) *The Leader's Guide to Storytelling: Mastering the Art and Discipline of Business Narrative*, San Fransisco, CA: Jossey-Bass.

Eldred, John (1999) "The New Face of Office Politics," interview by Polly LaBarre, *Fast Company* (28), September, www.fastcompany.com/magazine/28/newface. html?page=0%2C1 (accessed April 3, 2008).

Emerson, R. (1962) "Power Dependence Relations," *American Sociological Review*, 27: 31–40.

Emery, F. and Trist, E. (1965) "The Causal Texture of Organizational Environments," *Human Relations*, 13(1): 21–32.

Engelbart, Christina (2003) A *Lifetime Pursuit* (from a biographical sketch of C. Engelbart Douglas originally written in 1986). Douglas C. Engelbart and Kristina Hooper, "The Augmentation System Framework," in *Interactive Multimedia*, www.bootstrap.org/chronicle/chronicle.html (accessed Jan. 22, 2008).

ESMAP World Bank (1994) Energy Sector Assistance Program (ESMAP), "Power Sector Restructuring Program," Report No. 169194, Colombia: World Bank.

Fayol, H. (1949; original work 1916) *General and Industrial Management* (Trans. Constance Storrs), London: Pitman Publishing, pp. 19–42.

Follett, M.P. (1945; reissued 2003) *Dynamic Administration: The Collected Papers of Mary Parker Follett*, New York: Routledge.

Foucault, Michel (1981) *Power/Knowledge: Selected Interviews and Other Writings, 1972–1977*, New York: Pantheon Books.

—— Faubion, James D. and Hurley, Robert (2001) *Power: Essential Works of Foucault, 1954–1984*, Vol. 3, Leiden, Netherlands: New Press.

Freeman, R.E. (1984) *Strategic Management: A Stakeholder Approach*, in Pitman Business and Public Policy series, Boston: Pitman.

—— (2004) "The Development of Stakeholder Theory: An Idiosyncratic Approach," in Ken G. Smith and Michael A. Hitt (Eds.), *The Oxford Handbook of Management Theory: The Process of Theory Development*, Oxford: OUP, pp. 418–35.

Freud, Sigmund (1900*) The Interpretation of Dreams*, Standard Edition, 4 & 5, London: Hogarth Press.

—— (1915) *The Unconscious*, Vol. 14, pp. 161–215 (*The Standard Edition of the Complete Works of Sigmund Freud*, 24 vols, Ed. James Strachey *et al.*), London: The Hogarth Press and the Institute of Psychoanalysis, pp. 1953–74.

Frooman, J. (1999) "Stakeholder Influence Strategies," *The Academy of Management Review*, 24(2): 191–205.

Furugganan, Brenda and Lopez, Mario Antonio G. (2002) *Building Partnerships Between Government and Civil Society: The Case of Paiboon Wattanasiritham and the Government Central Bank*, Makati City, Philippines: Asian Institute of Management and New York, Synergos Institute.

Galbraith, J. (1973) *Designing Complex Organizations*, Reading, MA: Addison-Wesley.

—— (1977) *Organizational Design*, St. Paul, MN: Addison-Wesley.

—— and Nathanson, D.A. (1978) *Strategy and Structure: The Role of Structure and Process*, Reading, MA: West Publishing Company.

Gherardi, S. (2003) *Feminist Theory and Organization Theory: A Dialogue on New Bases*, *The Oxford Handbook of Organization Theory: Meta Theoretical Perspectives*, Oxford University Press, pp. 210–36.

Goethe, J.W. von (1982) *Theory of Colours* (Trans. Charles Lock), Eastlake, Cambridge, MA: MIT Press.

Gouldner, A. (1959) "Organizational Analysis," in R. Merton, L. Broom, and L. Cottrell (Eds.), *Sociology Today*, New York: Basic Books.

Graham, Pauline (1996) *Mary Parker Follett: Prophet of Management: A Celebration of Writings from the 1920s*, Cambridge, MA: Harvard Business School Press.

Greco, Janet (1996) "Stories for Executive Development: An Isotonic Solution", *Journal of Organizational Change Management*, 9(5): 43–74.

Greiner, Larry (1972) "Evolution and Revolution as Organizations Grow," *Harvard Business Review*, 50: 37–46 (July/August).

Gurdjieff, G.I. (1950) *All and Everything: Beelzebub's Tales to His Grandson*, New York: Harcourt, Brace & Co.

—— (1973) *Views from the Real World*, New York: E.P. Dutton.

Hardin, C.L. (1988) *Color for Philosophers: Unweaving the Rainbow*, Indianapolis, IN, and Cambridge, MA: Hackett Publishing Company.

—— (1997) "Reinventing the Spectrum," in A. Byrne and D.R. Hilbert (Eds.), *Readings on Color*, Vol. 1, Cambridge, MA: MIT Press.

—— and Maffi, L. (Eds.) (1997) *Color Categories in Thought and Language*, Cambridge and New York: Cambridge University Press.

Ho, Mae Wan (1993) *The Rainbow and the Worm: The Physics of Organisms*, Singapore: World Scientific.

—— (1998a) "Creating Colour-contrast in Light Microscopy of Living Organisms," in R.H. Newton, J.P. Haffegee, and M.W. Ho, *Journal of Biological Education*, 32(1): 29–33.

—— (1998b) *Organism and Psyche in a Participatory Universe in the Evolutionary Order. The Impact of the Human Agent on Evolution, Essays in Honour of Ervin Laszlo* (D. Loye, Ed.), Westport, CT: Praeger, pp. 49–65, www.ratical.org/org/co-globalize/MaeWanHo/organis.html#title (accessed, July 3, 2008).

—— (1998c) "Is There a Purpose in Nature?" 1998 Workshop papers (Ed. Ivan M. Havel), Prague, September, Center for Theoretical Study, Charles University, and the Academy of Sciences of the Czech Republic Jilská 1, 110 00 Praha 1, www.cts.cuni.cz/conf98/Procee-x.htm (accessed Feb. 8, 2008).

——, Saunders, P. and Fox, S. (1986) "A New Paradigm for Evolution," *New Sciences*, 109 (1497) (Feb. 27): 41–3.

Jackson, M.C. (2003) *Systems Thinking: Creative Holism for Managers*, [[PLACE??]]: John Wiley & Sons.

Jacques, E. (1967) *Equitable Payment*, New York: Pelican.

—— (1976) *A General Theory of Bureaucracy*, London: Heinemann.

Jantsch, Erich (1975) *Design for Evolution: Self-organization and Planning in the Life of Human Systems*, New York: George Braziller.

Jaynes, J. (1976) *The Origin of Consciousness in the Breakdown of the Bicameral Mind*, Boston, MA: Houghton Mifflin Company.

Jones, Peter *Better on a Camel: BOAC and BEA Reminiscences*, http://betteronacamel.com/ (accessed Jan. 2, 2008).

Jung, C.G. (1902–05) *Psychiatric Studies. The Collected Works of C.G. Jung*, Vol. 1 (1953) (Ed.) Michael Fordham, London and Princeton, NJ: Routledge & Kegan Paul.

Kaku, M. (2004) *Parallel Worlds: A Journey Through Creation, Higher Dimensions, and the Future of the Cosmos*, New York: Doubleday.

Kant, I. (1770) *De mundi sensibilis atque intelligibilis forma et principiis [On the Form and Principles of the Sensible and Intelligible World]*, Inaugural Dissertation, William Julius Eckoff, 1894, New York: Columbia College; reprinted 1970, New York: AMS Press, pp. 385–419.

Katz, D. and Khan, R.L. (1996) *The Social Psychology of Organizations*, Hoboken, NJ: John Wiley & Sons.

Kleiner, A. (2003) *Who Really Matters? The Core Group Theory of Power Privilege and Success*, New York: Currency, Doubleday.

Korab-Karpowicz, W.J. (2007) "Heidegger Internet Encyclopedia of Philosophy," www.iep.utm.edu/h/heidegge.htm (accessed Jan. 3, 2008).

Lawrence, P.R. and Lorsch, J.W. (1969) *Organizations and Environment*, Homewood, IL: Richard D. Irwin.

Leslie, Keith, Loch, Mark A., and Schaninger, William (2006) "Managing Your Organization by the Evidence," *McKinsey Quarterly*, 3: 65–75.

Lipnack, Jessica and Stamps, Jeffrey (2000) *Virtual Teams: People Working Across Boundaries With Technology*, 2nd rev. ed., New York: John Wiley.

Lyotard, J.-F. (1984) *The Postmodern Condition: A Report of Knowledge* (Trans. G. Benningon and B. Massumi), Manchester: Manchester University Press.

MacEvoy, Bruce (2005) *Color Vision: The Design of the Eye*, Handprint Water Colors, August (retrieved November 2006 from www.handprint.com/HP/WCL/color1.html).

McKee, Robert (1997) *Story: Substance and Style, and the Principles of Screenwriting*, 1st ed., New York: Regan Books.

MacLean, Paul D. (1978) "Mind of Three Minds: Educating the Triune Brain," *The 77th Annual Yearbook of the NSSE*, Part II, Chicago, IL: National Society for the Study of Education.

Mallaby, Sebastian (2004) *The World's Banker: A Story of Failed States, Financial Crises, and the Wealth and Poverty of Nations*, Yale, CT: Penguin Press.

March, James G. and Simon, Herbert A. (1958) *Organizations*, New York: John Wiley.

Marshall, Jeannie (2006) *Masculine and Feminine Energies*, available at www.mhmail.com/articles/masculine-feminine-energy.html (accessed Sept. 24, 2008).

Mitroff, I. (1983) *Stakeholders of the Organizational Mind: Toward a New View of Organizational Policy Making*, San Francisco, CA: Jossey-Bass.

Morgan, G. (1986) *Images of Organizations*, Beverly Hills, CA: Sage Publications.

—— (1997) Imagin-ization: *New Mindsets for Seeing, Organizing, and Managing*, Thousand Oaks, CA: Sage Publications.

Naguchi, Lynne (1996) *Case on Participation Thailand, ODII*, Application Papers. www.odii.com/Papers/LYN-RPT.htm (accessed Feb. 5, 2008).*

Navia de Guzmán, Olga (Ed.) (1997) *Resource Book on Participation*, Inter-American Development Bank (IADB), www.odii.com/sec7.htm (accessed Feb. 5, 2008).*

Nichols, E. (1976) *The Philosophical Aspects of Cultural Differences*, unpublished manuscript.

Nye, Andrea (1988) *Feminist Theory and the Philosophies of Man*, London: Croom Helm.

Nye, Joseph (2004) *Soft Power: The Means to Success in World Politics*, Washington, DC: PublicAffairs, new ed. (April 26, 2005).

Owen, Harrison (1997) *Open Space Technology: A User's Guide*, San Francisco, CA: Berrett-Koehler.

Ozbekhan, Hasan (1971) "Planning and Human Action," in Paul Weis (Ed.), *Hierarchically Organized Systems in Theory and Practice*, New York: A.S. Hafner Publishing.

Palmer, S.E. (1999) *Vision Science: Photons to Phenomenology*, Cambridge, MA: Bradford Books/MIT Press.

Parsons, T. (1967) *The Structure of Social Action*, New York: The Free Press.

—— and Shils, E.A. (1951) *Toward a General Theory of Action*, Cambridge, MA: Harvard University Press.

Pfeffer, J. (1981) *Power in Organizations*, Cambridge: Ballinger Publishing Company.

Phillips, Frederick B. (1990) "NTU Psychotherapy: An Afro-centric Approach," *Journal of Black Psychology*, 17(1): 55–74.

Pribram, Karl H. (1991) *Brain and Perception: Holonomy and Structure in Figural Processing*, Hillsdale, NJ: Lawrence Erlbaum Associates.

—— (Ed.) (1994) *Origins: Brain and Self-Organization*, Hillsdale, NJ: Lawrence Erlbaum Associates.

Prigogine, I. and Rice, S. (1985) *Orer Through Fluctuation: Self-Organization and Social Systems*, in Evolution. . . New York: John Wiley & Sons.

Prigogine, I. and Nicolis, G. (1977) *Self-Organization in Nonequilibrium Systems: From Dissipative Structures to Order Through Fluctuations*, Wiley: New York.

Pugh, D.S. (1971) *Organization Theory*, New York: Penguin Books.

Reed, Michael (2006) *Organizational Theorizing: A Historically Contested Terrain*, in *SAGE Handbook of Organization Studies*, 2nd ed., London: Sage, p. 25.

Riley, C.A. (1995) *Color Codes*, Hanover, Germany, and London: University Press of New England.

Rummel, R.J. (1975) *The Dynamic Psychological Field*, Beverley Hills, CA: Sage Publications. Available: www.hawaii.edu/powerkills/NOTE10.htm (accessed June 27, 2008).

Russell, B. (1945) *History of Western Civilization*, New York: Simon & Schuster.

Scottsburg, City of, Indiana (2006) *The Scottsburg Story: A Partnership of Leaders 1988–2005*, Bedford, IN: Rainbow Printing.

Senge, P. (1994) *The Fifth Discipline: The Art and Practice of the Learning Organization* (First Edition), New York: Currency/Doubleday.

—— (2004) *Presence: Human Purpose and the Field of the Future*, Boston, MA: Society for Organizational Learning.

Sermonti, G. (1998) *Science with Meaning, Symbol, and Beauty*, Workshop "Is There a Purpose in Nature?" Prague, September 1998, www.cts.cuni.cz, accessed 20 October 2008.

Shakunle, Leve O. (1996) "The ITSON—Beyond Field and Particle: The Matran School of Mathematics," Berlin, Germany, www.acsa2000net/matran/index.html (accessed July 1, 2008).

Smith, W.E. (1983) "Organizing as a Power Process: The Creation and Testing of a Conceptual Framework and its Application to the Design of Development Projects," Dissertation, University Microfilms International, Ann Arbor. Extract available: www.odii.com/Papers/the%20Development%20of%20Power%20concepts. pdf (accessed Jan. 4, 2008).*

—— and Charmoz, R. (1978) "Evolution of Control and Coordination in Multi-national Enterprises," in J. Galbraith and D. Nathanson (Eds.) *Strategy and Structure: The Role of Process*, Minnesota, MN: West Publishing.*

—— with Sato, T. (1996) "The New Development Paradigm: 'Organizing for Implementation,'" in Jo Marie Griesgraber and Bernhard Gunter (Eds.), *Rethinking Bretton Woods, Development New Paradigms and Principles for the Twenty First Century.*

——, Thoolen, B. and Thoolen, F. (1980) *The Design of Organizations for Rural Development*, World Bank, Staff Working Paper #375, available at www.odii. com/Papers/Design%20for%20Organization%20of%20Rural%20Development. pdf (accessed Jan. 4, 2008).*

Sommerhoff, G. (1950) *Analytical Biology*, London: Oxford University Press.

Sopchokchai, Orapin (1993) *Building Partnerships between Government and Civil Society*, Thailand Development Research Institute (TDRI).

Spranger, Eduard, Paul (1928): *Types of Men: The Psychology and Ethics of Personality*, Halle: M. Niemeyer.

Stamps, Jeffrey S. (1980) *Holonomy: A Human Systems Theory*, Seaside, CA: Inter-systems Publications.

Surowiecki, James (2005) *The Wisdom of Crowds*, New York: Anchor Publishing.

Taylor, F.W. (December 1916) *The Principles of Scientific Management*, an abstract of an address given by the late Dr Taylor before the Cleveland Advertising Club, March 3,1915, two weeks prior to his death.

Thompson, James D. (1962) *Organizations in Action*, New York: McGraw-Hill.

Trahair, R.C.S. (1984) *The Humanist Temper: The Life and Work of Elton Mayo*, New Brunswick, NJ: Transaction Books.

Tsoukas H. and Knudsen C. (Eds.) (2003) *The Oxford Handbook of Organization Theory*, Oxford: Oxford University Press.

Ulrich, W. (1983) *Critical Heuristics of Social Planning: A New Approach to Practical Philosophy*, Bern: Haupt; Reprint Edition, Chichester: Wiley, 1994.

Ushenko, A.P. (1969) *Dynamics of Art*, Bloomington, IN and New York: Indiana University Press and Kraus Reprint Co.

Vickers, G. (1965) *The Art of Judgment*, London: Chapman & Hall.

Weaver, W. and Shannon, C.E. (1949) *The Mathematical Theory of Communication*, Urbana, IL: University of Illinois Press.

Weber, M. (1946) *Max Weber: Essays in Sociology* (Eds. and Trans. H.H. Gerth and C. Wright Mills), New York: Oxford University Press, revised 1973 by H.H. Gerth.

—— (1962) *Basic Concepts in Sociology*, Vol. 1, Part 1, Ch.1 of *Wirtschaft und Gesellschaft*, extracts at www.mdx.ac.uk/www/study/xWeb.htm.

Weick, K. (1979) [1969] *The Social Psychology of Organizing*, Reading, MA: Addison-Wesley.

—— (1995) *Sensemaking in Organizations (Foundations for Organizational Science)*, Thousand Oaks, CA: Sage Publications.

Weis, Paul (1971) *Hierarchically Organized Systems in Theory and Practice*, New York: A.S. Hafner Publishing.

Weisbord, Marvin (1992) *Discovering Common Ground: How Future Search Conferences Bring People Together to Achieve Breakthrough Innovation, Empowerment, Shared Vision, and Collaborative Action*, 1st ed., San Francisco, CA: Berrett-Koehler Publishers.

Wheatley, M.J. (1992) *Leadership and the New Sciences*, San Francisco, CA: Berrett-Koehler Publishers.

Whelehan, Imelda (1995) *Modern Feminist Thought*, New York: New York University Press.

Wiener, N. (1948) *Cybernetics: or, Control and Communication in the Animal and in the Medicine*, 1st ed. (1948), 2nd ed., (1961), Cambridge, MA: MIT Press.

Wing, R.L. (1986) *The Tao of Power*, New York: Dolphin/Doubleday.

Winograd, T. and Flores, F. (1986) *Understanding Computers and Cognition: A New Foundation for Design*, Norwood, NJ: Ablex Publishing Corporation.

Witten, Edward (1988) "Magic, Mystery and Matrix," *Notices of the AMS*, 45(9) (October): 1124–9.

Young, Arthur M. (December 1976) *The Geometry of Meaning*, Cambria, CA: Anodos Foundation.

Index

Ackoff, Russell L. i, 55, 57–8, 61, 63, 66, 71, 83, 122, 240, 311
action plans 203–4, 251
actors 23, 35, 59, 66–7, 117–18, 124, 183, 199, 201, 204–5, 208, 217, 240, 249, 259, 264–5
adjustment, mutual 41–2, 45
aggregate
agreements x, 11, 33, 108, 112, 179–80, 203, 225, 227–9, 241, 271, 302
AIC i, xiv, xv, 1, 2, 4–6, 24, 31–2, 76–7, 85, 97–8, 103, 114, 135, 219, 235–7, 244–6, 256–7
    generic values map xiii, 251
    model i, ix, 49, 156–7, 159, 161, 163, 165, 167, 169, 171, 173, 175, 177, 179, 181
    model of culture xiii, 238, 309
    process 71, 75, 86–7, 90, 187, 204, 219–20, 255
    theory 1, 255, 259, 262
appraisal x, 64–5, 179–80, 203, 225, 227, 241, 246, 249, 302
appreciation 24, 42, 99, 178, 216, 262, 269, 291, 298, 301
    dimension 175, 177, 191, 257
    level of mind/spirit 266, 278
    organization ix, 25, 28, 173, 230, 242–4, 246–8, 256–7, 266, 269, 278
appreciative
    field ix, 18, 81, 83, 114–15, 120, 122, 124, 131–3, 170, 173, 190–1, 215–17, 236, 285–6, 291
    level xi, 3, 72, 94, 97, 122, 170–1, 192, 208, 227, 232–3, 236, 238–9, 241, 246, 267–8

phase xiv, 79, 83, 85, 115, 119, 122, 176, 184, 186, 194, 196, 198, 200, 250, 266
    process 118, 187–8, 190, 194–5, 197, 243, 270
Appreciative Inquiry 6, 98, 266, 312
at 11
atoms xii, 146–7, 154, 157, 181, 224

Basic Manifest Powers ix, 170
beauty 132, 139–40, 142, 167, 175, 225, 239, 268–9, 300, 316
being 115, 131, 133–4, 140, 149, 153, 157, 159, 173, 175, 177, 188–90, 194, 229, 267, 286–7
BOAC (British Overseas Airways Corporation) 1, 8–11, 13, 17–18, 20–1, 23, 37–8, 43, 45, 285
brain ix, 30, 106, 136, 141–9, 151–2, 154, 156, 158, 207, 218, 311, 315
breadth 61, 137, 157–8, 171, 179
Buddhism 89, 108–10, 112, 264
BWIA (British West Indian Airlines) 10–11

Campbell, J. 126, 128
capacity 46, 57–8, 88, 107, 112, 118, 129, 133, 141, 144, 159, 169, 173, 185, 191, 218
    human 130, 132–3, 136, 306
charismatic 24, 27–8, 231
circles, two-dimensional 159, 165, 167
circles of power xiii, 213
co-alignment 56
Colombia v, viii, 75–9, 82, 86, 124, 240, 286, 312

color ix, xii–xiv, 70, 132, 146–9, 151,
    153–4, 156–62, 164–74, 218,
    222–4, 226–8, 293–5, 297, 300–3,
    313–4
  choices xiii, 223, 293
  complementarity 132, 161
  constancy 148, 155, 199
  context 151
  contrast 149
  language 146, 149, 154, 167, 170
  numbers 293–4
  opponency xii, 150
  perception ix, xiv, 136, 142, 146,
    149, 151, 156
  physics of xii, 148
  primaries 159, 170
colors xiii, 132, 146–9, 151, 158–60,
    167, 169, 223, 227, 293–5,
    300
complements 130, 132, 161, 167–9,
    229
complex organizations 49, 305
concepts, stakeholder 55, 85
consciousness 6, 96–7, 106, 110, 115,
    125, 127, 129, 191, 314
control
  conditions 71, 229, 245
  culture 245, 277
  degree of 158–9
  demand dual 50, 305
  fields 3, 114–15, 121–2, 170, 185,
    208
  goal of 57, 288
  hierarchical 55–6, 134, 141
  level 72, 97, 112, 122, 171, 233,
    239–41, 256–7, 268
  locus of 41–2
  masculine 59, 274
  organization's 92
  patterns of 49, 305
  phase x, xiii, xiv, 85, 115, 118,
    199–202, 205, 253, 268–9, 288
  power 41–2, 123, 191, 292, 298
  purposes 288–9
  time 122
coordination 34, 41–3, 45, 48–9, 51,
    66, 158–9, 305, 316
Core Group Theory of Power Privilege
    314
cultures xi, xiii, 7, 8, 16–17, 86, 89–92,
    187, 235–41, 243, 245, 249–51,
    253–7, 275, 278, 289–90, 309

Dahl, A. B. 34–5, 312
dance vii, 32–3, 35–7, 39, 41, 43, 45,
    47, 49, 51, 53, 59, 176, 198, 245,
    263–4
death 28, 126–7, 164, 261, 289, 305,
    316
democracy 7, 62, 101, 264, 273–4, 311
design of complex organizations 49,
    305
Design of Organizations for Rural
    Development Projects 72, 75
design workshop 186
development i, v, xv, 2, 5–7, 24, 43–6,
    61–2, 75–6, 83–5, 88, 90, 106,
    144, 273, 278–9
  institutional 75, 77, 90
Dharmakaya 109–10
Dimensional Perspective ix, 154, 156
dimensions ix–xiv, 45–6, 49–51, 96,
    136–41, 154–9, 161–2, 164–7,
    169–75, 177–82, 191, 223–5,
    227–9, 271–3, 294–8, 301–3
diplomacy ix, 71, 179–80, 192, 217,
    225, 241, 244, 274, 302
discovery i, 2, 23, 32, 70, 82, 117,
    127, 133, 139, 142, 180, 191–2,
    243–4, 291, 302
duality 113

Economic Systems 24, 270–1
effectiveness 23, 56, 59, 61, 167, 199,
    244, 246, 250–1, 288–9
  Appreciative-Centered Organization
    xi, 242
  Control-Centered Organization xi,
    xiii, 246–7
  Influence-Centered Organization xi,
    xiii, 244–5
ego xiii, 125, 243
Einstein, A. 61, 72, 138–40, 146, 207
Eldred, J. xv, 242, 312
electricity sector v, 76–7, 79–82, 124,
    240
electrons 97, 146–7, 154, 181, 224
Emery, F. xii, 57–8, 61, 66, 117, 135,
    311–12
emotions 17, 27, 81, 83, 133, 143–4,
    151, 218, 266
empowerment 70, 88, 266, 317
energy 59, 69, 77, 80–2, 92, 98, 119,
    130, 133, 139–40, 144, 146, 148,
    172, 200–1, 224

Engelbart, Douglas 279–80, 312
enlightenment 109, 175, 225, 227–8,
231, 264–6, 268–9, 272, 300
environment 29, 35–6, 49–51, 53–4,
57–8, 66–70, 89, 90, 117–19, 135,
144, 186, 232, 274–5, 287, 295,
297–8
contextual 66–9, 135, 286
influenced 36, 50, 55, 58, 73, 93,
276
task 49, 65, 287–8
equity 268–9, 274, 281
ESMAP (Energy Sector Assistance
Program) 82, 312
essence xii, 35, 53, 76, 94, 107–8,
113–15, 121, 123, 125–6, 129,
185–6, 208–9, 218, 266,
287–8
Etzioni, A. xii, 26–7, 91, 96
evaluation 44, 180, 197, 225, 241,
244, 249–50, 253, 256, 302
evolution, organizational i, 1, 2, 5, 10,
41, 48, 54, 94, 101, 105, 107,
117–18, 141–2, 165, 264, 313–15
exceptional performance 32, 36, 38,
48, 59, 60, 72, 86, 258
experience 1, 3, 5, 20–1, 28–30, 39,
40, 59–61, 67–8, 83, 111–12,
116–17, 131–2, 207–10, 216–18,
283–5, 287
of Appreciation viii, 60–1, 63, 65,
67, 69, 71, 73, 305
conscious 131–2, 146, 216

facilitators 78, 82, 84, 87, 190, 194,
199, 201
faith 103–4, 118, 184–5, 258, 264–5
feedback x, 50–1, 53, 92, 99, 166, 169,
171–3, 180, 185, 192, 202, 205,
218, 223–4, 228
feedforward 164, 166, 171, 185, 192,
205, 223–4, 233, 256, 260, 262
feeling 59, 63, 70, 81, 94–5, 130,
132–3, 142, 191, 201, 210, 216,
218, 286
feminine 37–8, 59, 75, 86, 198, 245,
263, 268, 273, 277–8, 285
movement 276–8
fields 25, 61, 67, 70–1, 91, 102–5,
110, 117–20, 132–3, 135–6,
154–5, 158–9, 185, 190–1, 287,
291–2

aggregate 190, 198–9, 201, 235,
258
appreciative-centered 173, 230,
262
control-centred 201, 217, 230
influence-centered 59, 115, 121–2,
132, 170, 196–7, 230, 255, 268,
285, 287
fifth dimension xi, xiii, xiv, 98, 138,
140, 148, 151, 154, 162–3, 165–7,
171–5, 181–2, 184–5, 223–5, 271,
299, 300
field space 169
Organization ix, 141, 146, 162
Fifth Discipline 53, 316
Fiumicino 13, 19, 183
formation 26, 69, 143, 155, 178, 180,
182, 217, 288, 301–2
four-dimensional organization ix, 161
fourth dimension xi, xiv, 98, 138–9,
162, 166, 172, 176, 223, 225,
227, 229, 272, 301
fractal 165–6, 184–6, 224
dimensions ix, 165–7, 224
freedom, degree of 157, 161–2
Freeman, E. 55, 312
Freud, S. 124–7, 313

goals xiii, 24–5, 27–8, 35, 57–60,
65–6, 89, 93–4, 120, 179–80,
216–17, 223–5, 238–41, 248–50,
256–8, 298–9
God 81, 104, 106–8, 110–13, 121,
124, 126, 157, 265, 268, 306, 311
Gouldner, A. 25–7, 49, 96, 313
Government Service Administration
(GSA) 282
Graham, Bill 208, 218–19, 292
gravity 70, 99, 136, 138–41, 194, 263,
265
Greco, Janet 269
GSA (Government Service
Administration) 282

Heidegger 97, 114–15
Hierarchically Organized Systems in
Theory and Practice 315, 317
hierarchy, organizational 134, 157
Ho, Mae Wan 152, 154, 313
holistic leaders 231–2
holons ix, 97, 152, 172, 178, 224, 301
Human Resource 39, 41, 45, 47–8

humanity xiii, 106–11, 120, 208, 236, 238–40, 262, 264, 267, 269–72, 278–9, 283
Humpty Dumpty Rule xi, xiii, 260–1, 263, 265, 267, 269, 271, 273, 275, 277, 279, 281, 283

IADB (Inter-American Development Bank) 315
ideals xiii, 58–9, 113–14, 122–4, 131–2, 173–5, 185, 215–17, 223–5, 227–8, 239–40, 255–6, 261–2, 267–72, 274, 299, 300
identity 95–6, 173, 246, 266, 276, 306
infinity 169, 306–8
influence v, xiii, xiv, 42, 97, 170–1, 191, 233, 235, 241, 244, 258, 268, 277, 309–10
  circle 20, 188, 216
  colors 170–1
  influence-centered organization ix, x, 24, 28, 175, 231, 239, 244–7, 256–7, 290
  level 97, 170–1, 233, 235, 241, 244, 258, 268, 277
  phase xiv, 54, 85, 115, 119, 196–9, 201–2, 205, 209, 239–40, 288
infolding xii, xiv, 163, 165
information 7, 20–1, 43–4, 46, 92, 102–4, 129–31, 145, 148–9, 152, 155, 203, 205, 226, 229, 250
instincts 28, 125, 132–3, 143, 261–2, 264, 266
Institute of Science in Society (ISIS) 152
integration 29, 50, 64, 103–4, 131
integrity program, culture of 251, 254–5
intentions 99, 100, 120, 124, 235
International Development viii, 2, 6, 55, 65, 75, 77, 79, 81, 83, 85–7, 89, 91, 93, 95, 97
Intuition vii, viii, 1, 5, 6, 8, 12, 14, 16, 18, 28–30, 62–4, 78–80, 86, 92, 102–4, 129–30, 132–3
ISIS (Institute of Science in Society) 152
Islam 94, 111–13, 236, 269
itsons 169, 306–7, 316

Jackson, M.C. 6, 100, 314
Jacques, E. 51, 314

Jantsch, Erich 6, 94–5, 97, 314
Jones, Peter 8, 25, 314
judgment 68, 77, 92, 130, 151, 180, 255, 265, 267, 302, 317
Jung, C.G. xii, 126–9, 131, 314

Kaku, M. 314
Kaluza 139–40
Kant, I. 99, 113–14, 314
Katz, D. 314
Kleiner, A. 314
Korab-Karpowicz, W.J. 314

latent power 2, 73, 91, 186–8, 235, 239, 257, 264, 266, 269
Lawrence, P.R. and Lorsch, J.W. 314
leadership x, xiii, 24, 28, 46, 54, 63–4, 88, 100, 107, 111, 194–5, 199, 230–3, 261, 316–17
Leibnitz 114
Lere, S. 169, 306
Lethem, Francis 63–5, 72, 83
levels
  control-centered 94, 187
  ideal 122, 185, 228, 232
  influenced 94, 246–7, 257
  institutional 34, 50–1, 91, 259
  purpose 3, 187–8, 208, 238, 262
  third 62, 94–5, 187, 235, 287
  ultimate 97
light xvi, 108, 118, 136, 138–9, 146–9, 151–4, 157, 161, 164–7, 170–1, 181, 217, 223–4, 264–5, 291
  theory of 140
Lipnack, Jessica 209, 314
Lyotard, J.-F. 314

MacEvoy 150–1, 314
MacLean, Paul D. 143–4, 315
Mallaby, Sebastian 315
Management Planning Process, *see* MPP
manifest powers viii, xii, xiii, 107–8, 110–11, 113–15, 121, 123, 125, 129, 136, 155–7, 175, 178, 180–1, 234, 300–2
Marshall, Jeannie 278, 315
masculine 86, 198, 245, 263, 273, 277–8, 288
mass 7, 70, 92, 116, 139–40, 151, 266, 286

mathematics 26, 32, 48, 51, 57, 114,
137, 139, 152, 169, 224, 232,
236, 244, 264, 316–17
matrix organizations 50, 305
matter 7, 55, 70, 83–4, 138–40, 146,
198, 214–15, 217
MBA 5, 20, 32, 36, 49
McDonald 36–8, 241, 285
McKee, Robert 314
McNamara 64–5
Methods Time and Motion (MTM) 37
Michael xv, 38, 316
middle level, missing 73, 309
model i, v, 1–3, 66–7, 93, 96–7,
102–5, 112–14, 116, 154–6,
158–60, 166–70, 172–4, 180–2,
184–6, 196–8
holonomic 181–2
organizational 258
standard 139–40
motives 120, 124, 132–3, 266
movement, feminist 276–8
MPP (Management Planning Process)
46–8, 205
Murrell, K. 48, 63
myths 97, 128, 165, 266

Naguchi, Lynne 89, 315
NESDB (National Economic and
Social Development Board) 90
neurosciences 145
NGOs 85, 89, 90, 183, 194, 244, 246
Nichols, E. 315
Nye, Andrea 315
Nye, Joseph 6, 99, 277, 315

observer 84, 95
ODII team 88–9, 186
One-Dimensional Organization ix, 157
organizations 3–6, 23–8, 30–4, 36–41,
44–51, 53–6, 85–6, 92–4, 100–2,
134–6, 154–9, 207–8, 232–51,
253–60, 282–8, 314–17
circular 29, 159
design of 33, 72–3
development 6, 47, 63, 199
dimensions ix, xiv, 58, 157–8, 171
effective v, 63, 220, 257
environment relations viii, 49
fields 39, 48, 58, 91
ideal 157, 165
learning 171, 316

levels of xii, 18, 41, 187, 242, 247
model of v, 1, 157, 170
modern 27–8, 49, 305
multinational 5, 49
philosophy of 105, 121
political 244, 257
scientific management 10, 25, 30,
316
single 25, 58
theory 23, 25, 28, 48–9, 103, 145,
207, 246, 313, 315, 317
organizing process i, xi, 85–6, 135,
183–6, 188, 190, 197, 203–4, 235,
239–40, 242–3, 254, 256–7,
285–6, 290
orientation 122, 132–3, 170, 173,
186–7, 190, 214, 230, 232–3,
235–6, 246, 257
outfolding xii, 163, 165
Owen, Harrison 197, 266, 315
Ozbekhan, Hasan xii, 6, 51–2, 57, 60,
62, 91, 315

Paiboon 88–9, 187, 313
Palmer, S.E. 145, 315
Parsons, T. xii, 33–4, 46, 49, 51, 91, 241
performance 1, 5, 6, 9, 10, 13–16,
20–3, 31–2, 38–40, 45–6, 50–1,
64, 70, 90, 101, 249, 258, 284–5
Pfeffer, J. 56, 135, 315
phase x, 1, 10, 41–4, 47, 51–2, 57,
103, 183–4, 190–1, 196–9, 201–3,
210, 216–17, 249–50, 288
phases of organization 1, 42–4, 47,
51–2, 57, 66, 71, 81, 87, 190–1,
196–7, 199, 203, 216–17, 249, 288
Phillips, Frederick B. 237, 312, 315
philosophy i, v, viii, 1–3, 28, 70, 84,
87–8, 90, 102–22, 127, 133,
140–2, 207–8, 263–6, 298
photons xii, 146–7, 151, 315
plenty 8, 71, 132, 239, 269, 281
police 187, 254–5
Policy 23, 37, 41–2, 53, 61, 68, 80–2,
88, 90, 93–4, 179–80, 186–7, 204,
225, 249, 302
political systems xi, xiii, 62, 229, 239,
256, 270–3, 290
Power xiii
coercive 26, 29
dimensions 143, 173, 185–6, 190,
196, 220, 223–4, 227, 233

diplomatic 272, 298
exercise of 134, 169
fields ix, 69, 70, 73, 114, 118, 121,
    135–6, 155, 185, 188, 196, 217,
    224, 262, 286
hidden 169, 235, 290
kinetic 133, 155
levels of 273
manifest viii, 107–8, 110–11,
    113–15, 121, 123, 125, 129, 136,
    155–7, 181, 234, 266
models of 56, 135
multiplicative 47, 189
organizational 46, 56, 101
potential 118, 133, 155, 181, 235,
    262
Power Map x, xiii, xiv, 208, 218,
    221–2, 224, 226, 230, 233, 239,
    250, 271–2, 283, 293–303
power 'over' 34–5, 59, 105, 133–5,
    141, 181–2, 185
power 'to' 134–5, 141, 155, 181–2,
    185, 226, 238, 258
power 'with' 35–6, 59, 135, 141,
    181–2, 258
processes 33–4, 40, 44, 48, 58, 99,
    172, 256, 316
purpose 23–4, 28–36, 39, 40, 56–9,
    98–9, 101–8, 111–14, 118–21,
    133–6, 139–42, 169–75, 180–6,
    226–9, 263–70, 281–3, 298
relationships xiii, 2, 26, 35–6, 41,
    45, 57, 69, 84, 99, 101, 134–5,
    166–7, 181, 224, 227–9
spiritual 24, 263
unconscious 181, 266, 290
vectors 173, 185–6, 190, 196, 220,
    223–4, 227, 233
Power Map x, xiii, xiv, 208, 218,
    221–2, 224, 226, 230, 233, 239,
    250, 271–2, 283, 293–303
power vectors 173, 185–6, 190, 196,
    220, 223–4, 227, 233
Pribram, Karl H. 152, 207, 315
Prigogine, I. 95–6
probabilities 32, 35, 57, 59, 71, 87,
    115, 121–2, 132–3, 173–5,
    190–4, 214–15, 234, 258–9,
    262–3, 265–6
Process in Practice ix, 183, 185, 187,
    189, 191, 193, 195, 197, 199,
    201, 203, 205

psyche 125–7, 130, 314
purpose
    goals xiii, 24–5, 27–8, 35, 57–60,
        65–6, 89, 93–4, 120, 179–80,
        216–17, 223–5, 238–41,
        248–50, 256–8, 298–9
    human 28, 94, 99, 100, 260,
        316
    ideals xiii, 58–9, 113–14, 122–4,
        131–2, 173–5, 185, 215–17,
        223–5, 227–8, 239–40, 255–6,
        261–2, 267–72, 274, 299, 300
    levels of i, 58, 122–4, 165, 176,
        183, 186–7, 207, 278, 290
    values 39, 40, 51–2, 92–4,
        122–4, 132–3, 175–8, 184–5,
        197, 216–17, 223–5, 238–44,
        246–51, 256–7, 277–8, 301–2,
        309

RBT (Rhythm Based Time) xiii, 122,
    177
realities 71–3, 77–8, 80, 87, 95–7,
    115, 125, 132–3, 190–2, 196–7,
    203, 227, 234–5, 262–3, 269–72,
    290–2
Reed, Michael 316
religion
    Buddhism 89, 108–10, 112, 264
    Christianity 108, 110–11, 113,
        305–6
    Islam 94, 111–13, 236, 269
    major xii, 107–8, 111–3, 121, 264,
        267
reptilian brain ix, 142–3, 261
resolution 101, 118, 130, 149, 172–3,
    177–8, 181, 224, 240, 256, 267,
    273, 283, 288, 301
resources 7, 15, 22, 40, 52, 124, 158,
    175, 189, 215–16, 240, 242,
    257–8, 269, 283, 290
reveal 4
revolution, scientific 25
Riemann 136–40
Riley, C.A. 151, 316
role 10, 18, 20, 31–2, 34, 60, 63–4, 71,
    84–5, 97, 124–5, 194, 199, 242,
    254–5, 276
Rome vii, 5, 6, 13–15, 17–20, 23, 30,
    33, 46–7, 60–1, 67, 71–2, 78, 90,
    105, 183, 285
Rummel, R. J. xii, 117–21, 316

rural development 6, 55, 64, 66, 70, 72, 75, 87–90, 183
Russell, B. 316

Santa, Marta viii, 75, 78, 82, 287
Sato, Turid 75, 77, 79, 83, 88–9, 305
SBT (Signal Based Time) 177
SCG (Staff Coordination Group) 41, 45
science i, viii, 2, 48, 54, 70, 92, 102–6, 113, 136–7, 141–2, 263–6, 298, 311–12, 314, 316–17
  organizational 3, 102, 184
  physics 92, 113, 115, 140–1, 146, 156, 264, 307, 311
  quantum i, 30, 54, 63, 114, 140–1, 152–4, 181
  relativity 139, 141
  revolution 25
  string theory 140
scientific management 10, 25, 30, 316
Scottsburg 208, 218–22, 316
Searle 41, 45–6, 48, 58, 63, 67, 183, 285
self-control 36, 51
self-organization 54, 314–15
Senge, P. 6, 53, 99, 100, 316
Signal Based Time (SBT) 177
Situational level of power 273
Smith, William E. i, iii, iv, 12, 17, 19, 42, 72, 75, 134–5, 237, 241, 243, 245, 247, 276, 285
social sciences 29, 61, 63–4, 83, 94–5, 99, 118, 124, 181
Social Systems Sciences xv, 40, 51, 55, 57, 60–2, 65, 134, 136, 141, 315
Soft Power 6, 99, 315
space 2, 114, 119–20, 122, 136–7, 139, 159–60, 194, 201, 212, 215–8, 220, 239–40, 265, 280, 287–8
  ecological 119–20
  intentional 119–20
  multi-dimensional 137, 230
  physical ix, 96, 166, 223, 291
  spiritual 96
  three-dimensional 136–7
  two-dimensional 137, 159
sphere 26, 38, 137, 157, 160–1, 164–6

spiral geometry 307
spirit 82–3, 110, 112, 165, 173, 175, 195, 198, 209, 218, 226, 261–2, 269, 278, 287, 290–1
squares, magic 232, 244–5, 309
SRI (Stanford Research Institute) 55, 73, 279–80
Staff Coordination Group (SCG) 41, 45
stakeholders viii, 54–6, 59, 72–3, 76–7, 84–5, 132–4, 178, 186–8, 200–1, 203, 205, 242–3, 248–50, 253–5, 301–2
Stamps, Jeffrey S. 97, 209, 314, 316
Station Officers 8, 10, 13, 20–3, 32
stories i, x, 2, 3, 5, 8, 10, 14, 25, 75, 79, 109, 140, 212, 219, 281, 284–5
strategic planning x, xiii, 14, 40, 51–2, 73–4, 87, 180, 186–7, 197–9, 228, 240–1, 249–51, 253, 288, 302
structures 33, 50, 53–4, 56, 80–1, 98, 102, 134–6, 141–2, 166, 252, 273–4, 285, 305–6, 313, 315–16
  triune 146, 148–9
Surowiecki, J. 133, 251, 267, 270, 316
systems 2, 10–13, 15, 20, 23, 25, 29, 39, 42, 52, 57–60, 64–6, 69, 96–9, 273–4, 280
  appreciative 93
  closed 33, 49
  color-perception 141–2
  global 272, 283
  limbic 143–4
  natural 49, 142, 154
  purposeful 57–8, 61, 105, 311
  reticular 94

Tao Te Ching 108, 111–12, 266
TDRI (Thailand Development Research Institute) 87, 278, 316
Thailand v, viii, 6, 86–9, 109, 187, 189, 278
theology i, 104, 126
thinking 5, 22, 48, 50, 54, 63, 81, 83, 92, 97, 101, 120, 125, 130, 132, 162
Thompson, James D. i, 5, 32–6, 41, 45–7, 49–51, 56, 65, 305, 317

three-dimensional organization ix, xii, xiv, 158–9, 191
threeness 107–8, 110, 115, 121, 136, 142, 169, 207, 266
time orientations 112, 121–2, 155, 173–4, 176–7, 215–7, 228, 236, 239–40, 242
torus xii, 157, 161–6, 224
transactional 56, 61, 66–7, 117, 135, 286–7
transcendence 1, 3, 103, 113, 118, 131, 177, 183, 185, 194, 224, 234, 237, 239–40, 270, 277–8
transform 1, 178, 224, 241, 256, 283–4, 291, 301
transformation v, xi, xiv, 91, 118, 128, 162, 171, 177, 208–9, 220–1, 233–4, 283–4, 286–8, 290, 292
Trinidad vii, 5, 10, 13–15, 18–20, 33, 38, 46–7, 67, 71, 187, 285
Trinity 109–11, 122, 180, 268
Trist, Eric i, xii, 58, 61–2, 66, 117, 312
trust 175–6, 178, 187, 197, 205, 218, 227–9, 231, 239, 256, 261, 267–9, 275, 281, 290, 300
truth 115, 132, 175, 178, 239, 265–7, 269, 272, 300–1
Tsoukas, H. and Knudsen, C. 317
Turid Sato v, 75–6, 85–6, 292
Turnbull, Susan 282–3, 292
two-dimensional organization ix, 158, 171

Ulrich, W. 99, 317
unconscious 52, 91, 102, 106, 124, 127–33, 169, 172–3, 198–200, 205, 217–18, 227–9, 235–6, 261–2, 266, 290
   aggregate 91, 133
unconscious, fear 227–8
unconscious, purpose viii, 102, 124, 131, 200, 205, 218, 261
understanding 31–3, 36, 38–9, 53, 91–2, 96–9, 101–4, 106, 111–14, 127, 134, 185, 207, 242, 258, 262–3
   new level of 32, 207
Ushenko 118, 121, 317

value maps 250–1
value segments 251

values 39, 40, 51–2, 92–4, 122–4, 132–3, 175–8, 184–5, 197, 216–17, 223–5, 238–44, 246–51, 256–7, 277–8, 301–2, 309
   appreciative-level 250
   control-level 250
   cultural 38, 239, 242
   highest 237, 246
   organizational 244
   philosophical 244, 247
   political 227–9, 247
   strong control-centered 275
Vickers, Sir Geoffrey 68, 92, 317
visual system ix, 136, 141–2, 145–7, 151, 155–6, 199

wavelengths 147–9
Weaver, W. and Shannon, C.E. 317
Weber i, 24, 28, 35, 317
Weick, K. 97, 317
Weis, Paul 317
Weisbord, Marvin 266, 317
Wharton Graduate School of Business 6, 55, 60, 71, 73
Wheatley, M.J. 54, 63, 102, 317
Whelehan, I. 277, 317
wholeness viii, ix, 27, 59, 75, 91, 99, 100, 103–4, 108, 121, 127, 131, 152, 156, 168–9, 173, 175
Wiener, N. 92, 317
wisdom 2, 59, 102, 109, 169, 184–5, 194, 244, 258–9, 261, 265–6, 268, 272, 283
women 7, 37–8, 75, 86–8, 277–8
workshops 62, 73, 76, 78–82, 85, 87–90, 183–4, 187–8, 190–1, 198, 203, 210, 253–4, 282, 287–8, 314
world 91–2, 95–101, 107–10, 113–15, 128–30, 141–4, 175–6, 188–9, 207–12, 214–20, 228–36, 256–66, 274–84, 290–2, 297–8, 300
   appreciative 215, 226, 283
   appreciative-centered 262, 297
   control-centered 216, 234, 283, 290, 297
   external 143, 233
   five-dimensional 262
   four-dimensional 112, 141
   ideal 216
   material 104, 114, 208
   three-dimensional 141, 166
   timeless 234

World Bank v, viii, 6, 55, 63–6, 70,
72–8, 81–6, 88, 183, 276, 286,
312, 316
design of 1, 6, 65, 73, 85
experience viii, 6, 64, 71, 75, 83, 85
reorganizations viii, 6, 64, 71, 75,
83, 85

Young, Arthur M. 28, 37–8, 64, 75,
115, 140, 145, 184, 188, 211,
317

zero-dimensional point 158, 162, 164,
297
zeroids 307–8